India, Pakistan, and the Great Powers

INDIA, PAKISTAN, and the GREAT POWERS

William J. Barnds

Published for the

COUNCIL ON FOREIGN RELATIONS

by

PRAEGER PUBLISHERS

New York · Washington · London

PRAEGER PUBLISHERS
111 Fourth Avenue, New York, N.Y. 10003, U.S.A.
5, Cromwell Place, London SW7 2JL, England

Published in the United States of America in 1972
by Praeger Publishers, Inc.

Library of Congress Catalog Card Number: 72–115104

For a partial list of Council publications, see pages 387–88.

Printed in the United States of America

To my parents

WILLIAM H. BARNDS

1895–1965

VERONICA M. BARNDS

Contents

Preface   ix

1 *Introduction*   1

Part One: The South Asian Context

2 *Independence, Partition, and Conflict*   13
3 *India Fashions a Foreign Policy*   44
4 *Pakistan's Search for Status and Security*   68

Part Two: The Great-Power Involvement

5 *America Enters the Subcontinent*   83
6 *The Soviet Union Chooses India*   107
7 *China and India: The Spurious Friendship*   129

Part Three: Confrontations and Their Consequences

8 *The Sino-Indian Border War*   165

9 The Second Kashmir Conflict   183
10 Tashkent and After   209
11 India's Resurgence and Pakistan's Agony   237
12 The Policies of the Past   248

Part Four: America's Role in South Asia

13 U.S. Interests in the Subcontinent   257
14 Development Problems and Prospects   273
15 Regional Conflicts and the Great Powers   304
16 Defense of the Subcontinent   323
17 America and the Future of India and Pakistan   342

Notes   349
Selected Bibliography   369
Index   375

MAPS

1 South Asia and Surrounding Regions   12
2 The Sino-Indian Border with Disputed Areas   148
3 Kashmir and Jammu   202

TABLES

1-A India—Foreign Economic Aid, 1945–70   226
1-B Pakistan—Foreign Economic Aid, 1945–70   227
2-A India—Foreign Trade, 1950, 1955, 1960–69   230
2-B Pakistan—Foreign Trade, 1950, 1955, 1960–69   231
  3 Indian Parliamentary Election Results   275
  4 India and Pakistan: Defense Expenditures, 1955,
     1960, 1965–70   306
  5 India and Pakistan: Size and Composition of Armed
     Forces, 1960 and 1965–70   325

Preface

The cold war and the demise of European colonialism after the upheavals of World War II projected the United States into world affairs far beyond the imaginings of preceding generations. American involvement in areas that had been *terra incognita* a few short years earlier drew many young people, whose horizons a generation before would hardly have extended beyond their state or nation, into the study and practice of international relations. Domestic affairs are where the action is today in the eyes of the young; twenty years ago, foreign affairs occupied center stage.

It was for this reason that I joined the Central Intelligence Agency after leaving graduate school in 1952. At first, I worked as an analyst of political and economic affairs of the Soviet bloc. In 1956, fascinated by the contest between the Soviet bloc and the West for influence in the newly independent Asian countries and by the efforts of those new states to develop their societies, I began working on South Asian affairs.

It was clear even to a novice that India and Pakistan wanted a dignified position—as actors rather than objects—in a world still organized on the traditional basis of the European sovereign states. They wanted, furthermore, to maintain the essence of their ancient cultures and traditions, adapting them as necessary to modernize their societies so that they could deal with Western nations on an equal basis. This was proving to be far more difficult than was imagined at the time of independence, but they were intensifying their efforts rather than retreating into ineffectual demagoguery à la Sukarno. Although Indian and Pakistani leaders realized that their long-term tasks were domestic rather than international, they did not have the luxury of a lengthy quiet period to devote largely to addressing their internal problems. Ancient religious and cultural antipathies between Hindus and Muslims had taken on a political coloration during the struggle for independence, and led to bitter hostility between the two new states. Their hostility, together with Soviet-American antagonism and the rise of Communist China, drew South Asia into the cold war in ways that were both tragic (arms race) and beneficial (foreign aid for development).

If Indians and Pakistanis knew each other—or thought they did—all too well, the same could not be said for the other powers. The United States had begun arming Pakistan and helping India with its development program before learning much about them and their cultures. Khrushchev, Nehru, and Chou En-lai were exchanging visits and extolling nonexistent historical friendships among their peoples, while probing to understand and influence each other's policies. Whatever the future held, it would not be dull.

I spent most of the next ten years in the Office of National Estimates, where we tried to understand what was happening in other countries, to assess what the future held for them, and to suggest what this meant for the United States. The quality of my colleagues was as high as the task was difficult, and so our record, while uneven, was respectable.

The outbreak of war between India and Pakistan in 1965, and the attendant halt in U.S. military aid, indicated that the complex pattern of relations among India, Pakistan, and the great powers would undergo further shifts. American attitudes and policy toward the two countries also would alter substantially. All of this suggested the value of a study of the motivations and evolution of the foreign policies of the countries involved in the subcontinent and a reappraisal of American interests and policy. John C. Campbell, Senior Research Fellow at the Council on Foreign Relations, shared my interest and concern about these issues, and with his support I began working on this book, first as a Visiting Fellow and more recently as a Senior Research Fellow on the staff of the Council.

This book comprises four parts that are interrelated through narrative continuity. Part One is a study of the South Asian political environment in the years when Hindus and Muslims were contending with each other and the British for control of the subcontinent, and of the foreign policies the two new nations created and articulated. Part Two describes the arrival of the United States, the Soviet Union, and China on the South Asian scene, and discusses the complex relationships in the ensuing contest for influence. Part Three analyzes the major confrontations of the 1960s—the Sino-Indian and Indo-Pakistani wars—and the unforeseen consequences these conflicts had for all the powers involved. Part Four is an examination of American policy choices in South Asia in light of the past and the problems of the present and future.

This book concentrates on the relationships of the key states—India, Pakistan, China, the Soviet Union, and the United States. Discussion of Britain's role is more limited, and the activities of other European countries, Japan, and other Asian countries are treated only in so far as they affect the relations of the major powers.

While the book's purpose is not the historical study of the course of events, it does rely heavily on an understanding of the past as a guide (though not a strait jacket) for analyzing the present situation and for estimating future possibilities. All the participants have suffered from a lack of such understanding in the past; today, with the experience of two decades to draw on, there is less reason for misunderstanding.

The focus of Parts One through Three is on the direct relations of the five major countries involved in the subcontinent, but no study with such a broad focus can present a detailed, year-by-year analysis of their foreign policies as they affected each other. In order to present a useful interpretation without resorting to undue generalization or abstraction, this study centers on what I regard as the key policy issues and decisions of the countries at the turning points in their relations.

The policies of the five powers did not, of course, develop in a vacuum, being shaped by particular world views and over-all foreign-policy postures, as well as by domestic situations and aspirations. The links between domestic and foreign policy and between general foreign policies and those involving South Asia are discussed in the early chapters in the book, and at those points where they have a special impact, but considerations of space prevent more attention to these matters.

Any study that attempts to describe the pattern of relations among five major countries faces two dangers. The first is the hazard of presenting the policies and the motivations behind them as being more consistent and coherent than was actually the case. Many of the leaders in the postwar years—Nehru; Ayub Khan; Mao Tse-tung and Chou En-lai; Stalin and Khrushchev; Eisenhower, Kennedy, and Johnson—were involved. They sometimes demonstrated insight and courage, but at other times they acted out of ignorance and confusion or on the basis of distorted perceptions or personal pique. Moreover, the matters discussed here occupied most of them only sporadically: Other international concerns, a wide variety of domestic problems, and the purely personal matters that affect the actions of every public figure claimed most of their attention and energy.

The second and more subtle danger is that of ascribing points of view to governments or nations without distinguishing among the often divergent interests and views of different individuals, organizations, and other groups within a country. Although no one who has observed or taken part in the bureaucratic struggles of his own government is likely to be unaware of this pitfall, he may be tempted to regard other governments—particularly authoritarian ones—as less severely afflicted with it than is the case. There is no satisfactory solution to the problems this poses for an author. I try to describe the internal disputes when they seem important and the positions of different forces are reasonably clear, without, however, attempting systematically to describe the evolution of the views of all the significant groups in each country.

Part Four attempts a fresh look at American interests in, and policy toward, India and Pakistan in light of the changes that have occurred in the world since 1965. Everyone involved in international affairs uses the phrase the "national interest," often to cloak with respectability the particular policy he is advocating; efforts to analyze it are too infrequent. While the concept raises philosophical problems on account of the differing interests of groups within a country, it can be useful as a practical guide to policy. This is especially important today, when the United States is in search of a foreign policy.

To complete a book on U.S. policy toward the subcontinent when Pakistan is in the midst of a civil war, one which threatens to develop into a new Indo-Pakistan conflict, poses special problems. No author wants his work immediately to be overtaken by unforeseen events, but neither can he discuss the ramifications of every possible contingency.

A balance of certain calculated risks must be struck, because in the present upheavals many decisions concerning the subcontinent cannot be postponed. This book attempts to appraise both the present critical problems facing the United States and its longer term concerns in the light of basic American interests in the area as well as to suggest approaches to them in the context of the lessons of the past and the needs of the future.

A few words about terminology: Afghanistan, Ceylon, Nepal, Bhutan, and Sikkim are dealt with throughout this book only as they affect the relationships among the major powers on the subcontinent. Although "South Asia" normally includes these states as well as India and Pakistan, I have used the term throughout the text interchangeably with "India and Pakistan" to avoid naming the two countries an inordinate number of times. Because the two countries together comprise nearly all of the area and population of South Asia this seems justified, but the reader should keep this usage in mind.

Throughout this book I have used the conventional terms *foreign aid* and *foreign assistance* rather than the more accurate but unwieldy "transfer of resources." While some of the transfers were grants (pure aid), more were loans (at varying rates of interest) tied to purchases, thus reducing their value. Moreover, U.S. statistics list surplus foodstuffs at domestic prices rather than at the lower world market prices. Partially offsetting these factors are provisions for repayment of many loans in local currency. Even so, the amounts of true aid are much less than the figures given. Since this is not a book about foreign aid, I feel justified in using the official figures rather than making extensive calculations to determine the actual *aid* component involved in the transfer of resources. Nonetheless, this word of explanation seems desirable.

Every author is indebted to many people for assistance during the years of his intellectual pilgrimage. While it is impossible to remember, much less pay tribute to, all of those involved, an inadequate acknowledgment is better than none. Over the years, I have discussed South Asian affairs with many Indian and Pakistani friends, and these discussions have provided me with much of my knowledge about the views of the two countries.

During 1966–67, I benefited greatly from the assistance of a study group organized by the Council on Foreign Relations and chaired by Kenneth T. Young, Jr., to help me test my interpretations of the past and my thoughts about the future. The members of the group were Peter Black, George S. Franklin, Jr., George F. Gant, Col. Michael J. Greene, USA, Selig S. Harrison, William Henderson, Willem Holst, Townsend Hoopes, Ernest M. Howell, Thomas L. Hughes, John Huizenga, J. C. Hurewitz, Col. Amos A. Jordan, Jr., USA, Kenneth Kaufman, Donald W. Klein, Paul Kreisberg, David Linebaugh, David W. MacEachron, Philip E. Mosely, Gustav F. Papanek, Peter O. A. Solbert, James W. Spain, Col. Frederick C. Thayer, USAF, Wayne A. Wilcox, and W. Howard Wriggins. In addition to the regular members of the group, we benefited from the presence of Howard Boorman, John Devlin, Douglas Heck, Charles B. McLane, Hans J. Morgenthau, and A. M. Rosenthal at individual meetings. Their comments and suggestions were invaluable, and, though the final product represents my own views, these were influenced in many ways by the members of the group.

Throughout the period when I was writing this book I was encouraged and sustained by my colleagues at the Council on Foreign Relations: George S. Franklin, Jr., Executive Director; David W. MacEachron, Deputy Executive Director; and John C. Campbell and William Diebold, Senior Research Fellows. All of them provided invaluable assistance, and all have my deepest gratitude. I am also indebted to Helen Caruso, who was my research assistant as well as the rapporteur of the study group, and who continually came forth with helpful ideas and materials on her own initiative as well as in response to my sometimes confused requests.

I also benefited from the generous cooperation and assistance of the entire Council staff, particularly Rob Valkenier and Carol Kahn, Donald Wasson, Janet Rigney, Lorna Brennan, Jan Farlow, and Helen Balkin. My secretaries during this period—Susanna Taylor, Andrea Kim, and Susan Glass—were indispensable in the preparation of the manuscript.

I wish to thank the editors of *Asia, Foreign Affairs,* and *The World Today* for permission to use material from articles of mine that have appeared in their pages.

Finally, my gratitude to my wife and children goes beyond anything I am able to express. Without their patience, understanding, and support over a longer period than any of us originally envisioned, the writing of this book would have been an impossible task.

September, 1971

India, Pakistan, and the Great Powers

1

Introduction

The struggle of the great powers for influence in the former colonial territories is one of the striking phenomena of international politics since World War II. This struggle has been conducted first under cold war conditions and then against the background of a decline in bipolarity and a weakening of the Soviet and Western alliance systems. The great powers, no less than the new nations, had to face a multitude of new and extremely complex problems. Neither the United States nor the U.S.S.R., principal competitors to replace the receding European influence, had much experience in or knowledge of the Afro-Asian world; the newly independent governments, with no foreign policy experience, were forced to discover and further their national interests in a fast-changing international environment.

By virtue of its location, population, combination of actual weakness and potential strength, and efforts at nation-building, the South Asian subcontinent is an important example of that shifting struggle for influence. It illustrates equally well the complexity of problems in the postwar politics of Asia.

But is South Asia, in fact, a forum of world politics in the same sense that, say, the Middle East has been at the center of the contest between the Western nations and the Communist world? To be sure, India, Pakistan, the United States, the Soviet Union, Communist

China, and their various national interests come into striking juxta-position in South Asia. In sheer numbers they are the five most pop-ulous countries in the world, with China, the largest, having roughly six times as many people as Pakistan.

India and Pakistan, with perhaps 18 per cent of the world's popu-lation, have been locked in unyielding hostility that erupted into war twice within two decades. The U.S.S.R. and Communist China, once close allies, are pursuing sharply contrasting policies toward India now that Sino-Indian relations have moved from the super-ficial friendship of the 1950s to the open hostility of the 1960s. India tries to use both U.S. and Soviet support to deal with China—and with Pakistan. The suspicion and friction formerly noticeable in U.S.-Indian relations were gradually replaced by a measure of confidence and cooperation, which, however, have diminished sharply in 1971. In contrast, the close cooperation that once characterized U.S.-Pakistani relations has given way to uncertainty and suspicion; Pakistan has developed its relations with China (and, to a degree, with the Soviet Union) in hopes of enhancing its security vis-à-vis India. In short, international political relations in South Asia are so closely inter-twined that a change in one nation's policy almost invariably leads to a shift—sometimes subtle, sometimes dramatic—in the policies of the other nations.

Not only foreign policies but also ideologies, economic conditions and policies, and strategic considerations come into play in South Asia. The United States is a capitalist democracy; the U.S.S.R. is a "mature" Marxist society; and China is a young revolutionary Marx-ist state. India is officially a secular democracy, though with a strong Hindu coloration, whereas Pakistan is officially an Islamic nation, which, however, has recently been caught up in a civil war as a result of its failure to establish a durable political system. Despite major efforts to develop their economies, India, Pakistan, and China are among the world's poorest nations in terms of living standards. The Soviet Union, having become the world's second industrial power, affords its people a moderate standard of living, and the United States remains the wealthiest country. The U.S.S.R. and China are in geo-graphical proximity to the subcontinent, but the United States and other Western powers (and Japan) are many thousands of miles dis-tant. These pronounced differences among the principal actors on the South Asian scene influence perceptions of their national interests and consequently their policies.

It is neither necessary nor possible to answer with precision the question of whether the Indian subcontinent is as critical a focus of world politics as other areas of great-power confrontation. The powers demonstrate their foreign-policy interests in the subcontinent and regard it as an important area for maneuver. That has been the case historically, and it continues so today.

During most of the nineteenth century and throughout the first half of the twentieth, the Western position in Asia was based largely upon British sovereignty in India. Closely connected with this was Britain's role as the dominant outside power in the Middle East, where its aims were to prevent the region from falling under the dominion of any hostile great power, to secure the communications routes to India and the Far East, and to advance British commercial interests.

In South Asia Britain's position was virtually impregnable. The Royal Navy commanded the sea lanes and the Indian Ocean; the British Indian Army guaranteed the defense of the area from Burma in the east along the 3,000-mile line of the Himalayas to the Hindu Kush mountains in central Afghanistan. Behind them stood the scientific talent and industrial might of the United Kingdom. Nor was Britain's control ever seriously threatened. The Chinese Empire, crumbling under the impact of the West, posed no challenge. Russian expansion into Central Asia was checked in three Afghan wars, and Tibet became a buffer zone. As nationalist pressure mounted in the twentieth century, the European colonial powers, having come to accept each other's positions, even recognized a common interest in upholding the *status quo*.

World War II shattered the *status quo*, greatly altering the balance of power in Asia and the role of the subcontinent in international affairs. Though failing in its war aims, Japan undermined the domestic control of the Chinese Nationalist government and the position of the European colonial powers. The Soviet Union, victorious over Nazi Germany, extended its sway over Eastern Europe, shouldered the immense task of reconstruction with vigor, and quickly became the other nuclear superpower. China's strength after the Communist take-over in 1949 also increased both absolutely and relatively. The years of comfortable security along the northern frontiers of the Indian subcontinent were drawing to a close.

More dramatic was the British decision to withdraw from India in 1947.[1] The United Kingdom, emerging greatly weakened from World

War II, was under mounting pressure from nationalists in India and elsewhere. Leaders of the Labour government, who had long supported Indian aspirations for self-government, decided it was no longer feasible or desirable to rule India.

Although British authority was handed over to the nationalists, British power could not be transferred. Even a united India would have been weaker, but authority devolved upon two nations. The communications and administration of the subcontinent were badly disrupted. Where there had been a single economy, there now were two. And the defense of the area, assumed by mutually hostile governments, was correspondingly weakened.

Independence for the world's largest colony marked the beginning of the end of colonialism. Other Asians were encouraged by the example of India and Pakistan and acquired in them two enthusiastic and tireless supporters in the struggle against colonialism. Ceylon, with the important naval base at Trincomalee, gained its independence in 1948, as did Burma. The Dutch and the French were being pushed out of their possessions in Southeast Asia. The new states were, however, beset by grave internal weaknesses and, lacking any foreign-policy traditions, were as yet neither ready nor able to cooperate in meeting whatever external dangers might arise.

It was in the aftermath of these epochal changes that the United States first became seriously involved in the Indian subcontinent. Because of the intensity of the global struggle between the Western and the Communist nations, the United States attempted to rally the non-Communist nations of the world to prevent further Communist expansion. Seeking to disrupt the Western efforts, the Soviet Union tried to demonstrate to the new nations of Asia and the Middle East that they had nothing to fear and much to gain by refusing to align themselves with the West.

When the United States became involved in the affairs of South Asia after the Korean War, its interests were generally considered to be the following: (1) that the subcontinent be militarily secure from external attack; (2) that India and Pakistan assume some of the responsibility for the defense of Asia; (3) that the two countries cooperate politically with the United States and the Western powers; (4) that the quarrels between India and Pakistan, and between them and their neighbors, be settled or at least kept under control; (5) that both countries make sufficient political, economic, and social progress to enable their non-Communist governments to continue in power; and (6) that they be willing to provide the United States with transit rights, communications facilities, and perhaps even military bases if necessary. In sum, the United States wanted the two countries to be secure, to cooperate with the West, to hold the Communists at arm's length, and to enjoy political stability and economic progress. The interests of other Western countries were regarded as much the same, although it was generally recognized that the United States and the United Kingdom would be most directly involved.

A political and military balance had been restored in Europe and, more precariously, in the Far East after the Korean and Indochina wars. But Stalin's successors soon demonstrated new skill and flexibility in dealing with the underdeveloped countries. There was a growing belief that the struggle between the West and the Communists would be decided in the Third World. South Asia, with half the population of non-Communist Africa and Asia combined, and located between a turbulent Middle East and an unstable Southeast Asia, was regarded as an area of vital importance. Indeed, if India and Pakistan were unable to withstand the Communists and to make the transition from traditional to modern societies, what hope was there for nations less well prepared for the struggle?

Underlying this view of India's and Pakistan's importance was the widespread conviction that the underdeveloped areas, thought of almost as a unit, had to demonstrate to their peoples within a reasonably short time that they would succeed in the tasks of modernization as non-Communist societies. If they failed, it was expected that they would succumb to communism and become part of the Communist bloc, for the Moscow-Peking axis then seemed firm. This outcome would greatly change the world balance of power and imperil the survival of the West. It was also believed that, if the underdeveloped countries became Communist, they would succeed in their task of modernization. China, making rapid progress, seemed to demonstrate what could be achieved by a Communist government in a weak nation.

Such beliefs—or fears—were not shared by everyone, at least in the terms stated above. Yet, as oversimplified as they seem today, given the great changes that have occurred, they represented the general thought pattern of many officials and private citizens in the United States and the West as they tried to interpret the vast upheavals that were taking place in the world.

American attitudes varied over whether defense of the subcontinent or development of the two nations should receive top priority. The two views were more complex than a simple preference for placing either military or economic considerations first. Indeed, development and security are not really alternatives; because neither can exist without the other, both are sought. Economic aid is one instrument to foster development *and* security; military aid can be another to get security and *hence* development. Moreover, attitudes tended to shift back and forth over time. After the Korean War (and while the French were fighting in Indochina) military considerations were stressed. By the late 1950s there was a shift in emphasis toward economic development, but with the 1962 Sino-Indian border war the relative emphasis on military considerations came to the fore again for a time.

This issue was complicated by the fact that anything the United States did to bolster the defensive capabilities of either Pakistan or India caused a strong reaction in the other country. United States officials feared for a time that the U.S.-Pakistan alliance would lead India to seek much closer links with the U.S.S.R. and Communist China; after the eruption of the Sino-Indian quarrel and the provision of arms to India they feared that an alliance between Pakistan and China might result. On the other hand, U.S. economic assistance to India or Pakistan (even though it freed local resources for military spending) never aroused such intense opposition. Thus the United States has continually faced the problem of how to balance its interests in Pakistan, which was willing to cooperate quite fully in an alliance relationship in return for heavy U.S. support, and its interests in India, which was determined to remain nonaligned. The present civil war in Pakistan has greatly intensified this problem.

The other major powers have likewise been caught up in the dilemma of whether to balance their interests in India and Pakistan or to give top priority to relations with one or the other. The many shifts in the pattern of relationships suggest that no outside power has found a satisfactory solution. The subcontinent's recent experience in world affairs also demonstrates how major powers, in attempting to exploit local antagonisms and the need for economic assistance to further their own aims, can become enmeshed in these conflicts—especially when they lack knowledge of the area and, therefore, of the nature and depth of the quarrels.

The problems of the U.S.S.R. and China have been compounded

by the existence of local Communist parties, especially in India. Although the local parties are assets in some respects, they complicate the provision of aid and the forging of close relations with the bourgeois nationalist governments—a problem that has grown in complexity as the Communist movement in India has divided into three separate parties. Nor does the absence of "pro–United States" parties permit America to disregard the influence of its programs on the internal political scene if they are to be effective. United States arms aid had a substantial impact on the relative political strengths of various groups in Pakistan. American aid to India had a lesser impact, partly because of the nature of the aid and the strength of the Congress party, but also because India was never as dependent on the United States as Pakistan was.

It would be a mistake, however, to regard the outside powers as the active agents and India and Pakistan as passive spectators in the events of the past two decades. Indeed, they are prime examples of how countries that are actually weak can, by virtue of skillful leadership, exploit great-power rivalries for their own benefit.

Pakistani and Indian efforts to secure support, and the attempts of the major powers to gain influence on the subcontinent, have varied in intensity over the years but have not led to prolonged military involvement like that in East Asia or the Middle East. No outside power has been able to control the internal political life of either India or Pakistan, partly because of their size and partly because of their relatively stable governments and skillful leadership. From 1947 to 1967 India enjoyed a degree of domestic political stability that was virtually unique in the underdeveloped world. Pakistan, less fortunate in its early years, had stable government during the ten years President Ayub held power. And even today, when Pakistan is in desperate need of external aid, its leaders strongly resist outside pressures.

At the same time, the nature of the relationships continues to be profoundly influenced by the residual impact of colonialism on India and Pakistan. They remain, moreover, underdeveloped nations dependent upon large-scale economic and military assistance from abroad if they are to develop their economies and possess significant military strength. Cold war and global competition between Moscow and Washington have enabled India and Pakistan to secure large amounts of aid, often on terms that would have been regarded as remarkably lenient in any earlier age.

Conditioning all other elements of the relationships among India, Pakistan, and the major powers has been the age-old hostility between Hindus and Muslims, which intensified during the course of the independence struggle and became Indo-Pakistani hostility as a result of partition. Their enmity has been the major reason for the two countries' following strikingly different paths in the international arena, and it has created opportunities for, and presented limitations to, outside powers as they have attempted to advance their interests in South Asia.

As noted, no major power has been able to achieve really close relations with India and Pakistan simultaneously for more than a short period. Yet both countries are of such importance that a policy of "choosing" one over the other has always had obvious drawbacks. Thus the United Nations, the Western powers, and more recently the Soviet Union have attempted to promote settlements of the issues in dispute between India and Pakistan, especially the Kashmir quarrel, in hopes of resolving the dilemmas in building good relations with two hostile nations. The record of these attempts, while containing occasional successes such as the Indus Waters and Tashkent agreements, has generally been discouraging, underscoring the depth of the historical antagonisms.

With the relinquishment of Britain's sovereignty in 1947, India and Pakistan inevitably became a focus of great-power interests, and continued to be one throughout the hectic developments of the past two decades. Certainly, in the 1950s and 1960s the United States was convinced that the subcontinent was a focus of world politics. Today, the United States seems far less sure about the correctness of that assessment.

America has, to an extent, lessened its involvement in the affairs of the subcontinent. Since their war in 1965, it has not furnished military equipment to either India or Pakistan in any significant amounts, and, since 1968, it has cut back on new commitments of economic aid. This has been done despite the Soviet Union's supplying arms and economic aid to both countries and China's military and economic assistance to Pakistan.

As a carefully considered decision—if it was that—the U.S. decision to reduce its role during the latter half of the 1960s represented an assessment that India and Pakistan were perhaps less important than was once thought. They seem less vulnerable to possible external aggression and better able to withstand outside influence on their internal politics and foreign policies. Also, cut-backs in American economic aid have reflected skepticism, even disillusion, over the progress demonstrated by the underdeveloped countries. The measure of stability India and Pakistan have achieved in their foreign policies was not matched in recent years by corresponding stability in domestic affairs. To be sure, change—not rigidity—is the goal of the development process, but excessive turmoil can disrupt and reverse the process. The events of 1971 provide new challenges for the United States, and as usual there is reason for both hope and discouragement. Mrs. Gandhi's dramatic election victory offers India a new chance of a purposeful and effective government for dealing with its many problems. Yet overshadowing all else today is the civil war in Pakistan, which not only raises anew the most basic questions about that country's unity and viability, but also threatens to lead to a new Indo-Pakistani war with all of its attendant horrors and dangers.

It is, therefore, an appropriate time for a fundamental re-examination of American policy in South Asia—and of the circumstances that have created the setting and context in which it operates.

PART ONE

The South Asian Context

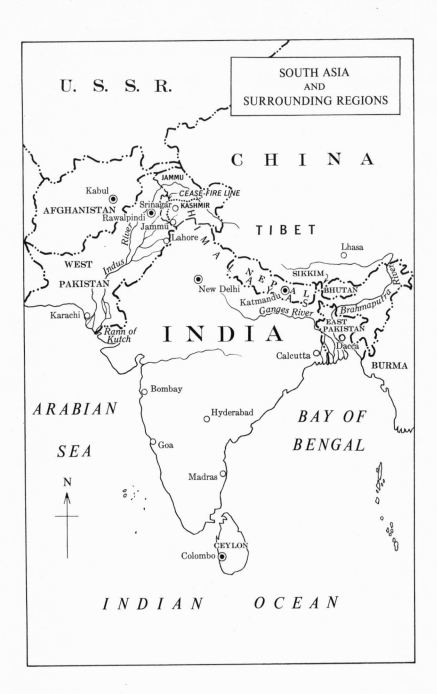

2

Independence, Partition, and Conflict

The circumstances leading to partition set the seal upon Indo-Pakistani hostility that has implacably shaped developments in South Asia since independence was won on August 15, 1947. At the root of this enmity has been the uneasy coexistence of Hindus and Muslims in the subcontinent ever since Islam made its appearance in the northwest around A.D. 1000. Partition occurred because most Muslims, fearing they would be second-class citizens in an independent and united India, believed that a state of their own represented the only way to ensure their security and perpetuate their way of life.

The Basis of Antagonism

No brief characterization of the relationship between Hindus and Muslims can do justice to its complexity. Cultural, historical and economic as well as purely religious differences are the causes of Hindu-Muslim communalism.[1] It remains a fact of daily life on the subcontinent for some 50 million Muslims in India and the sizable Hindu minority of East Pakistan.

The first and most fundamental difference between the two groups springs from their divergent religious outlooks. Islam, based upon divine revelations through a series of prophets, of whom Mohammed was the last and greatest, places a high value on doctrinal uniformity. Man's duty is to submit to these revelations and become a Muslim. Islam regards men as equal and believes that the Muslims should convert infidels to the truth revealed by God to the prophets. Hinduism, in contrast, permits almost any belief about God. Moreover, it holds that men are basically unequal in their intellectual capacities; thus they should not be expected to hold the same beliefs, nor should any attempts be made to create uniformity. With religion the central aspect of the two cultures, the divergent theological outlooks conditioned the cultural outlooks of both groups as well. Muslims looked with disfavor upon cultural diversity, which the Hindus regarded as normal, including the institution of caste. The Hindu's "human utopia is a state of philosophic anarchy; the Muslim's is the well-drilled regiment."[2] In consequence, the Muslims have always had a strong sense of community, which in India gave them strength out of proportion to their numbers, relative to the less cohesive Hindu community.

As is always the case when two such groups live side by side, numerous specific practices and prohibitions cause trouble. The Hindu worship of animals and idols is repellent to the monotheistic Muslims. Hindus decorate their temples with images and use music in them; the Koran forbids both in the mosque. Muslims eat beef; Hindus venerate the cow. Hindu efforts to enact and enforce bans on cow-slaughter antagonize the Muslims—an issue that flares up periodically, as it did in November 1966, when demonstrations in New Delhi to force the government to pass more rigorous laws led to widespread riots and the removal of a leading member from the Indian cabinet.[3]

History is another source of discord. The Hindus, especially in North India, remember the harsh treatment often received in the centuries of Muslim invasion and rule. The Muslims not surprisingly view these centuries in a different light; they could not calmly contemplate being ruled by those they once dominated, fearing they would stand little chance of securing justice or advancement in a Hindu-dominated India.

Cultural and historical factors were reinforced by two different kinds of economic problems. In some parts of the country, the landlords or moneylenders were predominantly of one community and the peasantry of the other. Perhaps more important were the differing positions of the Hindu and Muslim middle classes under the British. The Hindus developed a larger and better educated middle class for two reasons. The first was an accident of geography and history. The British entered India at the ports, where their influence and institutions were centered even after their activities spread over the countryside. It was in the ports, which were heavily Hindu, that the opportunities for acquiring new wealth and the new Western education existed. The Muslims were mainly located in the land-locked north of the country.[4] Nominally the rulers of much of the country when the British were taking over, the Muslims were penal-ized, especially after some rulers took part in the Mutiny in 1857. In the years after the Mutiny, Muslims, who had filled the majority of posts in the army, administration, and learned professions under the Mughal Empire and in the successor Muslim states, were able to win less than one-twentieth of the important government posts.

In addition, religious leaders urged Muslims to shun Western education in favor of traditional Islamic learning; in any case, many Muslims were more inclined to dream of past glories than to adapt themselves to new ways and acquire a new type of education. Not until near the end of the nineteenth century did many Muslims begin, at the urging of the far-sighted reformer and educator Sir Syed Ahmad Khan, to seek Western education. Throughout the period of British rule, the Hindus occupied a disproportionate num-ber of the positions in government services, the professions, and the business community. Muslims in time began to demand special con-sideration from the government, and to fear that their position of inferiority would be permanent in an undivided India.

Estrangement of the National Congress and the Muslim League

This is not the place to chronicle the growth of nationalism and the struggle for independence in South Asia. What is pertinent is to indicate some of the salient stages that led to partition, its atten-dant bitterness, and the continuing deep-seated hostility between the two countries.

Nationalist political activity in India began in earnest in the early twentieth century, although the Indian National Congress was founded in 1885 by a group of Europeans and Westernized Indians interested mainly in promoting social reform and greater opportu-nities for Indians. But the leaders of the Congress found that the government was often unwilling to accept their rather modest proposals calling for the application in India of some of the democratic principles Britain proclaimed at home. Actions that would have been accepted as inevitable if not right a few decades earlier generated resentment, and opposition to British rule became vociferous and even violent. Concerned, the British undertook the first important steps toward Indian self-rule.

The changes were set in motion by Lord Curzon, Viceroy from 1899 to 1905, whose extensive accomplishments were matched only by his alienation of Indian opinion through his methods, such as the notorious partition of Bengal.[5] East Bengal and Assam were separated from the rest of Bengal in 1905 and established as a new province, partly for reasons of administrative efficiency and partly to give Bengal's Muslims, who lived mainly in the east, a chance to develop their talents. The reaction, largely along religious lines, was not confined to Bengal but spread to the entire country. The Muslims, who had been a minority in united Bengal, welcomed the move as opening up new opportunities for them in a province they would control. The Hindus saw the partition as a British attempt to weaken their influence. The impact was to change the Congress party from a social reform movement into a political organization seeking home rule.

The deepening involvement of the Congress party in politics was accompanied by an intraparty struggle that continues even today. Congress had been established as a secular organization, and its Hindu members in the early days were reformist in outlook without abandoning their basic religious beliefs. They gradually came to believe that progress on their main interests in social reform, educational advancement, and improved economic conditions would be possible only if Indians acquired political power. Gopal Krishna Gokhale, a liberal Westernized Brahmin, was the leading exponent of this view, and the emphasis placed on such matters by the Congress party owes much to his efforts and influence. Considerable efforts were also made to win the cooperation of the Muslims, but with only modest success.[6]

During the first decade of this century, however, a representative of quite a different outlook became the most powerful figure in the party. Bal Gangadhar Tilak, a forceful conservative nationalist, was dedicated to the preservation of the Hindu religion and culture. Its values were endangered, in his view, not only by the foreigners who controlled India but also by Westernized Hindus seeking social change and religious reform. His advocacy of violence in the political struggle and his call for an India based on Hindu beliefs and values created apprehension among Muslims.

At the time that these trends emerged in the Congress, the British were making their first really significant concession to local political demands.[7] Lord Minto, then the governor general, and Lord Morley, the secretary of state for India in the British Government, attempted to reduce Indian unrest by expanding the size and scope of the legislative councils, to which nearly all unofficial members were to be elected. Many Indians thought the concessions were relatively insignificant, for the electorate was sharply restricted, the government retained official majorities in all the councils, and the councils had limited powers. Nevertheless, Indian members were now responsible to at least a section of Indian opinion and had a forum in which to express their views.

Shortly after the Minto-Morley reforms, however, Britain undid whatever political benefit might have been gained. King George V, in India in 1911 to be crowned Emperor, announced that the partition of Bengal was ended and that the capital would be moved from Calcutta to the Delhi area. The reunification of Bengal stunned the Muslims, who interpreted it as Britain's yielding to the Hindu majority. On the other hand, the Hindus, particularly in Bengal, regarded the transfer of the capital to the former seat of the Mughal Empire as a rebuke for their nationalist political activity.

The Muslims had reacted to developments in British policy and the Congress party by taking steps to protect their interests. In 1906 they organized the Muslim League, the political instrument that eventually won partition. They also pressed the government to grant them separate electorates under the Minto-Morley reforms, allowing Muslims to elect their own representatives to the proposed legislative councils, which the British did partly to assure the Muslims of a fair deal and partly to play them off against the more nationalistic Hindus.

Establishment of the Muslim League and the granting of separate electorates did not create an immediate and complete split between the Congress and the League. Some Muslims, including Mohammed Ali Jinnah, subsequently the leader of the Pakistan movement, were members of both organizations. Relations remained fairly good. Indeed, at the annual meetings in 1916, the two organizations concluded the Lucknow Pact, whereby the Congress agreed—reluctantly, to be sure—that the future constitution of India would guarantee Muslims a specified portion of seats in the central and provincial legislatures.

Opposition to British rule was not suspended during World War I, but it was noticeably curtailed. Both the Congress party and the Muslim League supported the war effort, and India made an impressive contribution of men and materiel. Indians expected their efforts would be rewarded. Aware that such expectations had to be met in some measure if moderate Indian opinion was to accept continued British control, the government announced in Parliament in 1917, "the policy . . . of the increasing association of Indians in every branch of Indian administration, and for the gradual development of self-governing institutions, with a view to the progressive realization of responsible government in British India as an integral part of the Empire." Even though no definite date was set for self-rule, the commitment was received with satisfaction by many Indians, who looked forward to the reforms that would carry out the pledge.

Britain also felt it necessary to suppress the extreme nationalists, some of whom had continued their terrorist activities. But the method chosen—secret trials without jury, counsel, or right of appeal—was so repressive that, instead of dividing the moderates and extremists, it antagonized Indian opinion. Indeed, the measures were so unpopular they were never used, but the intention to resort to them widened the gap between rulers and ruled.

The events of April 1919, at Amritsar in the Punjab, immeasurably widened the gulf. The area was in turmoil as a result of nationalist agitations and terrorist activities. The British, then engaged in the Third Afghan War, were tense and uneasy. In reaction to the killing of several Englishmen and an attack on an Englishwoman, all rights of assembly were suspended. The order was disobeyed by a crowd of several thousand, and General Dyer, in charge of military forces in the area, rushed troops to the scene. Soldiers opened fire without warning, killing hundreds and wounding well over a thousand. The government's harsh and humiliating actions after the shooting—widespread arrests and public floggings—further inflamed Indian public opinion.

Even to a world that had just emerged from the bloodletting of World War I, the Amritsar massacre of unarmed civilians was shocking. Instead of the lesson in obedience to authority that General Dyer had intended, nationalist determination to pursue a more forceful policy increased. Indians became convinced that a measure of control over the army was essential—an issue that was a major stumbling block in subsequent negotiations, especially during World War II. Amritsar damaged British stature in the eyes of the world; it also undermined the self-confidence of many officials, thereby weakening an essential ingredient of imperial rule, and raised doubts in the minds of British citizens about their government's policy.

In this atmosphere the measures for constitutional advance promised in 1917 were announced. Under the circumstances, they might have been unacceptable no matter how liberal they had been, but Britain, no longer hard-pressed by German arms, proposed only modest changes. The new constitution attempted to meet the nationalist objections to centralization of authority by shifting some powers to the provincial governments. However, elected Indian officials responsible to the legislatures would control only the less important provincial ministries, while the more important ones remained under British control. The responsibilities of elected officials in the central government were even less, and the central legislature could not even discuss the army or the budget. Communal representation was granted not only to the Muslims but also to the Sikhs, Anglo-Indians, and Indian Christians. Neither the Congress party nor the Muslim League was satisfied with these modest concessions, despite assurances that further reforms would follow if these worked satisfactorily.

Indian rejection of these proposals set the stage for the first nationwide clash between rulers and ruled. Congress, now led by Mohandas Gandhi, embarked on a program of nonviolent noncooperation to force major concessions and threatened a civil disobedience campaign if the British did not yield. The Muslims, aroused over what they regarded as Britain's unjust treatment of Turkey and its Sultan—the Caliph, or spiritual head of Islam—after World War I, regarded British policy as part of a general Western conspiracy against the Islamic world. By getting Congress to support the Khilafat movement for the retention of the Caliph, Gandhi was able to unite Hindus and Muslims against the British.

The 1920-22 noncooperation movement shook the foundations of British rule. Nationalists boycotted the elections, ignored the courts, left government schools, and refused to buy British goods. Government leaders feared a revolutionary situation was developing; thousands of Indians were jailed, and widespread military preparations to put down any uprising were undertaken. Early in 1922, at what was perhaps the crucial moment, when tension was near the breaking point and British officials were uncertain and divided, Gandhi called off the noncooperation movement because of one bloody but minor incident. His action baffled and angered many of his Congress supporters, who had not believed him when he said success is not worthwhile if achieved by violence. The Muslims, never convinced of the principles of nonviolence, were frustrated and angered. Shortly thereafter, the Khilafat movement also collapsed, for the new Turkey of Ataturk abolished the Caliphate.

Despite the failure to achieve any of the avowed objectives, noncooperation in 1920–22 was a big step forward. For the first time Indians were able to mount a coordinated nationwide effort against the British, with support in rural areas as well as the cities, and keep the movement going in a relatively disciplined fashion. The nationalists became more self-confident and won greater British respect.

The movement marked the emergence of Gandhi as the dominant figure of Indian nationalism. Basing his political ideas and actions on deeply felt and widely recognized Hindu values and attitudes, he transformed the Congress party from a middle-class to a mass organization. Gandhi, strongly influenced by certain Western ideas, was a Hindu reformer rather than an orthodox Hindu. While he upheld a purified caste system, he was opposed to untouchability and went to great lengths to combat it. Indeed, his principal aim was the moral and spiritual regeneration of the Indian people; national freedom was a necessary step toward this goal. Thus Gandhi was able to appeal to both the masses and the educated elite.

Gandhi's weapons probably were the most effective ones conceivable for use against the British. Just as civil disobedience, nonviolence, fasting, and boycotts struck a responsive chord within the Hindu community, they presented the British with a powerful yet embarrassing challenge. Almost no British officials wanted to resort to open force in ruling India, and Gandhi's policy of nonviolence made it possible for the independence struggle to be contained within tolerable bounds. Thousands were periodically jailed in the following decades, and force was used at times, though never again as at Amritsar. India had found a leader and a strategy for the struggle. But it was a strategy with a flaw. Much as Gandhi was opposed to Hindu-Muslim communalism, his efforts against the British were nonetheless a major element in raising Muslim political consciousness. Gandhi could win the political support of India's masses only by basing his appeal on religious values; this obviously meant Hindu values, which frightened and alienated the Muslim community.

After the collapse of the first noncooperation movement, the Indian nationalist movement entered a long period of drift and confusion broken only by the noncooperation campaign of the early 1930s. Of more lasting significance than the political activities that took place between 1922 and the elections in 1937 were the heightened communal tensions. The frequency and intensity of communal violence increased sharply in this period, which an observer described as one "of civil war between the Hindus and the Muslims of India, interrupted by brief intervals of armed peace."[8] Some of the disturbances were the usual ones precipitated by religious processions and services. Others had an economic character, reflecting the divergent religious affiliations of landlords and tenants and the competition between Hindu and Muslim middle-class elements for desirable jobs. As the nationalists stepped up their civil disobedience programs, there was a general decline in the respect for law and established authority.

As it became apparent that British power was receding, Indians turned more and more to questions about their political future. The Congress backed away from its agreement in the Lucknow Pact that Muslims would receive one-third of the seats in a future central legislature. The Muslim League, in turn, backed away from its willingness to see the establishment of a strong central government and demanded stronger representation in the provincial legislatures that it had agreed to at Lucknow. Self-rule had seemed remote in 1916, but, as it came to be viewed as possible, both communities reflected more deeply on their likely relationship in an independent India.

The Struggle for Independence

The first major test of the relative political strengths of the Congress and the League occurred in 1937, when elections were held under the new and more representative constitution that Britain had promulgated in 1935. The constitution, a significant advance toward self-rule, provided for full ministerial responsibility to elected legislatures at the provincial level, though the British governors retained important powers. Congress contested the elections and won a sweeping victory with about 70 per cent of the vote. The Muslim League, which was still a middle-class party, was able to win only about one-fifth of the seats reserved for Muslims. Other parties and leaders, particularly in the Muslim majority areas, overshadowed the Muslim League. Jinnah's prospects and those of his party looked anything but promising.

Ironically, the League was saved by the actions of the Congress party leaders. In some parts of India, particularly the large and populous United Provinces, the two parties had stressed the similarity of their aims, and apparently there was an agreement to form coalition ministries. Encouraged by the strong showing, Congress ministries took control of most of the provincial governments. In a move regarded by most scholars as a key to future Hindu-Muslim relations, they refused to allow Muslim League officials in the United Provinces to join the government unless they became members of the Congress and permanently dissolved the League's local parliamentary boards. As put by Ian Stephens:

> The effect of this, simultaneously on many Muslim minds throughout India, was of a lightning-flash. What had before been but guessed at, now leapt in horridly clear outline. The Congress, a Hindu-dominated body, was bent on the Muslims' eventual absorption; Western-style majority rule, in an undivided subcontinent, could only mean the smaller community being swallowed by the larger, as Syed Ahmad Khan had long ago pointed out; in the end Muslims would find themselves just one of the lower Hindu castes, dissolved in a general grey idolatrous mush. Those were the opinions formed; and that British Parliamentary precedents might readily be found to support the kind of decision the Congress had made, after so big an electoral success—and assuming no really firm promises had been broken—mattered not at all. For Britain was not India; conditions there were different; hers was a unitary society, not a plural or multi-racial one.[9]

Having aroused Muslim suspicions, the Congress ministries now proceeded to confirm Muslim fears. The Congress flag flew from government buildings, a Hindu hymn of anti-Muslim origin was adopted as the national anthem, and educational programs began to reflect Hindu culture. Land-reform programs aroused the fears of Muslim landlords. Numerous reports of discrimination against, and harassment of, Muslims circulated. That the number and scope of the incidents were probably exaggerated was of less political importance than the growing Muslim conviction that the reports had a basis in fact.

The events of 1937–39 shifted the locus of political power in the subcontinent as a result of the mounting apprehension of the Muslims and the dramatic change in Jinnah's role and strategy. At first a Congressman who had opposed the Muslim League's demand for separate electorates in 1909 and had striven for Hindu-Muslim cooperation, Jinnah had become disenchanted with the Congress when Gandhi, with his Hindu values and noncooperation program, became its leader. Brilliant and sensitive, honest but egotistical, he became the undisputed ruler of the League, which he reorganized, ran with an iron hand, and made into a powerful organization by stressing the theme of Islam in danger. The poet Iqbal urged Jinnah to work for a separate Muslim nation—an idea Iqbal had first publicly suggested in 1930. But Jinnah held back for a time, aware that the League had far from universal support in the Muslim community and uncertain whether such a drastic step was necessary.

Emboldened by its growing strength in by-elections and increasingly fearful of its probable place in a united and independent India, the Muslim League in March 1940 put forward its demand for a separate state. The area to be included was not defined at first, though in time the League demanded the four Muslim-majority provinces in the northwest and Bengal and Assam in the northeast. (Although Assam was only one-third Muslim, the League claimed it on the ground that it could not stand alone, separated from the rest of India.) At the outset, the support for Pakistan, as the proposed nation was to be called, came chiefly from Muslims in Hindu-majority areas. Where Muslims were in the majority, they felt more secure and their support for the League and for partition developed more slowly.

In seeking support for the creation of Pakistan, Jinnah went beyond the claim that such a state was necessary because of Hindu domination of a free and united India. The religious and cultural differences between Hindus and Muslims, he maintained, were so basic and extensive that they had to be considered as two distinct nations. The communities could live together under a single government only because it was controlled by an outside power, but they must follow separate paths to nationhood once the British relinquished control. This view was disputed by Muslims at both ends of the spectrum: Some, with a traditional religious outlook, held it to be a perversion of religion to equate it with nationhood, while others, who believed in secular democracy, regarded it as an outmoded view.

Nevertheless, Jinnah's driving energy and single-mindedness, together with the growing communal violence, gradually won most Muslims over to the two-nation theory.

Between 1939 (when the Congress ministries resigned because the government declared war without consulting the legislature on Indian opinion) and 1942, the British and Indians engaged in a series of maneuvers, exchanges, and negotiations but were never able to reach agreement. Although their positions changed somewhat, essentially Congress was willing to support the war effort only if a national government responsible to an elected legislature was established. Britain felt unable to take such risks, and particularly to relinquish control of the army to an Indian government during the war. In March 1942, when Japanese forces were approaching India, Prime Minister Churchill sent a special mission headed by Sir Stafford Cripps, who was sympathetic to Indian nationalism, to try to win acceptance of a new plan for constitutional reform. The plan provided that, in return for support of the war effort, Britain would grant dominion status after the war to an Indian union composed of those provinces and princely states that wished to be part of it, with the remainder free to seek separate dominion status. Congress leaders were far from united in their views, with Nehru particularly desirous of finding a way for India to join in the struggle against fascism and Japanese imperialism. After long and anguished consideration, the Congress refused to accept the Cripps plan, objecting most strongly to the postponement of any real constitutional advance during the war and to the provision for separate dominion status, which opened the door to partition. The League also rejected the plan, because it did not explicitly provide for the establishment of Pakistan, although, if the Congress had accepted, the League might have felt compelled to do the same. With the breakdown of negotiations the Congress launched a "Quit India" drive, and the government reacted by arresting thousands of Indians and outlawing the party. Political activity during the war was limited to the Muslim League, which cooperated to some extent with the government, the Hindu Mahasabha (a militantly anti-Muslim party), and the Communist party; they increased their strength substantially through the absence of the Congress leaders from the political arena.

With the end of the war in sight, Congress leaders were released from prison, and it was apparent that the demands of Indian nationalism could no longer be put off. British attempts to prosecute soldiers who had been captured by the Japanese and fought in the Japanese-controlled Indian National Army (INA) had to be abandoned because of massive popular opposition. Even more ominous was the mutiny in the Royal Indian Navy and the refusal of units in the Royal Indian Air Force to obey orders in the winter of 1945–46.

The Indian mood made it clear that the British could not remain in control without resorting to measures they despised. The resounding Labour party victory in the 1945 elections demonstrated that domestic reforms rather than imperial glory occupied first place in the minds of the British people, and Churchill's continuing attacks on the idea of Indian independence were futile. But it was far from clear who should inherit the mantle of authority.

Neither the Congress leaders nor the British knew quite how to evaluate the Muslim demand for partition. Nehru had long been scornful of the idea. As a nationalist he believed in the unity of India; as an advocate of secular democracy he was convinced the Muslims would receive fair treatment in an independent India; as an agnostic he found the idea of a state founded on religious loyalties abhorrent. Other Congress leaders with a Western outlook shared his opinions, while Hindus generally found the idea of a division of Mother India repugnant on religious and cultural grounds.

The problem of finding a solution acceptable to both sides was hampered by the widely divergent attitudes and claims of the two factions. Jinnah's insistence that the Congress party was a Hindu organization infuriated its leaders. His demands that the Muslim League be recognized as coequal with the Congress, that it be the sole representative of India's Muslims, and that it alone be given the right to appoint Muslims to office were completely unacceptable to the Congress leaders. They saw Jinnah's demands as negating the principles of democracy, just as they saw the League's separate existence and efforts as dividing and weakening Indian nationalism. Congress leaders (and Hindus generally) were convinced they had borne the brunt of battle and the Muslims had only joined the struggle after independence was in sight.

Most British officials were uncertain as to how to proceed; the unity of India was one of Britain's proudest accomplishments, which they were reluctant to see shattered. The idea of splitting the British Indian Army was particularly repugnant to them. Moreover, the Congress was espousing the same democratic ideals as the British, and few could accept the claims of the League that this was purely a façade that would vanish with the British departure.

Quite apart from these personal doubts, there were strong practical objections to partition. It would not really solve the communal problem, for there would still be religious minorities in both countries. Partition seemed to be administrative and economic folly. There were serious questions about the viability of a Pakistan divided into widely separated parts. The defense of the area would be weakened, particularly in view of the animosities of the two states. Advocates of Pakistan were also aware of these problems, but their deep-seated fear of Hindu domination and intense desire for self-rule predominated.

Between the release of the Congress leaders from prison in June, 1945, and the departure of the British just over two years later, two distinct but related activities dominated the political life of the subcontinent. The first was the long series of negotiations of the British Labour government, the Congress party, and the Muslim League in search of an acceptable plan for relinquishing power. The second was the growing communal violence on the subcontinent. The negotiations held the stage from mid-1945 to mid-1946; little real progress was made. Owing to this failure, from mid-1946 onward the rising tide of communal violence took over and forced both the pace and nature of the political decisions.

The two key issues in the negotiations were getting the parties to participate in an interim government, and thereby shoulder joint responsibility for the difficult days ahead, and persuading them to cooperate in drawing up a constitution for a self-governing India. Lord Wavell, the Viceroy, began the negotiations in the summer of 1945, but they soon collapsed over Jinnah's refusal to have the League join the interim government, because it would include Muslims who were members of other parties. The Congress adamantly insisted on its right to nominate Muslims if it chose to do so.

Although aware that the League had gained in strength, the Congress leaders were unprepared for the results of the elections held in the winter of 1945–46. The Muslim League won more than 80 per cent of the seats reserved for Muslims in provincial legislatures and all such seats in the central legislature, in a campaign based almost entirely on the demand for Pakistan. Jinnah's claim that the League represented the country's Muslims was confirmed.

On February 19, 1946, London announced that a Cabinet mission would visit India to prepare a program for granting the country its freedom. After two months of extremely difficult negotiations the Mission announced its plan, which was both complex and imprecise. Like previous plans, it provided for a large measure of decentralization in a complicated three-tiered structure. Basic governmental authority was to be centered in the provinces, with the central government's having clearly limited and enumerated powers—foreign affairs, defense, communications, and the financing of these subjects. Those provinces that so desired could join together in groups with more extensive powers than the central government had; the implication, although not specified, was that the groups could also leave the federal union. Three such groups were to be set up at once: two—the northeast and northwest—were Muslim-majority areas; the other comprised the rest of India. Special legal safeguards for communal issues were to be established. Finally, and this was specified as an integral part, an interim central government to implement the plan was to be set up with whatever parties were willing to join it. The Muslim League, with obvious reluctance because the plan did not clearly provide for Pakistan, accepted it nonetheless, thinking it might be possible to win the League's full goal. The Congress answer was a qualified acceptance of the basic structure, but a refusal to join the interim government on the terms offered.

After agonizing over the dilemma, Britain retreated before the Congress refusal and announced that it would not set up an interim government. The Muslim League was infuriated. More important, League officials, long suspicious that the British Labour party was pro-Congress, felt betrayed, concluding that Britain had decided that its long-term interest lay in good relations with the larger and wealthier Hindu community. Jinnah felt that henceforth he had to fight both the British and the Congress, and take an unyielding stance.

The Cabinet Mission left India at the end of June with one accomplishment to its credit. It had made it clear to all that Britain really wanted to relinquish power and that, if its plan—or something very much like it—was not accepted, the only alternatives were partition or civil war and chaos.

On July 7, Nehru, addressing an important party meeting in Bombay, asserted that the Congress had not in fact accepted the substance of the plan and that in the future it would be bound only by its own judgment of what was in India's interests. Three days later he went even further, predicting that no grouping of provinces would occur, that power would inevitably flow to the federal government from the provinces, and that the Congress would remain unbound by any agreements and completely free to decide issues as they arose. It is widely agreed that these statements had the most profound and disastrous impact. Even Maulana Azad, Nehru's life-long collaborator, insisted that Nehru's statements were not correct and that the Congress could not unilaterally modify the agreements.

Despite Nehru's remarks, the Viceroy issued a well-meant but ill-timed invitation to the two parties to form an interim government under conditions that the Congress accepted but that Jinnah felt had been made less favorable to the League. In a mood of growing apprehension and desperation, the Muslim League adopted a policy of all-out struggle against both the British and the Congress. Jinnah announced that the League would no longer limit itself to constitutional methods and fixed August 16 as "Direct Action Day." Alarmed at this, the British and the Congress made new attempts to get the League to enter the government, but all were spurned by Jinnah.

Nehru's provocative statements, the Viceroy's offer, and Jinnah's intransigent policy in effect marked the end of any chance, if indeed there ever was one, of transferring power to a united India. Although the League leaders apparently intended no violence on "Direct Action Day," Jinnah's words were incendiary. Most of India remained peaceful on August 16, but Calcutta experienced three days of the most savage communal riots in the city's history. Apparently some limited violence was planned by Muslim elements. Hindu organizations were prepared and struck back in force, and the Sikhs joined in pushing the riots beyond control. Thousands were killed; tens of thousands injured; and perhaps a hundred thousand made homeless by arson—with the Muslims (one-fourth of the city's population) the losers. Law and order broke down completely, and only the army was able to restore them.

The Calcutta riots inaugurated the second phase in the postwar situation, which was dominated by the steady spread of communal violence. Muslims in East Bengal retaliated by massacring the local Hindus; in Bihar, Hindus sought revenge by murdering their Muslim neighbors. As the virus moved westward it swept into the countryside, thus becoming more difficult to prevent or halt. More ominous were indications that the violence was increasingly the work of organized forces on both sides. The police were often unable or unwilling to intervene effectively, and the army was spread too thin to do more than halt the larger outbreaks after they had occurred.

In October, 1946, the Muslim League decided it could no longer afford to let the Congress alone hold office in New Delhi. It entered the government, but only to pursue a policy of noncooperation to undermine the government and prove that Hindus and Muslims could not work together. The arguments between the Congress and the League seemed pointless with communal strife sweeping across the subcontinent in the winter of 1946–47. Both parties condemned the violence, though usually blaming it on the other, but it was now beyond their control. The League maintained its intransigent position on partition and made no attempt to calm the fears of non-Muslims who would be in Pakistan, apparently determined to wield full power in the state it claimed for itself. Stalemate, frustration, and anger were rampant.

By December, communal violence had reached the Punjab and the Northwest Frontier Province (NWFP). These two provinces had always furnished a disproportionate share of the army's manpower, and continued atrocities would put a severe strain on the army's morale and discipline. Moreover, major political struggles were under way in both provinces. The Punjab had long been governed by the noncommunal Unionist party (a provincial coalition of Hindus, Muslims, and Sikhs), and the NWFP by a Muslim party affiliated with the Congress. Despite its gains in the 1946 elections, the Muslim League had been unable to win a majority of seats in either province, and it resorted to civil disobedience campaigns to bring down the provincial ministries. Communal incidents and political agitation finally led to a mass upheaval in the Punjab in March. All communities suffered, but perhaps none as badly as the Sikhs in the northern districts, where they were heavily outnumbered.

It became ever clearer in London in the winter of 1946–47 that major decisions, however unpleasant, would have to be taken. Conditions in the subcontinent were deteriorating swiftly, and the ability to cope would soon decline sharply, for during the twelve months beginning in April, 1947, the number of British officers in the Indian Army would drop from 11,400 to 4,000.

These factors led Prime Minister Atlee to make the most dramatic move of the postwar period on February 20, 1947. He announced in Parliament that Britain would cease to rule India by June, 1948, and that Lord Mountbatten would replace Lord Wavell as Viceroy. The announcement stunned the Indian political parties and finally gained Britain the initiative.

Upon surveying the situation in India, Mountbatten found the Congress leaders weakening in their opposition to partition but adamant that, if partition occurred, Assam (with its Hindu majority) be a part of India and Bengal and the Punjab be partitioned along communal lines. They felt that perhaps Jinnah would still back down if he could get only a truncated Pakistan and not the country he envisioned (which included all three provinces). Mountbatten also concluded that it was impossible to continue under the present governmental set-up for another year: The administration was dying on its feet; the Congress and the Muslim League would not work together; and communal violence would soon be utterly beyond control. Despite the immense difficulties, the only way out was an even earlier transfer of authority than contemplated in February. He quickly secured London's approval and early in June revealed that British authority would be transferred to two separate nations on August 15, 1947—just over two months away.

Jinnah and the Muslim League were disappointed with the proposed partition of Bengal and the Punjab and the assignment of Assam to India. Yet, having argued for the partition of the country along communal lines, Jinnah could not make an effective case against applying the same principle to provinces with large Hindu minorities in areas adjacent to the provinces that were to be part of India. It was clear that the British and the Congress were adamant on this point, and so with a grudging acknowledgement that "a moth-eaten Pakistan is better than none at all" Jinnah accepted the plan.

Acceptance was more difficult for the Congress. A division of India was equally abhorrent to Hindu nationalists and to those with a secular democratic outlook. Nehru and his colleagues had always believed that the end result of their struggle and sacrifices would be an independent India stretching from Burma to Afghanistan and from the Himalayas to Cape Comorin; they never expected the Muslim masses to support a party of landlords and bourgeois elements that had no social or economic program to alleviate their wretched conditions.

Desiring the unity and freedom of India, the Congress leaders now saw that they could not have both. Being human, they found it hard to blame themselves for the tragic choice they faced. Initially they had viewed the Muslim League's efforts as bargaining demands to gain limited ends. When it became clear that the League was determined to create a Muslim state, the temptation was great to blame either the British, charging that their divide-and-rule tactics stimulated Muslim demands, or "evil and power-hungry" leaders of the League. That the British resorted to such tactics in the past is true, but it is equally true that the divisions they exploited had long existed within Indian society. That Jinnah and his lieutenants were ambitious and at times irresponsible is also clear, but to describe Jinnah as one who would see hundreds of thousands die in communal upheavals merely to satisfy personal vanity is to portray him as an essentially evil man, which he was not. His efforts could never have called forth the strong response of the Muslims if they had not been deeply fearful of their future in a united and therefore Hindu-controlled India. As W. Norman Brown, a friend of Indian nationalism and Hindu culture, has concluded:

> . . . Indian nationalism rose, grew, and expressed itself in the religio-social group of Hindus. It was not possible for this nationalism to win to itself the Muslims, adherents to another religiocentric manner of life, which in its way was just as intent upon survival as ever was Hinduism. It is true that the Indian National Congress, the organ of nationalism, never conceded itself to be the voice of Hindu India alone as distinguished from India as a whole. It adopted a secular program meant to produce a secular state; many of its most prominent leaders sincerely and consistently upheld secular aims in politics and eschewed religious and narrow communal aims. Among them were certain Muslims. But the stubborn fact remained that nationalism was a phenomenon of the Hindu community and this community provided the strength and the direction of Congress, which, when it at last achieved power in 1937–1939 was not wise enough to win Muslim confidence. The rivalries already implicit in the situation were exacerbated by the communal activities of the Hindu Mahasabha, which frankly advocated violence against Muslims and goaded Congress as far as it could to communal action. The masses of each community, and more narrowly, the middle classes, which were those fostering political activity, never forgot the contrasts and antipathies of Hinduism and Islam. Hence they could not cross the barrier of communalism and press ahead in common effort to solve the problems posed before their country by the conditions of the mid-twentieth-century world.[10]

In the end, the Congress leaders one by one came to accept partition as less disastrous than any other course open to them. Azad, who as a nationalist Muslim loyal to the Congress was in an agonizing position, describes how Mountbatten was able to convince first Sardar Patel, the party boss, then Nehru, and finally Gandhi that partition was inescapable; their acquiescence led many lesser party officials to follow suit.[11] The reasons for acceptance varied. Some, still not fully convinced of Britain's determination to withdraw, feared that failure to reach agreement with the Muslim League would leave Britain in authority. Other leaders—particularly Nehru —felt that independence was not the end of their struggle; the tasks of social reform and economic development lay ahead. But could these tasks be carried out if an independent India had a weak national government unable to implement measures for reform and development, being hobbled by constant communal bickering, violence, and perhaps even civil war? Better to let some provinces go their way, and get on with the job; perhaps these areas would later see their error and rejoin India. The vote in the All-India Committee, despite an appeal by Gandhi, was only 29 to 15 in favor of accepting partition, an indication of how deeply the party and the country were divided even while formally accepting Mountbatten's plan.

In the Aftermath of Partition

The attention of the world and of the citizens of the two new countries was only briefly focused on the independence celebrations in August, 1947.[12] Communal violence had subsided in the last months of British rule, and there was hope that with an agreed settlement the worst was over. To everyone's horror, the communal fears and hatreds exploded in an orgy of murder, rape, and destruction on a scale beyond the most dismal fears.

The upsurge began in early August in the rural areas of the eastern Punjab, where the Sikhs began an organized campaign of revenge against Muslims for the massacres of March; soon Muslims were retaliating in areas that became West Pakistan. Indeed, across much of northern India, villages and cities quickly divided into two hostile camps, with members of each community half-fearful of being murdered and half-eager to murder their neighbors. Law and order broke down in the countryside and the cities of the Punjab. Local police were first overburdened, then overwhelmed. Neither country could control the situation; their armies, struggling to get organized, were able to do no more than mitigate the violence and prevent complete chaos. For a time it looked as though even New Delhi would be engulfed. The Indian Government "delegated" considerable authority to Lord Mountbatten, who had become India's first governor-general, and his military experience proved invaluable.

No one really knows how many were killed in the months after partition, or how many others perished because of disease, hunger, and exposure. Figures range from several hundred thousand to a million, with most estimates falling in the vicinity of half a million. Millions of families were affected, and each death added to the hatred between the two nations.

The massacres caused what was probably the greatest mass migration known to history, which, moreover, took place in the remarkably short period of a few months. Again, there are no accurate figures, but apparently some 5 million Muslims migrated to West Pakistan; roughly an equal number of Hindus and Sikhs moved in the opposite direction. As the massacres stimulated the migration, so the migration presented new opportunities for slaughter, and many who started the journey never completed it. By early 1948, virtually all the Sikhs and Hindus had left West Pakistan, and most Muslims who had opted for West Pakistan had arrived there.

The situation was different in the eastern part of the country after the division of Bengal. The migrations were smaller and more orderly, though the hardships were great for a people already living close to the margin. During the next few years some 2 million to 3 million Hindus left East Pakistan; about half as many Muslims entered the province. However, large numbers of Hindus—about 7 million—remained in East Pakistan, and several million Muslims stayed in nearby areas in India. The migration of these minorities has continued, rising and falling according to the treatment they receive and the state of Indo-Pakistani relations. The resettlement problem has been especially acute, because East Pakistan is heavily overpopulated and the Indian Government has failed to induce many refugees to settle outside of West Bengal.

The refugees added to the burdens of the two governments. Few of them arrived at their destinations with much in the way of worldly goods, for both states restricted what emigrants could take with them. Refugees who evaded the controls and traveled with their belongings found themselves easy targets for thieves. Upon arrival, the refugees clamored for food, housing, and land to begin a new life, and their tales of horror fueled the mutual hatreds. The pressures they brought on their governments made it difficult for leaders to restrain the firebrands and extremists calling for forceful action to avenge the wrongs. That the new governments were able to survive the upheavals and provide emergency care for most of the refugees is remarkable; that neither was able to settle and integrate them for many years is hardly surprising, however disappointing and difficult to accept for the refugees.

The migrations gave rise to one of the more disruptive problems in Indo-Pakistani relations, that of the disposition of evacuee property. Once it became clear that few refugees would return to their former homes, the two governments took control of the property left behind. Muslim refugees demanded that Pakistan either pressure India into compensating them for property they left behind or, at least, compensate them out of the property abandoned in Pakistan by Hindus and Sikhs. In India, Hindu and Sikh refugees made similar demands. Even if the value of abandoned property had been equal, its control, evaluation, and redistribution would have been extremely difficult. Most outside observers are convinced, however, that the non-Muslims left much more property in Pakistan than the Muslims left in India, which seems a reasonable judgment in view of the greater wealth of the Hindu and Sikh communities generally. Because this was one of the few issues on which Pakistan was in the stronger position, it was in no hurry for a settlement—nor could it have afforded to compensate India in the years just after partition.

Other financial disputes arose out of the division of the cash balances of British India. Pakistan was to receive a specified share, but when the time for payment came in early 1948 the two countries were fighting in Kashmir. India hesitated to make the payment lest Pakistan use the money to finance its military activities. Perhaps because Gandhi had begun a fast to secure better treatment for Indian Muslims, and also to induce the government to honor the financial agreement, India soon made the payment. Pakistan also claimed, apparently correctly, that India withheld millions of dollars' worth of military equipment and supplies that had been awarded to Pakistan, and that Pakistan never received its share of certain other assets. India contested these claims and countered with its own.

It was necessary to set up two special border commissions to establish the exact boundaries because of the division of the Punjab and of Bengal. Although reluctantly accepted by both governments, certain awards gave rise to much dissatisfaction. Pakistan objected particularly to the award of part of the Gurdaspur District in the Punjab to India. The district as a whole had a small Muslim majority, and its division provided India with its only access by land to Kashmir—a matter of great importance when the fighting in Kashmir began a few months later.

The conflicting claims to the waters of the Indus River system constituted one of the most serious disputes. The system comprises six major rivers: the Indus River itself and its tributaries the Jhelum, the Chenab, the Ravi, the Sutlej, and the Beas. The latter three flow for a considerable distance in India or Indian-controlled Kashmir before entering West Pakistan. The British had constructed the world's largest irrigation system in the Punjab to utilize these waters, but partition cut the system in two. India said it needed the waters of the three eastern rivers to develop its territory; Pakistan insisted that millions of its people depended on them for their livelihood. In March, 1948, India cut off the water supply for a few months, which led to fury and fear in Pakistan; an agreement was reached whereby Pakistan consented to a gradual reduction in the supply of water from the rivers flowing through India, but Pakistan later claimed that it had signed under duress, and it repudiated the agreement in 1950.

The Problem of the Princely States

Other problems arose from the existence of several hundred princely states, varying greatly from the large, populous, and wealthy to the minuscule and poor. Properly speaking, they were not even parts of British India. In theory, the princes were allies of the British Crown, although clearly subordinate to it, a relationship known as paramountcy. In return for ceding control of their foreign affairs the princes received protection from external threats and local insurrections; they enjoyed a large measure of freedom in internal affairs, provided their rule was not unduly offensive. In fact, the British had the final say on whatever they deemed important enough to warrant intervention.

Historical accidents and skillful diplomacy had enabled some princely states to maintain their separate existence as the British tide had rolled across the subcontinent. Before the Mutiny the British policy of gradually abolishing the princely states and bringing them under direct rule naturally aroused opposition, and this even led some of them to take part in the Mutiny. After 1857 the British came to believe that, through the device of paramountcy, the princely states would support British rule when it was challenged by other forces. But the value of that support became problematical when Britain began to institute self-government. The internal autonomy of the states made it practically impossible to bring about reforms and any measure of representative government without losing the support of the princes, which was the main reason for allowing the states to exist. Often the princes and their subjects were of different religions, and the princes generally favored the members of their own communities with state jobs and privileges, leaving the majority of people in an inferior status. The growth of democratic beliefs and religious nationalism made such situations explosive.

When Britain announced independence and partition in 1947, the princes were told that paramountcy would lapse and they could either join one of the two new Dominions or attempt to maintain their independence. If they chose the latter path, no British help would be forthcoming. In making their decisions, the princes should pay due regard to the religious composition of their people, as well as to geographical contiguity with the new Dominions.

The Congress had long been extremely critical of the princely states, whose continued existence would be dangerous for Indian unity, disruptive of the economy, and an affront to all nationalists; the leaders maintained that the new government would not recognize the right of the states to become independent. For Pakistan, they posed less of a problem because far fewer of them were within, or adjacent to, the areas destined to become Pakistan. Unlike the Congress, the Muslim League had no parallel organizations in the states, and so Jinnah espoused the cause of the rulers, supporting British policy on the right of the states to independence. He held out some hope that the states that acceded to Pakistan would continue to enjoy a substantial measure of autonomy. Jinnah was aware that he could not hope to entice the Hindu princes (or even the Muslim rulers of states well within Indian territory) to join Pakistan, but if they chose independence it would weaken India and indirectly strengthen Pakistan.[13]

It is noteworthy that serious trouble occurred in only three of the princely states. In most cases, India and Pakistan were able to integrate them with a minimum of disruption.[14]

The first and least important of the three disputes concerned Junagadh, an area of some 3,000 square miles, north of Bombay on the Kathiawar Peninsula; its only link with Pakistan was by sea. The population of about 700,000 at the time of partition was approximately 80 per cent Hindu, but the ruler was a Muslim. On September 15, he signed an instrument of accession to Pakistan. Resistance to the local government developed quickly, and a rival government was set up. Early in November Indian troops marched in, taking the state over in the name of the people. Pakistan took the issue to the United Nations but received no satisfaction. India held a plebiscite in February, 1948, and the people voted heavily in favor of accession to India. For all practical purposes that ended the issue, except for the exacerbation of Indo-Pakistani relations.

A more serious dispute concerned Hyderabad. Located in central India, Hyderabad was the second largest princely state on the subcontinent, with more than 80,000 square miles and a population of about 17 million at the time, about 80 per cent of which was Hindu. The Nizam, or ruler, and most of the governing class were Muslim. No moderate political party had been permitted in Hyderabad, which lagged far behind most of India in every way, and it had long been a special target of Indian nationalists. As the time for Britain's departure approached, communal tensions rose significantly, armed bands were formed by Muslim groups, and violence erupted frequently.

Unlike the ruler of Junagadh, the Nizam was not interested in acceding to distant Pakistan. When he proclaimed independence a few days after the British left, the Indian Government stated that Hyderabad was far too important to India's territorial integrity and economic needs to be permitted to choose independence. All India was willing to do was to sign a stand-still agreement with the Nizam in November, 1947, which provided that Hyderabad stood in the same relation to India as it had to Britain. Negotiations continued, but no satisfactory solution could be reached. Throughout late 1947 and early 1948 tensions and communal violence mounted. India, insisting that the Nizam improve and liberalize his government and curb the violence, organized an economic blockade to force compliance. The Nizam held fast and further infuriated India by lending money to Pakistan.

In the summer of 1948 India, frustrated in gaining its end indirectly, began preparing for invasion. Hyderabad appealed to the United Nations, but in September (before the Security Council had dealt with the case) India invaded and quickly won control in what it termed a police action to restore law and order. The Nizam was allowed to remain as nominal ruler under a new government responsive to New Delhi, and the complaint to the United Nations was withdrawn. India's action was strongly criticized in the Western press. Annoyed Indians claimed that the West simply did not understand the situation, refusing to admit that they had resorted to the straightforward power politics they condemned other nations for practicing.

In contrast to the take-over of Junagadh, Pakistan had no legal claim in the Hyderabad case. Nonetheless, to weaken India, it gave political support to the Nizam's position, recognizing that the arguments India had used would help Pakistan in the Kashmir case. Pakistan enjoyed seeing India's embarrassment before the world, which might reduce India's influence with other countries.

The Kashmir Dispute

Junagadh and Hyderabad, troublesome issues though they were, would have been of transitory importance in the absence of the struggle for Kashmir. This has been the focus of the threat that each country believed the other posed, raising their defense budgets, and has twice led to open though undeclared war. For over twenty years the Kashmir issue has rested unresolved on the doorstep of the United Nations.

Kashmir encompassed almost 85,000 square miles and had a population somewhat over 4 million at the time of partition. The ruler was Hindu, but approximately three-fourths of the population professed Islam—just the reverse of conditions in Junagadh and Hyderabad. The state was mostly mountainous, with only two small plains areas. The first was around Jammu in the southwest in the foothills of the Himalayas. The other was the fabled Vale of Kashmir, about 85 miles long by 20–25 miles wide in the central part of the state. Jammu and the Vale were the two key political divisions, each containing about 45 per cent of the population. Both were Muslim-majority areas—Jammu with a very large Hindu minority and the Vale with only a small one. Across the northern part of Kashmir, a miscellaneous collection of small principalities, mainly feudatory to the ruler, comprised three-fourths of the area of the state but less than 10 per cent of the population, which was Muslim except in the Ladakh area, where Buddhism was the predominant faith. In 1947 its transportation links and trade were almost entirely with West Pakistan.

Aside from its agricultural land and timber, Kashmir had few economic resources other than the magnificent scenery of the Vale. The upper reaches of four of the rivers on which West Pakistan depended for its irrigation were in Kashmir or bordered on it. Moreover, its location—between India, Pakistan, the Chinese provinces of Tibet and Sinkiang, and (beyond the narrow Wakhan corridor controlled by Afghanistan) the Soviet Union—endowed it with strategic importance in the eyes of both Indian and Pakistani leaders.

After defeating the Sikhs and taking direct control of the Punjab in 1845–49, the British did not want to assume direct responsibility for Kashmir, and they sold the Vale to Gulab Singh, the Dogra ruler of Jammu, who in turn acknowledged British paramountcy. Despite Kashmir's supposedly autonomous status, concern over princely misrule and Russian involvement in Central Asia led Britain to intervene in its internal affairs from time to time. Nonetheless, the reforms imposed by the British or wrung from a reluctant ruler by occasional upsurges of agitation in the 1920s and 1930s did not affect the essentials of the situation. The state in 1947 was run along orthodox Hindu lines by and for the Maharaja and two important Hindu castes, the Dogras of Jammu and the Kashmiri Brahmins in the Vale.[15] Political life centered on the conflict between the Maharaja and the Jammu and Kashmir National Conference, which was led by Sheikh Abdullah, a Muslim leader with an outlook similar to that of the left wing of the Indian National Congress and unsympathetic to the Muslim League. The more conservative Muslim Conference, which was favorably inclined toward the Muslim League, was much weaker. Sheikh Abdullah apparently felt that Kashmir's best interests called for an autonomous status within the Indian Union. The strength of the secularly oriented National Conference, headed by a prominent Muslim and ideologically oriented toward the Indian Congress party, was a bitter pill for Pakistani leaders to swallow, just as Sheikh Abdullah's later imprisonment in India became a political handicap for Indian spokesmen.

If the disposition of Kashmir had been made according to the principles applied to British India, the state—with the possible exception of a Hindu-majority area in Jammu adjacent to the Indian Punjab—would have gone to Pakistan. But with the lapse of paramountcy the power of decision rested with the Maharaja. Accession to a democratic India held no appeal for him, but his future looked even less promising in a Muslim Pakistan despite Jinnah's efforts to convince him that the state's autonomy would be respected if he opted for Pakistan. To complicate matters, he was suspicious of the

British and resisted Mountbatten's efforts to get him to make a definite decision. Hoping to achieve independence, the Maharaja arrested most of the state's politicians in mid-1947 and tried to arrange stand-still agreements with both India and Pakistan. The latter quickly agreed, thinking that the agreement meant it would not only maintain its transportation and communication links with the state but also assume Britain's responsibility for defense and foreign affairs, and that Kashmir would soon accede to Pakistan. This apparently was not the Maharaja's intention, for no accession was forthcoming. Visits by Congress leaders and Indian officials to Kashmir aroused the suspicions of Pakistani leaders, which grew in September when the Maharaja released Sheikh Abdullah from prison—though not the leaders of the Muslim Conference who favored Pakistan— and India began building a road from the Punjab to Jammu.

The communal rioting throughout the Punjab spread to Jammu, with Hindu and Sikh refugees' attacking Muslims there. In September a Muslim revolt against the government of Kashmir occurred in the western part of the state, and a provisional Azad (free) Kashmir government was established by the rebels.

At this point, with much of the northern and northwestern part of the subcontinent in near chaos and the Maharaja's position crumbling, the event occurred that transformed a political dispute into a military conflict. Muslim tribesmen, some from nearby areas in Pakistan but mostly Pathans from the Northwest Frontier Province 100 miles to the west who had heard of atrocities against the Muslims of Jammu, began an invasion of Kashmir. Pakistani officials, probably relieved that the tribesmen were not raiding areas within Pakistan, did not have the means to halt them. In fact, they helped the tribesmen to pass through and allowed them to use Pakistan as a base for operations. The tribesmen soon reached the Vale and moved on Srinagar, looting and raping while demonstrating their loyalty to Islam by wresting the area from the Hindus. The Kashmiri state militia was no match for them. The Maharaja fled to Jammu and called for military help from India, but Indian leaders and Mountbatten said that forces would be sent only if the Maharaja acceded to India. Left with no choice, he did so on October 26, 1947. Upon accepting his accession, Mountbatten wrote to the Maharaja that the question of the state's future should ultimately be settled by reference to the people of Kashmir. India immediately sent troops, which landed at the airport in Srinagar just in time to prevent the tribesmen from taking the city. Gradually the Indian troops pushed the tribesmen out of the Vale and began advancing on other areas.

Jinnah saw the acceptance of the accession by Mountbatten (whom he regarded as strongly biased in favor of India) and the subsequent dispatch of Indian troops as parts of a well-planned conspiracy. He ordered General Gracey, who was the acting chief of the Pakistani Army, to send in Pakistani forces. However, General Auchinleck, who was at the time still Supreme Commander of both the Indian and Pakistani armies, would not agree to become involved in a war between two dominions. He ordered Gracey to inform Jinnah that sending regular Pakistani forces into Kashmir would lead to the resignation of all British officers from the Pakistani Army. They were essential, and Jinnah was forced to yield. However, fearing that India would soon control the whole state and post its forces along the northern border of the Pakistani Punjab, Pakistan gave the Azad Kashmir government materiel and weapons and sent Pakistani soldiers to serve in Kashmir as "volunteers."

Early in November Nehru informed the public and the Pakistani Government that the ultimate disposition of Kashmir would be made in a plebiscite, but not before the invaders had been removed and peace restored to the area. In his radio broadcast Nehru stated:

> We have decided that the fate of Kashmir is ultimately to be decided by the people. That pledge we have given, and the Maharaja has supported it, not only to the people of Kashmir but to the world. We will not, and cannot back out of it. We are prepared when peace and law and order have been established to have a referendum held under international auspices like the United Nations. We want it to be a fair and just reference to the people, and we shall accept their verdict. I can imagine no fairer and juster offer.[16]

Pakistani Prime Minister Liaquat agreed to the plebiscite, saying he would work to ensure that the Azad Kashmir forces agreed to a cease-fire and disbanded. However, he added several conditions to his acceptance: Indian forces should also be withdrawn; the state militia immobilized; and the recently installed government of Sheikh Abdullah (whom Liaquat characterized as a quisling and an agent of the Congress) replaced by a coalition.

Nehru refused to accept these conditions, and, with both political discussions and military operations bogged down, India referred the matter to the United Nations. It charged Pakistan with complicity in the tribal invasion and asked the Security Council to have Pakistan halt its assistance to those fighting in Kashmir. Pakistan had no intention of letting the discussion center on the Indian charges. Instead Foreign Minister Zafrullah Khan launched an all-out counterattack, charging New Delhi with genocide because of the massacres of Muslims at partition and with aggression against Pakistan by its take-over of Junagadh. India's unwillingness to give Pakistan its share of the assets and military equipment of British India was also attacked. Pakistan, which had never recognized the validity of the Maharaja of Kashmir's accession, claimed it was obtained by fraud.

These charges painted a picture of an India that, far from being an innocent victim, was itself doing all it could to destroy Pakistan. India was clearly taken aback by the force and range of the Pakistani case, and many members of the United Nations were impressed. From then on, U.N. attention centered on the whole question of Kashmir and Indo-Pakistani relations, rather than only on the Indian charges. Pakistan had won the first round, but possession still rested with India. Moreover, Pakistan's admission in July, 1948, to the U.N. mission dealing with Kashmir that its troops had been fighting in Kashmir for several months somewhat compromised its position and correspondingly helped India.

During the next several years the dispute was almost constantly before the United Nations, and the Security Council produced numerous resolutions and appointed a series of mediators to find some method that would permit a settlement.[17] The United Nations had one clear accomplishment during these years; a Security Council resolution of December, 1948, providing for a cease-fire was accepted by India and Pakistan, and, as of January 1, 1949, the line between the troops of the two countries became the official cease-fire line.[18] The United Nations had no success, however, in moving beyond this real but limited achievement to the more basic task of devising an acceptable method of settling the dispute. India and Pakistan both professed confidence that they would win a fair plebiscite. Pakistan believed that the tie of Islam and the past injustices suffered by the Muslims under Hindu rulers would cause the Kashmiris to vote to join Pakistan. Indians claimed that the popularity of Sheikh Abdullah —until he was arrested in 1953 for his unwillingness to see Kashmir absorbed by India—combined with resentment over the behavior of the tribesmen and appreciation of Indian economic aid would incline the people toward India. But both sides felt that the conditions under which a plebiscite was conducted would have much to do with its outcome. Pakistan had no confidence in any plesbiscite conducted by Sheikh Abdullah under the watchful eye of the Indian Army. India was determined to maintain its position of strength and prevent the issue from being decided on a religious basis.

*   *   *

Hindu-Muslim communalism, the historic curse of the subcontinent, had lead step by step to an unyielding hostility that imprisoned the leadership and the peoples of India and Pakistan. It increased their burdens and limited their freedom. Each country, believing itself threatened by the other, felt compelled to allot desperately needed resources to defense. Each became dependent upon outside support and susceptible to outside influence in ways that still affect not only them but the pattern of world politics as well.

3

India Fashions a Foreign Policy

The Kashmir dispute plunged India and Pakistan into their most important foreign-policy issue—their relations with one another—before there was any time to weigh the basic foreign policies to be adopted. Pakistan's leaders, previously absorbed in the struggle for partition, were immediately swept up in the task of establishing a government. India was more fortunate, for it had a functioning, if badly disrupted, government. Nehru had long reflected and spoken on the foreign policy a free India should pursue, though he had always assumed that a free India would be undivided. The creation of Pakistan would obviously require major changes.

The foreign policies gradually worked out by the two governments were influenced by certain similarities, such as poverty and the experience of colonialism, with its residue of European influence on institutions and habits of thought. Among obvious differences were the disparities in size and resources and a secular orientation versus an Islamic commitment. Both countries set very ambitious goals despite their lack of actual, as distinct from potential, power. Indian leaders saw their country as a leader in Asia and as exercising influence in the world as a whole; Pakistanis were determined to achieve security from, and equality with, India. In neither case, however, could the attitudes and aspirations be said to constitute a foreign policy. Only when tested by specific issues, when alternative policies and the resources they required were assessed and the implications for domestic goals weighed, could a definable foreign policy emerge.

Any categorization of the foreign-policy issues both countries faced has a certain artificiality about it because of their close interrelations. Nevertheless, in the early years of independence, policy concerns centered on five or six issues: (1) the overriding matter of their mutual relations; (2) the nature of the ties, if any, with the United Kingdom and the British Commonwealth; (3) relations with other Asian nations, some of them independent, others still struggling for freedom; (4) territorial integrity, especially defense of the northern and northeastern frontiers of the subcontinent; and (5) nonalignment, the great powers, and the developing cold war. Pakistan was also saddled with the Pushtunistan dispute. Defense policy and establishing effective military forces figured prominently in several of the issues for both countries.

This chapter and the next examine the foreign policies India and Pakistan fashioned in grappling with these key questions.

India's Dual Heritage

The new Indian Government was heir to two distinct traditions in foreign-policy thinking. One was the foreign policy of British India; the other, the ideas on international affairs expressed by the Congress party in the years before independence.

The British Indian tradition was centered on the most vital element of national policy, territorial integrity. Officials had evolved a well-thought-out policy for dealing with threats to the security of South Asia, particularly on the mountain frontiers. In the broader international context, however, that tradition was clearly directed toward advancing British, rather than Indian, interests.

The Congress party had stressed quite different elements. There had been no clear concept of the defense of the frontiers in the pre-independence pronouncements of the Congress. Yet the mountains were to be the scene of the major conflicts in the subcontinent after 1947. On the other hand, Nehru's thinking on foreign affairs was closely in touch with many of the realities of postwar Asia, and it was India's efforts to apply his precepts that attracted attention in the early years.

It is difficult to exaggerate Nehru's importance in the development of Indian foreign policy. Largely at his urging, the Congress party began to make regular pronouncements on world affairs in the 1920s and the 1930s. Nehru's concern reflected his wide-ranging interests, his extensive travels and reading, and his recognition that science and technology were increasing the interdependence of nations. The progress of independence movements, he was convinced, was linked with trends in world politics, and Asian leaders could hardly afford to neglect thinking about foreign affairs until the day they acquired the responsibility for their countries' destinies.

Although a convinced democrat, Nehru had great doubts about the sincerity of the Western democracies, because of their refusal to apply their professed principles to their colonies. He was strongly repelled by Western capitalism, which he regarded as unjust in itself and intricately linked to colonialism and later to fascism. Capitalism's further evolution, Britain's eventual stand against fascism, and the decolonization process after World War II led him gradually to modify his views, but he never entirely abandoned them. The desire for a strong nation and an improved lot for the masses, combined with his antipathy to capitalism, propelled Nehru in the direction of socialism as the only just and effective way of dealing with India's domestic problems. His socialism was pragmatic, rather than rigid, and at bottom amounted to a belief that a system based on cooperation rather than competition offered the only hope of creating the India he envisioned.

Nehru looked with favor upon the drive for economic development and social welfare in the Soviet Union, and some of his statements in the 1920s and 1930s were extremely laudatory. The anti-imperialistic stance of the U.S.S.R. also impressed Indians favorably, and Nehru held office in the Comintern-sponsored League Against Imperialism. But his attitude toward the U.S.S.R.'s foreign policy changed after the Nazi-Soviet pact. Moreover, Nehru had never been a blind admirer of life in the U.S.S.R., the harsher aspects of which repelled him. While in jail in 1934–35, he wrote in his autobiography:

> . . . I am very far from being a communist. My roots are still perhaps partly in the nineteenth century, and I have been too much influenced by the humanist liberal tradition to get out of it completely. This *bourgeois* background follows me about and is naturally a source of irritation to many communists. I dislike dogmatism, and the treatment of Karl Marx's writings or any other books as revealed scripture which cannot be challenged, and the regimentation and heresy hunts which

seem to be a feature of modern communism. I dislike also much that has happened in Russia, and especially the excessive use of violence in normal times.[1]

The attitudes of Nehru and many other Indian nationalists toward the Communist Party of India (CPI) shifted over the years. When the CPI switched from opposition to support of the British war effort after the German attack on the Soviet Union, many Indians, who refused their support unless Britain met nationalist demands, were alienated. Thus, Nehru wrote from jail during World War II:

> . . . I know that in India the Communist party is completely divorced from, and is ignorant of, the national traditions that fill the minds of the people. . . . So far as it is concerned, the history of the world began in November 1917 and everything that preceded this was preparatory and leading up to it. Normally speaking, in a country like India . . . communism should have a wide appeal. In a sense there is that vague appeal, but the Communist party cannot take advantage of it, because it has cut itself off from the spring of national sentiment and speaks in a language which finds no echo in the hearts of the people.[2]

As the Congress party continued to leave foreign-policy matters largely in Nehru's hands after independence, he enjoyed an unusually large measure of freedom. He did not ignore popular attitudes, however, being very much the practical politician, and professional diplomats and military men, accustomed to thinking in the British-Indian tradition, also influenced him to a degree. Yet few Indians had more than vague opinions on foreign policy, and as long as his policies did not run directly counter to their attitudes he enjoyed considerable leeway.

India's foreign policy attracted worldwide attention, mainly because a large and important country was developing a policy independent of the two power blocs then forming. Its many articulate spokesmen were presenting the policy as based on an approach and attitude quite different from what was customary. Nehru's voluminous, wide-ranging, and often improvised comments on international affairs provided the raw material for extensive discussion and analysis. One of the most succinct statements summarizing his ideas on Indian foreign policy was made at Columbia University on a visit to the United States in 1949:

> India is a very old country with a great past. But it is a new country also with new urges and desires. . . . Inevitably she had to consider her foreign policy in terms of enlightened self-interest, but at the same

time she brought to it a touch of her idealism. Thus she has tried to combine idealism with national interest. The main objectives of that policy are: the pursuit of peace, not through alignment with any major power or group of powers, but through an independent approach to each controversial or disputed issue; the liberation of subject peoples; the maintenance of freedom both national and individual; the elimination of racial discrimination; and the elimination of want, disease, and ignorance which affect the greater part of the world's population.[3]

A persistent theme in Nehru's speeches is his view that a new epoch in Asian history began after the end of World War II. After centuries of decline and foreign rule, Asian nations were free to demonstrate their ability to regain in the future the greatness of the past, but they had to close the gap between themselves and the western world.

Thus India's primary task would be nation-building. Not only was the newly won freedom important in itself and as a repudiation of the racist implications of colonialism, but, equally, freedom was an imperative if Asian countries were to realize their full potential. Nation-building involved much more than economic growth, although that was an essential element. For Indian leaders, it also meant drafting and adopting a constitution, holding general elections, carrying out social and economic reforms, and—although little was said about it—setting up an effective military establishment and, in time, attaining an adequate level of defense production.

Nevertheless, economic progress remained the essential ingredient. India's poverty weighed heavily on the minds of its leaders, and they were determined to eliminate it as fast as possible. Many Indians believed that their living standards had declined under colonial rule, despite the technological advances made during the period. Convinced that British investors had exploited their country, they envisioned little scope for private foreign investment. There was a broad consensus, from businessmen to economic planners, that the government had an important role to play in economic affairs, although naturally there were differences on how extensive that role should be.

While recognizing the enormity of the economic task and the need for outside help, India felt under little immediate pressure to secure foreign aid. British India's foreign liabilities amounted to approximately $4.5 billion before World War II, far more than its slender assets. Its exports during the war years, the unavailability of many imports, and the expenditures of British and American forces in South Asia virtually wiped out the liabilities and provided assets of more than $5 billion by 1946, of which India received about 80 per cent at partition. Because of the United Kingdom's stringent financial position, these assets could not all be drawn at once, but gradual drawings enabled India to overcome the wartime neglect of its capital plant and begin an economic development program.

Unless there was peace in the world, the task of nation-building, difficult in the best of circumstances, would be impossible. "Without peace," Nehru said, "all our dreams are vanished and reduced to ashes." The desire for world peace was no Indian monopoly, though India's spokesmen at times seemed to suggest this. They took the position, however, that there was a basic difference between their policy and that of most other powers, especially those aligned on either side in the cold war. Power politics was the cause of wars, Nehru held, and continued reliance on this unsavory and discredited method could lead the world into another and more terrible war. India would refuse to play the game and would not join either bloc. Its policy would attempt to achieve security by promoting peace and building a world community.[4]

Indians sometimes claimed that their foreign policy was the expression of peculiarly Indian ways of thinking. As an agnostic steeped in the Western humanistic tradition, Nehru did not claim that India's foreign policy was a result of spiritual superiority, though he saw a close connection between some aspects of traditional thought and the policy of nonalignment.

> Peaceful co-existence is not a new idea for us in India. It has been our way of life and is as old as our thought and culture. About 2,200 years ago, a great son of India, Ashoka, proclaimed it and inscribed it on rock and stone, which exist today and give us his message. . . . This is the lesson of tolerance and peaceful co-existence and co-operation which India has believed in through the ages. In the old days, we talked of religion and philosophy; now we talk more of the economic and social system. But the approach is the same now as before.
>
> From this it has naturally followed that we should keep ourselves free from military or like alliances and from the great power groups that dominate the world today.[5]

Whatever its history, every country operates within the system of independent national states and must deal with a variety of issues for which its culture and traditions provide few specific answers. A nation's way of thinking tends to be ascribed more to general policy issues than to such vital matters as territorial integrity. Certainly, Indian distaste for power politics in global affairs was neither the guiding force behind nor the rationale for policy toward Pakistan.

It is easy to overlook the relevance of the British-Indian tradition in the development of Indian foreign policy, for much more than the unity of the subcontinent changed in 1947. Indian leaders were convinced that upon the transfer of power they would pursue a completely different foreign policy, and in some respects they did. The altered stance on colonial questions and great-power rivalries was inevitable.

But, if the interests and inclinations of Indian leaders markedly changed some global aspects of policy, their freedom of action was much more limited in dealing with the problem of India's territorial integrity. They were slow to recognize this point, for they were convinced that British claims about external dangers to the subcontinent were at least partially designed to justify British control. To the extent such claims were valid, they were due to British imperialism, which involved India in quarrels of no interest to it; these quarrels would disappear when India gained control of its affairs. With the diminution of the Russian threat after 1917 and Britain's seemingly impregnable position, this Indian attitude was understandable. For example, at its annual meeting in 1921 the Congress party proclaimed:

(1) that the present Government of India in no way represent Indian opinion and that their policy has been traditionally guided by considerations more of holding India in subjection than of protecting her borders;

(2) that India as a self-governing country can have nothing to fear from the neighboring states or any state as her people have no designs on any of them . . .[6]

Yet, from the outset, India asserted all the British claims along the northern frontiers of the subcontinent, thus facing many of the same problems that had confronted the British. The Himalayan mountains were a problem for any government to the south attempting to control them and a formidable obstacle to any army attempting to cross them from the north. The political arrangements by which these areas were governed, and the underlying British-Indian attitude toward their inhabitants, were part of the legacy of British India. Changes could be and were made, but over the decades British-

Indian officials had worked out a system for the protection of the area.

When the British established themselves on the subcontinent, their first concern was for the security of the sea lanes across the Indian Ocean, and by the early nineteenth century they had gained control of the key points along its shores from South Africa in the west to Singapore in the east. Nor did the British expansion over the southern and central part of the subcontinent and across the great plains in the north present any lasting strategic problems or issues. British authority was imposed even where the local prince was allowed to retain his throne. When expansion reached the foothills of the great Himalayan range and its western spurs, however, the British faced major strategic problems, which still confront the subcontinent today.

British-Indian officials, realizing they could not permit a potentially hostile power to control the mountains if the position in the plains below was to be secure, concluded that authority had to be extended into the mountains. To some this meant a defense strategy based on control of the crests and passes. But, given the topography of the mountains, which rise from sea level to over 25,000 feet in less than a hundred miles, others argued that control of the crest line was possible only if the reverse slopes of the ranges were also controlled—or at least neutralized. The substance of such a forward policy was relatively clear in the northeast, where for nearly a thousand miles the topography was simple; as long as no hostile power was established on the Tibetan plateau the British position was secure. A more complex topography in the north and northwest presented a far more difficult problem.

On the related issue of the form British control or influence should take, there was a spectrum of possibilities. The British could annex the territory and exercise direct control. They could lay claim to, and establish sovereignty in, the area without exercising administrative control. They could maintain the existing political entities as subsidiary or buffer states with British officials really running things from behind the scenes, or they could permit such states internal autonomy while assuming responsibility for their foreign affairs and defense. Finally, they could allow the states to retain their independence on condition that they not ally themselves with Britain's enemies. In fact, all of these methods were tried at different times and places along the frontier.

It was not merely the traditional British indifference to administrative neatness that led to such varied policies. The British encountered the problems of working out a Himalayan frontier policy piecemeal as they advanced across northern India. Different conditions called for different responses, and experimentation was inevitable. Moreover, the many governments and officials who formulated British policy over the decades sometimes disagreed on these matters.

Despite the various political arrangements, there was an underlying theme to British policy: Form a ring of protectorates and buffer states to ensure the security of frontier areas. In the east, Britain pushed northward and took direct control of Upper Burma. In time it annexed the Northeast Frontier Agency (NEFA), the area of primitive tribal structures between the plains of Assam and the Himalayan peaks, but only gradually brought it under British administration. Bhutan was allowed to maintain a separate identity and internal freedom, but its foreign relations were in effect controlled from New Delhi. Sikkim was made a protectorate, with British control of its foreign affairs, its defense, and certain aspects of its internal affairs. Nepal retained its identity and internal autonomy; its foreign relations were controlled by the British until after World War I, when it acquired a measure of international status and freedom of action. The central area from Nepal to Kashmir was under direct British control, and Chinese suzerainty over Tibet was upheld to maintain it as a buffer state when Russia showed an interest in the area. Kashmir, though its rulers enjoyed nominal internal autonomy, was in fact under the ultimate control of New Delhi.

During most of the period of British rule, however, the main threat to the subcontinent came from the northwest. Here the geography is less clear-cut. From Kashmir westward the Himalayas fan out into many ranges, making the natural frontiers of the subcontinent difficult to determine. Beyond the mountains the expanding Russian Empire loomed. And the warlike inhabitants of the northwest frontier and of Afghanistan were more resistant to British control than any of the mountain peoples previously encountered. At times British policy was based on the premise that the Hindu Kush mountains across central Afghanistan were the logical frontier, and Britain accordingly tried to make Afghanistan a subsidiary state. The policy was never fully successful, and eventually Britain concluded that a friendly neutral government in Kabul was all that was necessary or possible. In 1893 the Durand Line, running from northeast to southwest, was established as the boundary between Afghanistan and

British India, with the key passes through the mountains on the British side. Even after 1893, however, the British never tried to administer all the territory they claimed, being content with control of key areas through a network of communications and fortifications.

Central to the defense of the subcontinent, of course, was the role of the armed forces of British India. With independence, India had to adopt a defense policy as well as to reorganize the military services.

Under the British the Indian Army had been carefully selected from those groups or castes regarded as possessing "martial" characteristics and firm loyalty to the British Raj. These forces were supplemented by a large number of mercenaries—the Nepalese Gurkhas, who were immune to the appeals of Indian nationalism. Troops were garrisoned away from cities, and soldiers were inculcated with a nonpolitical outlook. Naval and air forces were kept small—India could rely on the Royal Navy and the Royal Air Force. Although Indians began to move into the officer ranks after World War I, nearly all senior officers, a large part of the officer corps, and most holders of technical posts were still British officers and enlisted men as late as World War II.

To convert the armed forces into an effective and reliable military instrument capable of defending the country would have been a difficult task even in the absence of partition. It was necessary to train Indians to replace British officers and technical specialists and to work out an arrangement with Nepal for the continued service (at least for a time) of some Gurkha units. The new government had to establish its authority and win the loyalty of the men who had served the British throughout the independence struggle and, instead of accepting only certain groups, gradually open up recruitment to the armed services to all the people of India.[7] The army was given top priority because of the conflict with Pakistan and the need for forces to maintain internal order. A gradual build-up of the air force began. Despite thousands of miles of coastline, the navy had low priority—indicating little or no fear of attack by sea and disruption of important sea links.

Summing up the dual heritage of independent India, Bisheshwar Prasad has commented:

> . . . Indian thinking on foreign policy has flowed into two parallel streams. . . . The official attitude . . . involved the adoption of a policy to dominate the states on the frontiers of India and subordinate their foreign relations. . . . This attitude continued to govern India's

foreign policy throughout, up to the end of British rule in India. The non-official attitude, on the other hand, was critical of imperialism and was definitely favorable to the emergence of independent Asian states, free of imperialist domination of whatever variety. It stood for peace, international cooperation and good will and supported the growth of nationalism in Asia and Africa.[8]

However, the two traditions provided no guidance on the most important issue facing the new Indian Government—relations with Pakistan.

Policy Toward Pakistan

History and geography made it impossible for India and Pakistan to be indifferent toward each other. Peace, trade, and cooperation in a variety of endeavors were the desiderata; conflict and enmity were their legacy. Inevitably, each country had an intense interest in the ties of its neighbor to outside powers, which would complicate their relations.

Broadly speaking, India had two choices open to it. It could endeavor to win Pakistan's cooperation, even if that involved making substantial concessions. Or it could pursue a hard line, seeking as the larger and stronger nation to impose its will on Pakistan and establish hegemony in South Asia. But to set forth the two choices as equally open would be grossly misleading.

The Muslim League leaders, who now ruled Pakistan, had shattered the dream of a free and united India. Communal violence, which reached a state of virtual civil war at partition, had raised bitterness and hostility to levels previously unknown. Indeed, in many respects the two countries were *de facto* enemies from the day of independence. It would have required the foresight of genius and a long view of history at a time when hatreds were burning fiercely for Indian leaders to have made a serious attempt to win Pakistani cooperation. However tragic, it was practically inevitable that India would follow a hard line.

Indian leaders were convinced that Pakistan would not survive as a nation—a judgment shared by some outside observers. The distance and differences between the two wings of the country, the lack of educated talent, and the paucity of natural resources did not inspire confidence in its future. Moreover, Indian leaders believed that Pakistan could not survive because it should not survive. As Nehru said:

Pakistan is a mediæval state with an impossible theocratic concept. It should never have been created, and it would never have happened had the British not stood behind this foolish idea of Jinnah. . . . It should be so natural to have with Pakistan the closest possible cooperation. We want to cooperate and work toward cooperation, and one day integration will inevitably come. If it will be in four, five, ten years—I do not know.[9]

How Indian officials envisioned the reunion of the two countries is not clear.

India's leaders were convinced they made substantial efforts to win Pakistan's cooperation. They felt—and still do—that they had gone more than halfway in agreeing to partition and to a plebiscite in Kashmir, while Pakistan had taken everything it could get and continued to press for more. Not only was India opposed on legal and moral grounds to making concessions to a country it regarded as an aggressor; it also doubted that concessions would have a beneficial result.

On three separate occasions in the early years, Indo-Pakistani hostility threatened to erupt in war, with the treatment of minorities often a precipitating factor. Muslims in India who chose not to migrate to Pakistan were Indian citizens; those Hindus remaining in the areas awarded to Pakistan were citizens of Pakistan. In 1947 about 55 million Muslims were in India (chiefly in the north) and about 17 million Hindus were in Pakistan, nearly two-thirds of them concentrated in the eastern wing. The mass migrations following partition reduced the size of the minorities in India and East Pakistan only moderately, though nearly all the Hindus in West Pakistan fled.

Such a sizable minority of Muslims posed no theoretical problems for India, whose leaders were committed to secularism. For Pakistan, however, its Hindu minority posed a difficult theoretical problem, for what was the status of minority groups in a land established on the premise that Hindus and Muslims were separate nations? (Once partition was ensured, Jinnah in effect abandoned the two-nation theory domestically, repeatedly stressing that all citizens of Pakistan were equal.) In fact, the minorities created serious problems in both countries. The governments tried, but were not always able, to protect them from the aroused feelings of the majorities, whose interest in the political theories of their governments was less than all-absorbing.

The first war scare occurred immediately after partition, during the savage communal violence and the fighting in Kashmir. Each government accused the other of failing to protect its minorities and, worse, of instigating communal animosities, though they also issued joint appeals for peace and joint declarations designed to calm and protect the minorities. The U.N. Commission for India and Pakistan was especially active in urging restraint. Whether or not Nirad Chaudhuri's contention that on two or three occasions only American and British efforts kept India from attacking Pakistan is true, Britain certainly urged restraint on both countries.[10] That the Kashmir fighting, erupting before the mass migrations had ended, did not lead to general war was perhaps due as much to a recognition by both countries of their inability to wage full-scale war as to a realization of the tragic consequences.

Another crisis arose late in 1949, when the United Kingdom devalued the pound by 30.5 per cent. Most countries whose currencies were linked to sterling followed suit, but Pakistan declined to do so, thereby greatly depreciating India's currency relative to Pakistan's. India refused to trade with Pakistan at the official exchange rate. The wheat and cotton of West Pakistan, the raw jute of East Pakistan, and the manufactured goods of India no longer moved in trade. The economic consequences led first to discrimination against the minorities in both East and West Bengal and then to communal violence. Stories were spread and exaggerated by travelers and newspapers; soon both countries were moving troops to the borders. Many in each country thought the other government was carrying out a deliberate plan to drive out the minority community, and each government was under great pressure to take strong action to protect the minority in the other country. Nehru and Liaquat publicly spoke of a willingness to resort to other means if peaceful measures were not successful, but both worked hard to bring the situation in their own territory under control. By April of 1950 they had largely succeeded. They met and reached an agreement in which each country again recognized its responsibility to protect its minorities and reiterated that the minorities must look to their own governments for redress of their grievances. War had been avoided, but the economic ties between the two nations were further eroded.

The third crisis occurred in 1951 because of the continuing conflict over Kashmir. India had been actively attempting to portray the situation in Kashmir as one of normality, hoping to forestall further U.N. recommendations unfavorable to India. Early in April India rejected one of the many resolutions on Kashmir passed by the Security Council. These moves and claims created a storm of anger and frustration in Pakistan. Its leaders were particularly opposed to the announced convening of a Kashmir constituent assembly before a plebiscite was held. Indian intransigence, they asserted, might force them to resort to new methods; Pakistani newspapers spoke openly of a readiness to resort to war if necessary. Incidents occurred along the cease-fire line in Kashmir, and in July Indian troops were moved to the frontier, undoubtedly as a warning that a new conflict might ultimately be decided on the Punjab plains rather than in Kashmir.

Pakistan's relative military weakness made the prospect of war unappealing. India, by this time essentially satisfied with the *status quo*, was disinclined toward a new round of hostilities with the consequent danger of greater U.N. involvement. Tension remained high, then gradually subsided, and the assassination of Liaquat in October turned Pakistan's attention to domestic affairs.

Relations with Britain and the Commonwealth

Whether or not India remained in the Commonwealth of Nations depended on the new relationship with the United Kingdom. Although membership in the Commonwealth was the more visible issue, the basic questions were the retention, modification, or abandonment of the numerous ties with Britain.

There was a general expectation that India would leave the Commonwealth, for the Congress had repeatedly proclaimed its intention to sever all political ties with the United Kingdom when India was free. This seemed to preclude dominion status and Commonwealth membership. Britain and India were not linked by ties of blood or a common heritage. Many Congress leaders, angry over Britain's willingness to partition the subcontinent, resented the strong criticisms of Labour's policy by Conservative party leaders, particularly Churchill. Indians were also resentful of racial discrimination elsewhere in the Commonwealth. Finally, there was a fear that Commonwealth membership would seem to link India with the West in the cold war.

Yet there were also weighty considerations for a close relationship with the United Kingdom, and membership in the Commonwealth might offer the best method of advancing Indian interests. History had given both countries similar political institutions, and British culture had made deep inroads among key groups in Indian society. Economic ties were extensive, but it was not clear that India could retain its trade preferences and access to British capital markets if it left the Commonwealth. Similarly, the status of some 2.5 million to 3 million people of Indian origin living in other Commonwealth countries would be altered, but by remaining in the Commonwealth India might be able to influence their situation. India was still dependent upon British personnel to keep its administrative and military services functioning effectively. Its military forces were equipped with British arms. There were few other countries able to provide adequate new equipment, and none from whom India could secure arms with fewer political implications. Close association with a worldwide group of nations offered India a variety of contacts it would not otherwise possess.

Despite these arguments about the value of remaining in the Commonwealth, India might well have left had partition not occurred. With Pakistan's intending to remain in the Commonwealth, however, India had second thoughts about leaving, lest Pakistan thereby gain British backing in its disputes with India. Its power was in decline, but Britain still could damage one country's position if it sided with the other. Although seldom mentioned, this consideration probably weighed heavily in the decision.

India began discussions with two basic stipulations—that membership not restrict its independence and freedom of action in any way and that the Commonwealth change so that India would not be required to abandon its plans to become a republic. It gradually came to see that the first point presented no real problem. Much to Pakistan's consternation, the Labour government was willing to work out a formula, making the Crown merely the symbolic head of the Commonwealth and accepting India as a republic.

It would have been a blow, both politically and psychologically, to Britain and to the Commonwealth if India had left, for the organization would have represented a greatly diminished population. Such an action would have deprived the Commonwealth of a certain status in world affairs, which, while nebulous and of declining significance in the postwar world, was still important in the late 1940's and early 1950's. Moreover, if India had left, other former British colonial territories would have found it difficult to stay. India's example made it much easier for them to remain and for the Commonwealth to become multiracial in nature.

In a speech moving a resolution to remain in the Commonwealth, Nehru told the Indian Constituent Assembly on May 16, 1949:

> I think there can be little doubt that it does us good, that this continuing association at the present moment is beneficial for us, and it is beneficial, in the larger sense, to certain world causes that we represent. And lastly, if I may put it in a negative way, not to have had this agreement would certainly have been detrimental to these world causes as well as to ourselves.[11]

Although attacked by Indian Communists and by the U.S.S.R., as well as by some nationalists, the decision was accepted by the Constituent Assembly.

India and Free Asia

After two centuries under European domination, it was natural for India to pursue a strong anticolonialist policy. The combination of European political domination and Western attitudes of racial superiority left Indians suspicious of Western motives and sensitive to real and imagined slights. Nehru spoke for most Indians when he said that "the crisis of the time in Asia is colonialism versus anticolonialism." The colonialist evils they had known were more of a threat than distant Communist evils. This difference in assessment made it difficult for Indians and Americans—who did not regard themselves as colonialists—to communicate, much less to arrive at a common position on international issues. Why, asked many Americans, did India not recognize that colonialism was on the wane and that communism was the real threat to the newly won independence of Asian nations?

The feeling of Asian solidarity was the other side of the coin of anticolonialism. Asia's resurgence was more than freedom for former colonies; it was the beginning of a new epoch in world history in which the Asian nations would again count for something. This called for close cooperation. But first these countries, whose ties had been almost exclusively with their colonial overlords, had to get to know one another.

Even before India won independence it convened the first Asian Relations Conference in New Delhi in March, 1947. Twenty-eight Asian countries, including several republics of the Soviet Union, discussed the status and prospects of various national independence movements, the common problems of Asian peoples, and the ways of handling them. It was Western political and economic influence that was feared, and Asian countries gave notice they would be on guard in their dealings with the West.

India organized a second Asian Relations Conference in New Delhi early in 1949, after Dutch attacks on the nationalist forces of Indonesia. Fifteen Asian nations attended, but no Soviet republics were present. The Conference adopted strong resolutions against the Dutch and forwarded them to the United Nations. Several participants imposed sanctions by denying the Netherlands transit facilities, landing rights, and refueling privileges in their territories. Although of no great immediate effect, particularly on U.N. deliberations, these actions may have hastened the Dutch decision to grant Indonesia independence late in 1949.

A third cooperative effort was the Colombo Plan, proposed by the foreign ministers of India, Pakistan, Ceylon, Burma, and Indonesia early in 1950. Its basic purpose was to help Asian countries overcome their problems by sharing their experience, their facilities, and, to the extent possible, their resources, but it soon became dependent upon outside, that is, Western, help.

India's anticolonial policy had pronounced psychological motivations: a feeling of kinship with other Asians in their shared poverty, experience of colonial rule, and high hopes for the future. Until all of Asia was freed, it would be weak and divided and thus subject to the influence of outside powers seeking their own advantage. This, rather than old-style colonialism, was what India viewed with apprehension. India's policy also reflected an awareness that it could not hope to acquire much influence in Asia until the colonial powers departed. While Nehru on numerous occasions disclaimed any desire to have India act as a leader of Asia, he did not pretend that its size and location could be ignored.[12] Many other Indians were less restrained and saw India as a great power, at least in Asia, around which the smaller countries could be grouped. More than a little harm was done to India's cause by the way many representatives and citizens acted when visiting other Asian countries in the years after independence.

Most Indians felt themselves culturally closer to the countries of Southeast Asia than to those of the Middle East. Yet India regarded the efforts of Middle Eastern countries to shake off colonial rule in much the same terms as its own independence struggle. With most of its trade ties still with Europe and most of its oil supplies coming from the Middle East, India clearly had an interest in political developments in the area. Most important, perhaps, India was determined to maintain political credit and good relations in the Middle East lest Pakistan acquire the support of the Muslim countries. Thus India voted against the partition of Palestine when that issue came up in the United Nations. (Even before independence, the Congress had proclaimed solidarity with the Arabs in opposing Western plans to colonize Palestine with Jews.) No doubt India's opposition to the partition of Palestine also reflected its own dislike of partition. India eventually recognized Israel but only after several Muslim countries did. If it did not pursue as strongly an anti-Israel policy as Pakistan, its position nevertheless prevented Pakistan from garnering all the good will and support of the Arab states. A desire not to offend its own Muslims was probably also an element in India's policy toward Israel.

India was, of course, pleased with the worldwide retreat of colonialism, but publicly, at least, it was impatient with the slowness of the movement. Moreover, it insisted on complete independence when colonial rule ended. One example of India's attitude was its refusal to attend the San Francisco Conference and sign the Japanese peace treaty. The refusal reflected India's views that Japan would not be wholly independent as well as concern over China's exclusion and Soviet opposition. India also disapproved of the retention by the United States of certain islands in the Pacific that were ethnically and historically Japanese. A separate peace treaty with Japan was signed somewhat later.

The situation in Indochina caused special concern. While India recognized the strong Communist position in the anticolonial movement, it was also concerned that the alleged dangers of communism might be used in Indochina or elsewhere as an excuse to perpetuate colonial rule.

India and the New China

The evolution of Sino-Indian relations is discussed in detail in Chapter 7, but a few comments on India's China policy are necessary at this point. Congress party leaders had been friendly toward the Chiang Kai-shek government, supporting it in its struggle with Japan. Yet, when the Nationalist regime collapsed, India had no problem accepting the Communist regime as the legitimate government of China, extending recognition on December 30, 1949. Nevertheless, Indian views of Communist China were complicated by three separate but related issues. The Chinese were fellow Asians, and the rise of Communist China was part of the great Asian upsurge in search of freedom, status, and progress. Thus international issues involving China had to be considered in terms of India's policy toward colonialism and Asian solidarity. At the same time, China was a Communist state allied with the Soviet Union, which had implications for Indian policy toward the cold war. Finally, India and China were neighbors, whose ideas on the proper status of Tibet and even the location of their border in the Himalayas were to prove quite different.

Initially, many Indians viewed the new Communist Chinese Government as an ally in the struggle against imperialism. The new China was admired not so much because it was Communist as for its international assertiveness and domestic achievements. "Whether we like it or not," Nehru said, "China has been reborn." Some Indians clearly liked it; returning visitors usually sang its praises, and India-China Friendship Associations were formed in both countries. India called for the transfer of the Chinese seat in the United Nations to the Communists, for the absence of the Peking government was regarded as an affront to Asia and a handicap to the world organization.

This generally friendly attitude toward China was damaged but not destroyed by Peking's assertions that Nehru's government was a Western puppet and by the Chinese Communist take-over of Tibet. India maintained that as the successor to British India it had inherited all of the territory and rights of its predecessor. This included a special position in Tibet, which consisted of treaty rights regarding trade, control of telegraph facilities, and the right to send small contingents of Indian troops to accompany its traders in the area. In any case, in 1947 the Nationalist Chinese Government was in no position to extend its control into Tibet and to challenge India's rights there, though it did maintain that Tibet was an integral part of China. When the Chinese Communists came to power, they too set forth the traditional Chinese claim, but India hoped that any differences over the status of Tibet and its rights there could be handled by diplomacy. In effect, India hoped the area could remain autonomous and continue to be a buffer between India and China.

With little if any warning, Communist China moved troops into Tibet in October, 1950. India formally protested, but Peking curtly told New Delhi that Tibet was a part of China and the Chinese actions were of no concern to India. After a few battles the Chinese gained control of Tibet and began a program of political action to consolidate their position. They did not interfere with the Indian forces or activities in the area, and the two sides settled down to an uneasy coexistence.

However much India would have liked Tibet to remain a buffer zone, it obviously lacked the military capability to challenge the Chinese. Relations with Pakistan were tense despite the cease-fire in Kashmir, and any Indian military involvement in Tibet might have tempted Pakistan to renew hostilities. Indian leaders may also have feared that to challenge China's actions would only have made sense if India had been willing to encourage a U.S. involvement in the dispute, thus increasing the chances of war and endangering India's nonalignment policy. India therefore decided there was little it could do beyond protesting Peking's actions. It moved to strengthen its position in Bhutan and Sikkim (a process which had already begun when India negotiated new treaties in 1949) and supported the overthrow of the feudal regime in Nepal in 1950.

Nonalignment and the Cold War

The cold war, which began in earnest as India was winning its freedom, cast its shadow across a world desperately in need of peace. Although the magnitude of the conflict forced every country to become at least indirectly involved at times, India was determined not to line up with either side.

India's nonalignment policy rested on four fundamental considerations: (1) The country's major tasks were the internal ones of political, social, and economic development, on which it should concentrate rather than becoming involved in a struggle between the West and the Communist powers that did not directly concern it; (2) taking either side in the conflict would be divisive among a people badly in need of greater national unity; (3) as a weak though large nation, India would lose some measure of freedom if it allied itself with any major power; and (4) as the strongest power in the area, India had no need for external support to bolster its regional position. (The opportunity that such a policy provided for extracting foreign aid from both sides had not yet been discerned.) As the difference in perspective has been summed up, "The cold war means to the West a struggle for the survival of a certain way of life; to

India it means a most inconsistent and exasperating insistence on the settling of Western problems on other people's soil."[13]

In general, Indian attitudes were ambivalent toward the United States and the U.S.S.R.[14] There was admiration for the Soviet attempt to lift itself from poverty, and a feeling that the Soviet experience in economic planning might hold some lessons. At the same time, the harsher aspects of the Soviet dictatorship were recognized. Soviet political and propaganda support of anticolonial movements outweighed concern over Soviet policy in Eastern Europe. Yet Indo-Soviet relations were cool and distant, the Indian government being treated by the Soviet press and propagandists as a tool of the West. Indian leaders, aware of the ties between the Indian Communist party and the Soviet Union, had to put down Communist-sponsored violence and insurrections at the time of independence, which made them wary of the U.S.S.R. In any case, Stalin's policy of isolating the U.S.S.R. made close relations impossible.

The majority of educated Indians knew little about the United States. Their education, if it had been abroad, probably had been in the United Kingdom; if in India, it probably had been under British teachers. They saw no Americans, except possibly an occasional businessman, missionary, or GI during World War II. Nevertheless, the standing of the United States was high at the war's end by virtue of the contribution of American industrial production and President Roosevelt's efforts to persuade Churchill to be forthcoming in his dealings with Indian nationalists. Indians knew that the United States was a practicing democracy—though with the serious blemish of racial segregation—but they felt that the American economy, geared to a high standard of living, provided no pertinent example for India. In their categorization of the world into "haves" and "have-nots," they saw Russia somewhere between the extremes of the United States and India.

But the high U.S. standing soon began to decline. Indians, frightened by the atom bomb, were dismayed that it had first been used against Asians. As the cold war developed, the position of the United States on colonialism seemed more concerned with maintaining good ties with its European allies than with upholding its own tradition of anticolonialism. India was also disappointed and sometimes angered by American policy on the Kashmir issue. Finally, Indians felt that the United States was doing little to aid them, while it was passing out billions of dollars to the wealthier, if temporarily hard-pressed, European nations. Willingness to provide India with funds to purchase American wheat after the poor monsoon of 1951 was offset by the extended haggling in the U.S. Congress and the harsh things said about Indian policy in that forum.

Despite its nonalignment policy India leaned toward the West, as Nehru himself acknowledged in a major speech on March 22, 1949:

> . . . we should not align ourselves with what are called power blocs. We can be of far more service without doing so and I think there is just a possibility—and I shall not put it higher than that—that at a moment of crisis our peaceful and friendly efforts might make a difference and avert that crisis. . . . When I say that we should not align ourselves with any power blocs, obviously it does not mean that we should not be closer in our relations with some countries than with others. . . . At the present moment you will see that as a matter of fact we have far closer relations with some countries of the Western world than with others. It is partly due to history and partly due to other factors. . . . These close relations will, no doubt, develop and we will encourage them to develop, but we do not wish to place ourselves in a position where, politically speaking, we are just lined up with a particular group or bound up to it in regard to our future foreign activities.[15]

The U.S.S.R. also viewed India as leaning toward the West and vigorously attacked its leaders for "having made a deal with Anglo-American imperialism and Indian reactionaries to fight their own people." But many Americans, unaware of the underlying pro-Western inclinations of the Indian Government, were convinced that it was more sympathetic to the Communists and consequently were antagonistic.

With the outbreak of the Korean War in June, 1950, India's attitude and policy shifted toward a somewhat anti-Western nonalignment, with a consequent severe deterioration in relations with the United States and other countries. Most non-Communist countries were convinced that the security and peace of the world depended upon a successful collective resistance to the North Korean aggression. Initially there was no difference between India and the West on what to do. Speaking to the Indian Parliament, Nehru had outlined India's response as follows:

> Our policy is, first, of course, that aggression has taken place by North Korea over South Korea. That is a wrong act that had to be con-

demned, that has to be resisted. Secondly, that so far as possible the war should not spread beyond Korea. And thirdly, that we should explore the means of ending this war.[16]

But India soon found that its support of collective security collided with its determination not to favor any bloc and with its fear of a major war.

If the Korean War had been only a conflict between North Korea and the United Nations, India might have remained a firm supporter of the U.N. effort. However, on June 27, President Truman announced that the U.S. Seventh Fleet would neutralize the Formosa Strait. In the words of Berkes and Bedi:

> It may not have been wise, but India began to see the Korean War less and less as a vital demonstration of collective security, and more and more as an American-Kuomintang threat to reopen the Chinese civil war, and to resettle one of the greater stakes in the Great Power rivalry. Nor should it be said that this was so wild a possibility as to make very ridiculous India's fear of consequent general war.
>
> It is at this point, and surely in the light of this background, that the reversal of priorities in Indian policy took place. India's interest in a clear stand against aggression became overwhelmed by a driving urge to terminate the war. The added conviction that the key to the joint puzzle of ending both the aggression and the war rested with Communist China's admission to the United Nations took possession of Nehru's outlook.[17]

Communist China's admission to the United Nations, Nehru believed, was essential in order to get the U.S.S.R. to end its boycott of the Security Council and to help bring the war to a settlement. His efforts to link the two issues were naturally supported by the Communist powers and opposed by the United States.[18] Further strains developed over India's opposition to the U.N. forces' crossing the 38th parallel to unify the country after defeating the North Korean Army in September. (K. M. Panikkar, India's ambassador in Peking, had reported Chou En-lai's warning that Communist China would respond with force if U.N. troops crossed the 38th parallel.)

With the entry of Communist China into the war, India's fears were confirmed. Its policy moved toward one of peace at almost any price to prevent World War III from developing out of the conflict between Chinese and U.N. and U.S. forces. Deprived of military victory and a stunning demonstration of the free world's cooperation for collective security when both had seemed within grasp, Americans reacted with determination and anger. The American Government and people felt more strongly than ever the absolute necessity of demonstrating that aggression did not pay. Their anger was directed not only against the Chinese and their supporters but also against India for its active opposition to condemning the aggressor. According to India, condemnation of Peking would make negotiations for a cease-fire and settlement impossible when ending the conflict must be given top priority. In the American view, India's stand was encouraging Peking to hold out for conditions that the United States should not and would not meet to initiate negotiations.

Each country was convinced that the policy of the other would lead to disaster, and the fact that India had been correct in its judgment of Chinese military intentions probably only added to American vexation. Officials of each government measured their public words carefully while attacking the policies and proposals of the other. Private citizens did not, and the changes reflected the deep hostility toward the policies of the other country. When an Indian military contingent was used in Korea to help settle disputes concerning North Korean and Chinese Communist prisoners, U.S. officials noted with wry satisfaction that India's efforts to find the basis for a compromise settlement sometimes subjected it to Communist attacks and vilification. The experiences of the Korean War left a legacy of suspicion between India and the United States that lasted for years.

* * *

Despite strained relations with the United States, most Indians—and many other observers—regarded India's foreign policy as fairly successful during the first years of independence. India held the most valuable part of Kashmir and was able to deal with Pakistan from a position of strength; the United Kingdom and India developed a formula that allowed India to remain in the Commonwealth as a republic; India's nonalignment and anticolonialism won it great attention and much respect in many parts of the world; and India's foreign policy, given widespread acceptance by politically conscious Indians, strengthened national unity. Communist Chinese control of Tibet was something beyond the impenetrable Himalayas and seemed of little consequence to most Indians. If the United States did not approve of India's foreign policy, that was too bad, but India would follow its own course regardless of what others thought.

4

Pakistan's Search for Status and Security

Pakistan faced no problem of blending two traditions in foreign policy and applying them to a situation that neither had foreseen—a partitioned subcontinent. Its problem was the lack of a tradition to guide it.

Before partition, the men who were to create Pakistan had given little thought to international affairs, except to express a desire for close ties with other Muslim nations. Politically aware Pakistanis did have certain attitudes, of course, but these were vague and hardly constituted a basis for a foreign policy. They wanted their government to pursue an "Islamic foreign policy," but they had no real idea of what this meant. (As Pakistan was to discover, trying to base domestic policies on a faith born in another era that did not distinguish between the spiritual and the secular realms was difficult enough; trying to base a foreign policy on Islam was all but impossible.) They agreed that the colonial countries had been exploited by European nations, and they supported other independence movements. Pakistanis also tended to see the difficulties between Europe and the Middle East (including Pakistan) in the light of the Christian-Muslim conflict of earlier centuries. These attitudes did not, however, add up to antipathy or opposition to the West, for they were partially offset by admiration of Western technological progress and some aspects of Western culture and by recognition of the need to maintain certain links with the West.

Keeping East and West Pakistan together as parts of one nation was the key element in creating a sense of national unity. Periodically during the struggle for independence Bengali Muslims had called for a united but independent Bengal, arguing that its culture, history, and economy had given the province sufficient cohesiveness to enable its Hindu and Muslim communities to live together. The proposal was never a realistic alternative, for the intense communalism made it all but impossible for most inhabitants of the subcontinent to think other than as Hindus or Muslims. Nonetheless, the idea that Bengalis had certain things in common was not completely lost in the communal upheavals. East Pakistanis, although wanting no more of the Hindu landlords or moneylenders who had dominated them before fleeing to West Bengal after partition, saw certain advantages to a working relationship with India. The attitude of the West Pakistanis has been quite different.

The problems created by differing attitudes toward India were intensified by haggling over the division of power and allocation of resources between East and West Pakistan.[1] It was almost inevitable that the western wing, as the home of most of the soldiers and civil servants and with the national capital, Karachi, would have power out of proportion to its population.[2] The disparities were a source of dispute and disunity. Many West Pakistanis entertained doubts about the loyalty of East Pakistanis and feared that someday the province would attempt to secede and rejoin India or would gradually be absorbed by "Bharat."[3]

East Pakistanis generally supported the central government in its disputes with India. Yet distance alone meant that they could hardly be as absorbed by the desire to gain Kashmir as the West Pakistanis were. And they could hardly avoid noting that the addition of more territory and population to the nation would strengthen the West Pakistanis relative to themselves.

Even after the shock and disruption of partition had been absorbed, Pakistan faced monumental economic problems and gloomy economic prospects.[4] Pakistan comprised two of the least developed parts of an underdeveloped subcontinent. Lacking most raw materials, deficient in transportation facilities, and almost devoid of industrial facilities, the two territories had depended on the shipment of wheat and raw cotton and jute to India.[5] One motivation behind the Pakistan movement was the feeling of many Muslims that both as individuals and as a community they were exploited by the Hindus as well as the British. Therefore with independence they were determined to lessen if not eliminate their dependence on India by reorienting their trade, setting up textile and jute mills to process their raw materials, and eventually building other factories to supply their needs for industrial and consumer goods. This was as much economic "planning" as Pakistan could do for many years. Some reduction of dependence on India was achieved within a few years, but the task of lifting two of the most neglected areas of Asia out of poverty was obviously going to take decades if not generations.

In addition to Pakistan's fragile political unity and economic weakness, the external environment was unpromising. India and Afghanistan, its two neighbors, were hostile. Pakistanis wondered where they could find strong and loyal friends. Indeed, the new nation was hardly known and expended much diplomatic effort to make other nations aware of its existence and its problems.

Because of the animosity of its neighbors, the lack of strong supporters, and the martial traditions of most West Pakistanis, high priority was given to national defense and the creation of effective military forces. The Punjab had supplied over half of the forces of the British-Indian Army before World War II. A large proportion of these were Muslims who opted for Pakistan, and they, together with the soldiers from the Northwest Frontier Province (another important recruiting ground), gave Pakistan the nucleus of an army. However, because of problems with the Muslims at the time of the Mutiny, the British had not permitted the establishment of all-Muslim regiments, so the Pakistani Army had to be organized almost from scratch.[6] There were few technicians, and arms and equipment were in short supply, for Pakistan never received its allotted share of the equipment of the British-Indian Army. Almost all the facilities for the production and maintenance of military equipment were in the areas that went to India. Pakistan therefore faced the difficult and expensive task of building armed forces able to defend a divided territory with thousands of miles of frontier.

Attitudes toward the over-all situation were an uneasy mixture of confidence and fear, and often the two were found in the same person. Pakistanis were confident that the determination that had enabled them to create a country would also enable them to overcome its many problems. At the same time, they feared that internal weakness and external threats might prove more than they could cope with. As a result, a feeling that it was impossible to take a calm and circumspect approach to foreign policy imparted a certain harshness of tone and inflexibility of thinking, particularly on issues involving their neighbors.

The most striking feature of Pakistan's foreign policy was its extremely ambitious goals. Here were two unorganized and impoverished pieces of territory, as yet a nation in name only, seeking to gain security through strength rather than accommodation and to wrest a sizable area away from a neighbor four times as large. Yet, under the disorganized conditions prevailing on the subcontinent, when present boundaries had not yet hardened, such goals may have seemed ambitious but not unrealistic. Through sheer reliance on the will to succeed, Pakistanis had already accomplished what most observers a few short years earlier had thought impossible. Having established a nation, was it inconceivable they could surmount one more obstacle and gain control of the additional territory that would make their country complete?

In the Shadow of India

Although the Indo-Pakistan relationship was the central issue for both countries, for Pakistan it assumed transcendent importance. It was the base point for policy on all other issues; indeed, the position other countries took on Indo-Pakistani disputes determined Pakistan's attitudes toward those countries.

Most Pakistanis—East and West—were convinced that the Hindus were determined to dominate the political and economic life of the subcontinent. It was this desire to dominate, they felt, rather than any noble belief in Indian unity and the possibility of creating a secular state that motivated the opposition of the Congress party to partition. Further, they saw the acceptance of partition by the Congress leaders as a cunning and temporary expedient to ensure a British departure, after which India would be free to dominate and even absorb Pakistan as it saw fit.

Statements by India's leaders reinforced this Pakistani belief. The

All-India Congress Committee resolution of June 14, 1947, accepting partition, still spoke in terms of the essential unity of India:

> Geography and the mountains and seas fashioned India as she is, and no human agency can change that shape or come in the way of her final destiny. Economic circumstances and the insistent demands of international affairs make the unity of India still more necessary. . . . The A.I.C.C. earnestly trusts that when the present passions have subsided, India's problems will be viewed in their proper perspective and the false doctrine of two nations in India will be discredited and discarded by all.[7]

The reaction of the right-wing Hindu Mahasabha, which opposed partition, was even stronger: "India is one and indivisible and there will never be peace unless and until the separated areas are brought into the Indian Union and made integral parts thereof."[8] Other Indian leaders, such as Maulana Azad and Sardar Patel, foresaw a "short-lived partition" and thought that "Pakistan was not viable and could not last."

The view that India was convinced that Pakistan could not last and was even working for its collapse was held not only by Pakistanis. Sir Claude Auchinleck, the commander of the Indian Army in 1947, told the British Government on September 28, "I have no hesitation whatever in affirming that the present Indian Cabinet are implacably determined to do all in their power to prevent the establishment of the Dominion of Pakistan on a firm basis. In this I am supported by the unanimous opinion of my senior officers and indeed by all responsible British officers cognizant of the situation."[9]

Against the background of such Indian statements (and there were many others like them) its actions in the period just after partition appeared ominous. The take-overs of Junagadh and Hyderabad, the curtailment of irrigation waters in the Punjab, and the withholding of funds and military equipment were seen not as the normal hard-line politics that often characterizes the actions of independent nations but as evidence of the intention to destroy Pakistan. Any doubts about India's hostility vanished with New Delhi's acceptance of the Maharaja of Kashmir's accession and the sending of troops to control the state. Indian arguments that the Maharaja's accession was perfectly legal and that the issue was simply one of Pakistani aggression through its tribal agents and later its soldiers infuriated the Pakistanis. They were convinced that the majority of the Maharaja's subjects were in revolt against him and his rule had in effect ceased to exist in most parts of the state; consequently it was a travesty on justice and reason to claim that he had the right to determine the future of Kashmir by his personal decision.

What assurance was there, many Pakistanis asked, that a desire for territorial expansion and a determination to protect Hindus would not lead India to move against East Pakistan? An Indian take-over of the eastern wing of the country would provide a more secure link with Assam and might even finish Pakistan as a country.

The Pakistani interpretation of India's attitude during these years was accurately summarized by K. Sarwar Hasan:

> [The Hindus] genuinely believed the new state would collapse—they were convinced it would not be economically viable and that the Muslims had no administrative capacity. And when it collapsed, they thought, they would have Muslims of Pakistan as well as those of residuary India in the bag! It was their hope that it would collapse by itself and it was their plan to assist it to collapse. Indeed they did everything to bring about its collapse. But it did not collapse.[10]

India's explanations of its attitudes and actions, which in the eyes of outside observers ranged from the probable to the dubious, were brushed aside by most Pakistanis as hypocritical. Nor did they see any significance in India's acceptance of a cease-fire in Kashmir or in its failure to attack Pakistan in 1950 and 1951. They were annoyed that few outside observers saw India as determined to destroy Pakistan, and incensed at the acceptance by many of Indian claims that the central goal of Indian foreign policy was peace.

Thus even those Pakistani leaders who recognized that there were many practical reasons for good relations with India regarded it as diplomatically useless and politically impossible to search for compromise and an accommodation. Even in the economic field, which was least charged with emotion, cooperation implied a degree of dependence, which was exactly what Pakistanis wanted to avoid. Therefore they felt the Indian challenge had to be faced, whatever the difficulties. Government leaders refused to exclude war as a possible outcome: Popular anti-Indian attitudes would have made it politically risky to rule out a resort to force and sign the no-war pact India wanted. In any case, strength and power were the only things that could move India toward a just settlement.

What then did Pakistan want from India? While it had a long

list of grievances, there were two essential and interrelated demands. It wanted India to acknowledge that partition was both inevitable and right and thus grant the validity of both the two-nation theory and the implication that India and Pakistan had equal status. It also wanted Kashmir, partly for strategic and economic reasons but basically because the state's accession to Pakistan would have been tangible evidence that India did in fact accept the permanence of Pakistan. Only in this way could Pakistanis have a feeling of security. As Keith Callard has said:

> For Pakistan, 1947 marked the end of the seven-year struggle to secure recognition of the claim to a separate state. The eleven years that followed saw Pakistan determined to assert first, that the creation of the state was right and proper; second, that Pakistan is a permanent addition to the map of Asia; and third, that Pakistan and India are equal successors to the Indian Empire. There are those in India who continue to question each of these propositions. . . . For India to concede the validity of the two-nation theory would be a denial of the basis of the Congress Movement and a threat to the Muslim minority remaining in India. For Pakistan, anything less than such an admission casts doubts upon the legitimacy and permanence of the national homeland.[11]

Pakistanis, at least those in the west, were convinced that man for man they were better than the Indians, but unless India suffered near disintegration, Pakistan could only hope to deal successfully with its adversary by securing assistance from outside the subcontinent. Thus it embarked upon its long search for external support in the classic pattern of a state confronting a strong and hostile neighbor.

Pakistan and the Commonwealth

At first Pakistan turned to the United Kingdom and to other Muslim nations in seeking external support for its disputes with India. The Commonwealth, Pakistan argued, could hardly expect to play an important role in promoting peace and understanding in the world if it did not even attempt to settle disputes between its own members. But the United Kingdom and other Commonwealth members wanted to avoid becoming involved. Britain had no desire to antagonize India by applying pressure while the latter was weighing the question of its future relationship with the Commonwealth. Pakistan protested: In 1951, for example, Prime Minister Liaquat, under considerable domestic political pressure on the Kashmir issue, said he would not attend the Commonwealth Prime Ministers Conference in London unless he was assured the issue would be on the agenda. By his refusal to attend the opening sessions, he won agreement that informal discussions would be held, but this inexpensive and inconsequential concession from India and Britain was all he could obtain.

Pakistani attitudes toward Britain in the early years can best be described as ambivalent. Few Pakistanis believed that British policy either before or after independence was basically pro-Muslim. Indeed, most felt that Britain had not even been neutral but had sided with the Hindus. The pro-Indian inclinations of the Labour government, Lord Mountbatten, and certain other officials were seen to outweigh the pro-Pakistani sympathies of more conservative British elements.

This was not the whole story, however. By education, training, and personal inclination, Pakistan's political leaders, civil servants, and military officers were on the whole deeply influenced by British culture and wanted to retain links with the United Kingdom. Even more than India, Pakistan was dependent on Britain for arms and officers to organize its armed forces, for civilian officials to help set up its governmental units, and for professors and teachers to staff its universities and schools. And Britain was its key trading partner.

Ultimately, however, the necessities of international politics kept Pakistan in the Commonwealth. The initial inclination to remain a dominion was based not only upon the sentiments of the ruling class and the need for assistance but also on the belief that when India left the Commonwealth, Britain and the other members would back Pakistan in its quarrels with India. That India was allowed to remain in the organization after becoming a republic provoked surprise and dismay. But once the decision had been taken, Pakistan could not afford to leave lest it forfeit the neutrality of the Commonwealth members on Indo-Pakistani disputes.

Decolonization and the Muslim World

Countries still under colonial rule gained a strong supporter when Pakistan became independent. Both in and outside the United Nations, Pakistan was a skillful and effective spokesman for granting freedom to Burma, Ceylon, Indonesia, and eventually the African nations. But because it was less prominent than India, was more preoccupied with domestic affairs, had fewer men trained in international affairs, and (after the deaths of Jinnah and Liaquat) had no leader of Nehru's stature, Pakistan's opposition to colonization attracted less attention. Occasionally, too, it took a less dogmatic anticolonial position, as when it acknowledged that the struggle in Indochina was not a purely anticolonial conflict and when it agreed to sign the Japanese peace treaty.

Pakistan also gave less weight to appeals for Asian solidarity. As a state born of the profound differences between Asians, Pakistan could hardly overlook the problems Asians would face in attempting to work together. As a nation looking for external support in its quarrels with India, Pakistan could not be rigidly opposed to Western influence or involvement in Asian affairs—provided it helped Pakistan.

If Pakistan was realistically aware of the limitations to Asian solidarity, it was naïvely optimistic about the prospects for Muslim solidarity. It placed great hopes in the creation of close ties with other Muslim nations, especially in the Middle East, to help offset Indian preponderance on the subcontinent. If Muslims were to achieve again the greatness they had known in the past, they would have to work together and pool their strength. For many years, therefore, Pakistan automatically supported any Muslim country involved in a dispute with a non-Muslim nation. Pakistani leaders frequently exchanged visits with other Muslim statesmen, and treaties of friendship were signed, but Pakistan was not satisfied with these modest achievements. It pushed for institutional ties. In 1949, an international Islamic Economic Conference was held in Karachi under governmental sponsorship, and two years later, a World Muslim Conference. In 1952, Pakistan invited the prime ministers of twelve Muslim countries to meet in Karachi to see if a system of high-level consultation on matters of common interest could be worked out. The project seemed innocuous enough on the surface but generated so little support that the meeting was never held. Turkey rejected the invitation outright, saying it was a secular nation with no interest in political alignments based on religion. Nor were the Arabs uniformly pleased. Many not only were suspicious of Pakistan's motives but thought of themselves as the aristocrats of the Islamic world and viewed Pakistanis with some disdain. A more fundamental problem was that Arab rulers increasingly believed that culture and nationalism rather than Islam should be the motivating force behind their policies. Unable to make any headway even with merely consultative institutions among Muslim nations, Pakistan had to fall back upon a policy of working for close bilateral relations.

Of particular importance to Pakistan in this period were its advocacy of the cause of the Palestinian Arabs in the United Nations and its opposition to the Western-sponsored plan to partition Palestine. Pakistan, regarding the plan as an attempt by the West to atone for its own failings toward the Jews at the expense of the Muslims, repeatedly insisted upon a fair settlement of the Palestine issue before Pakistan would be interested in close relations with the Western nations.

The failure of other Muslim states to back Pakistan in its dispute with India was a bitter disappointment. Yet the Muslim nations could not have provided much more than diplomatic support, which would hardly have led India to pursue a basically different policy. Pakistanis needed economic and military assistance if they were to develop their country and deal with India from a position of strength.

The Pushtunistan Dispute

Compounding Pakistan's frustrations was the dispute with Afghanistan over the Pushtunistan issue. In the last years of British India the Northwest Frontier Province (NWFP) was governed by a Muslim party affiliated with the Congress party and led by Abdul Ghafar Khan, known as the "frontier Gandhi." This party was ideologically opposed to partition along communal lines, and its leaders saw no role for themselves in the proposed state of Pakistan. Ghafar Khan urged a boycott of the referendum organized by the British to let the people choose between India and Pakistan; he insisted the choices include an independent or at least autonomous "Pushtunistan." The British refused and held the referendum. Only 51 per cent of those eligible in this overwhelmingly Muslim province voted, but 99 per cent of them opted for Pakistan, and on this basis the area was incorporated.[12]

Afghanistan, comprising various ethnic groups ruled by a royal family of Pushtun extraction, refused to accept the outcome. When Pakistan's application for membership came before the United Nations in September, 1947, Afghanistan cast the lone dissenting vote, asserting it would not recognize Pakistan's right to control the NWFP and the Pushtun tribal territory. Pakistan had hoped that the replacement of Christian by Muslim rule would induce the previously ungoverned hill tribes to accept its authority, but Kabul's actions dimmed that hope. Reacting strongly, Pakistan claimed that as one of the successor states to British India it had inherited all the territory east of the Durand Line, maintaining that whatever happened east of that line was of no concern to Afghanistan.

Afghanistan continued to press the issue, although its ultimate goals (assuming any had been formulated) have never been clear. The boundaries of the proposed Pushtunistan varied, sometimes limited to the Northwest Frontier Province and adjacent tribal areas and sometimes embracing all the territory between Afghanistan and the Indus River as far south as the Arabian Sea. Afghanistan claimed to be interested only in seeing that the Pushtuns had a true opportunity to exercise the right of self-determination.[13] More likely, the Afghan leaders thought that with the removal of the British the splintering of the subcontinent would not stop with the creation of two nations, and they may have concluded they could once again extend their rule eastward as their forebears had done in the eighteenth century. This would have greatly increased the Afghan Government's control of the tribes, whose ability to play off first the Afghans against the British and later the Afghans against the Pakistanis was one factor in enabling them to enjoy considerable freedom. Thus considerations of defense against their own tribes—who had overthrown Afghan governments in the past—and of national aggrandizement led the Afghans to challenge Pakistan, despite landlocked Afghanistan's heavy dependence on the transit route through Pakistan to the sea and the world.

A constant barrage of propaganda hostile to Pakistan was directed at the Pushtuns by the Afghan Government. Subsidies were paid to tribal leaders to intensify trouble between them and the Pakistanis, who in turn resorted to the same device. The contest went on as it had in centuries past:

> The main target of both sides are the great "independent" tribes . . . who constitute the inner core of the Pathan borderlands. These and similar clans, whose tribal structure is still intact and vigorous, dwell in a strip of relatively inaccessible hills from fifty to a hundred miles wide and perhaps three hundred miles long. There are four to five million Pathans in the inner core, something more than half of them dwelling on the Pakistan side; the remainder on the Afghan side. Some tribes . . . have part of their membership in one country and the rest in the other.
>
> The border hills are almost completely lacking in economic resources. The pressure of population is intense. The hill Pathans have

traditionally lived by raiding the fertile lowlands and by taking toll of the commerce which moves through their famous passes: the Khyber, the Malakand, the Kurrum, the Tochi, and the Gomal. They have been forced to desist from these practices only by strong governments and then only when subsidies were paid in return for their good behavior in "guarding" rather than preying on the lowlands and the passes. These subsidies were paid by the great Mogul Emperor Akbar in the last part of the sixteenth century; the use of them became almost a fine art under the British; supplemented by an occasional hospital or school, they are paid today by the governments of both Pakistan and Afghanistan.[14]

The territorial conflict with Afghanistan along the northwest frontier obviously weakened Pakistan's position vis-à-vis India, and for years Pakistanis accused India of supporting if not instigating the Pushtunistan dispute.[15]

The Cold War

During the first years of independence, Pakistan was not involved politically or emotionally in the cold war. Concerned that world peace be preserved, it had no illusions regarding its ability to play a role of any consequence in global disputes. As it did not then see either the Communist or the Western nations as threats to its security, it saw no reason automatically to side with either group.

Knowledge of the U.S.S.R. was very limited, aside from a vague admiration for its material achievements. No Pakistani leaders and few intellectuals were attracted to Marxism as Nehru and many younger Indians were; the local Communist party was insignificant; and the occasional talk about socialism was generally in terms of a vague Islamic socialism.

Though Pakistan was oriented toward the United Kingdom, even the many links with London were not a sufficient reason in Pakistani eyes to side with the Western powers. In addition, Moscow was less critical of Pakistan than of India in the late 1940s. Many observers believed that Prime Minister Liaquat's 1949 announcement of a state visit to Moscow was designed to prod Washington for an invitation after Nehru's trip to the United States. Whatever the reason, Liaquat never went to Moscow, and his visit to the United States in 1950 was generally regarded as a success for Pakistan. However, the United States though it supported U.N. efforts to achieve a settlement in Kashmir, did not feel that considerations of justice or international politics called for full support of the Pakistani position.

Pakistan's knowledge of China was no greater than its knowledge of the Soviet Union or the United States. But China was an Asian nation, and Pakistan was eager for good relations. It recognized Communist China and initially supported its assumption of the Chinese seat in the United Nations. Pakistan supported the action of the United Nations in Korea and voted to declare North Korea an aggressor; its spokesmen also urged that U.N. forces unify Korea after the military power of North Korea was destroyed. When Communist China entered the war, Pakistan pulled back a bit, however, and was opposed to branding China an aggressor and imposing an embargo on trade. Its position in most respects did not greatly differ from that of India, but neither did it attempt to play as prominent a role nor was it as outspoken in its criticism of U.S. policies in Korea and the Far East generally. In short, its policies and activities never created much resentment in the United States, a matter that later proved important.

* * *

Events made it increasingly obvious that Pakistan had to secure much greater external support than it had obtained thus far. The initial shocks of partition had been absorbed and a functioning government established, but the basic weaknesses of the country stood out starkly. The collapse of world prices for many raw materials in 1951 hit Pakistan particularly hard and forced it to devalue its currency. Food production was stagnant or declining, while the population continued to grow. The armed forces had been able to obtain only a fraction of the military equipment they felt was necessary to defend West Pakistan, much less the entire country. It was clear that India held the upper hand, and Pakistan did not believe India would agree to a fair solution to their disputes in the circumstances. Pakistan had looked to the United Kingdom, to the United Nations, and to the Muslim world for support, but adequate help was not forthcoming. The internal political situation was deteriorating; Jinnah, the founder and ruler of the nation, had died in 1948, and Liaquat Ali had been assassinated in 1951. The politicians who followed had neither their abilities nor their popular support. To the men of the civil service and military establishments who soon came to the fore, it was time for Pakistan to look elsewhere for support. The advent of the Eisenhower Administration early in 1953 suggested one possible source.

PART TWO

The Great-Power Involvement

5

America Enters the Subcontinent

The United States entered the subcontinent principally by way of the Middle East. But the first ventures of American policy toward India and Pakistan must be seen in the larger context of worldwide developments in the years immediately after World War II.

Entertaining few illusions during the war about making the world safe for democracy, American leaders nevertheless hoped that a peaceful world order could be built upon the postwar cooperation of the victorious Allies. But serious miscalculations were made of the intentions and capabilities of the U.S.S.R., no less than of Britain, France, and China. Hopes were sanguine, and Western military strength was precipitously demobilized.

Despite the vast wartime devastation it had suffered, the Soviet Union was able, in a remarkably short time, to restore production to prewar levels and beyond. Even before V-E Day, the U.S.S.R. was seizing the opportunity to strengthen its security by filling the power vacuum left in Eastern Europe upon Germany's defeat. Far different from the traditional influence of a great power on its smaller neighbors, Soviet domination of the region meant the imposition of Communist rule, controlled from Moscow, and the severing of traditional links with Western Europe. Nor were Soviet moves limited to Eastern Europe. Denouncing its prewar treaty with Turkey, the Soviet Government pressed for a new regime for the Straits, which were to be defended jointly by Soviet and Turkish forces. It also demanded that Turkey cede two eastern provinces. Moscow refused to withdraw the troops it had stationed in northern Iran during the war, using them to protect and promote a revolutionary government in Azerbaijan. Local Communist parties instigated trouble, ranging from major strikes in Western Europe to civil war in Greece.

The other Allies proved to be much weaker than expected. Britain, in severe economic difficulties that required large infusions of American aid, and undertaking great social changes, was less able to maintain a global or even an imperial position. By early 1947 it could no longer furnish the assistance Greece and Turkey needed. Realizing that if it were to exercise power in some areas it would have to pull back elsewhere, the British Government decided to concentrate on maintaining its influence in the oil-rich Arab lands astride the communication routes to the Far East and Australasia.

France was in a worse situation. Drained by war and torn by internal dissension, it was able to do little more than hold on to its colonies. Nationalist China soon proved to be in the most desperate straits of all. By the fall of 1949 Chiang Kai-shek's government had been driven from the mainland to Taiwan by a militantly anti-American Communist regime. The U.S. position in the Far East seemed gravely jeopardized.

At first the United States responded to Soviet moves with uncoordinated actions. It supported Turkey's rejection of Soviet demands. It sent naval vessels to the Persian Gulf and took a firm stand against Soviet troops remaining in Iran. Stalin yielded, and Tehran regained control of northern Iran.

But it was soon apparent that, in facing the momentous Soviet challenge to the West, a comprehensive policy rather than a series of *ad hoc* improvisations was required. Containment, the policy devised, received perhaps its most persuasive statement in George Kennan's *Foreign Affairs* article "The Sources of Soviet Conduct." The essence of the policy was the conviction that "the Soviet pressure against the free institutions of the Western world is something that can be contained by the adroit and vigilant application of counterforce at a series of constantly shifting geographical and political points, corresponding to the shifts and maneuvers of Soviet policy." If the United States were successful in this, it would "force upon the

Kremlin a far greater degree of moderation and circumspection than it has had to observe in recent years, and in this way promote tendencies which must eventually find their outlet in either the break-up or the gradual mellowing of Soviet power."[1] Although the containment policy was attacked as too ambitious, it gained wide acceptance as the rationale for the Western response—military, economic, diplomatic, and ideological—to Soviet pressures. Later, opponents of containment charged that it was not ambitious enough in that it did not aim at the liberation of Eastern Europe and a roll-back of Soviet power. Ironically, Kennan contends that the ideas were misunderstood and misapplied, and that he intended containment to be basically a political rather than a military strategy.[2]

American efforts to build situations of strength were first centered in Western Europe and the Eastern Mediterranean, where both the threat and the stakes seemed greatest. Under the Truman Doctrine, aid was quickly sent to Greece and Turkey. In Western Europe the emergency aid of the immediate postwar years gave way to the Marshall Plan, which became an element in the containment policy when Moscow forced Czechoslovakia to repudiate its previously announced intention to participate in the plan. As a result of the systematic and massive infusion of U.S. resources, Western Europe began to recover. But economic strength was not sufficient to ensure security. As Soviet pressure continued, the Western nations realized that military strength was also necessary; such events as the Czechoslovak coup and the Berlin blockade prodded the Western nations step by step toward signing the North Atlantic Treaty and military cooperation in the North Atlantic Treaty Organization (NATO).

In contrast to its relatively clear-cut policies in Western Europe, Greece, and Turkey, the United States was uncertain about to what extent and in which manner it should become involved in the great arc of countries stretching from Morocco to China. France was still the paramount external power in North Africa and Indochina, as was Britain in the Middle East and parts of Southeast Asia, and the United States was not looking for new responsibilities and burdens.

Events soon forced a change in U.S. policy. The North Korean invasion in June, 1950, threatened a take-over of non-Communist South Korea, which would undermine the U.S. defense position in Japan and destroy the United Nations as an organization that could help maintain peace. Under the U.N. aegis, the forces of many nations, led by the United States, entered the battle. The U.S. Seventh Fleet was ordered to seal off Taiwan from mainland China, and U.S. aid to the French in Indochina was stepped up—ancillary decisions that were to have profound and lasting consequences.

The North Korean attack and the Chinese entry into the war late in 1950 decisively changed the attitudes of American officials and other citizens. Previously, the Communist bloc had not resorted to open and direct aggression. The predominant view in the West had been that the Communists would be deterred from aggression by the risk of a major war between the U.S.S.R. and a nuclear-armed United States. After the Soviets exploded their first nuclear device in 1949, this view underwent little if any change, for Americans thought that their larger nuclear arsenal and vastly superior bomber force still provided an adequate deterrent. When this proved too complacent an estimate of Soviet intentions, U.S. public opinion generally swung far in the other direction. Public opinion elsewhere also saw aggression by the Soviet bloc as a serious threat. Communism ruled the vast area from China to Central Europe. The Western world felt its back was to the wall and feared that further Communist gains would decisively shift the balance of power against it. The Western powers rearmed to make NATO a more effective deterrent to Soviet attack and provide the necessary military and psychological security if Europe's promising recovery was to continue. Additional U.S. divisions were sent to Europe, and an integrated NATO command under General Eisenhower was set up.

Middle Eastern Defense: The Initial Effort

Europe and the Far East received top priority, but it was feared that much of Asia was open to attack. The Middle East seemed the most vulnerable of all. The immediate postwar threats to Greece and Turkey had been surmounted, and the two countries had become members of NATO in 1952, but the situation in much of the area was worrisome. Britain, still the paramount Western power there, was embroiled in bitter struggles with Iran over nationalization of the Anglo-Iranian Oil Company and with Egypt over the Suez military base and control of the Anglo-Egyptian Sudan. Politically stable Israel had an effective though small military force, but Arab hostility made it impossible to bring Israel into any regional security grouping.[3] Indeed, Arab bitterness over Western support for the establishment of Israel, and resentment of Western colonialism, made the creation of any Middle Eastern security organization a formidable undertaking. Nonetheless, Western leaders decided to try.

The West had certain assets for working out some type of security arrangements. The British, with extensive military installations throughout the area, took the lead. Turkey, a Muslim nation, was willing to join once its entry into NATO was assured. As yet, the West was the only supplier of the arms desired by Middle Eastern governments, and judicious offers of military equipment might induce them to cooperate at least minimally. Finally, Soviet propaganda attacks on Middle Eastern governments were virulent and continuous, which probably led Western leaders to believe mistakenly that Arab governments considered the Soviet Union a serious threat.

Egypt was regarded as the key because it was the largest Arab state and the site of the Suez base, considered essential to the defense of the area. The Western plan was to offer Egypt formal control of the Suez base (and a greater role in Sudanese affairs) if it were willing to become a member of the planned Middle East Command and place the base under this command. In short, the hope was to make the base, and the presence of Western forces, less offensive to Egyptian nationalism by changing it from a British to an allied base. The proposal was made in October, 1951, when Egyptian nationalism was at fever pitch against the British; the Western governments—at least at the top levels—failed to realize the poor timing of their offer. The Egyptian government immediately rejected the proposal; abrogated the Anglo-Egyptian Treaty of 1936, upon which Britain's base rights rested; and began a campaign of harassment and terrorism against British forces and interests in Egypt.

The Middle East Command was stillborn, for none of the subsequent Western arguments altered Egypt's opposition to the plan. Without Egyptian participation other Arab states were unwilling to cooperate; nor was the West desirous at this time of including them in Egypt's absence. With British-Iranian relations so antagonistic, it was impossible even to approach Iran, geographically one of the key areas to be defended. The lessons to be drawn from the Western failure (and only partially absorbed in subsequent efforts to create a Middle Eastern security organization) were several:

> What went wrong? Certainly the tactics and timing of the approaches left something to be desired. More fundamentally, the real difficulty lay in the attempt to create a military command and base structure

without sufficient underpinning of political understanding and agreement. Even the promise of arms and of "social and economic advancement" was not enough to overcome the effects of the deep political cleavages separating some of the Middle Eastern nations from each other and from the West or the general disbelief among the Arab governments in the reality of a Soviet military threat. . . .

Any progress on arrangements for defense had to await progress toward settlement of the major political disputes. Second, clearer understanding was necessary as to the interests and political commitments of the nations concerned, so that the limitations as well as the possibilities of defense would be apparent. . . . If anything could be concluded by American policy makers . . . it was that the old roads led nowhere and that some new approach would have to be tried.[4]

The Republican Reappraisal

General Eisenhower's election to the Presidency was due to a variety of factors, but perhaps none was as important as a widespread popular feeling that American foreign policy had become unduly burdensome. Accordingly, the new Republican administration assumed office in January, 1953, and took a fresh look at the international problems the United States faced. Considerable progress had been made toward rebuilding Western Europe and reestablishing a balance of power on that continent. An uneasy stalemate existed in the Far East; in the vast array of lands stretching from Morocco to Indochina, the United States had few responsibilities and little influence. Decolonization was proceeding at a pace that both pleased and worried the United States. The freedom of subject peoples was widely if somewhat vaguely regarded as a good thing by most Americans, but decolonization also meant a great reduction if not a complete withdrawal of Western power, about which U.S. leaders were of two minds. The United States wanted to make use of European power in dealing with the Communist challenge; at the same time, it was uncertain as to how closely it could work with the former colonial powers in Asia without being labeled a supporter of colonialism. Naturally, this attitude created a certain ambivalence in U.S. policy.

Many thoughtful Americans were troubled about becoming involved in areas so largely outside their knowledge or experience. Even American scholars who specialized in Asian studies did not find it easy to interpret the significance of what was happening or to evaluate the attitudes and actions of Iranians, Indians, or Indonesians. Ancient cultures, life under colonialism, and nationalist struggles had gone into the making of the newly freed nations; how these diverse ideas and experiences would be woven together was as problematical for the peoples themselves as for outside observers, and the difficulties in judging the extent to which their shared experience of humiliation at the hands of the West would override their ancient differences and modern conflicts were as real for the Asians as they were for Western scholars and officials. The United States could hardly avoid making mistakes; it could only hope that they would not prove fatal.

As for the policies, it was far from clear whether the United States should adopt a basically military approach, seeking allies and building up local forces, or an economic approach, supporting economic development as a better means to counter the appeal of communism, or some combination of the two. The decision, depending on the estimate of the danger facing these countries and the American interest, was not one that could be immediately resolved.

In any case, the first order of business for the new administration clearly was a settlement in Korea, despite the fear of new Chinese pressures in Southeast Asia. The willingness of Stalin's successors to sign a Korean armistice was an argument that the contest was shifting from the military to the political and economic. Nevertheless, the fear that the Communists might resort to force once again remained, a fear that was not lessened as the crisis in Indochina heightened in late 1953 and early 1954. Nor, it was widely felt, could the free world risk the loss of more countries and peoples to communism. Thus the U.S. government concluded that the immediate danger was military and that it should commit itself in some manner to the defense of the area. Although aware of the necessity for economic development, Washington regarded these problems as less critical in the short term and subordinated them to military considerations.

President Eisenhower, Secretary of State Dulles, and Admiral Radford, the principal architects of the new strategy, decided to prosecute the cold war more vigorously at less cost by exploiting U.S. technological superiority more fully. This became the policy of massive retaliation, designed to reduce manpower needs and cut the costs of U.S. defense policies, making them politically and economically more supportable over the long term. At the same time, a new effort would be made to develop local situations of strength both for the direct benefits and as a means of drawing other nations into cooperative political relationships, for the political advantages of close relations with Asian countries loomed large in U.S. calculations. Local defense forces would be built up, with U.S. forces held in reserve.

Before turning to the stages in America's entry into the affairs of the subcontinent, a few words should be said to characterize its relations with India and Pakistan. India's prestige was initially rather high in the eyes of many Americans: Its grappling with monumental domestic problems and its active role in the United Nations enhanced its stature, though some were critical of its policy toward Pakistan. Nonalignment had not become a source of friction with the United States, which was not yet seeking allies in Asia. The outbreak of the Korean War and then the entry of Communist China forced India and the United States into closer but more antagonistic contact politically, bringing to the fore the underlying disagreement about policies toward the Communist nations.

Nehru saw much to admire (and much to criticize) in Russia and China; the United States saw little to admire in either. Nehru believed the Soviet and Chinese leaders were nationalists first and Communists second, and not basically aggressive. The United States had concluded from the actions of the Russian leaders after World War II that they were motivated by an aggressive communism as well as nationalism. Largely on the basis of its reading of the lessons of Nazism and Japanese militarism, the United States was convinced that the only way to deal with potential or actual aggression was to rally as many nations as possible to confront the aggressor with stronger force. Nehru feared that military bases, alliances, and buildups were likely to provoke the very aggression they were intended to prevent. As he became steadily more annoyed with American policies, the United States became more irritated by his moralistic stance and criticisms.

Policy differences and public pronouncements made it difficult to maintain mutually beneficial bilateral relations, which fluctuated considerably.[5] The emergency shipment of some 2 million tons of wheat to help meet India's critical food shortage in 1951 is a case in point. When the bill was finally passed, there had been so much delay and so many acrimonious remarks about India had been made by congressmen and sections of the U.S. press so as to erode sharply whatever good will the United States might have gained, though good will was not—or should not—have been the primary aim. India gave approximately equal publicity to the 50,000 tons of wheat the

U.S.S.R. sent. But the actual arrival of the U.S. wheat shipments, new economic aid commitments under President Truman's Point Four program, and the efforts of Ambassador Bowles to explain the policies of each country to the other improved relations in late 1951 and 1952. The lull in Far Eastern fighting also eased tensions.[6]

During these years Pakistan's international stance was not markedly different from India's, but relations with the United States were much less troublesome. Pakistan benefited from being a smaller country. It said less, spoke less moralistically, and what it did say was not as widely reported. Only on the Israeli issue did Pakistan take a more critical position on the West than India, and, on the Korean War and the Japanese Peace Treaty, Pakistani and U.S. policies were not so far apart as were those of India and the United States. Thus there was little experience of past clashes to overcome when the United States and Pakistan decided it was in their interest to establish closer ties.

First Step: Arms for Pakistan

The idea of a U.S.-Pakistani military relationship first came under serious consideration in Washington in 1951, at the same time that General Ayub was thinking of the United States as a source of military equipment. The U.S. Air Force was interested in possible sites for air bases; other military strategists considered the manpower the Pakistani Army might furnish for use elsewhere in Asia. There was a vague but general feeling that by extending military assistance Pakistan's friendship could be won and its opposition to the Communist nations strengthened.

Selig Harrison has traced official American thinking on defense of the subcontinent to the writings of Sir Olaf Caroe, a former Governor of the Northwest Frontier Province and Foreign Secretary of the British-Indian government.[7] In his book *Wells of Power* (1951) Sir Olaf set forth his argument, which was openly directed to the Americans, that Western defense of the Middle East should be based on Pakistan, just as British defense of the Middle East had previously been based upon control of the subcontinent.[8] His argument gave clear expression to a vague outlook already held by some U.S. officials, among whom there was much respect for British thinking on strategic issues in unfamiliar lands.

Apparently, U.S. officials envisioned no formal military alliance or explicit defense commitment, at least in the near future. Soon after the appointment of Brigadier General Henry A. Byroade as Assistant Secretary of State for the Near East, South Asia, and Africa, in December, 1951, the Pentagon was given approval by State to discuss with Pakistan a limited arms assistance program. Talks were held the following spring, and agreement in principle was apparently reached by mid-1952.

The Indian government soon learned about the prospective program and privately made its objections known. Ambassador Bowles in New Delhi also strongly opposed any arms aid for Pakistan. Nonalignment, he was convinced, was a firmly established Indian policy and not incompatible with U.S. needs in Asia. If the United States extended military assistance to Pakistan, it would be exacerbating the tense relations between India and Pakistan, partly by upsetting the established balance of power and partly by adding differences over their approaches to the cold war to their already formidable antagonisms. Ambassador Bowles also argued that U.S. arms assistance to Pakistan would antagonize Afghanistan, moving it closer to the U.S.S.R. George Kennan was similarly opposed, and Secretary of State Dean Acheson had never been enthusiastic. In any case, because of the objections of Bowles and Kennan, the uncertainties of other officials, and the fact that the Truman administration was in its last months, the United States held off on a final decision.[9]

The Middle East and South Asia were not top priority areas for the newly elected Republican administration when it assumed office in early 1953, but soon thereafter they came under serious consideration. The visit of Secretary of State Dulles to eleven countries in the Middle East and South Asia in May confirmed his thinking that no area-wide defense organization would be possible for some time, particularly one based upon Egypt and the Suez Canal base. However, Dulles thought that bilateral arrangements with individual states could lead to a more formal regional security system.

Dulles reported his impressions in a speech delivered over nationwide radio and television networks on June 1. One of his conclusions was that:

A Middle East Defense Organization is a future rather than an immediate possibility. Many of the Arab League countries are so engrossed with their quarrels with Israel or with Great Britain or France that they pay little heed to the menace of Soviet communism. However, there is more concern where the Soviet Union is near. In general, the northern tier of nations shows awareness of the danger.

There is a vague desire to have a collective security system. But no such system can be imposed from without. It should be designed and grow from within out of a sense of common destiny and common danger.

While awaiting the formal creation of a security association, the United States can usefully help strengthen the interrelated defense of those countries which want strength, not as against each other or the West, but to resist the common threat to all free peoples.[10]

The United States would stand behind and strengthen those countries that wanted help, but Western membership in a defense pact was not foreseen for some time.

Turkey was obviously the key nation in any Middle Eastern security scheme. It was the strongest state in the area, firmly anti-Soviet, and willing to work closely with the United States and the United Kingdom to create defensive strength on its eastern borders to prevent being outflanked by a Soviet attack. The Western position in Iran was going from bad to worse, for under Mossadegh's rule, rabid anti-British nationalism and Communist influence were both growing rapidly. The situation improved dramatically with the overthrow of Mossadegh and the return of the Shah in the summer of 1953, though the new government's preoccupation with strengthening its hold on the country and uprooting the Communists entrenched in government services kept Iran from focusing on foreign affairs. Beyond Iran was Pakistan, which seemed a potential source of strength. The British-Indian army had fought in defense of the Middle East before; perhaps its successor forces would again have that mission.

If a Turko-Pakistani tie could be fostered, a good beginning would be made. In time it might be possible to bring in Iran and some Arab countries to the south, but not until some of the quarrels between them and the West were settled. American leaders apparently believed that the specific quarrels then in the headlines, rather than basic antagonisms, caused much of the problem. Moreover, the United States believed it could be accepted as a noncolonial Western power. But to the Arabs the fact that it was Western, allied to colonial powers, and a supporter of Israel, were the key points. To help alleviate Middle Eastern disputes, the United States tried to foster compromise settlements concerning the Iranian oil dispute, the Suez base, and the Sudan; it also pulled back somewhat from Israel and tried to take a more even stance in Arab-Israeli affairs.

Despite the decision to move ahead with the Northern Tier scheme, there was no great hurry within the administration on the project, partly because of many other concerns and partly because there was a limit to how fast a system that was "designed to grow from within" could develop. Military equipment and economic aid would be the instrumentalities. Acting Assistant Secretary of State John P. Jernegan told Congress that "Military leaders in most of these states are relatively progressive and friendly toward the West, and are acutely conscious of the deficiencies of their own forces, and their need for additional military equipment." He added that most of them would "cooperate with the West, at least on a limited basis, provided this cooperation brought them significant benefit in the form of military equipment and did not involve any encroachment on national sovereignty."[11]

While Washington was moving ahead slowly, Pakistan was becoming increasingly anxious to obtain U.S. military and economic assistance. Pakistan had followed a policy of nonalignment in fact though not in name since 1947. It did not want to depart too far in international politics from the other Muslim states, and Arabs had generally shown their opposition to Western defense alignments and organizations. Although the Pakistanis had no desire to antagonize the U.S.S.R., this was hardly an imperative of Pakistani foreign policy. Indeed, at this point Pakistan could not be too particular. Its economy was in trouble and it badly needed arms. Neither the Muslim states nor the U.S.S.R. could or would provide the support required.

After Prime Minister Liaquat Ali's death the Muslim League proved unable to govern effectively. There were frequent cabinet crises and constant political instability. There were troubles in the army, as in the Rawalpindi Conspiracy, when several generals were arrested in 1951 and charged with preparing to seize power for a foreign country. Widespread Muslim communal riots in West Pakistan early in 1953 forced the government to declare martial law and use the army to re-establish order. The attempt to cut the army's budget during a period of general economic retrenchment led Governor General Ghulam Mohammad to dismiss the government and install a new cabinet headed by Mohammad Ali of Bogra, then ambassador to the United States, who had no substantial political following.

Pakistan was now under the control of the men aptly labeled the "hierarchs"—the senior military officers and civil servants. The hierarchs, the most prominent of whom were Governor General Ghulam Mohammad, Defense Secretary Iskander Mirza, and Army Commander-in-Chief General Ayub Khan, had initiated the earlier attempt to secure military assistance from the United States. On September 1, 1953, the government announced a halt to retrenchment in the armed forces. In an attempt to pressure Washington into an early decision on military aid, word of U.S.-Pakistani discussions was leaked to the press. The Karachi correspondent for *The New York Times* stated that discussions on a military alliance were to begin soon and that Pakistan "was 'willing' to consider an exchange of air bases for military equipment."[12] The visit of Ghulam Mohammad and Ayub to Washington in November was described in the Pakistani press as designed to conclude negotiations on an arms agreement.[13]

The initial reaction of the U.S. government to Pakistani pressure was negative. Not only did it dislike being pressured, it also had not laid the political groundwork for an arms program. The State and Defense departments had not yet received Presidential clearance or clarified and coordinated the precise shape and scope of such a program. The State Department denied a story put out by the Pakistani Embassy in Washington that the two countries were about to conclude an arms pact, claiming that only "general conversations" had taken place.[14] In his news conference on November 18, the President said the United States would be "most cautious" about any action that might cause trouble for India.[15] Moreover, some officials still doubted the value of such a pact in its effect on U.S. relations with India and, to a lesser extent, with Afghanistan. There was awareness that Pakistan's first concern was India, and there was much dispute as to just what Pakistan's attitude toward the U.S.S.R. was, although some officials saw Pakistan as willing to cooperate with the West against the Communist bloc. But a pact with Pakistan did fit in with the general scheme that the United States was working toward in the Middle East and South Asia.

The public knowledge that negotiations were under way presented Prime Minister Nehru with a dilemma. He could hardly let the Communists or the right wing Hindu parties seize the issue to exploit it; yet, if he protested too vigorously, he might force Pakistan and the United States to move ahead. His initial public comments on November 15 were only that the reports were a matter of "intense concern to us" and that he was "watching these developments with the greatest care," but the next day he warned that a U.S.-Pakistani alliance would bring the cold war to India's borders, with far-reaching consequences in South Asia. Determined to protect his domestic position, Nehru directed the Indian Congress party to mount public protests and demonstrations against the program. India tried to dissuade Pakistan by warning that a military pact would damage the chances of reaching a settlement on Kashmir, and to get the United States to hold back by hinting that arms aid might cause India to move closer to the U.S.S.R.

The Soviets and the Chinese also denounced the proposed program. Once again the picture in American minds was that of India in agreement with the U.S.S.R. and China, and in opposition to the United States, or at least "neutral on the side of the Communists." Indignation in the United States was widespread; American newspapers, led by *The New York Times*, denounced the Indian government for "playing with fire" by the manner in which it opposed the program. Vice President Nixon, who visited Pakistan and India in December, apparently concluded that any attempt to back out of the program would strengthen neutralism throughout Asia.

Nonetheless, the Indian opposition led to a new delay, although it is unclear whether the purpose was to mollify India or to reappraise the whole program. In any case, Secretary Dulles and other leaders seemed to feel that any backing down at this point would amount to letting Nehru control American foreign policy. They were convinced of the general validity of the program despite arguments that the United States would be playing the old British game of divide and rule in a new context, ignoring the natural interdependence of India and Pakistan. The arms agreement was approved on February 8, 1954, by the National Security Council. The decision was generally accepted in the United States, though a few public figures, such as Senator Fulbright and former Ambassador Bowles, some Asian scholars, and an occasional newspaper, like the St. Louis *Post Dispatch*, were opposed.

While the United States went ahead with its plans to aid Pakistan over Indian objections, it was anxious to limit the damage to U.S.-Indian relations. President Eisenhower wrote to Prime Minister Nehru, stressing that military aid for Pakistan was not directed against India, assuring him that the United States would come to India's aid if Pakistan were ever to use the arms for aggression against India, and offering to give sympathetic consideration to any

Indian request for arms. The letter had the opposite effect from that intended. Nehru regarded such assurances as meaningless even if well-intentioned and was incensed at the implied suggestion that India's opposition to military aid was based on calculation rather than on principle. Having earlier said that if Pakistan accepted American military aid "she became progressively a war area and progressively her policies are controlled by others," he replied to the President, "If we object to military aid being given to Pakistan, we would be hypocrites and unprincipled opportunists to accept such aid ourselves."

A treaty of political consultation and cooperation that Pakistan had been negotiating with Turkey during the second half of 1953 was signed in April, 1954. Although a step toward the concept of the Northern Tier, it was not a defense treaty. While it is not clear that this treaty was an explicit condition of U.S. military assistance, there was an understanding that Pakistan would in time move in the direction of a regional defense pact. The State Department's press release on the Turko-Pakistani Treaty, referring to Secretary Dulles' earlier statement on the desire in the area for a collective security system, concluded that it was "of this character" in an attempt to make the decision to aid Pakistan more appealing by placing it in the context of America's general alliance strategy.[16]

Second Step: The Formation of SEATO

Before events resolved Pakistan's nebulous status in a Middle East security arrangement, developments in Southeast Asia led to a formal U.S.-Pakistani alliance. After the defeat of the French at Dien Bien Phu and the Geneva Conference on Indochina it was evident that France was no longer willing or able to remain a major power in the area. American policy-makers did not think they could leisurely approach the creation of a regional defense organization, allowing it to develop out of the efforts of indigenous forces. If such an organization was to be created, it would depend upon a strong American initiative. Therefore, the United States decided to rally as many of the nations in the area as were willing, together with the interested Western powers, to set up a regional defense organization to mobilize their strength and develop cohesion. Such a defense organization, it was hoped, would serve to deter Communist aggression or subversion by creating the basis for any future Western military intervention

that was required in the area. Not only did Pakistan, bordering on
Southeast Asia as well as on the Middle East, seem a logical member, but its membership would also serve to link this organization
with the one that Washington hoped to create in the Middle East—
just as Turkey would be the link between NATO and the Middle
East defense organization. Moreover, with only Thailand and the
Philippines eager to join the organization, Pakistan would augment
its Asian component.

The attitude of Pakistani leaders toward a Southeast Asian defense organization was ambiguous. They enjoyed satisfactory if distant relations with Communist China and had no desire to antagonize Peking. At the same time, they realistically recognized that if,
contrary to American urging, Pakistan refrained from joining the
Southeast Asia Treaty Organization (SEATO), its claim on U.S.
military and economic assistance would be weakened. Pakistan's
leaders, who had previously been oriented largely toward the Middle
East, now stressed that their country was a Southeast Asian as well
as a Middle Eastern nation.

At the Manila Conference which set up SEATO, Foreign Minister
Zafrullah Khan strongly opposed making the treaty applicable only
to Communist aggression. He even threatened to leave without signing when the United States refused to have the treaty apply to any
conflict between India and Pakistan. Eventually the American delegation agreed that the text would simply refer to the treaty as being
directed against aggression, but insisted on attaching an understanding that only Communist aggression would automatically be considered by the United States as endangering its own security and thus
bringing the operative clauses into effect. Pakistani leaders were able
to present the treaty to their people as covering all armed aggression
(for example, by India) but not being aimed at any particular country and thus not formally involving Pakistan in the cold war. How
many people took this at face value is questionable.

Third Step: The Baghdad Pact

During this period the Baghdad Pact was taking shape in the Middle East. The first step, referred to above, was the treaty of friendship and cooperation between Turkey and Pakistan, which also
provided that they would explore how they might cooperate in defense matters. The distance separating the two countries and their

inability to help each other militarily suggested other countries as potential members. Iran, the geographical bridge, was still seeking political stability after the overthrow of Mossadegh; for it, a settlement of the oil dispute with Britain held top priority.

Iraq seemed a better prospect than Iran in the short run. In contrast to the attitudes of most Arabs, Iraq's leaders saw the Soviet threat as real, partly because of geographic proximity, but also because of fear of Communist influence within Iraq, particularly among its large Kurdish minority. Turkey was willing to enter a defensive alliance with Iraq as a step toward regional security. But signing a bilateral treaty with Turkey was bound to cause trouble with Egypt, Iraq's long-time rival. Egypt, regarding itself as the leader in the region, wanted all the Arab states to stand united and refuse military ties with outside powers, at least until the Suez base issue had been resolved in a manner satisfactory to Cairo. In fact, as the strongest Arab state, Egypt had no desire to see any of its rivals strengthened by gaining access to outside arms. Nevertheless, Iraq went ahead with its plans, and the Turkish-Iraqi Pact was signed in February, 1955.

Britain enjoyed close relations with Iraqi leaders and was anxious to participate with Iraq in the emerging regional defense organization.[17] Its military base rights in Iraq were due to expire in a few years, and the anti-British riots which had occurred earlier when the Iraqi government agreed to extend them had demonstrated the futility of a strictly bilateral approach. The best way of holding onto its bases, Britain concluded, was to give them the protective coloration of a multilateral defense organization, even though that device had not worked with Egypt and the Suez Canal. In April, 1955, Britain adhered to the Baghdad Pact; Pakistan joined in September, and Iran in October.

Attempts to bring in other Arab states failed, but a Middle Eastern defense organization was nonetheless in existence. Although the Western position in the northern part of the Middle East was improved, the Pact—or the inclusion of Iraq—alienated the countries to the south. An opportunity was developing for the U.S.S.R. to exploit Arab resentment. Moreover, the United States decided not to join the Pact, in the hope of maintaining good relations with Egypt and because of Israeli opposition. But the nonadherence of the United States weakened the Pact and whatever chance there was of attracting other nations.

Questions and Reflections

The impact of the U.S.-Pakistani arms agreement and alliance on the international relations of South Asia raises a number of questions and reflections. What led each country to enter the relationship? What did they expect of it? What kind of problems did it create for them? A listing and some brief comments may illustrate the complexity of the motivation involved.

(1) The U.S. government was convinced of the desirability, if not the absolute necessity, of building collective security organizations in Asia. While officials recognized that no Asian defense treaty would provide any immediate increase in non-Communist strength and cohesion, they felt that such organizations could in time be strengthened to the point that they would attract further Asian support and increase the ability to contain Communist power.

(2) Officials were impressed with the quality of Pakistani soldiers. Although no Middle Eastern or South Asian army could have withstood any large-scale Soviet attack, the 250,000-man Pakistani army had considerable potential for the defense of the northwest frontier of the subcontinent until outside forces arrived, provided it could acquire an adequate and assured supply of modern military equipment.[18] Its officer corps was capable although, because of rapid promotion, senior officers lacked experience in the command of large units. The Pakistani soldier, heir to a long martial tradition, was an excellent infantryman, but lacked modern technical skills. The army had done a good job pulling itself together at the time of partition and appeared to be a potentially effective fighting force.

(3) Adequately equipped and trained Pakistani troops might be available for use outside the subcontinent—if Pakistan could be diverted from its preoccupation with India. Yet this was a mountainous "if," given Pakistani attitudes toward India. Some officials may have thought that if the United States equipped a large enough Pakistani army (expanded to several divisions more than were ever supplied), India would have been economically unable or unwilling to match the buildup; in return for such large amounts of arms, Pakistan would be willing to send some of its troops abroad if needed for purposes of collective security.[19] This view underestimated the domestic political constraints on sending Pakistan's troops abroad (at least without a firm guarantee of its security).

(4) Some U.S. officials, and particularly senior Air Force officers, regarded military bases in Pakistan as both desirable and obtainable. At the time the United States had no air bases between Turkey and the Philippines, and bases in Pakistan (or even the right to land on airstrips in wartime) would extend America's power to strike at the U.S.S.R., thereby adding to Soviet air defense problems. While neither the arms agreement nor the alliance provided for military bases in Pakistan, the possibility of acquiring such facilities was obviously better in an allied nation than in a neutral one.

(5) Given the general U.S. policy of seeking to encourage and develop Asian security organizations, and the opposition of Asian neutrals to such pacts, the United States had little choice but to accept those nations willing to join.

(6) Many American leaders were convinced that the struggle between the free and the Communist worlds was a struggle between good and evil. Hence, it was important for nations to stand up and be counted.

(7) The political support that was expected to accrue from allies as compared to neutrals was regarded as important, particularly their votes in the United Nations. In part this reflected the traditional American desire for friends, but calculations of political support were interwoven.

(8) Many U.S. officials believed that a strong Pakistani military establishment would be an important element of stability in a country which was having a difficult time developing a satisfactory political system. The army had to restore order after the Lahore riots early in 1953, and the need for such action might arise again.

(9) Finally, Pakistan was looked upon as a target of opportunity, and close ties might be useful when new dangers or opportunities arose. As we shall see, this was later to provide the most specific benefits derived by the United States from its relationship with Pakistan.

Underlying most of these reasons, of course, was the view that Communist aggression was a real danger in Asia and the conviction that local situations of strength (with the United States committed to supporting its allies) would serve as a deterrent to such aggression.

The reasons Pakistan pursued the course it did are less complex. The primary goal was to obtain military equipment to modernize the armed forces. Pakistan's leaders apparently also believed that being an ally of the West would afford them some military security against India beyond that provided by arms, and would help them in dealing with Afghanistan's attempts to undermine Pakistan's position along the northwest frontier.

Although security considerations were paramount, Pakistan's need for economic assistance was important. Agricultural stagnation and the collapse of the prices of raw material after the Korean War boom left the economy in a precarious position. Outside help made it possible to avoid choosing between defense cutbacks or critical hardships, either of which would have serious political repercussions. Allies were heavily favored over neutrals by the United States in the distribution of economic assistance during these years—although some of it was then labeled "defense support" to make it more politically acceptable to Congress.

In return for these benefits Pakistan was willing to abandon its policy of nonalignment—or its policy of friendship for all, as it had been called by Pakistani leaders. Signing up with the West, thereby abandoning the mainstream of Asian politics, was hard for many Pakistanis to accept. The countries that shunned the alliances often accused those that did join of having betrayed the Asian cause and traded their freedom for material benefits from the colonialist West. Since Pakistanis generally were somewhat defensive about this charge, their leaders stressed the Indian danger to justify the policy.

If the need for the support of a major outside power was fairly obvious to Pakistani leaders, there was some uncertainty and division within the government over the form of the relationship that was desirable with the United States, the mixture of aid to be sought, and the channels through which it should flow. Having acquired some political support within the Muslim League after assuming office in April 1953, Prime Minister Mohammad Ali was concerned more with political and economic considerations than were the hierarchs. He was also more concerned with domestic attitudes on international affairs, and hence more apprehensive about the effects of an open U.S.-Pakistani alliance on public opinion. The hierarchs would, of course, have been happy to get extensive military and economic assistance from the United States without making any commitments, but they were prepared to incur the necessary obligations. By the fall of 1953, however, Mohammad Ali was resisting the attempt to get U.S. military aid, preferring economic assistance. Arms aid, he feared, not only would be at the expense of economic assistance but would also increase the autonomy and independence of Ayub and the military in the government. But real power within the establishment lay with the hierarchs, and Mohammad Ali remained largely a front man.

What made it relatively easy to win public approval for alliance with the West was the Indian reaction to the shift. By reacting so strongly, India made it difficult for any Pakistani to argue against the new policy without appearing to be pro-Indian. Even Nehru's efforts to convince the Pakistanis that accepting military aid would endanger negotiations on Kashmir had no success. Thus Indian leaders greatly reduced any domestic political problem the change in course might have posed for the Pakistan government. Indeed, Pakistanis were generally delighted to see India furious but frustrated. For the first time since 1947 Pakistan had, they felt, clearly come off better than India in a major international episode, and it was sweet to savor.

What did the United States think were Pakistan's reasons for signing up with the West? Was the administration unaware that Pakistan's primary motive was to strengthen its position vis-à-vis India and that it was much less worried about a Soviet military threat? That India was Pakistan's major concern was reflected in Dulles' statements from the beginning. However, the United States was not well informed about Pakistan's attitude toward the U.S.S.R. Policy-makers seemingly believed that Pakistan assessed Soviet military pressure as a significant danger, which made cooperation with the West desirable. In effect, at least some important officials apparently thought that Pakistan regarded the Soviet threat a close second to that posed by India. How close is impossible to determine; that perception certainly varied within the government. The United States, engrossed with what it regarded as a life-and-death struggle with the Communist powers, found it hard to believe that others did not, to some extent, share its view of the world.

It is also clear that the U.S. government realized India would be strongly opposed to its policy of building up Pakistan's military strength. For this reason the United States was initially unenthusiastic about a military tie with Pakistan, and even hesitated late in 1953 before completing the negotiations. Despite India's objections, which were largely foreseen, the United States went ahead with the policy, which probably reflected a feeling that the damage it would cause to U.S.-Indian relations would not be unduly severe over the long run. Beyond this, it was apparently felt that the benefits from the alliance would more than offset the problems it would cause.

For many years there was a widespread impression that the Pakistani military establishment, like its British model, was nonpolitical. The impression had some validity, for Ayub could have taken over the government on more than one occasion but declined to do so. He did not want the military to be held directly responsible for the record of the Pakistani government and thus criticized for its failures. Within the government, however, the armed forces, and especially Ayub, played a very active political role in the struggle for the division of the available resources.

Moreover, although Ayub did not act counter to government policy during 1952, he had initiated the efforts to get U.S. arms and in the course of the negotiations acted with some independence of the faltering Muslim League government. Naturally, his freedom of maneuver increased after the hierarchs came to power. Ayub, engaged in establishing his predominance in the Pakistani military, was attempting to deal directly with the United States on the amount and type of equipment and defense-support assistance to be supplied. The larger the program and the greater his autonomy in acquiring and using aid, the greater impression he could make as the one who could get what the military wanted. While civilian politicians were hardly enthusiastic about an autonomous status for the Pakistani military, Ayub's public restraint during a period of pronounced political instability limited their concern or resentment over his maneuvers.

The alliance involved the United States in the internal politics of Pakistan in several distinct but related fields. Military aid strengthened the hand of the officers vis-à-vis the civilian politicians. American prestige was thus committed not just to Pakistan as a country but primarily to a particular group, which reduced contacts with other groups. By dealing with the officers and their civilian allies, U.S. aid also strengthened the position of West Pakistan relative to that of East Pakistan, for most of the officer corps and the civil servants were from the West where the disputes with India were also centered. Finally, by stressing military rather than economic assistance the U.S. program influenced the government's priorities on defense and development. It is clear that policy-makers were only dimly, if at all, aware that such effects on internal affairs would follow a decision to provide military assistance. Furthermore, they seemed not to be fully aware that by committing the United States in the way they did they were limiting their options in the subcontinent for many years to come, for once the alliance was formed it became a matter of prestige to justify and preserve it.

Pakistan naturally sought to gain support within the U.S. government and among the American public, thus inevitably becoming involved in the debate on policy toward Asia. In cultivating those who were primarily worried about the Communist military threat, it urged the United States to give top priority to military aid for those willing to cooperate with the West. Support for Pakistan, which was virtually nonexistent in 1951, became particularly strong in the Pentagon, with advocates also in the Congress, the State Department and elsewhere. Because of the general support for the decision to provide arms to Pakistan, no split along party lines took place, although a Republican administration set up the alliance and most of those who initially favored a higher priority for India were Democrats.

The operations of the alliance created practical problems. No sooner did Pakistan and the United States reach agreement on supplying arms than disagreements arose over the size and composition of the program. When the National Security Council approved the program in February 1954, something like $25 million in arms was apparently contemplated. A military survey team sent to Pakistan to assess the needs soon discovered they could hardly be met by such a small program. Agreement was finally reached between General Ayub and the Joint Chiefs of Staff and ratified by the two governments. But its terms were vague, or at least subject to sharply different interpretations, for the United States agreed to support certain force goals rather than to provide specified items and amounts of military equipment. In particular, the United States agreed to provide arms to modernize five and a half Pakistani divisions, and to support various other units in the army, the air force, and navy. The United States apparently expected this program to cost $171 million over the first three to four years. Differences over the meaning of the agreement plagued both countries for years, for they not only had different definitions of a division but also had to wrestle with what constituted modernization in a period when weapons technology was changing rapidly. It is not clear whether this was due to carelessness on the part of the negotiators or whether the two nations, wanting to move ahead with the program but unable to agree on its scope, consciously and deliberately left its terms broad and uncertain.

In any case, the Pakistani military, especially Ayub, constantly pressed for larger allotments of arms and other aid. Although Ayub, who occasionally resorted to public pressure (as in his October 1955 letter to Admiral Radford which was leaked to *The New York Times*), never secured the amounts of assistance he wanted, he was able to extract much more than $171 million. His arguments were supported by many within the U.S. government who, convinced that Pakistan had adopted a firm anti-Communist policy, argued that it could only play a role in regional defense if it were given more arms than originally planned.

Another aspect of the U.S. position raised problems. By seeking Asian allies, it was more difficult for the United States to keep out of Asian regional quarrels, in which its interests in the specific terms of any settlement were limited since its primary concern was that such disputes not explode and draw in the great powers. Moreover, the United States was generally associated with the weaker party to these quarrels—Pakistan vs. India, Iraq vs. Egypt—for naturally it was the weaker nation that sought outside support.

Finally, one underlying problem presented potential difficulty for U.S.-Pakistani relations. Each country clearly understood that it had taken on certain obligations and its ally had done the same, but both thought that an unspoken and unsigned agreement going further was implied. The United States thought that Pakistan was well aware it was expected to pursue an anti-Communist policy generally. Pakistan thought the United States understood that if it was not expected to pursue an anti-Indian policy, it surely was not to adopt a pro-Indian stance. These different underlying assumptions were later to cause much trouble.[20]

6

The Soviet Union Chooses India

Unsuccessful in preventing the United States and Pakistan from following their chosen course, the leaders in New Delhi, Moscow and Peking were faced with the need to make adjustments in their policies. Nehru had always wanted India to have good relations with its two large neighbors to the north, the U.S.S.R. and Communist China. All the more reason now that U.S. arms aid for Pakistan was likely to shift the previously favorable balance of power in the subcontinent. One of India's first moves after the U.S.-Pakistani arms agreement was to conclude the prolonged negotiations with Peking on the status of Tibet, for Nehru wanted to avoid having both Pakistan and Communist China as enemies. India renounced the rights in Tibet it inherited from the British and recognized Tibet as a part of China. Peking, while unwilling to yield anything of real importance, was at this time adopting a less antagonistic stance toward its Asian neighbors, and the treaty was regarded with satisfaction in New Delhi as well as in Peking.

India had already hinted at expanding its relations with the Soviet Union if the United States armed Pakistan. The threat had not dissuaded Washington. Having thereupon decided to explore the possibility of closer relations with Moscow, Nehru and his associates were uncertain how far it would be wise to move, in view of the cold war atmosphere, the abrupt reversals which had characterized Soviet foreign policy in the past, and the links of the Communist Party of India (CPI) to the Soviet Union.

In Search of a Policy and a Party

From the time of the Bolshevik revolution until World War II, the men who ruled Russia paid little heed to the Indian subcontinent. Despite the precedent of czarist efforts in the area, Lenin and his collaborators centered their attention on regions they regarded as more important, such as Europe or China, or on closer neighbors, such as Turkey and Iran. Soviet leaders were also handicapped by their lack of knowledge and experience concerning Asia. To the extent that they were informed about the world outside Russia, their knowledge was of Europe; and the few Orientalists who remained after the revolution did not concentrate on current affairs.

Under Lenin's theory of imperialism, European colonial control enabled the capitalist states to delay the inevitable socialist upheavals. Thus, Asian revolutions would undermine imperialist strength. But in India the British were firmly in control, the nationalist forces were led by bourgeois elements, and there was no organized Communist party. There was a brief upsurge of hope among some Russian Communists in 1920 that revolutionary situations were developing in Asia. By 1921, however, Soviet leaders saw that revolution was a distant rather than an immediate prospect in Asia. Accordingly, the Soviet Union turned to the arduous but necessary task of building up local Communist parties in the Asian countries. Party organizers and ideologists came to play an important role in Soviet policy, and short-run requirements of Soviet national interests were not yet in competition with ideological considerations as they were in later years. Marxism gave the men in Moscow certain insights into relationships between competing groups and social forces in Asian countries and the antagonisms between Asia and Europe, but this reliance on Marxism also led to distortions.

Two major ideological issues regarding Asian countries had to be faced from the beginning. The first concerned the correct Communist view of, and policy toward, the nationalist movements. Should Communists oppose these movements, or collaborate with them in an effort to weaken the colonial powers? The second and related issue (though of less immediate significance) concerned the possibility of Asian countries skipping the capitalist stage of development. Was it possible for them to move directly from precapitalist to socialist societies, as Russia had done?[1] Though Lenin had no great faith in cooperation with Asian nationalist movements, he saw no practical alternative to making tactical alliances with them because of the scarcity of Asian Communists. Few if any social forces in Asia were ready for radical revolution in the 1920s, as the few Asian Communists themselves recognized. Yet support of nationalist movements was not without its own dangers. After the Chinese Nationalists ended their cooperation with the Chinese Communists and wiped out many of them in 1927, Stalin shifted the party line from cooperation to attacking the nationalists as bourgeois tools of imperialism. The new line came at a time when Stalin was also adopting harsher domestic policies to carry out the First Five-Year Plan.

Any Soviet decision to support or oppose the Indian nationalist movement would have little practical importance until a Communist party was well established there. A few small groups within India and some scattered bands of emigrés who were inclined toward revolution and socialism became the nucleus of the Communist Party of India.[2] Progress was slow and uneven; periodic changes of the party line confused some Indian Communists and alienated others. There were disagreements between Lenin, who argued for tactical cooperation with the Indian nationalist movement, and M. N. Roy, the Comintern representative in India, who favored a more independent and radical course. British intelligence constantly infiltrated the movement, and the British Indian government at times repressed it. There were personal struggles for power and conflicts between Indians like Roy, who wanted a direct relationship between Indian Communists and Moscow, and the Communist Party of Great Britain (CPGB), which aspired to guide the Indian movement and emerged as its mentor by the mid-1920s. In 1934 the party apparently had only about 150 members, but thereafter it grew more rapidly as interest in radical social and economic ideas increased; by 1942 the party had about 5,000 members.[3]

The position of the CPI grew steadily stronger during World War II, its membership rising to about 30,000 in 1945 and 53,000 in 1946.[4] To a degree, the CPI gains in this period reflected the party's pursuit of a moderate rather than a revolutionary course. Perhaps more important, however, was the CPI's position in the Indian political context during the war years. After the Nazi attack on the Soviet Union, the CPI quickly shifted from opposition to support of the Allied war effort. It urged acceptance of the plan produced by the Cripps mission in 1942 and made it clear that the CPI would fight to defend India against Japan. The British Indian government responded by announcing in July that the party was now legal. It released many Communists from jail, and accepted the Communist offer to train some units in guerrilla warfare, although this program was discontinued as the Japanese threat faded. The CPI also bene-fited from the absence of the Congress party, which had been de-clared illegal and its leaders imprisoned when they launched the "Quit India" movement in August 1942 after the failure of the Cripps mission. By strengthening its organization, by winning or solidifying its control of mass organizations of workers, peasants, students, and by creating a wide array of front groups, the CPI was in a much stronger position when the war ended. But its demonstrated willing-ness to subordinate nationalistic considerations had alienated most Congress leaders and made them wary of cooperation with the CPI.

South Asia remained an area of secondary concern and activity for the Soviet Union in the years just after World War II. Soviet com-mentators discussing the Indian situation seemed uncertain and confused, and Moscow apparently did not provide any clear guidance to the CPI. Soviet and Indian Communist leaders found it difficult to believe that Britain's new Labour government meant what it said about freeing India. During 1946–47 the CPI officially proclaimed a policy of loyal opposition to the interim Nehru government, but the party floundered and at one point even went so far as to support the division of India into seventeen separate sovereignties on the basis of linguistic nationalism. For a time the moderate leadership of the CPI was able to beat off the challenge of those urging a more radical pol-icy and to remain in control (although the traditional factionalism and indiscipline of the party made such control less than all-embrac-ing). In June 1947 the CPI pledged its support to the Nehru govern-ment, and the party's stand was backed by their British Communist mentors, who continued to guide the CPI until after independence. However, this policy appealed only briefly to the more radical and militant leaders and cadres; late in 1947 they seized control of the CPI and began to reverse its moderate course.

The position of the radicals was greatly strengthened by the shift that occurred in Soviet policy during 1947. As early as June, Soviet commentators were attacking the Nehru government, but the Soviet party apparently did not get the message across to either the CPI or the British Communists for several months. The new and more militant Soviet policy was not, of course, caused by or limited to developments on the Indian scene, but reflected a stepped-up campaign against non-Communist states and forces. These were the years of Andrei Zhdanov's ascendancy and of the hard line generally, when Soviet political leaders foresaw an intensifying global conflict, with the world divided into two camps—and anyone not in the socialist camp was a lackey of the imperialists. Unable to recognize that Asian countries were winning their independence through nationalist parties with bourgeois leaders, Moscow called their independence a sham. To a Communist observing the British officers in the Indian and Pakistani armed forces, the British businessmen operating in both countries, and their membership in the Commonwealth, it seemed obvious that both remained dependencies of their former colonial master.

This view prevailed in Moscow for several years; in 1950 a Soviet Asian expert could write: "The political and military-strategic dependence of both dominions on England and the United States had found its expression in agreements which were concluded between these two countries and England at the Imperial Conference in October 1948, and in April 1949. . . . On January 26, 1950, to deceive the masses, India was proclaimed an independent republic."[5] Another typical example of Soviet views was, "The National Congress in India, Quirino and Romulo in the Philippines, etc., are obedient executors of the will of the British American imperialists, their mainstay in the colonies."[6]

The CPI Tries Revolution

It was in the atmosphere of an intensifying cold war and sharp antagonism toward Asian nationalists that the Communist Party of India adopted a policy of orthodox revolution against Nehru's government at its Second Congress in Calcutta in February 1948. Indian Communists felt that the U.S.S.R. supported such a course. They were strongly influenced by the writings of Yugoslav leaders and by the speeches of their delegates to the Calcutta meetings, who spoke and acted as if they possessed the authority of the international Communist movement, and urged Asian Communists to follow a radical course. Moreover, many CPI leaders in the radical wing of the party felt Indian conditions called for revolution. As events in 1948 demonstrated, the strategy was not confined to India, for Communist parties adopted revolutionary tactics and started civil wars in Burma, Malaya, and Indonesia. Although many non-Communist leaders and students of communism have argued that such actions were carried out under Moscow's *orders*, in recent years some have questioned this interpretation.[7] But the tenor of Soviet propaganda and acts encouraged the recourse to direct action at this time.

Initially the CPI attempted to stage an orthodox, urban-based revolution. While it was able to spark considerable labor unrest and violence, its efforts were sporadic and uncoordinated. It soon became apparent that the party did not have an adequate organization or sufficient resources to carry out anything approaching a revolution. The central and state governments cracked down hard on the CPI and arrested many of its leaders; and there was no underground apparatus capable of carrying on the struggle in such an eventuality.

The failure of the party's orthodox revolutionary strategy was becoming clear to all but its most dogmatic adherents, though not all who admitted its failure were willing to abandon any thought of immediate revolution. Since 1946 a group within the CPI had been leading an agrarian revolt in the Telengana area of Hyderabad, where local conditions and the disruption that accompanied the struggle between the Nizam and the Indian government had enabled the revolutionaries to gain and hold many villages. Encouraged by their success, they urged the CPI to adopt a strategy based on agrarian revolution against large landlords (but not wealthy peasants) as better suited to Indian conditions than the more orthodox revolutionary posture. Additional support for the arguments of the Telengana revolutionaries and their sympathizers in the Andhra section of Madras state just across the border was the success achieved by the Chinese Communists' adherence to an agrarian strategy.[8] They were not bashful about claiming that their experience provided the proper example for other Asian Communist parties, and in 1949 the U.S.S.R. began to urge a shift from a leftist to a neo-Maoist strategy.[9] The shift was accepted in January 1950 in the official Cominform journal.[10]

Fortified with apparent Soviet support, the Andhra Communists gained control of the central CPI organs and tried to put their strategy into action. Despite the early successes of the Telengana insurgents (who at one point claimed they controlled 3,000 villages), the attempt to seize power by guerrilla action was a failure. This strategy was no better suited to Indian conditions than was the earlier orthodox strategy. The Nehru government, proving to be far stronger than the Chinese Nationalist regime, suppressed the groups trying to seize additional rural areas, and in time put down the Telengana revolt, too. Confused and disrupted, the party was unable to pursue any policy effectively, and the leaders of its moderate wing and of the Communist trade unions who had argued against "adventurism" slowly began to work their way back into leading positions.

Two conclusions emerge from this brief account. First, the party's sense of timing and judgment of the conditions and basic power relationships in India was faulty. It gravely overestimated its own strength and the popular appeal of revolution in the years 1948–51, and it underestimated the government's capability to deal with the upheavals it tried to instigate. If there ever was a chance for revolution—which seems doubtful—it was in the chaotic period just after independence, but the CPI waited nearly a year before challenging Nehru's government. Second, communications between the Soviet and Indian Communist parties left much to be desired, and Soviet guidance was sporadic and ineffectual.[11]

The party was gravely hurt by its adventurism. Membership declined from approximately 90,000 in 1948 to between 20,000 and 30,000 in 1951. Many nationalists became aware of its true nature, and the government regarded it as a threat to the country and a competitor for power. Both Moscow and the CPI saw that a change in strategy was necessary, but the former was confused and the latter disorganized and exhausted.

By mid-1951 the international scene had stabilized to a degree. The Korean War was stalemated; most Asian revolutions led by the Communists had either failed or been contained, and a Western military buildup was underway in Europe. There were a few hints during Stalin's last year that he was exploring a more flexible policy, but essentially Soviet policy was marking time, a phase that continued until after his death.[12]

The Post-Stalin Relaxation and the New Offensive

The men who took charge after Stalin's death decided to relax tensions within the U.S.S.R. and with the non-Communist world.

Stalin's methods of rule were no longer suitable to the society that had developed, and local wars as in Korea were too dangerous. These conclusions probably were the considered judgments of the Soviet leaders, but may have also reflected their initial lack of self-confidence and the need to sort out their relationships with each other before embarking on new foreign-policy initiatives. In any case, it appears that what the new leadership initially desired was a relaxation of tensions rather than a general liberalization of relations between the Soviet government, its citizens, and foreign nations.

As part of their reassessment of the world situation and their policies, the new Soviet leaders took a fresh look at the Asian countries. No dramatic shift in viewpoint or policy occurred, but a gradual change in outlook was evident in Premier Malenkov's address to the Supreme Soviet on August 15, 1953. He hailed India's "significant contribution" among the "efforts of the peace-loving countries towards ending the Korean War," and expressed hope that "in the future, relations between India and the U.S.S.R. will grow stronger and develop in a spirit of friendly cooperation." India's initial reactions were cautious, but New Delhi clearly welcomed the change and hoped for more. When the U.S.S.R. and Communist China appeared to urge Ho Chi Minh and the Vietnamese Communists to accept a compromise settlement of the Indo-Chinese conflict in 1954 —a settlement giving the Viet Minh less than a continuation of the armed struggle would have achieved—Indian hopes rose further.

Soviet leaders soon realized that more than a few kind words and an end to insults were needed if Soviet interests in the Middle East and South Asia were to be advanced. In 1954 and 1955 Stalin's successors were faced with a major problem as well as a major opportunity. The United States was establishing military, political, and economic ties with many countries in the Middle East and Asia as British and French power receded. It seems unlikely that the Soviet Union feared the Baghdad Pact as such, for its local members were obviously too weak to pose any threat. But Moscow's denunciations of the pact suggest that it was regarded as a cover for the continuation of British influence and for setting up additional U.S. military bases—particularly air bases—in the member countries.

The U.S.S.R. had two assets to counter the American and British effort. The first was the willingness of the new leaders, particularly Khrushchev, to make a fresh appraisal of the Asian scene. They did not underrate the existing tensions between many Asian states and the West, which were being heightened by the efforts to establish regional security systems. They recognized that the governments of India, Egypt, and Indonesia, far from being in league with the imperialists, were strongly opposed to most kinds of Western influence in the area. In short, the post-Stalin leaders saw that their neutralism or non-alignment was not only genuine but could be usefully exploited. Furthermore, the quarrels between various Asian countries also were possible targets for exploitation. By supporting one side or the other in the disputes between Arab states and Israel, between India and Pakistan, and between Pakistan and Afghanistan, the U.S.S.R. could exacerbate the difficulties facing the West and perhaps gain some influence. Such a policy would mean abandoning at least temporarily any hope of gaining a foothold in the countries attacked, but a partial position in the area was better than none at all.

In order to exploit Asian resentment of the West or intra-regional quarrels, the U.S.S.R. could not rely on propaganda and diplomacy alone, though such support was welcome to the Asian countries involved. Material assistance was also required. The second asset possessed by the Soviet leaders was the ability of their economy by the mid-1950s to produce enough so that arms and industrial equipment could be offered to Asian countries. Military equipment of the early postwar years was becoming obsolescent by Soviet standards and could be supplied at limited cost. Industrial goods represented more of a sacrifice; but the economy was growing rapidly, and deliveries did not need to be heavy for a number of years. In any case, an investment of Soviet resources held the prospect of reinforcing the inclination and ability of such countries as India and Egypt to oppose the West. By helping Asian governments do some of the things they wanted to do, the U.S.S.R. would be able to establish itself in the area.

Because Soviet policy toward the Middle East and Asia in the mid-1950s was so obviously concerned with advancing the national interest and was dependent upon the conventional tools of contemporary statecraft—military and economic assistance—it is easy to overlook its ideological element. The nationalist tides in Asia had a revolutionary potential, Soviet leaders felt. They reasoned that the nationalist leaders and governments would prove incapable of effectively promoting social and economic reforms and economic development as long as they maintained their bourgeois attitudes and policies. As a result of their difficulties in moving ahead and also of their association with the Soviet bloc, such regimes would gradually become more radical and ultimately choose the socialist (Communist) path. Hence economic and military assistance—and even political support—for non-Communist governments was justified. (Some Soviet leaders may have also been concerned lest these countries look toward China for a model, although this probably was not yet a major worry.) Those Communist officials with long memories (and an orthodox cast of mind) probably were dubious of or opposed to the new policy, remembering how earlier nationalist leaders had turned on their Communist "supporters" in China in 1927. However, Soviet leaders felt there was less danger of this than in the past: the Soviet bloc was stronger, and local nationalists would be less inclined to risk Soviet displeasure. Moreover, what alternative was there? Local Communist parties had been unable to seize power through revolutionary struggle; and if the U.S.S.R. was hostile or even indifferent toward nationalist regimes, the United States might become firmly established in the area. Thus national interest and a more sophisticated ideological approach both argued for a new policy. The Soviets discarded the old view of the world divided into two camps, and acknowledged the existence of a third or neutral camp.

The extent to which Moscow was operating according to a well-thought-out policy can be overstated. At the time it obviously was not clear to Soviet leaders what the situation in Asia was, what their prospects were, and what moves they should make. There was some uncertainty and experimentation on their part. But what has been described above was the policy that gradually emerged to guide Soviet actions.

India's Response

The serious setback Indian foreign policy had suffered with the conclusion of the U.S.-Pakistani arms agreement increased receptivity to Soviet overtures. India's leaders probably had no very clear picture of the precise implications of the new relationship. Was the United States abandoning hope for even tolerable relations with India, and planning to support Pakistan fully in its quarrels with India? President Eisenhower had said he would continue to work for better relations, but Indian leaders may have felt that this was either a *pro forma* statement or else he did not realize the extent of the challenge to India that the new U.S. policy represented.

Although Nehru's major objection to the U.S. regional security policy was its direct effect on India, he was also convinced that military buildups and alliances were the wrong way to deal with the Soviet Union and China. These measures would only cause the Communist countries to react in the same way, thereby increasing the dangers of war. What was called for, in Nehru's view, was an effort to ease tensions and improve relations between the Western and Communist worlds; the West should be willing to take some risks in face of the indescribable disasters that would flow from another world conflict.

While the American search for Asian military allies may have been the immediate cause of the Soviet offensive and the Indian response, the U.S.S.R. and India probably would soon have manifested an interest in closer relations in any case. In 1954 and 1955 India was engaged in drawing up its Second Five-Year Plan (1956–61), which called for expenditures of about $15 billion, or twice as much as was spent on the First Plan. The Second Plan required over $1 billion in foreign aid. Moreover, in 1955 the Congress party had called for a "socialist pattern of society" and a large expansion of the public sector of the economy. Nehru, who had long desired a move to the left, now felt ready to carry the policy through. Western aid was still quite modest; and, clearly, some Western countries—particularly the United States—were not inclined to provide much help for building state-owned industrial establishments. Although India's move to the left was not made to please the U.S.S.R., it probably made it easier for Soviet and Indian Communists skeptical about aid to non-Communist governments to accept Moscow's new policy.

Other considerations argued for closer relations with Moscow. India believed the post-Stalin policies reduced the danger of war. The attention and praise bestowed by Moscow, enhancing Indian prestige, probably led Indian leaders to conclude that their opportunities for playing a moderating and mediating role between East and West were increasing. Although not invited to the Geneva Conference in June 1954 because of American objections, India felt it had played a useful unofficial role; it also felt the U.S.S.R. and Communist China showed a commendable willingness to compromise. Nehru hoped that more contacts between the U.S.S.R. and countries like India would indirectly foster liberalization within the Soviet bloc. Improved relations with Moscow could also serve as a warning to Pakistan and its ally that India had powerful friends. In particular, it might even be possible to get Moscow to shift from its generally neutral position on Kashmir to a pro-Indian stance, which would be valuable, given the U.S.S.R.'s permanent membership in the Security Council.

Despite its policy of rapprochement, India showed little interest in acquiring Soviet arms to carry out the military buildup it began as a result of U.S. arms deliveries to Pakistan. Nehru stressed that India felt free to buy arms from any source, and would not hesitate to seek Soviet arms if that should seem desirable. But India wished to standardize arms as much as possible and was reluctant to rely heavily on either the United States or the Soviet Union. As India's defense spending increased from about $400 million in 1955 to over $550 million in 1959, it continued to buy military equipment from its traditional suppliers in Western Europe, principally Britain and France.

The Untroubled Years

With both countries eager for better relations and closer cooperation, events moved quickly. At the February 1954 conference of the United Nations Economic Commission for Asia and the Far East, the Soviet delegate pledged assistance for those countries which had advanced the cause of peace. Shortly thereafter, negotiations began for Soviet assistance in constructing a steel mill, and in September it was announced that the U.S.S.R. would supply the necessary equipment for a one-million-ton mill. Under the agreement signed in February 1955, the Soviet Union extended a loan equivalent to $112 million to be repaid in Indian goods over twelve years once the project was completed. Moscow also offered expanded trade opportunities, much welcomed by Indians, which promised diversification of trade and supplies of industrial equipment to be paid for in Indian products rather than hard currency.

Throughout 1954 and 1955 there was a general rapprochement between Asian neutrals and the Communist countries, while relations between the neutrals and the Western countries and their Asian allies worsened. The year 1955 also saw an important exchange of visits by Nehru to the U.S.S.R. and by Khrushchev and Bulganin to India. Nehru and his entourage toured extensively in the Soviet Union, and held lengthy discussions with the new Soviet leaders. Indicative of the importance attached to India as a country and to Nehru as a person was the fact that he was the first non-Communist leader to address the Soviet people directly. He spoke to a crowd of 100,000 gathered in a Moscow stadium, balancing praise for Soviet efforts to reduce international tensions with words stressing that each country was different and should choose its own way of achieving national objectives.

The most spectacular visit, however, was the Khrushchev and Bulganin tour of India (and also Burma and Afghanistan) in November and December. The Soviet delegation of some fifty people spent nearly three weeks in India, which seemed a great honor to ordinary Indians. Encouraged by the Indian government, tremendous crowds greeted the Soviet leaders, who responded warmly; Khrushchev skillfully mingled praise for the beauty of the Taj Mahal with regret over the sufferings of the workers who built it. He denounced colonialism vigorously and repeatedly, and Britain and America so extravagantly that many Indians were embarrassed. However, the embarrassment was more than offset by Soviet support on Kashmir and the Goa dispute with Portugal. The final Indo-Soviet communiqué called for the admission of Communist China to the United Nations and the banning of atomic weapons, opposed regional military pacts, and urged a new summit conference. Issues on which disagreement existed, such as the status of East Germany, were not mentioned. The CPI leaders, who were allowed no official role in the visit, were bitter at the praise showered on the Congress leaders and could only hope the increased respectability of communism would ultimately benefit them.

The dramatic exchange of visits caught the world's attention for a time, even though they were as much spectacle as substance. Less observed by most outsiders though symbolic of the closer Indo-Soviet cooperation that was developing was the exchange of numerous delegations concerned with cultural, trade, agricultural, industrial, and parliamentary affairs. Soviet books and periodicals were made available at low prices in India, and Soviet radio broadcasts (in a variety of Indian languages) were stepped up. There was a revival of Asian studies in the U.S.S.R., and many Indian and other Asian students were invited to study there.

The Communist Party of India had also been revising its policy between 1951 and 1956, shifting from its advocacy of armed struggle to a concept of "constitutional communism." Not an easy change for the party to make, it was accompanied by bitter disputes in which ideological convictions and personal struggles for power were intrically interwoven and caused repeated trouble. The key issue turned on the nature and policy of the Nehru government. Were the government and its policies progressive or reactionary? A corollary was the extent to which the needs of international communism should take precedence over national issues. Subordinating the party's local concerns to Soviet requirements called for support of the Nehru government in its opposition to U.S. foreign policy, but this would make it difficult to challenge the Congress party within India.

Initially the CPI avoided a clear choice, supporting Nehru's foreign policy while opposing his domestic policy. As Ajoy Ghosh, the CPI Secretary General, said upon returning from a trip to Moscow in December 1954, "The internal policy of the Nehru Government does not suit the interest of the masses, while the foreign policy does."[13] The CPI tried to maintain this position during its campaign in the important Andhra state elections in February 1955, but the Congress party counterattacked vigorously, charging that the CPI was loyal to a foreign power. Communist prospects, initially bright, were further damaged by an article in *Pravda* shortly before the election which praised Nehru's domestic policy as well as his international stance. The resounding Congress victory and the steadily increasing Soviet support confirmed for Nehru that he was following a sound strategy. During the following year, 1956, the CPI also had to contend with the confusion and demoralization brought on by Khrushchev's revelation of Stalin's crimes and his de-Stalinization campaign, and by Soviet acceptance of Nehru's "socialistic pattern of society" as a progressive policy and not the sham the CPI had claimed it was. Battered and disoriented, the CPI decided it had no choice but to accept the favorable Soviet judgment of Nehru's policies.

Nehru felt encouraged by the signs of liberalization within the Communist world. Soviet leaders were curbing the role of the police and showing more concern for the welfare of their people. They had admitted mistakes in dealing with Tito and were striving for a better understanding with Yugoslavia. The Cominform was dissolved in April 1956. The U.S.S.R. agreed to an Austrian Peace Treaty and ended its occupation of the eastern part of that country. Nehru took the de-Stalinization policy adopted at the Soviet party's Twentieth Congress as confirmation that the U.S.S.R. had embarked on a new course "based on a more realistic appreciation of the world situation and [representing] a significant process of adaptation and adjustment."[14] The West, he argued, should attempt to increase its contacts with the Communist countries. His approach was "to bind the Soviet Union (and China) to international obligations and responsibilities from which it would become increasingly difficult to withdraw."

During these years India was bitterly attacking the United States on a wide variety of issues besides its military aid to Pakistan. In criticizing its basic approach toward the U.S.S.R. and Communist China, India repeatedly said Washington should agree to China's admission to the United Nations and to Peking's control of Taiwan. India strongly opposed any U.S. military involvement in Indochina in 1954, and resented Washington's opposition to Indian membership in the Geneva Conference. It also vigorously attacked the United States for supporting Nationalist China's defense of the offshore islands late in 1954. Secretary Dulles' statement in December 1955 referring to Goa as a province of Portugal created an uproar in India, as did his assertion in 1956 that neutralism was "immoral." The antagonism between Nehru and Dulles—two self-righteous men representing two self-righteous nations—began even before independence with Dulles' comment early in 1947 that "Soviet Communism exercises a strong influence through the interim Hindu government" and constantly flared up during the 1950s. India also resented the communiqués issued at the conclusion of the Baghdad Pact and SEATO meetings in March and April 1956 calling for a settlement of the Kashmir dispute. Such calls, which fell short of what Pakistan wanted, seemed unexceptional to the Western members. India felt, however, that pressure was being applied, and that Kashmir was no concern to professedly anti-Communist military groupings.

Complexities and Complications

As 1956 wore on, the situation became more complex. The rising tide of nationalism and popular discontent in Eastern Europe began to pose serious problems for the U.S.S.R. The Soviet leadership, uncertain how to handle the situation, tried to keep control without returning to Stalinist methods. When the upheaval finally came in Poland in October, Khrushchev and his colleagues rushed to Warsaw and appeared for a time ready to resort to force to reassert control. But the newly installed party leader, Wladeslaw Gomulka, was able to convince them that it was better to rely on a good Communist, which he claimed to be, than to try to repress the upsurge of Polish nationalism.

Hungary was not so fortunate, however, and there the upheaval became an outright anti-Communist revolution which the Soviet Union suppressed with its troops. With the issue in the United Nations, India—alone among the nonaligned nations—voted with the Soviet bloc countries against a resolution urging the removal of Soviet troops from Hungary and the holding of elections under U.N. auspices. There was briefly speculation that Krishna Menon, India's special U.N. delegate, had acted without direct authorization, but Nehru defended the vote in parliament a few days later, saying that forcing an election under U.N. auspices on an unwilling government could be a dangerous precedent for Kashmir. While Nehru never admitted misjudging the matter, within a week he recognized the revolt as a nationalist uprising and called for the evacuation of Soviet troops and the exercise of the right of self-determination for the Hungarian people—though without U.N. pressure or involvement. Stung by Western criticism, some Indians privately argued that the West had done little but talk at the crucial point; why should India damage its relations with the U.S.S.R.—uselessly—in the circumstances?

Such a stand was not satisfactory to many other Indians, who felt their government had acted dishonorably after years of noble talk. For the first time since independence, Nehru's conduct of foreign policy was vigorously attacked by Indians whose nationalist credentials and adherence to nonalignment left them immune to charges of fronting for the West.

The world's attention in October and November of 1956 was not focused solely on Hungary. In the eyes of Asian countries once ruled by Europe, the Israeli invasion of the Sinai and the British and French attack on Suez were even more repugnant than Soviet actions in Hungary. The strains on the Commonwealth were great, and apparently were one reason behind Britain's decision to halt the attack when it did. If Britain and France were acting like the bad old imperialists, and the U.S.S.R. was acting like a bad new imperialist, the behavior of the United States was no less surprising. On the eve of a presidential election the United States broke with its allies Britain and France and with its close friend Israel. It condemned their action and put extremely heavy pressure on all three countries to halt the fighting and then to withdraw. For several years Indian leaders had been lauding the U.S.S.R. as a peace-loving nation and (while acknowledging U.S. desires for peace) attacking U.S. policies as increasing the chances of war. Now Soviet troops were suppressing a nationalist revolt while the United States was acting to halt the Middle East fighting. It was obviously food for thought.

The events in Eastern Europe and the Middle East late in 1956 marked both the low point in U.S.-Indian relations and the starting point for their improvement. The collapse of the Hungarian police state amidst a popular uprising aroused powerful emotions in the West, first exhilaration, then dismay and despondency, and finally shame as the Soviets brutally suppressed the struggle for freedom while the West fearfully and idly stood by. India's vote in the United Nations and Nehru's equivocation were regarded as reprehensible even by India's best friends in the United States; his subsequent call for the departure of Soviet troops never overcame the feeling that India had faltered at a crucial moment. New Delhi's actions and the criticism they aroused within India apparently also affected the attitudes and policy of India's leaders; from this time forward their general tendency to sit in moral judgment upon other nations was held somewhat in check. The West was the principal beneficiary of this restraint, which, combined with a new respect for the United States, laid the basis for a steady improvement of Indo-U.S. relations.

Soviet-Pakistani Relations

The Soviet policy of supporting those Asian countries desirous of closer ties with the U.S.S.R. by taking their side in their quarrels made it inevitable that Pakistan would be written off. In November 1953, when reports of Pakistan's alignment with the West began to circulate, Moscow sent a note of protest against any alliance with the United States and asked for clarification of what was taking place in the negotiations for military aid and air bases. Pakistan, while assuring the U.S.S.R. of its desire for friendly relations, rejected the note and said air bases for the United States were not even under consideration.[15] In March 1954 Moscow again sent a note criticizing the recently announced U.S.-Pakistan military aid agreement as unfriendly; it too was rejected. Moscow also protested the signing of the Turkish-Pakistan agreement in April 1954, and Pakistan's membership in SEATO in 1955, as Soviet propaganda constantly attacked the Baghdad Pact and SEATO.

The most spectacular Soviet attack on Pakistan came in late 1955. Since Khrushchev's and Bulganin's Asian trip was cause for serious concern, Pakistan attempted to persuade the Soviet leaders not to visit either Kashmir or Afghanistan. Khrushchev was not to be deterred, and in Kashmir he publicly revealed the Pakistani objections to the visits and denounced the attempt to tell the Soviet leaders where they should go. More importantly, he supported New Delhi's position that Kashmir was part of India.

During their visit to Kabul the Soviet leaders supported Afghanistan's position on the Pushtunistan dispute, with no embarrassment about upholding the right of self-determination for the Pushtuns while opposing it for the Kashmiris. There was worry in the West that the U.S.S.R. would incite the Afghans to pursue a reckless course that would lead to military clashes, with the West obliged to support Pakistan and with Afghanistan completely dependent on the U.S.S.R. These fears mounted when, shortly after Khrushchev's visit, it was announced that a $100 million Soviet loan had been granted to Afghanistan. Arms agreements with the Soviet Union and Czechoslovakia followed in 1956. But Afghanistan asserted it would maintain its independence and neutrality. And the leaders of both Afghanistan and Pakistan recognized the need to curb their hostility; official visits gradually eased tensions and led to tolerable though not friendly relations for a time.

Early in 1956 there was a temporary warming of Soviet-Pakistani relations. Perhaps Moscow felt it had gone too far in siding with India and Afghanistan—or at least had antagonized Pakistan unduly. Perhaps it was probing to test the firmness of Pakistan's alignment with the West. At any rate, in March 1956 Molotov, attending the national day reception at the Pakistan embassy in Moscow, stressed the U.S.S.R.'s desire for friendship and hinted that it might supply a steel mill to Pakistan as it had done to India. Deputy Premier Mikoyan visited Pakistan at the same time, talked of aid and trade possibilities, and attempted to make some political capital by stating on March 26 that "the future of Kashmir is not for us to decide. This is for the people of Kashmir to decide." However, Pakistani hopes that the U.S.S.R. was adopting an even-handed approach were dashed when Mikoyan, visiting India the next week, referred to Kashmir as a part of India. Mikoyan's visit led to the first Soviet-Pakistan trade agreement, signed in June 1956, but nothing else developed. The lines in the cold war were still too sharply drawn for either the Soviet Union or the United States to look with favor upon friendly relations between Moscow and the Asian allies of the West.

The Indo-U.S. Rapprochement

During 1955 and 1956 those Americans who had objected to the alliance with Pakistan when it was established continued to argue that the United States was alienating India. They maintained that a higher priority should be given to ties with India, the key country in South Asia. Since Soviet policy was not proving to be militarily aggressive toward the underdeveloped world, the United States should de-emphasize military pacts and military assistance and give economic aid a higher priority. India's Second Five-Year Plan was regarded as particularly crucial, on the grounds that the real issue for the future of Asia was likely to be the outcome of Indian and Chinese efforts to develop their economies and societies by different methods. While no one ever quite said that every peasant in Asia was watching the contest between India and China with bated breath, or was making his judgments about the future only after comparing the Indian and Chinese rates of economic growth, some claims came close to this.

These ideas were not new. Secretary Dulles, hardly the hero of those urging an "economics first" strategy, had mentioned after returning from his first official visit to India in 1953 that

> There is occurring between these two countries [India and Communist China] a competition as to whether ways of freedom or police-state methods can achieve better social progress. This competition affects directly 800 million people in these two countries. In the long run, the outcome will affect all of humanity, including ourselves. Our interest fully justifies continuing, on a modest scale, some technical assistance and external resources to permit India to go on with its Five-Year Plan.[16]

What was new, however, was that the administration was changing its policy somewhat. Testifying before the Senate Foreign Relations Committee on March 24, 1958, Dulles acknowledged that too much attention had been given to military considerations, and said an adjustment in priorities had already been made.[17] However, the administration was not making any dramatic shift from allies to neutrals or from military to economic aid; it had merely concluded that a shift in emphasis was desirable.

Thus the United States and India sought to improve their relations. India's needs for foreign aid during the Second Plan were even larger than originally estimated. Foreign exchange reserves fell from $1.87 billion at the end of 1955 to $942 million at the end of 1957, as imports surged far above planned levels. Some Indian merchants were acquiring an industrialist orientation, and private investment was growing rapidly. Progress was being made, but it also meant that the demand for imported industrial goods and raw material was rising much more rapidly than anticipated. Moreover, because of a poor monsoon, India's food-grain production declined for the first time since 1950–51. Obviously, the United States could help.

Many factors made an Indo-U.S. rapprochement desirable and politically feasible. Not only did their views of each other change during these years, but each could claim that the change had occurred principally in the policies of the other. U.S. Ambassador Ellsworth Bunker played a major role in this by his ability to present American policy in a manner Indian leaders could appreciate and to explain Indian actions skillfully to Washington. His efforts reduced the distrust between the two governments, leading them to understand and emphasize their common interests rather than their differences.

The two countries still differed on some issues. India thought that the United States was not going far enough toward seeking better relations with the Soviet Union, and Nehru was strongly critical of U.S. nuclear testing. India hardly could approve of the promulgation of the Eisenhower Doctrine early in 1957 or of American opposition to Nasser's brand of Arab nationalism, nor could it condone the landing of U.S. troops in Lebanon in 1958 or U.S. support of Nationalist China's efforts to hold the offshore islands that year. But while it could not approve of these American actions, it could and did keep relatively silent about them.

When India sought special U.S. economic assistance in 1957, the administration regarded it as economically desirable and politically feasible to provide the aid. A loan of $225 million was extended, the first of many to follow. Nehru had always been dubious about too much reliance on foreign aid lest the leaders of recipient countries become more responsive to the donors than to their own people. Yet India was now forced to take the risk if its development program was to be carried out.

The damping down of antagonisms and the growing understanding and support of India's development effort on the part of the United States were disquieting and worrisome to Pakistan. There was little it could do, however much it objected. Washington assured Karachi that no major change in policy was occurring or planned, and that Pakistan would continue to be regarded and treated as a close friend. U.S. military and economic aid continued to pour into the country, and key personnel in the military and civil services were still firmly committed to the alliance as offering the best hope for Pakistan. Opposition politicians sometime attacked its Western ties and U.S. aid to neutrals. At the time of the Suez invasion there were severe strains on Pakistan's continued membership in the Commonwealth and Britain's membership in the Baghdad Pact and SEATO. However, Prime Minister Suhrawardy turned to advantage against domestic neutralists Nasser's refusal of Pakistani assistance, and in early 1957 he asked for and received a vote of support from the National Assembly for Pakistan's policy of alignment with the West. Finally, U.S. backing of Pakistan on the Kashmir issue in the United Nations in 1957 won widespread approval among Pakistanis. They were further reassured when the United States negotiated and signed a new bilateral security agreement with Pakistan after the 1958 Iraqi revolution brought to power a group of nationalists who took Iraq out of the Baghdad Pact.

* * *

At the end of the first ten years of independence India and Pakistan had achieved a measure of stability in their relations with each other and with the major powers. Indo-Pakistani relations were set in a mold of inactive hostility. Kashmir seemed firmly under Indian control, and the United Nations Security Council action in 1957, while pleasing to Pakistan and a source of embarrassment to India, did not change anything. U.S.-Pakistan relations appeared to be going reasonably smoothly. Pakistan's military forces were acquiring the arms they needed, if not all they wanted, and it felt a certain sense of security despite the expanding Soviet role in India and Afghanistan. The U.S. military relationship with Pakistan was not proving as harmful to relations with India as its opponents had feared, and the necessity and purpose of the continued arming of Pakistan in view of the less threatening Soviet stance was not really questioned. Indo-Soviet relations had cooled somewhat as a result of Soviet actions in Hungary, Soviet annoyance over Indian attempts to further liberalization within the Communist bloc by urging upon Moscow a generous policy toward Tito, and better Indian relations with the United States. Furthermore, in 1958 Nehru wrote an article condemning dogmatic ideologies in general and communism in particular.[18] Its purpose apparently was to justify India's moderate course and modest progress to those Indians who were dazzled by the economic progress of the U.S.S.R. and Communist China. (The CPI had increased its vote from 5 to 10 per cent of the total in the 1957 general elections, and had won control of the state of Kerala.) But Moscow, suspicious that India was moving to the right politically and economically, denounced Nehru's critique, and he dropped the subject.[19]

Thus the polarization that at one point appeared to be a distinct possibility, with Pakistan, the United States, and (to a lesser degree) Britain lined up against India, the U.S.S.R. and Communist China, never came about. Among various reasons for this, the most important was that neither India, the United States, nor the Soviet Union pushed things beyond a certain point. While India wanted expanded relations with Moscow, it had no intention of becoming a partner of the Soviets. Nor did the United States carry the alliance with Pakistan to its logical—or illogical—conclusion. It supported Pakistan, but only to a point. In particular, it never attempted to place really heavy pressure on India to compromise on Kashmir. Washington had no means of exerting such pressure before the Indian dependence on American aid increased in the late 1950s and early 1960s, and then Washington thought that its interest in India's economic development was too important to take serious (and unpromising) risks by withholding aid pending a Kashmir settlement. Finally, as the decade of the 1950s wore on, the U.S.S.R. began to realize that while it was easy to gain an important presence in an area by dispensing aid, there were limits to the influence that could be acquired, at least in the short run, and that there would be setbacks as well as advances. This awareness, combined with the sheer size and magnitude of India's problems and aid requirements, kept the U.S.S.R. from pushing too hard to upset the pattern of relationships that had evolved. Yet this measure of stability was not to last for long, for subsequent events in the Himalayas disrupted these patterns.

7

China and India: The Spurious Friendship

The task of understanding the policy of any nation, difficult enough in ordinary circumstances, is compounded when its government is controlled by men whose ideological outlook as well as conception of their country's national interests define their foreign policy. Or perhaps it would be more accurate to say that their ideological commitments shape their concept of national interest. Doak Barnett outlined the problem when he wrote:

> It is necessary, in evaluating Peking's aims and strategy, to attempt to differentiate between those aims which it regards as vital Chinese national interests and those which constitute its long-term revolutionary objectives. This attempt must be approached with caution, for aims of differing origins often tend to merge.[1]

Other difficulties arise from the differing backgrounds and approaches of those analyzing the actions of Communist China—whether the Old China hands, the theorists of power, or the specialists in Communist doctrine.[2]

While such *caveats* are necessary, they do not make it impossible to understand Chinese policy, for China, like other nations, has had to operate within the constraints of its domestic situation and of the international system. And, perhaps more so than is the case in other nations, the outlook of China's leaders has been formed by their country's long and unique historical experience.

The Communists gained control of a China that had experienced a century of weakness, disruption, and humiliation at the hands first of the intruding Western powers and then of the Japanese. The bitterness and humiliation suffered by the Chinese were made all the more acute because of their enduring ethnocentrism, cultural pride, and sense of superiority. Although China was never reduced to the status of a colony it was unable to prevent the Western powers from detaching many of its tributary states and carving out spheres of influence inside China itself. China thus went from dominance to inferiority without ever experiencing life in an international society composed of independent states of equal status or power. For a short ten years or so under the Kuomintang regime, China had made progress toward unification and modernization and was gaining international respect, but the outbreak of war with Japan in 1937 halted and then reversed the progress.

Against this background, the basic desires of almost all politically aware Chinese were national unification, economic development, and social progress at home, and power and status for China abroad. The inability of the Chinese Nationalists to achieve these goals during and after the Second World War weakened first their appeal, and then undermined their cohesion and strength. The Communists' capitalization on these weaknesses, combined with their remarkable organizational talents, enabled them to move against the Nationalists with steadily mounting effectiveness. Within five years after the Japanese surrender the Communists were in control of China. Once in power, they set about to realize these aims as quickly as possible. As with practically all new governments, their major tasks were internal. Viewed against the disorganization, periodic famine, inflation and corruption that had plagued China in the preceding decades, the record of the Communists in the years just after their ascendancy to power was most impressive.

Although the concerns of the new regime were primarily internal, they were by no means exclusively so. In the first place, some that Peking regarded as mainly domestic had international implications. National unification meant gaining control of Taiwan and Tibet, which were matters of interest to the United States, Japan, and India. The Communists' determination to eliminate Western influence and nationalize Western investments in China were other examples with international implications. In any case, a strong China would play a key role in Asian affairs; and because of Marxist ideology and their experience in winning power, the new leaders were certain that the new China had a revolutionary message for all of Asia.

As Communist forces gained the upper hand in the struggle with the Nationalists in 1947 and 1948, the leaders concluded that Asia was on the verge of a revolutionary upheaval. They added their voices to those in the world Communist movement arguing for a militantly revolutionary policy, and their success provided additional support for that course. Mao himself in mid-1949 said that the world was divided into only two camps; no third road existed.[3] Peking demonstrated open contempt and hostility toward most Asian leaders, although Nehru was sometimes portrayed as more progressive than other Indian leaders. But India was not regarded as truly independent; Mao, in reply to a greeting from the Communist Party of India, cabled on October 19, 1949:

> I firmly believe that relying on the brave Communist Party of India and the unity and struggle of all Indian patriots, India certainly will not remain long under the yoke of imperialism and its collaborators. Like free China, a free India will one day emerge in the Socialist and People's Democratic family.[4]

All this was in line with Soviet thinking and policy at the time, and probably stemmed from a similar appraisal of the world scene rather than from any compulsion to follow the Soviet lead blindly. Indeed, during this period the U.S.S.R. accepted Mao's strategy as basically correct for most Asian Communists under prevailing conditions.[5] Though there is little indication that the Chinese tried to control Asian Communist parties, they naturally promoted their version of Marxism as the appropriate strategy. Chinese leaders may, for example, have regarded the Congress party as similar to the Kuomintang, destined to be swept aside shortly; their statements reveal quite clearly their ignorance of the difference in conditions in China and elsewhere in Asia. At the time they could not render much help to the Asian parties beyond some aid provided to the Vietnamese Communists struggling against the French.

Tibet: Peking Asserts Its Control

Despite Chinese insults and hostility, Prime Minister Nehru and most Indian leaders sought friendly relations with the Communist regime, having promptly recognized it when it assumed power at the end of 1949. Nonetheless, there was uncertainty as to what kind of relationship could be established. K. M. Panikkar, the Indian ambassador to China and one of the few besides Nehru who were influential in the development of Indian foreign policy, stated his view of the situation in mid-1950 in these terms:

> When I came to Peking I had imagined my mission to be nothing more than that of witnessing the development of a revolution and of working for a better understanding between China and India. I knew, like everyone else, that with a communist China cordial and intimate relations were out of the question, but I was fairly optimistic about working out an area of cooperation by eliminating causes of misunderstanding, rivalry, etc. The only area where our interests overlapped was in Tibet, and knowing the importance that every Chinese government, including the Kuomintang, had attached to exclusive Chinese authority over that area I had, even before I started for Peking, come to the conclusion that the British policy (which we were supposed to have inherited) of looking upon Tibet as an area in which we had special political interests could not be maintained. The Prime Minister had also in general agreed with this view. So there was nothing which I could then foresee that would make my mission unduly difficult, exciting, or troublesome.[6]

The events of 1950, however, were to demonstrate that the problem was far more difficult and complex, as Panikkar soon recognized. Peking had announced in January 1950 that Tibet would be "liberated" by the People's Liberation Army. The Tibetan government had been practically independent during the latter years of the Chinese Nationalist reign. Having no desire to be ruled from Peking, the authorities at Lhasa claimed that Tibet was an independent nation and sought international support for their position. A Tibetan mission went to India in April 1950 in the hope of arranging talks with the Chinese Communists in neutral territory. But the Chinese government insisted that talks be held in Peking, and the Indian government apparently urged the Tibetans to agree.

The outbreak of the Korean War, which occurred while these maneuvers were taking place, brought a marked shift in Chinese policy. Although the idea of revolutionary struggle throughout Asia was not abandoned, concern for China's security and direct national interests became overriding. Since China had almost no naval forces, it could not militarily challenge the U.S. announcement that the Seventh Fleet would neutralize the Taiwan Strait. But when U.N. troops approached the Yalu River, the border between Manchuria and North Korea, Peking entered the war late in 1950. In October of that year it had sent military forces into Tibet, which, after some initial clashes, were able to advance without much fighting.

The decision to shift from political maneuvering to military operations to gain control of Tibet probably reflected Chinese suspicion of Western and perhaps Indian intentions in Tibet. It provoked anxiety and indignation in India. In a parliamentary debate Nehru expressed shock at the resort to force, terming it unnecessary since Tibet posed no threat to China. Some Indian political leaders argued that China's move into Tibet, together with its propaganda attacks, signified that India's policy of seeking friendship with China was ineffectual and that a firm line should be taken. Nehru tried to reassure them and maintained that to continue to work for friendly relations was desirable in view of their importance to all of Asia. While acknowledging Chinese suzerainty over Tibet, he stressed his conviction that ultimately the fate of Tibet should be determined by its people.

There was a sharp exchange of diplomatic notes between New Delhi and Peking. India expressed regret that China had resorted to force despite previous assurances that peaceful means would be used, and "amazement" at Peking's charges that its policy was the result of sinister foreign influences. New Delhi assured Peking that no foreign nation determined Indian policy, which aimed only at peacefully "adjusting legitimate Tibetan claims to autonomy within the framework of Chinese suzerainty." China's replies were strong and unyielding: Tibet was a domestic problem of China, which exercised "sovereign rights," and no outside interference would be tolerated.

A Tibetan attempt to secure United Nations consideration of the issue failed because India, Britain, and Russia were opposed, holding that there had been no further clashes since the initial Chinese moves, and that in any case the legal position of Tibet was not clear. The issue gradually receded from public attention. On May 23, 1951, Peking announced that an agreement had been signed which provided that the Chinese government would control Tibet's external affairs but would respect its autonomy.

Why did Nehru acquiesce in the Chinese take-over of Tibet and attempt to put the best face possible on it? Perhaps the most important reason was India's inability to do much about the matter. India, still uncertain whether there would be new fighting with Pakistan, lacked the military power to contest China's moves. By itself, India could have done little more than provide aid to Tibetans. Probably the only way India could have effectively challenged China over Tibet would have been by doing just what the Chinese had charged Nehru with—reaching a military understanding with the United States and the United Kingdom designed to create an independent Tibet.[7] Such a course would have posed major obstacles as far as Nehru was concerned—if he ever even considered it. It would have meant India's military alignment with the West against the Communists under circumstances in which, Nehru believed, India could not be truly independent. India's struggle for independence could not be cast aside so easily. Alignment would add to the dangers of a larger war, and India's hopes for peace and development would fade. Having recognized China's suzerainty, Nehru could only protest against its methods and urge Peking to respect Tibet's autonomy. What Nehru really wanted was that Tibet remain a *de facto* buffer zone with few if any Chinese troops. Any Indian attempt to challenge China's position, he probably concluded, would only cause Peking to increase its forces in the area.

Nehru had already demonstrated his concern over the security of India's northern frontier by strengthening India's position in the Himalayan border states. In June 1949 Sikkim became a protectorate as Indian troops moved in and New Delhi took charge of the state's foreign relations, defense, and communications. In August an Indo-Bhutanese treaty was signed, replacing the former treaty with British India. India increased the subsidy to the Maharajah, who agreed to be guided by India's advice in foreign relations. In November New Delhi helped the Nepalese monarch and political parties to overthrow the anachronistic Rana regime of hereditary prime ministers, for Nehru was convinced that if there was no reform, communism would appeal to politically conscious Nepalese. Once the Rana regime was ousted, India negotiated a treaty with Nepal which provided for consultation between the two governments if either should face an external threat. From that time on, while admitting Nepal's independence, New Delhi maintained special rights and provided economic and military assistance. Nehru stated publicly that Nepal's northern border was India's strategic frontier.[8]

China Changes Course

Beginning approximately in mid-1951, China began to shift from its emphasis on revolutionary militancy and reliance on armed might. Probably no one of the many reasons for this shift was sufficient in itself to cause the change in policy, but together they led the leadership to decide a new line was appropriate.

The U.S. and U.N. forces, after being driven south of the 38th parallel, had reorganized themselves, withstood new Chinese assaults, and were slowly moving north once again. Communist China had not accomplished all it had hoped for, but at least its minimum aim of keeping U.S. forces away from its Manchurian frontier had been achieved. Thus the Chinese apparently agreed with the U.S.S.R. on the desirability of opening truce negotiations in Korea in the summer of 1951.

The Chinese leaders also recognized by this time that the prospects for radical revolution in Asia—except for Indochina—were not bright. The Asian nationalist leaders had managed to crush or at least isolate the insurgents and to stabilize conditions within their countries. Moreover, their criticisms of America's policy in the Far East demonstrated to the Chinese that these Indian, Burmese, and Indonesian nationalist leaders were not really the "running dogs" of Western imperialism. A policy of cultivating them through political action and normal government-to-government relations seemed worth trying, particularly in view of Nehru's helpful stance during the Korean War.

Domestic considerations probably contributed to the shift. The economy was being strained by the war, and the Chinese were eager to begin their First Five-Year Plan in 1953. The gains from the Korean War—a heightened sense of pride and national feeling, the consolidation of Communist rule, and a major inflow of Soviet arms —had been achieved; little more seemed likely to be gained from militancy.

From mid-1951 until early 1955 the Chinese line, like the Soviet line, changed. In mid-1953 Peking yielded on the issue of the disposition of prisoners who did not want to be repatriated, thereby clearing the way for a Korean armistice. The Indochina crisis remained a danger spot. The French were obviously becoming warweary, and the Vietnamese Communists were growing stronger. If it were only a matter between them, the prospects for the Communists would be bright. But there was the possibility that the United

States would become militarily involved. The Korean War had greatly increased the U.S. military presence in the Far East, and a prolongation of the Indochinese war might result in a further expansion of U.S. military power. Therefore the Chinese Communists were agreeable to exploring the possibilities of a negotiated settlement, as proposed by the Foreign Ministers of the Big Four when they decided in early 1954 to convene a special conference on Indochina and Korea. At the Geneva Conference Chou En-lai sensed China's opportunity to advance its interests by political means if it followed a more moderate line of action, and apparently he urged the Vietnamese Communists to agree to a compromise settlement.

Meanwhile, India and China had settled down to an uneasy coexistence over Tibet. Although Panikkar believed that there were no outstanding issues between India and China at the time of his departure from Peking in mid-1953, it was not until December of 1953 that the two countries began formal negotiations over Tibet. A treaty was signed on April 24, 1954, shortly after the U.S. decision to extend military aid to Pakistan was announced. India acknowledged that Tibet was part of China, thus formally recognizing Chinese sovereignty; it gave up the special position and facilities it had there, but received specific trading rights. Nehru told Parliament that it had been the multitude of minor issues rather than India's willingness to recognize the existing situation in Tibet (indicated two or three years earlier) which had taken so long. Although there were some attacks on the treaty for recognizing Chinese sovereignty, and a few regrets that it did not specify the McMahon line as India's northern border, Indian opinion was generally favorable to the agreement.[9] Indeed, within a short time both in India and abroad, major interest was focused less on the provisions of the treaty relating to Tibet than on the preamble, which contained the famous five principles of peaceful coexistence—the Panch Sheel.

The Panch Sheel Period

The Panch Sheel, or five principles on which the two countries agreed to base their relations, were (1) mutual respect for each other's territorial integrity and sovereignty, (2) mutual nonaggression, (3) mutual noninterference in each other's internal affairs, (4) equality and mutual benefit, and (5) peaceful coexistence. Neither the phrases themselves nor the ideas they expressed were new.

In their essentials they can be variously traced in the U.N. Charter, the September 1949 Common Program of the Chinese People's Political Consultative Conference, Soviet legal concepts of relations between nations, and in long-held and articulated Western concepts of international law. Nehru said the principles had deep roots in the Indian moral tradition, but the connection with ancient Buddhist teachings about personal conduct is vague. Van Eekelen, in his study of this subject concludes that "Panch Sheel is, therefore, better regarded as a catch-word, suggestive of ancient concepts but without any real links with the past other than a spirit which can be found in the heritage of all known religions."[10]

Yet to many Asians Panch Sheel represented something new and valuable in international politics—something that stemmed from their effort to adapt their ancient concepts to modern needs rather than an outgrowth of the Western political tradition. The five principles seemed at times to be regarded as a foreign policy in themselves. Asian leaders were hardly so naïve as to think that once a country proclaimed its belief in and willingness to abide by the principles it would never break them; but some did think that a nation which had accepted Panch Sheel would be most hesitant to act in a manner incompatible with them for fear of antagonizing other nations. Lacking the traditional elements of national power, they tried, understandably, to shift the focus of international politics to the moral plane where they felt they were on stronger ground. But in arguing their concepts they came to see moral considerations as having a greater impact than later events proved to be warranted.

The importance attached to the five principles was indicated by their reiteration in innumerable communiqués and statements of Asian and African countries on the exchange of official visits among themselves or with Communist countries during the next few years. Occasionally they were modified, as in the communiqué issued during Nehru's visit to the U.S.S.R. in 1955, which proclaimed "noninterference in each other's internal affairs for any reason of economic, political or ideological character."

The attitude of Western leaders toward the five principles was ambiguous. They were hesitant to voice approval of a set of principles that fitted neatly into the Communist ideological framework and that had assumed prominence as a result of a treaty with Communist China. Such principles could easily be broken, and they were convinced the Communist nations would do so if it suited their purposes. The Communist campaign of peaceful coexistence, they felt, was designed to lull the free world into a sense of complacency while the Communists strengthened themselves and improved their position. Nevertheless, recognizing the importance attached to Panch Sheel by many Asians, they stressed the similarity between the principles and Western ideas.[11]

The Bandung Conference, held in April 1955, represented the dramatic highpoint not only in the general Asian resurgence but also in good relations between the Asian neutrals and the Communists. A conference of Asian and African countries had first been proposed by Indonesia at a meeting of the Prime Ministers of India, Pakistan, Burma, Ceylon and Indonesia in April 1954, just before the conclusion of the Geneva Conference. Although initially skeptical, India and Pakistan agreed to have Indonesia explore the idea. Indonesian persuasiveness and the lack of any good reason to oppose the conference won the support of other states, especially once it became clear that the formation of a new bloc was not envisioned. The trend of events in 1954, bringing closer relations with the Communist states and sharper frictions with the West, inclined the more cautious Asian neutrals to accept the idea of such a meeting.

The official purposes of the conference were the unexceptional ones of promoting good will and cooperation among Asian and African nations, discussing their social, economic and cultural problems and the contribution they could make to world peace. There were other important if unspoken purposes, such as getting to know other leaders and nations, giving Asia a more active role in world affairs, and taking advantage of China's professed peaceful intentions to bind Peking to a peaceful policy.

Although the U.S.S.R., classified as a European state, was not invited to join the twenty-nine participating Asian and African nations, Moscow supported the conference in the hope it would take on an anti-Western tone. While not opposing the affair, the United States was clearly unenthusiastic about it, fearing it would follow the course hoped for by Moscow. Some pro-Western Asian and African countries were initially dubious about attending, but it soon became apparent that participation offered a chance of keeping it from assuming an anti-Western character.

As it turned out, neither the hopes of Moscow nor the fears of Washington were justified, although many harsh things were said about the United States.[12] Krishna Menon made his customary acid comments about the United States and its Asian allies, and Nehru seemed to be in general agreement with the Soviet position on most important issues. He contended that the Eastern European governments were independent of the U.S.S.R. and he was critical of the United States, arguing that the countries represented at the conference should be forbidden to enter alliances with the United States. But the conference was less than a clear success from India's viewpoint. Nehru's remarks antagonized several countries, and he was overshadowed by Chou En-lai, who expressed affability toward all nations, even the United States. His conciliatory statement on Taiwan, coming when there was widespread fear that Peking would soon renew the bombardment of the offshore islands held by the Nationalist regime, impressed most delegates. Moreover, many of the leaders of pro-Western nations openly and vigorously denounced Soviet colonialism. The split between neutralist and pro-Western nations made it necessary to adopt compromise resolutions on the two key issues, colonialism and the question of collective self-defense. No reference was made to Soviet colonialism or even to the pointed phrase, "the new colonialism." Instead, colonialism in all its manifestations was condemned. It was also impossible to reach agreement on the five principles, and eventually a list of ten was accepted, including the right of collective self-defense.

The general Indian reaction to the Bandung Conference was one of pride and hope, tempered in a few cases with skepticism. There was pride that Asian countries had skillfully organized and conducted a conference of such magnitude before a watching world, which seemed to spell the coming to full stature of countries only recently unheeded by the West. There was hope that the ability Asian and African countries had shown in working together was a harbinger of future cooperation, and that Chinese reasonableness and a peaceful line would continue. The skepticism, and it was not widespread, concerned these same points; some Indians doubted that cooperation on specific actions to reach agreed goals was likely, or that China could be counted on to demonstrate its devotion to peaceful coexistence. Even the skeptics, however, shared the pride in the accomplishments of the conference.[13]

These were the years when Asian statesmen were visiting each other frequently and constantly reaffirming their desires for peace and cooperation. Chou En-lai visited India four times between June 1954 and January 1957, and received a warm welcome on each visit, and Nehru visited China in October 1954. The outward signs indicated a relationship of friendship and cooperation, and the slogan "*Hindi Chini bhai bhai*" (Indians and Chinese are brothers) was chanted by Indians, who seemed convinced that China had only good will and peaceful intentions toward India.

To the West, and especially to the United States, the conferences, exchanges of visits, and friendly communiqués between neutral nations and China were distasteful and possibly dangerous. Such activities made it more difficult to isolate Peking and to build and maintain an Asian security system. Moreover, the words and actions of India and its friends seemed to indicate a naïveté about the true nature of the Chinese Communist regime if not an outright pro-Communist attitude. What the United States, and to a lesser degree the Western European countries, wanted was that Asian countries accept the view of Communist China as expansive and aggressive and cooperate in containing China and developing countervailing power to maintain security and peace. In Washington's view, a successful policy of this type offered the best hope of inducing China to accommodate itself to the existing structure of international life in Asia.[14]

That course appealed to a few Asian countries and to some citizens of all Asian countries, but to most it offered few advantages and many dangers. Asian statesmen were not unaware of past Chinese tendencies toward expansionism, and few thought that communism would attenuate rather than stimulate them. Yet if they were publicly to admit such apprehensions, except in the most guarded fashion, they would have had to deal explicitly with the question posed by some Asians and by the West: Why not align themselves with the West and rely on Western protection?

Most Asian nations felt that this was not a practical or desirable policy. They were keenly aware of their own lack of power and, while desirous of Asian cooperation in some fields, did not think they commanded sufficient power to amount to much even when combined.[15] Any countervailing power would be American, with the Asian countries in a subsidiary role. Relying on the West for defense, with the implied acceptance of the general thrust of Western foreign policy, would be giving up control of precisely those matters they regarded as the hallmarks of independence.[16] To nations still dependent on the West for trade, technology, arms, and (by the mid-1950s) for economic aid, alignment would seem to be a decisive step back toward dependency and colonialism. Alliance with the West would also create severe domestic political strains in view of the still strong though declining anticolonial attitudes of key elements in the population. Furthermore, alignment could, by making China feel encircled and in danger of attack, provoke the military action it was designed to prevent. Finally, it would divert the attention and energies of the government and people from nation-building and development.

India was the great exponent of the views set forth above, just as it was the most eloquent champion of the five principles. As long as nothing happened on the international scene that clearly demonstrated the inherent limitations of Panch Sheel, it was politically and psychologically important in Asian affairs. As long as Chinese foreign policy followed a moderate line and India was at odds with the West, and as long as Tibet was quiet, Nehru's policy of friendship for China appeared to be successful. Whether such conditions would prevail in the future was another matter, and one that soon took an ominous turn.

From Friendship to Animosity

Chinese policy, both at home and abroad, shifted markedly in the direction of a harder and more militant line during 1957 and 1958.[17] Mao and his colleagues were surprised and alarmed by the upheavals in Eastern Europe in 1956, which revealed the fierce animosities existing between the rulers and the ruled. To keep his regime in touch with popular attitudes and to prevent similar troubles, Mao organized the "Hundred Flowers Campaign" for the more open discussion of public issues. The eruption of bitter criticism by party members as well as others shocked the regime, and it moved quickly to suppress the dissent. In reappraising their position, the leaders concluded that the advantages to be gained from soft or moderate policies were quite limited in both domestic and foreign affairs. They became more responsive to those within their ranks urging a harder or more radical line.

The socialist camp, the Chinese reasoned, had a great opportunity following the Soviet Union's dramatic success with Sputnik in October 1957, which led Mao to proclaim that "the East wind has prevailed over the West wind." When Khrushchev did not press his advantage harder in dealings with the West, Peking reacted with frustrated scorn. The limited Soviet support received during the 1958

Taiwan Straits crisis also angered Peking. Friction over this issue as well as Khrushchev's coexistence policies, Soviet reluctance to provide the nuclear assistance desired by Peking, and Soviet disapproval of Chinese policies and ideological claims during the "Great Leap Forward" of 1958 were driving the two Communist giants apart—of which the world knew nothing at the time.

The changing Chinese attitude created some apprehension in India, but as there was much ambiguity in Chinese policies, New Delhi could do little except remain silent and hope for the best. For a while Peking seemed to continue its friendly line toward the Afro-Asian neutrals. In his report to the People's National Congress in February 1958, Chou En-lai spoke favorably of Nehru and India. Neutralist opposition to the Eisenhower Doctrine and to U.S. support for Nationalist China's efforts to retain the offshore islands found favor with Peking. But the rash of military coups in Africa and Asia during 1958 probably led the Chinese leaders to discern a trend toward the right and China's declining prospects in these areas. India's economic dependence on the West was growing, which suggested to Marxists that India was moving into the Western camp.

Certain Chinese actions had a more direct bearing on matters of interest to India. China established diplomatic relations with Nepal in 1956 and gave 10 million rupees in cash as aid. India could not really object, in view of Nepal's independence, but was uneasy. Nehru's policy of recognizing Chinese supremacy in Tibet was based upon an implicit understanding, or at least a hope, that China would acknowledge the territory on the southern slopes of the Himalayas as being within the Indian sphere of interest. But the problem with such arrangements is their vagueness. Did they mean China should have no relations with Nepal, or only that it should not seriously contest Indian influence there?[18]

Another source of concern was the continued issuance of maps that showed areas New Delhi regarded as Indian territory as part of China. These included the Northeast Frontier Agency (NEFA), the Indian-claimed part of the Aksai Chin area in the Ladakh section of Kashmir, and certain other smaller areas. The Chinese claims amounted to about 50,000 square miles. New Delhi raised the matter of these maps with Peking several times, and each time the Chinese answered that these were only copies of old Chinese Nationalist maps and that the Chinese People's Republic would issue its own maps when it was able to. India was uneasy, but again could do little.[19]

Indian concern increased sharply in 1958, when an Indian patrol sent into the Aksai Chin discovered that the rumors about a Chinese road across this area were correct. New Delhi protested in a note on October 18, asserting that the territory crossed by the road had been part of the Ladakh region of India for centuries. The note also mentioned that an Indian patrol in the area had been missing for several weeks and inquired whether the Chinese government knew of its whereabouts.[20] Peking replied on November 3, stating that the territory across which the road had been constructed was Chinese, acknowledging that the Indian patrol had been detained when discovered there but would shortly be returned, and complaining of Indian aircraft flying over Chinese territory on reconnaissance missions since September.[21]

Prime Minister Nehru, deciding higher-level consideration was required, wrote a long letter to Chou En-lai on December 14, 1958, stating that India had always made its position plain on the location of its boundaries. He reminded Chou how they had discussed the subject personally in 1954 and 1956, when Chou had said that while China had not had time to survey the boundaries and disliked the phrase "McMahon Line," it thought it should recognize the line since it was an accomplished fact and since India and China had friendly relations. Nehru then went on to complain that recent Chinese maps showing parts of India and Bhutan as Chinese territory nine years after the establishment of the People's Republic of China was hard to understand or explain to the Indian public.[22]

Chou's reply to Nehru on January 23, 1959, must have confirmed his worst fears. Chou contested the Indian view that the boundary between the two countries was clear and settled, asserting that it had never been delimited, that no treaty between the two governments dealing explicitly with this matter had ever been signed, and that a dispute over its location did in fact exist. While stressing that the McMahon Line, as a product of British imperialism, could not be considered legal, he acknowledged that it could not be completely disregarded when the time came to settle the issue. Finally, he appealed for maintenance of the *status quo* lest border patrols clash and cause trouble that neither party wanted.[23]

Tibet Revolts

The focus of Sino-Indian relations was soon diverted from the developing border dispute by events within Tibet. The outcome was new Sino-Indian suspicion, which exacerbated the border dispute.

The agreement signed with Tibetan authorities in May 1951 stipulated that Peking would, in return for conducting Tibet's foreign relations, respect its autonomy and political system. During most of the 1950s the Chinese apparently pursued a dual course. Peking refrained from imposing Communist reforms upon Tibet but at the same time tried to manipulate the Tibetan political system by strengthening the authority of the Panchen Lama, who was then inclined to cooperate with the Chinese, at the expense of the Dalai Lama.[24]

The Dalai Lama later claimed that while in India in 1956 he was disinclined to return to Tibet because of the Chinese pressures and interference, but that Nehru had advised him to return after Chou En-lai (also visiting India) had given Nehru assurances that China would respect Tibetan autonomy and not impose communism there.[25] Nehru, however, strongly denied that he was involved in such an episode. In 1956 he would have been reluctant to have had the Dalai Lama ask to remain in India in view of the problems this would have created in Sino-Indian relations at a time when they were still friendly.

Apparently, Nehru wanted to make a return visit to the Dalai Lama at Lhasa in 1958 but was prohibited from doing so by Peking. Tensions were increasing inside Tibet, especially in the Khampa region in eastern Tibet. Peking sent a strong note to New Delhi on July 10, 1958, charging that the U.S. and Chinese Nationalist agents were using the Indian border town of Kalimpong as a base for carrying out subversive activities in Tibet. The note recalled that China had previously raised this matter with India but that no action had been taken against activities which "cannot but enrage the Chinese government" since they were "a direct threat to China's territorial integrity and sovereignty."[26] India's reply, while conciliatory in tone, stated that the Chinese charge was based upon "a complete misunderstanding of facts" and assured Peking that no activities hostile to China would be permitted on Indian soil.[27]

By early 1959 the unrest in Tibet had spread beyond the Khampa region, and in March fighting broke out in Lhasa. Official Indian statements had depreciated the seriousness of the unrest, but Nehru soon acknowledged that the fighting in Lhasa added a new dimension to the situation. It had indeed, for the Tibetan revolt was a humiliating setback for Peking at a time when the leaders were riding the crest of the Great Leap Forward. Suppression of the Tibetans altered the attitude of many Asians toward China, and nowhere was the change as great as in India. Nehru, in an attempt to hold rising anti-Chinese feelings in check, told Parliament that while India's tradition of cultural ties with Tibet made whatever happened there of interest, the government could not interfere in what was essentially an internal Chinese affair. But indignation increased when the Chinese Embassy in New Delhi asserted that the revolt was masterminded from Kalimpong, and a statement by the Communist Party of India congratulating Peking for leading the Tibetan people "from medieval darkness to prosperity and equality" further inflamed many Indians.[28]

Nehru's difficulties in preventing a major deterioration in Sino-Indian relations were compounded when the Dalai Lama and thousands of Tibetans fled across the border seeking political asylum. The Indian government felt it had no choice but to admit them, although, when informing China of its decision, it stressed that it was disarming the Tibetans before permitting them to cross the border and it would not permit the Dalai Lama to carry on political activities in India. Nehru persisted in trying to limit the damage to Sino-Indian relations and proclaimed his continued faith in Panch Sheel, saying that "If we believe in Panch Sheel, we follow it, even if no country in the wide world follows it."

The Tibetan revolt humiliated the Chinese, who seemed convinced that India was guilty of great duplicity. Speakers at the Second National People's Congress in Peking in April 1959 claimed that the Dalai Lama had gone to India under duress, and the Chinese press and radio lashed out at India.[29] Nehru's freedom of maneuver was now being reduced by Chinese charges as well as Indian popular feeling. Peking was not impressed by his measures to hold anti-Chinese feeling in check. On May 16 the Chinese ambassador made a harsh statement to the Indian Foreign Secretary, accusing Indian political leaders and newspapers of slandering China and supporting the Tibetan rebels. Although the statement spoke of the continued desire for friendship with India and added that "China will not be so foolish as to antagonize the United States in the East and again to antagonize India in the West," it concluded on the ominous note that "you too cannot have two fronts."[30] Peking clearly was concerned that those elements in India (the "big bourgeoisie") opposed to Chinese Control of Tibet were gaining ascendancy in New Delhi.

The Tibetan revolt led China to end the measure of Tibetan autonomy it had permitted. While Nehru had recognized that India could not maintain Tibet as a buffer state in any legal sense, his willingness to accept Chinese control of it was based on the implicit assumption that Peking would limit its military presence there. Suppression of the revolt had required a large increase in Chinese troops. Fearing that the refugees who fled to India might acquire arms and return to Tibet, China moved military forces to the border and attempted to close it.

The Border Dispute Becomes Public

India had always held that its borders were clearly established. Since the boundary was legally defined at independence, technically there was no border dispute, and the issue of its basic (as distinct from its precise) location was not open to negotiation. But this policy was now to be tested, for the movement of the troops of both countries into areas where they had overlapping claims led to clashes between border patrols in the summer of 1959 in both Ladakh and NEFA. At this point Nehru apparently concluded that it was no longer possible or desirable to hush up the troubles. Given the rising Indian suspicion of and animosity toward China, Nehru probably felt he would be in a difficult position if the existence of a serious border dispute and a series of armed clashes were revealed by the Chinese or discovered by opposition elements in India. As a second consideration, India's policy of friendship and quiet diplomacy did not seem to be influencing Peking.

When the prime minister rose in Parliament on August 28, 1959, to acknowledge publicly the existence of the border dispute, he not only brought to a close the short-lived Panch Sheel era but also raised questions for all the major nations as to the extent and implications of the Sino-Indian dispute. Would India try (and be able) to maintain its policy of nonalignment? What stance would Moscow take in a quarrel between its Chinese ally and its Indian friend? How would Pakistan and the United States react? What would be the effect on other Afro-Asian countries? Was the shift in Sino-Indian relations the forerunner of a major change in the strategic picture in Asia? Some of these questions were answered fairly soon, but some relationships were affected in ways that are still working themselves out.

The most dramatic effect of Nehru's statement was on Indian opinion, and it was immediate and profound. He revealed that China and India had been involved (secretly) in a dispute about the border since shortly after the signing of the agreement on Tibet in 1954, that Indian patrols had been attacked, that China claimed nearly 50,000 square miles of territory India regarded as its own. He also acknowledged that China had built a road across the disputed Aksai Chin territory in Ladakh. Labelling Chinese actions aggressive and ominous, Nehru announced that the Indian army had been ordered to man and defend the border.

The press reacted with anger and bitterness. Peking's behavior, *The Indian Express* said, demonstrated that "imperialism is not a European monopoly but can extend to an Asian power," and *The Hindustan Times* insisted that India had "no need to buy Chinese good behavior at the cost of our self-respect." Other papers took a similar line, with some castigating the Indian government for not having earlier made public the extent of Sino-Indian differences.

The dispute posed an acute problem for the Communist Party of India (CPI), already in irate disarray over New Delhi's removal of the Communist government of the state of Kerala in July.[31] The CPI had been united in supporting the suppression of the Tibetan revolt and had even echoed Peking's charges that the revolt was organized and controlled from Kalimpong. Both positions had antagonized an aroused Indian public opinion and brought strong attacks on the CPI. But the party's real dilemma began with Nehru's announcement of the border dispute. It was (at least at the time) ideologically impossible for Indian Communists to admit that a Communist state was guilty of aggression; yet it seemed like political suicide not to support their own country's territorial claims with popular feeling running so high. At first the CPI attempted to avoid taking a stand and in September urged negotiations without any preconditions. In November the National Council endorsed the McMahon Line as India's border, but by then the party was far from united on the issue, with the more radical elements refusing to accept this and thus taking a pro-Chinese position.[32]

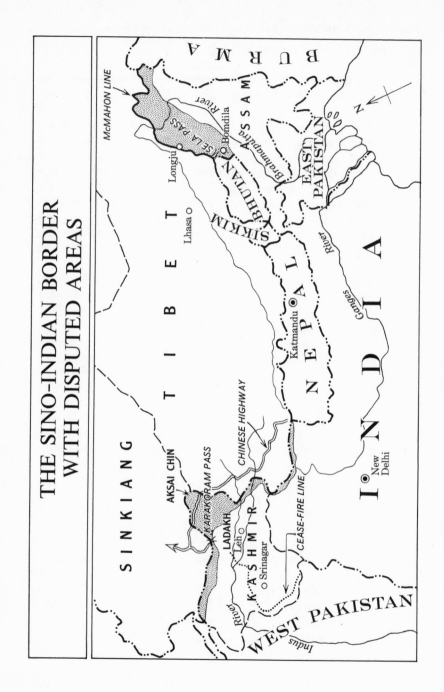

THE SINO-INDIAN BORDER
WITH DISPUTED AREAS

SINKIANG

T I B E T

McMAHON LINE

SE LA PASS

Bomdila

Brahmaputra River

A S S A M

B U R M A

Longju

Lhasa

SIKKIM

BHUTAN

EAST PAKISTAN

AKSAI CHIN

KARAKORAM PASS

CHINESE HIGHWAY

N E P A L

Katmandu

Ganges River

LADAKH

Leh

K A S H M I R

Srinagar

CEASE-FIRE LINE

I N D I A

New Delhi

Indus River

WEST PAKISTAN

It is necessary at this point to describe briefly the areas in dispute. The Sino-Indian frontier is over 2,000 miles long, which can conveniently be divided into three sectors: The eastern sector is the portion of the Himalayas running from Burma to Bhutan, a distance of just over 700 miles. The middle sector runs about 400 miles along the crest of the Himalayas from the western end of Nepal to the point where the Sutlej River flows through the Himalayas and is the boundary between Tibet and the Indian states of Uttar Pradesh and Himachal Pradesh. The western sector runs for over 1,000 miles from the Sutlej to the Karakoram Pass in the north separating Kashmir from Tibet and Sinkiang.

The dispute in the eastern sector involves approximately 38,000 square miles. India claims that the boundary is the McMahon Line, which generally follows the crestline of the Himalayas. China claims that the boundary runs along the foot of the Himalayas. (See map.) The area in dispute, known as the North East Frontier Agency (NEFA), has nearly 400,000 people divided among several tribal groups just beginning to emerge from a rather primitive way of life.

The disputed area in the middle sector is apparently less than 200 square miles and consists of only a few scattered points along the crest of the Himalayas. Although the friction over this sector of the border arose in 1954, this part of the dispute is relatively minor.

The amount of contested territory in the western sector seemed to be about 10,000 square miles in 1959, although Peking has since expanded its claims. The major dispute here involves part of the Aksai Chin (Soda Plains), a desolate and unpopulated area which India claims is the northeast part of the Ladakh region of Kashmir. There are also several areas in dispute along the boundary between the Aksai Chin and the Sutlej river.

The Chinese maintained that the entire boundary had never been delineated in the past (except for the small part that separates Tibet and Sikkim) and that the two countries should through negotiations first agree on the alignment of the boundary and then demarcate it —a process which would, in the best of circumstances, require many years because of the terrain. Their own general boundary claims, they asserted, were supported by Chinese maps, administrative records and practice, commercial and travel accounts, and other evidence. The Indians, on the other hand, argued that the entire length of the boundary had been defined by custom, tradition, and administrative practices which go back beyond the British period to medieval and ancient Indian kingdoms. Moreover, the Indians maintained that their claims in both eastern and western sectors were supported by treaties: in the east by the Simla Convention of 1914, and in the west by the Tibet-Ladakh agreement of 1684, which was affirmed in the Dogra-Ladakh agreement of 1842 and an Anglo-Chinese exchange of notes in 1846–47.

The merits of the claims are considered in Chapter 15. Most Indian scholars have adopted the firm position of their government, while Western scholars are divided in their opinions.

Motivations, Problems, and Strategies

The motivation behind Chinese policy toward India in the late 1950s perplexed many people. India had to decide whether it was basically a border dispute and not much more, or part of a broader challenge. If it was the first, an effort to work out a settlement that met the needs of each country made considerable sense.

Briefly, the argument in favor of the first interpretation runs as follows: The direct routes from western China to Tibet pass through extremely difficult terrain and are sometimes impassable in winter. A less direct but more dependable route is through Sinkiang into Tibet from the northwest. But that route has to pass through the disputed Aksai Chin territory to avoid the rugged terrain to its north. Therefore, possession of the area is of extreme importance to Peking if its position in Tibet is to be secure. Some of Peking's later actions lend credence to this interpretation. Moreover, Chinese leaders may have felt that an exhibition of Chinese power in Tibet and along the frontier would awe India. New Delhi would come to see that it had little choice but to adopt a flexible policy on the border dispute— clearly a serious miscalculation by Peking.

If, on the other hand, the border dispute was part of a broader and more ominous Chinese challenge to India, then New Delhi faced a different and more difficult problem. Perhaps Sino-Indian tensions reflected an inevitable rivalry between the two largest nations of Asia for influence in the continent and beyond, and the border dispute was just a manifestation of their rivalry. If that were the case, the advantages to be gained by a compromise border settlement would be limited and might even be nonexistent, serving only to whet the Chinese appetite. This conclusion would seem to follow whether the border dispute was due to aggressive Chinese expansionism or revolutionary Communist zeal, or a combination of the two. Finally, if Chinese actions were a function of China's internal difficulties or its desire to disrupt Indo-Soviet ties or the developing Soviet-American dialogue (Khrushchev visited the United States in September 1959), then any serious attempt to reach a settlement would have to be postponed until Chinese policy on these matters shifted. In fact, India's words and actions during the next few years revealed its continuing uncertainty about China's motivations.

During the remainder of 1959 and 1960 both prime ministers spoke of the need to prevent border skirmishes, but neither wanted to concede much to prevent them lest he appear weak and subject to pressure. A serious border clash in Ladakh in October 1959, in which nine Indians were killed forty miles inside Indian-claimed territory, further inflamed Indian opinion and led New Delhi to accuse China of acting in a manner "reminiscent of the old imperialist powers."

At this point China shifted tactics if not strategy in an effort to contain the dispute, perhaps at the urging of Khrushchev, who visited Peking in October. On November 7 Chou wrote Nehru suggesting mutual troop withdrawals in Ladakh and NEFA and a meeting between the two prime ministers as soon as possible.[33] In his reply on November 16 Nehru was agreeable to a withdrawal in Ladakh—though on a basis more favorable to India—but was dubious about a meeting before an adequate basis had been established.[34]

Chinese policy on borders was not directed to India alone. A border agreement with Burma was reached on January 28, 1960. The treaty, signed in Peking on October 1, 1960, was based on an implicit acceptance of the validity of the McMahon Line, although with certain modifications. China reached a preliminary agreement with Nepal on March 21, 1960, calling for "scientific delineation and formal demarcation" of their common frontier; a formal treaty, which provided that the boundary would run at the peak of Mt. Everest, was signed on October 5, 1961. But New Delhi believed that Chinese willingness to reach these settlements was designed to isolate India from its neighbors. Furthermore, China built an extensive system of border roads along the Indian frontier, stationed more troops there, and established and stocked supply depots. Peking was determined to negotiate from a position of strength.

Whatever the reasons behind China's actions, Nehru's foreign policy came under sustained and serious attack in India in a way it never had before, even during the brief flare-up over his reaction to the 1956 Hungarian uprising. Henceforth there were continual disputes over foreign policy within the government, and the sometimes open disarray over China policy complicated Nehru's task.

Nehru wanted to avoid a prolonged and costly conflict with Communist China for many reasons, but he was also determined to uphold India's basic claims and remain in the forefront of nationalist sentiment on foreign policy issues—which was one way he had maintained control in the past. If he did not adopt a firm nationalist line, he feared he would be vulnerable to right-wing elements in the Congress party and the opposition, as well as those in the military with a similar outlook. (The military take-overs in Burma, the Sudan, and Pakistan in 1958 clearly worried Nehru.) Since Nehru had always felt that rightists posed the major threat to his policies of socialism and nonalignment he was determined to prevent them from seizing upon the border issue to increase their power.

At the same time, the adoption of an anti-Communist posture and a turn to the West might also strengthen rightist forces. A firm policy required increased military strength, which might contribute to an upsurge of prestige and influence for the military—something Nehru had worked to hold in check ever since independence. In addition, any long-term ability to stand up to China would depend heavily on India's economic progress, which a major defense buildup would handicap. There seemed to be no end to the dilemmas involved.

In his attempt to cope with the many problems, Nehru announced that India would build up its military forces and strengthen the border defenses, while at the same time seeking a settlement with Peking. Between 1959 and 1962, India's annual defense budget nearly doubled to just under $1 billion; the manpower of the armed forces grew by about 25 per cent to 550,000. Roads into the border areas were built, and new equipment was procured to improve logistic and combat capabilities in the Himalayas. More funds were also made available for development, education and welfare of the people living in frontier areas to assure their loyalty and cooperation.

The benefits derived from the increased resources and attention devoted to security affairs were limited by the rising political frictions within the military establishment. The controversial and acid-tongued Krishna Menon had been appointed Minister of Defense in 1957. Charges were soon made that he was placing in key positions officers who shared his views and were willing to support him, possibly as a means of building up his weak political base. His actions angered many Congress party leaders and senior military officers, and at one point were said to be the cause of the proffered resignation of the Army Chief of Staff, General Thimayya. Although Nehru prevailed on Thimayya to serve out his term under Menon, the atmosphere of suspicion and distrust within the military was hardly ideal for a nation facing new and difficult problems.

As a separate aspect of strengthening its position, New Delhi increased its efforts in the Himalayan border states.[35] Additional Indian troops were stationed in Sikkim; more aid was given to Bhutan, especially for transportation and communications, and to Nepal. In the first national elections held in Nepal in 1959, the Indian-oriented Nepali Congress party won an overwhelming victory, which was naturally pleasing to India. But the pleasure was short-lived. When King Mahendra, fearful for his power and position, ousted the Nepali Congress government and arrested several of its leaders late in 1960, Nehru publicly attacked the King's action and permitted those leaders who had escaped to operate a resistance movement from Indian territory.

The chances of reaching a settlement of the border dispute were never great after the issue became a matter of public dispute. New Delhi's practice of publishing its correspondence with Peking every few months reduced its diplomatic flexibility. In his letter of November 1959 suggesting a personal meeting, Chou En-lai had proposed to Nehru that both sides pull back an equal distance "from the so-called McMahon Line in the East, and from the line up to which each side exercises actual control in the West." This Nehru was unwilling to accept, as it was essentially based on recognition of the *status quo*. Instead, he suggested that each side treat the McMahon Line as the frontier in the east and pull its troops in Ladakh out of the disputed territory. Chou refused to accept this proposal, but winter weather reduced patrolling and the chances of clashes even without an agreed pullback.

Chou continued to press for a meeting. Nehru hesitated, apparently under heavy pressure from some members of the cabinet and much of the public, who did not trust Nehru to maintain a firm stand and were opposed to anything that might be even the first step toward compromising India's claims. In January 1960 he finally agreed to a meeting with Chou in April in New Delhi (perhaps at

Soviet urging), an agreement which was widely criticized in India.

When the two men met for six days in April they made no discernible progress. All they could agree to was that officials from each country should meet to examine the relevant historical facts and documents and report their findings.[36] But at a press conference held the day before he left New Delhi, Chou En-lai set forth his proposed solution, and it seems likely that he made the same proposal in his talks with Nehru. Although "the so-called McMahon Line is absolutely unacceptable to China," he said that China would nonetheless be willing "to accommodate the Indian point of view in the eastern sector" if India would "accommodate China in the western sector." In effect, Chou was urging a settlement of the dispute on the basis of the *status quo*.

Chou's proposal probably seemed a reasonable and sensible compromise to the Chinese. India would have to yield about 10,000 square miles of uninhabited territory it claimed in Ladakh, but China would be yielding about 38,000 square miles of territory it claimed in NEFA. Moreover, each would be getting what was strategically important to it; India would have sound title up to the crestline of the Himalayas, and China's claim to the Aksai Chin with its important roads would be recognized. (By 1959 China had built a second road to the south of the first.) What could India possibly want the Aksai Chin for, unless it was to weaken China's position in Tibet? It was north of the Karakoram Range, which was India's natural defense line. India's refusal of the settlement must have been puzzling to the Chinese.

The picture appeared quite different in Indian eyes. India considered it had a good title to both NEFA and Aksai Chin, and was not prepared to sacrifice either, particularly to a country that had, it felt, betrayed its trust and friendship. Indians had no interest in accommodating China's strategic needs, since Chinese military power was there either to suppress the Tibetans or to threaten India. Chou's compromise was dismissed as a typical Chinese Communist maneuver of making totally outrageous claims and then expecting a settlement after indicating a willingness to yield a portion of them.

Nehru himself probably recognized that the situation was not wholly clear-cut. While not inclined to yield on Aksai Chin, he saw that the roads there were important to China. He offered to let China use them for civilian traffic, and once even hinted that India might be willing to lease them to China for 99 years. But he never went beyond this, probably partly because the political cost of a settlement—if he could have won parliamentary approval for one—would have been too high, partly because he believed in India's claims and did not want to set a precedent for Kashmir, and partly because he was doubtful that concessions on the border would bring China to pursue a friendly policy toward India.

When the dispute first became public, Nehru claimed to have been aware of the dangers involved from the early 1950s. The release of the official correspondence shows that to a degree he was, although he thought the major danger was in the northeast rather than the Aksai Chin. Yet the public stance of India's leaders was so different from their private worries that the public was unprepared for the disclosure. Nehru's position had been a difficult one; he could hardly have stated openly that he was trying to reduce the chance of aggressive Chinese action by friendship and kind words. Moreover, some of his statements about China's peaceful intentions had been made in response to critics, both domestic and foreign, who held that the Chinese Communists were a great danger to peace and had to be opposed at every turn. This attitude, in Nehru's view, was itself a great danger. In the final analysis Nehru had bet on Chinese behavior and lost; in losing his gamble he greatly reduced his power to work out a compromise border settlement.

The Line to Moscow

Strengthening India's military position and working out a settlement with China were the two major thrusts of Indian policy announced by Nehru when the border dispute was disclosed. Obtaining Soviet support was an unannounced component of Indian policy. Although the U.S.S.R. had supported the Chinese suppression of the Tibetan insurgents earlier in 1959, Moscow had not been directly critical of India. In July, New Delhi's removal from power of the Communist government in Kerala after prolonged anti-Communist demonstrations in the state (in which the local Congress party played a prominent role) prompted only mild protests in the Soviet press. Despite this setback for the "parliamentary path" adopted by the CPI and endorsed by Khrushchev, the U.S.S.R. made no move to rescind its commitment for the new $378 million credit it had made just before the ouster of the Kerala Communists.

It is difficult to judge exactly what India's goal—or more appropriately, India's hopes—were concerning Soviet policy in the Sino-Indian dispute. Nehru obviously hoped that the U.S.S.R. would not actively support China, with India thus facing a united Communist stand on the issue. This might have meant openly turning to the West for assistance, thereby emasculating the policy of nonalignment to which Nehru had such a heavy commitment, or forcing India to seek a compromise on the border issue. Either would have been extremely distasteful and, in the eyes of Indian leaders, a setback in terms of India's national interests. If preventing open and direct Soviet support for China was India's minimum aim, it probably hoped that the Soviet desire for good relations with India—and concern lest it be forced to turn to the West—would cause Moscow to urge restraint on Peking. Nehru's willingness to meet with Chou in April 1960 may have been due in part to Soviet urging of such a course.

In any case, the Soviet response was not long in coming. For the first time the U.S.S.R. refused to support a Communist state involved in a quarrel with a bourgeois government. It adopted a neutral position, which the Soviet news agency TASS announced on September 9, 1959, and the bulletin was printed in *Pravda* and *Izvestia* the following day. Soviet concern that Indian policy would move toward the West was obvious, although the criticism of those seeking to undermine peaceful coexistence probably was directed at Peking as well.

> Certain political circles and the press in Western countries recently opened up a noisy campaign about an incident that occurred not long ago on the Chinese-Indian border, in the region of the Himalayas. This campaign was obviously directed at driving a wedge between the two largest states in Asia, the Chinese People's Republic and the Republic of India, whose friendship has great importance in ensuring peace and international cooperation in Asia and in the whole world. Those who inspired it are trying to discredit the idea of peaceful coexistence of states with different social systems and to prevent the strengthening of the Asian people's solidarity in the fight to consolidate national independence.
>
> . . .
>
> It would be wrong not to express regret that the incident on the Chinese-Indian boundary took place. The Soviet Union enjoys friendly relations with both the Chinese People's Republic and the Republic of India. The Chinese and Soviet peoples are tied together by indestructible bonds of fraternal friendship based on the great principles of

socialist internationalism. Friendly cooperation between the U.S.S.R. and India according to the ideas of peaceful coexistence is developing successfully.

   . . .

   Soviet leaders . . . express the conviction that both governments will settle the misunderstanding that has arisen, taking into account their mutual interests in the spirit of the traditional friendship between the peoples of China and India.[37]

Nehru was obviously pleased, commenting that the statement was "a fair one and an unusual one" for the Soviet Union to make. India's hopes were raised further when Khrushchev, in a speech to the Supreme Soviet on October 31 after his return from Peking, once again equated both sides in his remarks deploring the dispute and urging a settlement. Thus encouraged in their policy of keeping a line open to Moscow, Indian leaders began to seek Soviet support. This took the form of Indian purchases, for rupees, of Soviet transport aircraft and helicopters for supplying Indian troops along the frontier with China. The purchases had the double advantage of increasing India's military capabilities and serving as a warning to China to adopt a moderate position on the dispute. Under such circumstances, it was worth permitting the U.S.S.R. to gain a toehold in the Indian Air Force.

From the Soviet point of view, the economic aid commitments made to India during 1959, a neutral position in the border dispute, and the sale of aircraft were regarded as the necessary price to pay to maintain the Soviet position in India and to keep it from moving toward the West.

In retrospect it is clear that a major reason for Soviet unwillingness to support China on the border dispute was that Moscow and Peking were at odds on many other issues. Mao seems to have been obsessed with the idea that Khrushchev was willing if not actively planning to sell out China—whatever that meant—and to have imputed a passive meaning to Khrushchev's policies of the parliamentary path and peaceful coexistence that the Soviet leader never intended them to have. To Khrushchev, his détente policies represented a less dangerous strategy for pursuing Soviet and Communist interests in a nuclear age; to Mao, they represented an incorrect line and a sacrifice of Chinese interests, and they clearly did require at least a postponement of such Chinese objectives as recovering Taiwan. Perhaps Mao feared that the U.S.S.R. would in time become committed to such policies as ends and not means. In addition, Soviet and Chinese views of bourgeois Asian nationalists were also diverging at this time.

How important a role did differing Soviet and Chinese attitudes and policies toward India play in the development of the Sino-Soviet split? Although among the first to be publicly known, differences on policy toward India were not of the same rank of importance as the question of peaceful coexistence, the extent of Soviet support for Chinese nuclear development, and—perhaps most important of all— the issue of political and doctrinal authority in the world Communist movement. Policy toward India nonetheless involved conflicting ideological considerations of how to deal with the neutral nations and the obligations of one Communist state toward another, as well as questions of national interest and power. Peking's November 1963 account of its efforts since 1959 to convince Soviet leaders they should support their Chinese ally—or at a minimum refrain from publicly taking a "neutral" position—reveals the extent of Chinese bitterness at Soviet behavior.[38] Thus divergent Soviet and Chinese attitudes toward India worsened their relationship at a time when it was already under strain.[39]

Effects on Pakistan and the United States

In contrast to India's active involvement with the major powers, Pakistan's links were almost entirely with the United States during the 1950s. But domestic changes in Pakistan, as well as the Sino-Indian dispute, were to alter this.

Since the death of Liaquat Ali in 1951, the Pakistani political system had been a model of instability; in October 1958 General Ayub Khan seized power. Although uncertain of their course at first, Ayub and his colleagues gained experience and self-confidence as they tackled some of Pakistan's many problems with new vigor. Most of Ayub's first year in office was devoted to domestic affairs, though he indicated his intention to seek solutions to the long-standing Indo-Pakistani disputes.

The initial Indian reaction to Ayub's take-over had been sharply critical, Nehru attacking the new regime as a naked military dictatorship. The sharpness of Indian criticism gradually subsided as New Delhi began to view Ayub's government in a rather different light;

perhaps Pakistan now had a leader who could make an agreement and carry it out.

But India was not about to rush into anything. Shortly after the Sino-Indian border dispute became public knowledge in August 1959, Ayub proposed that India and Pakistan cooperate in the joint defense of the subcontinent—at least to the extent of repositioning the military forces of the two countries so that they faced their northern neighbors rather than each other. This arrangement was subject to agreement on a method to settle the Kashmir dispute if not on an outright settlement. Nehru immediately turned down the suggestion. He wanted no link with Pakistan and the Western powers in opposition to both the U.S.S.R. and Communist China, nor was he willing to make Indian concessions sufficient to effect a settlement of the Kashmir dispute. Why give up the Vale of Kashmir in order to hold Aksai Chin? Indeed, how could India face China in Ladakh unless it controlled the supply lines running through the Vale? The question was pertinent if the Sino-Indian quarrel was primarily a border dispute over particular pieces of territory. If, however, the quarrel was basically a conflict between two large nations for influence in Asia, then a settlement with Pakistan would have made sense. Many Indians accepted the second interpretation but without drawing the logical conclusion regarding policy toward Pakistan.

Nonetheless, during late 1959 and 1960, agreement was reached on a number of issues outstanding since partition, including a settlement of most of the remaining border disputes between India and Pakistan. More important, the dispute over the division of the waters of the Indus River system was settled with the help of the World Bank and some friendly nations.[40] Hopes were high in many quarters that the two leaders would begin serious negotiations on the critical Kashmir issue when they met in September 1960; Ayub clearly wanted to do so. He hinted that Pakistan would no longer insist on a plebiscite, and stated that "all the things achieved in other fields will be nullified if the Kashmir dispute is not solved." Nehru balked, however, and it soon became known that he had refused even to discuss Kashmir seriously with Ayub.

As far as can be determined, Nehru never thought that a genuine compromise settlement with Pakistan on Kashmir was necessary or desirable. By September 1960 he felt confident of Soviet support and thus was even less inclined to yield anything of importance on Kashmir. Shortly after his talks with Nehru, Ayub publicly stressed

Pakistan's intention to push for a satisfactory Kashmir settlement and was sharply critical of Indian policy. Relations began to deteriorate to their customary level of animosity. The agreements reached between the two countries in late 1959 and 1960 thus represented not the beginning of a new and sounder Indo-Pakistani relationship but rather the short-lived high point in their post-independence relations.

India was now engaged in territorial disputes with both Pakistan and China, each of which was allied to one of the superpowers. Yet rather than seek a compromise settlement with either one so as to be better able to face the other, India held firm in both cases.

The decision to hold fast was partly based upon the natural reluctance all governments have to cede territory or even abandon territorial claims, particularly when domestic political feelings are inflamed. Beyond this, however, India's decision apparently reflected three conclusions: first, that it would be possible to induce the United States and the Soviet Union to adopt essentially neutral positions in the Indo-Pakistani and Sino-Indian disputes respectively; second, that the antagonisms of both Pakistan and China were broader and deeper than the border disputes, and that their settlement would not lessen the underlying hostility; and third, that India could afford the military burden of having both neighbors as enemies.

India was clearly correct as to the first judgment, but the soundness of the second is still problematic. As to the third, India clearly was overly optimistic about its ability to embark upon such an ambitious foreign policy and assume the attendant defense burden without damaging its economy.

Washington took no official public notice of the developing Sino-Indian border dispute in the summer of 1959. Undoubtedly the Indian government and public were pleased that Washington did not point to the innumerable past occasions when India had criticized the United States for asserting that China was a threat to peace. Nevertheless, many Indians were puzzled and unhappy that the United States did not take India's side in the dispute; but the government, which was maneuvering for Soviet support, probably was satisfied with the U.S. stance.[41] The United States was uncertain about the complex claims and counterclaims, and also aware that its Chinese Nationalist ally upheld the claims India disputed, but neither quandary explained American reticence. Nor was the restraint based upon a petulant desire to let India stew in its own troubles. In an address in New Delhi on August 8, 1962, Ambassador Galbraith said that both Chester Bowles and John Sherman Cooper, two former U.S. ambassadors who were friendly toward India, had urged restraint lest American support of India make the problem more dangerous by seeming to make it a part of the cold war.

If the United States was officially silent, however, there was a general satisfaction that India was becoming more aware of the threat posed by China. U.S.-Indian relations, it was widely believed, would improve considerably, and India would be more cooperative with U.S. efforts to oppose communism; perhaps, too, fear of China would lead India and Pakistan to settle their differences. Despite the unhappiness of some Indians that the United States did not rush to its side, the general Indian belief that the two countries stood together was behind the massive and wildly enthusiastic reception given President Eisenhower on his state visit late in 1959. It was a dramatic change from the bitter attacks on the United States less than five years earlier.

The United States continued to increase its aid, and in 1960 agreed to supply 17 million tons of wheat to India for rupees over the next five years, the largest surplus foodstuff agreement ever signed. In the same year the United States and the World Bank set up the consortium of foreign aid suppliers to deal with India's growing aid requirements.

Any period that has seen improvement in U.S. relations with either India or Pakistan has also seen a strain in relations with the other, and these years were no exception. During the mid-1950s Pakistanis felt more secure as a result of their links with the United States and the United Kingdom and the arms they were receiving. In time, however, Pakistanis began to take the flow of arms for granted, and became concerned that they had alienated the U.S.S.R. as well as many Asian and African countries; moreover, they were annoyed that they were making no discernible progress toward acquiring Kashmir.

U.S. relations with Pakistan became less close, although there was no dramatic change. Indeed, two of the reasons behind the change had nothing to do with India. The Ayub government was more self-confident and assertive than its predecessors. After concluding that Pakistan had followed the United States too closely, it gradually began to adopt a more independent course. At first this was not due to any significant new divergence of views, but rather to Pakistan's determination to decide for itself where its interests lay on each issue confronting it. However, the U-2 incident of May 1960, the revelation that the plane had taken off from Peshawar, and the manner in which the U.S. government handled the affair led Ayub and his colleagues to reappraise Pakistan's position. With his confidence in the United States declining somewhat, Ayub decided it would be wise to take out some insurance with the U.S.S.R. in order to reduce Soviet antagonism. He accepted a Soviet offer of a $30 million credit to be used for oil exploration in Pakistan—such being one way a smaller power apologizes for its actions against a major power in the modern world.

Nevertheless, as President Eisenhower prepared to leave office early in 1961, he could conclude that conditions in South Asia and the U.S. position in the subcontinent were developing in a reasonably satisfactory manner in a far from satisfactory world.

PART THREE

Confrontations and Their Consequences

8

The Sino-Indian Border War

The course of the Sino-Indian quarrel led to shifts in the relationships among India, Pakistan and the major powers, but during 1959 and 1960 none of the shifts was dramatic. The United States leaned a bit more toward India—or a bit less toward Pakistan—and the U.S.S.R. refused to sacrifice its relationship with India despite Chinese claims on its support. In effect, the powers were able to adjust their relationships without making basic alterations. This period was short, however, for the advent of the Kennedy administration and the rising intensity of the Sino-Indian dispute soon brought major changes.

The Kennedy administration took office convinced that the trend of world affairs was running in favor of the Communist world. President Kennedy and his colleagues believed that because the Eisenhower administration had not done enough to meet the Communist challenge, the United States had to make a greater effort lest the balance of forces shift decisively against it. An increase in U.S. conventional and nuclear forces—particularly long-range missiles—was required, at the same time that greater efforts were needed to work out an accommodation with the U.S.S.R.

Much greater efforts were also needed in the underdeveloped areas in view of the gains the U.S.S.R. had made since the mid-1950s. President Kennedy thought the United States had attached too much importance to formal military alliances and military assistance and had devoted insufficient attention and inadequate economic resources to the nonaligned nations, although he thought that policies had shifted in the right direction during the later years of the Eisenhower administration. Thus a key aspect of his foreign policy was to demonstrate greater understanding and support of nonaligned nations such as India, Indonesia, the United Arab Republic, Ghana, and Guinea. A growing humanitarian concern and a strong belief that the long-run dangers in these countries were poverty and social injustice led to the conclusion that the United States had no choice but to become involved not only in economic development, but in the processes of political development as well. Although aware of some of the complexities and pitfalls, the President and many officials were convinced that progress in overcoming economic stagnation and social injustice was dependent on improving the effectiveness of the local governments.

The minimum goal of this policy was to limit Soviet and Chinese gains in the nonaligned nations. Beyond this, there was a general belief that if the United States demonstrated greater understanding and support of the neutralists, they would in time respond with more understanding and support for the United States in the struggle with the Communist world. The Kennedy administration did achieve more cordial relations with many of the neutralists, at least for a time, which was worrisome to Soviet leaders, who feared these "bourgeois nationalists" might move into the Western camp and adopt an anti-Soviet stance. Yet for all its efforts, the Kennedy administration was unable to win lasting neutralist support in world affairs.

There were several reasons behind the administration's lack of success. The United States tried to win the support of the neutralists without abandoning—as distinct from loosening—ties with its allies, which limited the neutralist response. Moreover, many of the neutralists had quarrels with neighbors (who were often allied with the United States) and the American tendency to avoid a clear-cut stance on these issues had drawbacks as well as advantages. Basically, however, the neutralists wanted to remain nonaligned; they felt this enhanced their freedom and enabled them to play off the Communists and the West against each other. In retrospect, the Kennedy administration misjudged the importance of the various reasons behind Afro-Asian neutralism and placed too much credence on the arguments of neutralist leaders that their anti-Western attitudes were a reaction to specific Western policies and actions.

John F. Kennedy had shown a special interest in India while still a senator. He was one of the sponsors of the Indo-American Conference in Washington in 1957; he sponsored an amendment to the Mutual Security Act of 1958 which expressed the interest of the United States in the political stability and the economic growth of India. India and China, he believed, were engaged in a struggle "for the economic and political leadership of the East."[1] That he reached this conclusion at a time when Indian influence (never as great as believed by sympathetic Westerners) was declining in Asia and Africa was of less immediate importance than the fact that these were the views of the newly elected president of the United States.

U.S.-Indian relations continued to improve in 1961–62. Chester Bowles, Phillips Talbot, and John Kenneth Galbraith, who were known to be friendly to India, held influential positions, and an element of warm rapport was established between the two governments. The official Indian reaction to the Bay of Pigs was critical but short-lived, and New Delhi was pleased at Washington's efforts to reduce the danger of military conflict with the Soviet Union. Indian willingness to assume greater international responsibilities by sending combat troops to the Congo in 1961 also pleased Washington.

Moreover, the advent of the Kennedy administration coincided with the beginning of India's ambitious Third Five-Year Plan (1961–66), which called for expenditures of about $25 billion and was predicated upon the receipt of at least $5 billion in foreign aid. Although the U.S. government had spoken favorably of India's plans and had increased aid considerably during the Second Plan, it had carefully avoided a position where it was committed to the success of the Indian plans. This attitude changed in 1961, and while the United States never formally committed itself to the success of the Third Plan, it moved in that direction and urged other Western donors to provide more aid on easier terms. U.S. economic aid (excluding surplus foods) rose to over $400 million a year, to be matched by the other members of the consortium, with the IBRD supplying the remainder of the $1 billion annual requirement.

Yet the path of U.S.-Indian relations was far from smooth, as certain events caused much friction and demonstrated the limitations in the relationship even while its potential was increasingly being realized. Kennedy and Nehru did not hit it off well when they met in Washington in November 1961. A more serious problem was continued American support of Pakistan. Another was India's exploration during 1961 and 1962 of the possibility of acquiring MIG aircraft from the U.S.S.R.[2] Official statements held that the MIGs were needed to offset the advanced aircraft the United States supplied to Pakistan. Defense Minister Krishna Menon was strongly of the view that Pakistan rather than China was India's main enemy, and he wanted—over the opposition of most Indian military leaders—to shift from complete reliance on Britain and France for arms to at least partial reliance on the U.S.S.R. American officials were loath to see the Soviet Union gain a major foothold in the Indian military establishment, but were also reluctant to supply India with the same quality aircraft Pakistan was receiving.[3] By mid-1962 U.S. opposition to India's course and efforts to get it to purchase British or French planes had caused relations to deteriorate sharply. (The U.S. vote for a Security Council resolution calling for fresh negotiations on the Kashmir issue added to Indian irritation.) Nehru denounced the United States in Parliament, saying he was doubtful of American goodwill toward India, and the Indian press echoed him.

Another source of discord was the Indian invasion of the Portuguese enclaves of Goa, Damão, and Diu, in December 1961 and the American (and Western) reaction. Anger over Portuguese intransigence, nationalist domestic pressures on the eve of general elections, fear that India was losing influence in radical Afro-Asian circles because of its moderation, and perhaps a desire to demonstrate to China that India could take military action when deemed necessary were all behind the move. Understandable as the take-over was, it was viewed by the U.S. government as a move that removed one more inhibition against violence in a strife-ridden world. India's assertion that the whole affair was begun by the Portuguese was so transparently false that it convinced almost no one in the West. Adlai Stevenson attacked India strongly in the United Nations, and soon the press in each nation was once again pointing out the errors and hypocrisy of the other.

More important than either the friction over the MIGs or the Goa affair was continuing U.S. support for Pakistan. It is not clear what policy India expected the Kennedy administration to follow toward Pakistan. New Delhi must have hoped that the United States would at least reduce its military assistance, stand aloof from the Kashmir issue, and be more appreciative of nonalignment without, however, embracing India so closely as to bring its stance into question in the Afro-Asian world.

The U.S.-Pakistani relationship did not deteriorate to the extent that might have been expected. When President Kennedy took office he discovered that there were reasons for giving Pakistan a higher priority in his over-all strategy than he had recognized as a senator.[4] In part, this was the discovery of past commitments which any new administration inherits. Far more important, however, the United States had established important intelligence installations in Pakistan. Moreover, the new administration recognized the increasing regard in which President Ayub was held by Congress, and it was averse to seeing U.S. alliances crumble at a time when the Soviet and Chinese military challenges still seemed threatening. (This was the year 1961 when Soviet pressure in Europe was symbolized by erecting the Berlin wall, and when Moscow mounted an intense campaign of threats against the CENTO countries.)

Vice-President Johnson, who visited India and Pakistan in May 1961, was favorably impressed with both countries and on his return wrote a memorandum to the President stating that the United States should continue to back Pakistan while trying to establish its friendship with India on a lasting basis.[5] His remarks at a news conference on June 28 about India's important role in Asia alarmed and angered Pakistan.

President Kennedy invited Ayub to Washington for a state visit in July in an effort to reassure him. Before his visit Ayub made known his worries that the United States would upset the military balance on the subcontinent by providing military aid to India or ending its aid to Pakistan. He also indicated his belief that the United States was now in a position to use its economic aid to pressure India into accepting a reasonable Kashmir settlement. Ayub was given a lavish reception and made a very favorable impression, especially on Congress. Kennedy made it clear the United States would continue military aid to Pakistan and that the F-104 aircraft (more advanced than anything on the subcontinent) previously promised would soon arrive. He assured Ayub that the United States would not give military aid to India unless the security of the subcontinent was threatened, and even then, Pakistan would be consulted in advance. On the other hand, Kennedy also made it clear that he would not agree to withhold economic aid if India refused to compromise on Kashmir. He did not believe such a move would succeed in view of the importance India attached to Kashmir, and it would certainly undermine U.S. efforts to forge closer ties with India.

The United States sharply stepped up its economic aid to Pakistan, which was now able to absorb larger sums. While there was some Pakistani annoyance over U.S. urging that more be done for East Pakistan, the increased aid was nonetheless welcomed. Ayub, who probably had not really expected a favorable response to all his requests, proclaimed himself satisfied. U.S.-Pakistani relations appeared to have withstood a time of testing.[6]

Thus during 1961 and 1962 the American attempt to maintain useful relations with both India and Pakistan appeared, at least on the surface, to be proceeding satisfactorily if not smoothly. Both countries were making domestic progress. Pakistan was moving toward the adoption of a constitution. The Congress party won a solid victory in the third general elections in 1962, and India's remarkable political stability seemed likely to continue. Increased economic aid was available and India's chances for continued economic progress looked promising. But events in the Himalayas were soon to upset some of these calculations.

India's Forward Policy

The failure of the Chou-Nehru talks in April 1960 ended any serious search for agreement. Each party continued to proclaim its desire for a settlement, of course, but only on terms that the other had demonstrated it would not accept. Thus in February 1961, for example, Nehru asserted that India did not recognize the existence of a border dispute, and would not negotiate on the basis of China's claims. Indian leaders had been surprised and shaken when in the 1960 meetings the Chinese had altered their description of the boundary line in Ladakh in a way that added several thousand square miles to their claims. When confronted with this change from their previous claims, the Chinese blandly denied there was any difference in the two lines. These actions (and the Chinese tendency to attack Indian evidence without providing much evidence in support of their own claims) caused many Indians to believe the Chinese had ominous and large-scale designs.

Strong words and legal arguments, the Indian Government recognized, would be of limited avail in view of China's military control of the territory Peking really valued. New Delhi therefore decided that its political pressure should be supplemented by military measures in the Ladakh area. It adopted a policy of reclaiming lost ground by sending Indian patrols behind Chinese-held posts and setting up Indian posts. The combination, it was hoped, would lead China to agree to a satisfactory settlement.

This policy represented a misreading of both the respective military strength of the two countries and China's likely response to military pressure. Why Indian leaders thought that China, which was then defying both the United States and the U.S.S.R. on the political battlefront, would be moved by Indian pressures is hard to understand. Equally difficult to fathom was their judgment that India could apply military pressure to China and not meet with a determined response. Perhaps they felt that China could not afford to ignore political pressure because of India's influence in the underdeveloped world. Perhaps they believed that concern over the Western and Soviet reaction would deter China from risking war of uncertain dimensions because of India's growing ties with the United States and the U.S.S.R.. The gap between Indian thinking and reality quickly became apparent.

Tensions increased between the two nations. On November 2, 1961, the Chinese protested India's military activities in "China's territory and territorial air," stating:

> The Chinese Government has been following with great anxiety the Indian troops' steady pressing forward on China's borders and cannot but regard such actions of the Indian side as an attempt to create new troubles and to carry out its expansion by force in the Sino-Indian border areas. . . . The Chinese Government hereby demands that the Indian Government speedily change its present practice and order all the intruding Indian troops to put an end immediately to their violations of China's territory.[7]

On November 30 the Chinese, protesting India's assertions that whatever it did in Indian-claimed territory was none of China's concern, warned that New Delhi's unwillingness to respect the *status quo* in Ladakh could lead to trouble in the eastern sector, where

> . . . the Chinese Government has always held that this sector of the boundary lies along the Southern foot of the Himalayas . . . If the

Indian Government's above logic should be followed, the Chinese Government would have every reason to send troops to cross the so-called "McMahon Line" and enter the vast area between the crest of the Himalayas and their Southern foot. But the Chinese Government has never done so.[8]

The Chinese sent a patrol south of the McMahon Line in January 1962 to show that they were serious.

India was determined to continue its policy, however, and had so informed China in a strongly-worded note on December 9:

> In face of growing Chinese aggression on Indian territory since 1957-58, . . . it ill-behooves the Chinese Government to ask the Government of India to desist from taking measures to safeguard its territorial integrity. The Sino-Indian border was always a border of peace and friendship until the Chinese Government embarked on a course of aggression. To restore peace and tranquility . . . Chinese forces should first of all withdraw from Indian territory into Chinese territory. It would serve no useful purpose for the Chinese Government to go on pressing faked charges about Indian intrusions into Chinese territory in order to justify its own aggression on India.[9]

New Delhi followed this with a note of February 26, 1962, stating "The Government of India takes strong exception to the Chinese attempt to reply to the Government of India's protest against Chinese aggression in the Western sector by threatening aggression elsewhere."[10]

In still another note on March 13 India pointed out that it agreed that both sides should maintain the *status quo*, but whereas China favored the *status quo* as of 1959 India insisted on "a restoration of the *status quo* through the withdrawal of Chinese forces from Indian territory, into which they have intruded since 1957."[11]

The steadily stronger protests of Peking did not deter New Delhi from its course. Indian leaders were thoroughly outraged at Chinese behavior, quite willing to trade accusations and insults, and convinced that only by winning firmer control of the disputed territory could India hope to negotiate from a position of strength. Moreover, its military tactics seemed to be working, for patrols were slowly pushing forward and establishing themselves behind Chinese posts, causing the Chinese to pull back at some points. It is inaccurate to speak of operating behind enemy lines; there merely were outposts and patrol routes, and a country could claim it controlled a particular area because it sometimes sent patrols there. Nonetheless, Indian leaders were determined to continue the forward strategy of the energetic and ambitious Lieutenant General B. M. Kaul, who became the driving force in the army after General Thimayya's retirement.

With Peking informing New Delhi at the end of April that Chinese forces were resuming patrolling in Ladakh, tensions rose throughout the spring and summer of 1962. The announcement in May of an agreement between China and Pakistan to "negotiate a border settlement" set off a furious reaction in India, which claimed that since it was the rightful sovereign of all of Kashmir, no border between Pakistan and China existed. The announcement also caused apprehensions in Washington, for Pakistan, which professed to follow an anti-Communist foreign policy, was undermining the position of the one major Asian nation that was confronting Communist China.

India also refused to renew the 1954 agreement regulating trade with Tibet, which would expire in June 1962, unless China agreed to evacuate its forces from all Indian-claimed territory. China refused, and the agreement lapsed. Chinese trade agencies in India were closed, as were Indian agencies in Tibet. This also led to angry exchanges concerning the status and rights of Chinese nationals in India, demonstrations over Chinese consulates in India, and other matters.

Perhaps fearing by this time that the dangers were becoming too great, New Delhi proposed in a note on May 14 that "the two governments should take necessary steps to prevent armed clashes on the border and lay a proper foundation for peaceful negotiations." Nehru went on to suggest that in Ladakh both withdraw their forces behind the border as claimed by the other party, adding that in the interest of a peaceful settlement India was prepared to permit the continued use of the Aksai Chin road for Chinese civilian traffic.[12] These suggestions were repeated in Indian notes in June and July, but when the texts were published late in July, the implication that the Indian government was prepared to renew negotiations raised cries of "appeasement" in Parliament and in the press. The government quickly backed off by claiming that it only sought talks to reduce border tensions and would not enter formal negotiations until the Chinese vacated their aggression.

China was in no mood to pull back, saying in a note on June 2, "Why should China need to ask India's permission for using its own road on its own territory? What an absurdity!"[13]

Sometime in the summer of 1962 the Chinese Government apparently decided that it would take a firmer stand, and began to build up its forces along the border. It was also preparing an ideological justification for war, should it come, by drafting a major policy statement vituperatively attacking Nehru's foreign policy, which was published on October 27.

Early in September Chinese troops crossed the Thagla Ridge, in Western NEFA on the McMahon Line, and showed they were determined to remain. On September 20 Peking warned New Delhi that it was resuming active patrolling along the entire frontier, and on the same day a major clash occurred on the McMahon Line. The exchange of notes went on in early October, with China urging talks and India refusing to negotiate "under duress." On October 12 Nehru publicly announced that the army had been told to clear Indian territory in NEFA of Chinese intruders unless they pulled back. An editorial in the *People's Daily* two days later warned Nehru that he was on the "brink of the precipice" and added, "If there are still some maniacs who are reckless enough to ignore our well-intentioned advice and insist on having another try, well, let them do so. History will pronounce its inexorable verdict."[14]

The Indian Government and its critics seemed quite unaware of the relative military strength of India and China along the Himalayas. *The Hindustan Times*, for example, while unwilling to accept the government's claims regarding its border preparations, still commented: "For the first time since Chinese aggression in Ladakh began, we are on the point of reaching the stage where the Chinese military threat could be contained with a relatively minor effort on our part."[15]

Ignorance of the real state of affairs was perhaps understandable on the part of those outside the government. Yet government leaders, to judge from their actions, were not much better informed about Chinese military capabilities despite the apparently systematic and continuous series of reconnaissance flights over Tibet.[16] Whatever information was derived from these flights either had little effect on Indian policy or the Indian army was considered vastly more capable than it proved to be.

The War

In contrast to the long buildup of tension, the war itself was sharp and short, lasting little longer than a month. On October 20, China launched major attacks at several points in both Ladakh and NEFA. India's advance posts were quickly overwhelmed, as were many of the defensive positions a few miles back. Nehru went on the radio the same night to tell the nation of the defeats India had suffered. Determination to stand up to the Chinese was mingled with shock, and Nehru spoke of India being "awakened from a dream of our own making."

The shock was worldwide, for in these weeks people everywhere witnessed not only war between the world's two most populous countries but also the Cuban missile confrontation between the two superpowers. These crises, occurring at the same time, profoundly affected the policies of all the powers.

After its initial victories, China on October 24 proposed an armistice, contingent upon both armies withdrawing 20 kilometers (about 12.4 miles) from the lines they actually controlled. Although worried about the losses and the trend of battle and shaken by the initial Soviet support for the Chinese armistice proposal, India was still unwilling to agree to keep its troops out of the territory it claimed. Men and materials were rushed to the Ladakh and NEFA battlefronts.

On November 16, Chinese troops again took the offensive and quickly won a stunning series of victories. Within three weeks they won back all the territory India had gained in nearly two years of patrolling in Ladakh, although the Indian forces there gave a good account of themselves despite their inadequate clothing and equipment. India's defense at the eastern end of NEFA was less effective, but the troops retreated in a semi-orderly manner. At the western end of NEFA, however, the fighting quickly turned into a rout and near panic set in. The Chinese outflanked and defeated the Indian forces which had been rushed up to the Se La Pass and were awaiting a Chinese attack through it. The key town of Bomdila was captured, and Chinese troops proceeded south until they were at the foothills of the Himalayas. Stunned, the Indian Government made frantic appeals to other nations for great quantities of military assistance.

Then, as suddenly as they had attacked, the Chinese announced on November 21 that they were withdrawing their forces 20 kilometers back of the lines of actual control of November 7, 1959, which was north of the position India had earlier conceded to them. This unilateral withdrawal was subject to an armistice, noninterference with the Chinese withdrawal, Indian acceptance of the 20 kilometer demilitarized zone, and no Indian attempt to re-establish any of the Indian posts captured by the Chinese in Ladakh. Although even at this point India was unwilling formally to agree to such conditions, Peking did not insist on it. In any case, India was unable to interfere with the Chinese withdrawal and disinclined to send its troops beyond the line suggested by China.

India's defeats shook the nation's self-confidence to the core. The government's strategy had exploded in its face; it was unwilling to negotiate and unable to fight. There was a widespread desire on the part of millions of Indians to do something, but their eagerness to help ended in frustration and disenchantment when it became clear that the government was unable to direct their energies into useful channels. Though still defiant, India's leaders seemed dazed and confused. The Himalayas, the barrier to any attack from the north, were no longer impregnable. For a brief time the country seemed open to invasion, and the hard-won freedom from foreign rule in peril. The public reacted with anguish and anger upon discovering that its leaders had been inept and its army ineffective. Krishna Menon's manipulation of military assignments and promotions and the consequent poor military leadership became known. In late October widespread pressures, especially from other political leaders eager to settle old scores, forced Nehru to remove Menon as defense minister. (Ironically, Menon had favored a more cautious military strategy than was adopted.) Although he was given another post, the opposition within Parliament and the public was so strong that he was soon forced to resign from that as well. General Kaul's reckless strategy and poor command performance—he had taken charge of the NEFA front just before the fighting began—brought his downfall as well.

The war with China created a dilemma for the Communist Party of India (CPI) and created greater strains within its ranks. Most of the top leaders favored support of the Indian government and condemnation of China's military actions, but a vociferous minority dissented. The U.S.S.R. had attempted to keep the party united and loyal to Moscow, and had even sent M. Suslov, its top ideologue, to India to help guide the 1961 party congress. But in October and November 1962 Moscow was too preoccupied with the Cuban missile crisis to give guidance to the CPI, although by this time the split within the party was too wide to be papered over. In any case, the pro-Chinese wing of the party was roundly condemned throughout India for its unpatriotic and antinational stand.

With the Chinese pullback the fear of invasion disappeared, but the shattering blow to India's pride and self-confidence lingered.

India had projected a certain image of herself, and perhaps she had also come to believe in her own relative importance in the world. . . . A nation whose military weakness had been revealed in so brutal but effective a manner could not continue to enjoy the same prestige as she had before. Instinctively and perhaps spontaneously, India reacted bitterly to this humiliation, with a half-conscious awareness that what she had lost was not merely some mountain passes, soldiers, and equipment but her entire international position.[17]

In the months and years that followed many and varied reasons for the Chinese action were put forward. Some Indians stressed the relatively limited nature of China's aims as far as the attack was concerned. Chinese military pressure was designed, according to the editor of *The Times of India*, to "compel New Delhi to accept a negotiated settlement in Ladakh." If negotiation was the Chinese aim, there was a gross miscalculation on Peking's part, for India's attitude hardened rather than softened.

Another judgment was that the Chinese action

can be explained almost exclusively in terms of China's determination not to give up the Aksai Chin and the strategic highway so vital for controlling the difficult provinces of Tibet and Sinkiang. . . . The Chinese military action was an exercise in limited war in pursuit of limited objectives; in the context of the existing military situation along the border, the force employed was adequate for the purpose. At one stroke it restored the *status quo* in the western sector which Indian nibbling over the previous three years had undermined; reopened China's claims south of the McMahon Line which the Indians had ignored during three years of relative tranquility in the area; and re-emphasized China's determined stand on the boundary question.[18]

Yet the same author thought that any explanation which focused entirely on the border dispute was too limited, for "the border dispute is only one instrument in the protracted war Mao Tse-tung has declared on India."[19]

More typical of the Indian reaction was the view that the border dispute was a part of an effort to pressure India "to follow the Chinese line, both in her domestic and external policies, or risk disintegration in the process of resisting that pressure." Prime Minister

Nehru seemed to accept the more ominous view, for he called China "a country with profoundly inimical intentions toward our independence and institutions."[20]

Contrasting International Responses

Whatever the explanations accepted at the time, defense against the Chinese threat was the overwhelming preoccupation of Indians at the end of 1962. Foreign countries were judged for a time largely by the way they reacted to the crisis, and the unexpected reactions—along with the defeat itself—called into question the bases of Indian foreign policy. Most of the Afro-Asian neutralists, whose cause Nehru had championed so long and eloquently, were awed by China's demonstration of its disciplined use of power. They stood mutely neutral instead of rallying to India's side as expected. The support India received from Afro-Asian countries came almost entirely from nations allied with or inclined toward the West. This too was a sobering lesson for India. While India did not cease to work with the neutralists, New Delhi's scorn for the Asian nations that had chosen a different path was henceforth muted. In time, six neutral nations—Ceylon, Cambodia, the United Arab Republic, Burma, Ghana, and Indonesia—met and tried to take a more active role by making certain proposals for bringing about new talks between India and China. India was suspicious of their activities in view of their failure to condemn China's attack, but found it difficult to answer their assertion that China could not be expected to consider the proposals of a group of nations that had condemned its actions. Moreover, India was unwilling to hold discussions with China until it vacated the aggression, that is, withdrew from all Indian-claimed territory. Eventually, however, India was able to interpret the proposals of the six in such a way as to make acceptance possible, while China found it difficult to do so, which eased India's feeling of isolation.

The reaction of the Afro-Asian nations was only one of the surprises. The Soviet Union, then deeply and dangerously involved in the Cuban missile crisis, retreated from its earlier neutral stance, and in an October 25 *Pravda* editorial attacked the McMahon Line, criticized "certain reactionary circles in India which have tightly bound their destiny with foreign capital and imperialist forces," and suggested that India accept the Chinese offer of a pullback.[21] New Delhi had sent urgent requests for help to the United States, Britain, and the Soviet Union. Indian policy had counted on the U.S.S.R. to restrain China or, failing that, to assist India. The first hope vanished with the Chinese attack; the second with Moscow's silence in response to the Indian appeal. Those Indians who had urged reliance on the U.S.S.R. were shocked and confused; those who had doubted the wisdom of such reliance felt confirmed in their judgment. A *Pravda* editorial on November 5 (after Khrushchev had agreed to pull the missiles out of Cuba) drew back from support of China, but only partially undid the damage to the Soviet position.

The Soviets suffered not only from the inadequacy of their stance but also by contrast to the Western reaction to India's call for help. Planes loaded with American and British arms began landing within a brief time, and arrangements were made to provide New Delhi with emergency supplies of arms to fill in its most glaring deficiencies. If the response of the American press was to look backward as well as forward, the American government did not publicly yield to the temptation.

The United States and Britain also attempted to persuade Pakistan to assure New Delhi that it would make no trouble for India in its hour of danger, arguing that a generous Pakistani stance might make possible a new and fruitful relationship with India. Pakistani leaders, however, found India's humiliation too enjoyable and the U.S. and U.K. arms aid to India too worrisome to extend any such assurances (see Chapter 9).

The unexpected reactions of the Afro-Asian neutrals, the U.S.S.R., and the West shook the foundations of Indian foreign policy. Nonalignment itself came under direct assault. In the words of one Indian columnist: "Yet another, a Dullesian, truth brought home to us is that in this world sharply divided between the Communist and non-Communist blocs, there is no room for neutrals—not when the chips are down."[22]

Nonalignment in a New Context

Faced with the disintegration of so many of their beliefs and illusions about themselves, their country, and the world, India's leaders set out to revise their foreign policy. This must have been especially onerous to Prime Minister Nehru, who had labored so hard since independence for the development and advancement of his country.

Now aging and ailing, with his self-confidence and prestige shaken, he wearily began guiding India along a difficult path in a changed world.

Yet the eventual changes in India's policies were less dramatic than the changes in its view of the world. The events of 1962 did cause India to place less emphasis on its role as a world peacemaker and devote more attention to its direct national interests. Since neither the Himalayan barrier nor the armed forces were adequate to assure the nation's security, a major military buildup was set in motion. Throughout 1963 a review of India's military needs was underway in the Ministry of Defense, and in early 1964 the government published a five-year defense program which called for defense spending, which was $1 billion in 1962, to rise to approximately $2 billion in 1969. (This represented a rise from about 3 per cent to 5 per cent of national income.) The army was to expand from approximately 600,000 to 825,000 men and the number of divisions (which had gone from 9 to 15 between 1962 and 1964) was to increase to 21 by 1969. The air force was to add 15 new squadrons for a total of 45, and large numbers of obsolescent planes were to be replaced with the most modern types. Practically all the expansion was to be in fighter or fighter-bomber aircraft; in 1964 there was no thought of acquiring any significant bomber capability for striking deep into China. Although the Chinese naval threat to India was difficult to discern if not positively nonexistent, the Indian navy was also to have more modern ships. India was determined to develop its own defense industry so that in time it would be free of undependable foreign suppliers and the problems created by having so many diverse types of equipment.

If India's goal was independence of foreign suppliers, its immediate needs forced it to seek much larger amounts of military equipment from abroad to carry out the planned expansion and modernization of the armed forces. Hitherto India had acquired its military equipment from abroad on basically commercial terms, though it, like other Commonwealth countries, sometimes received discounts on arms purchased in Britain. Nehru had poured scorn on Asian governments that accepted military aid from the West. Now India needed large quantities of modern weapons and lacked the money to pay for them. In the circumstances, Nehru had no choice but to continue to seek military aid from the West on a grant basis.[23]

The general hardening of Indian attitudes toward China led to the abandonment of any thought of a diplomatic settlement of the dispute. It also caused India to take a vigorous anti-Chinese stand in many Afro-Asian and world forums, although New Delhi continued to support (though not actively to urge) Communist China's membership in the United Nations. But at the same time that Indian political policy became actively anti-Chinese, its military policy along the frontier became very cautious. India was slow to send its main forces much beyond the foothills of the Himalayas, and careful not to resume anything that Peking would interpret as a military challenge.

Even with so many of his cherished beliefs shattered and his past policies under bitter attack, Nehru clung tenaciously to the policy of nonalignment. This was not just the simple decision to remain unallied with any outside power. Actually, no one was seeking to draw India into a formal alliance. The Western governments were not actively seeking new members for SEATO or CENTO, nor were they eager to assume any obligations for India's security through formal bilateral ties. The United States and Britain did hope that closer if informal military cooperation would develop, but, aside from a joint U.S.-U.K.-Indian air exercise in July 1963, this hope was not realized. Some of the reasons for adherence to nonalignment involved domestic Indian politics and national prestige, but these were not the only considerations. Nehru's insistence on keeping a certain distance from the Western powers once the fighting stopped in November 1962 probably also represented a shrewd assessment on his part that certain interests of India still diverged from those of the United States and the United Kingdom and that Indian and Western policies would once again come into conflict.

In this he was more foresighted than many of his critics, for the Harriman and Sandys missions, which arrived on November 22 and 23 to assess India's military needs and capabilities, both urged Nehru to agree to open negotiations with Pakistan on the Kashmir dispute. A settlement of that dispute was more important than ever to the British and American governments in view of the seemingly more serious Chinese military threat to the subcontinent. Nehru apparently felt it unwise to refuse to negotiate with Pakistan in view of India's dependence on the West, and so agreed. Yet within a few days he made it clear to the members of Parliament, all of whom were angry about Pakistan's unsympathetic reaction to India's defeat and some of whom were fearful that the West was insisting on a Kashmir settlement as the price of arms, that India would not make any significant concessions to Pakistan.

Once the Kashmir issue came into public focus again, the advantages of preserving good relations with the U.S.S.R. became apparent to more Indians. Although Moscow's equivocal position during India's moment of crisis was not forgotten, Indians became more aware of the difficult choices facing Soviet leaders at the time. Thus much of the clamor for abandoning nonalignment subsided.

The Soviet decision to continue its support for India—made after a policy reappraisal early in 1963—could not have been easy. Leftist elements were losing strength in the Indian government; India's ties with the United States were expanding; and India was locked in what promised to be a long and bitter quarrel with a major Communist country. But the alternative to increased Soviet support was greater Indian reliance on the West, and so Moscow lowered its ideological sights in order to maintain its position in India. With the revival of Soviet military aid, which both Moscow and New Delhi claimed had been delayed rather than halted during the fighting, Indian foreign policy could once again be called nonaligned—though it could also be described as double alignment.

9

The Second Kashmir Conflict

Western arms aid and the Indian defense buildup following the Sino-Indian war foreshadowed for Pakistan a seriously adverse shift in the balance of power. Seeking ways to offset India's growing strength, Ayub and his colleagues gradually changed the orientation of their foreign policy. Pakistan remained formally (if unenthusiastically) aligned with the West, just as India remained formally nonaligned, despite changes in the substance of the foreign policies of both countries. During these years Pakistan took the initiative in altering the power relationships affecting South Asia, and its moves culminated in the second Indo-Pakistani war in 1965.

Pakistan's Search for a New Policy

Pakistan's reaction to India's defeat by China was a complex mixture of pleasure, fear, and frustration. "The first reactions to Indian reverses in Pakistan were both sweet and sour. The sweet part, and it was savored, was the enjoyment one gets from seeing a neighborhood bully meeting a bigger bully. The sour part was in knowing that there was an even bigger bully in the neighborhood."[1]

During the Sino-Indian conflict, the United States and Britain had urged the Pakistani government to invest heavily in Indo-Pakistani reconciliation by assuring New Delhi that it would not take advantage of India's troubles. Specifically, on October 28 President Kennedy wrote to President Ayub, suggesting that he assure Nehru that Pakistani troops would do nothing to harm India. This would enable India to shift troops from the Pakistani to the Chinese frontier to strengthen its defenses. Kennedy added that as he was familiar with the history of the Kashmir dispute he did not make his suggestion lightly. But India, he believed, was coming to recognize the threat from the north as more dangerous than regional quarrels in the subcontinent. In the circumstances, a generous Pakistani move could open the way for reconciliation.[2]

Pakistani leaders did not believe beneficial results would follow if they gave such assurances. They saw India rather than China as the major threat to Pakistan's security. Furthermore, they felt that India's lack of response to their efforts at rapprochement in 1959 and 1960 showed its lack of interest in any genuine compromise. It seemed far more likely to them that India would simply accept any assurances it received as its due and continue its past policies toward Pakistan. Therefore in his long reply to Kennedy on November 5, Ayub refused to give the assurances requested; but neither did Pakistan alter its troop dispositions to make life more arduous for India.[3]

Although the position of the government was proper, if not helpful, the Pakistani public made no secret of its delight in seeing India humiliated. At last, someone was able to cut India down to size. Comments in the press gloating over India's defeat touched sensitive nerves and remained embedded in Indian minds. Once the conflict was over and the Chinese had pulled back, Pakistan's delight gave way to frustration and anger over its inability to take advantage of India's troubles to gain its demands, especially on Kashmir. Their provision of military aid made Britain and the United States special targets of Pakistani anger. This created a crisis for Pakistan's foreign policy of alliance with the West; and since Ayub had been a principal architect of that policy, the crisis was personal as well as political.

Ayub felt aggrieved on several counts. Worry when the United States had begun to dilute its opposition to neutralism in the late 1950s sharpened when the Kennedy administration took office. For reasons set forth in the preceding chapter, Pakistani apprehensions had been held in check by careful U.S. steps to balance policies toward India and Pakistan. But the Anglo-American decision to provide military aid to India was another matter. Divergent interests and policies could be accepted, but not policies that clashed as directly and openly as this. Logically, arms aid to India should not have created such an uproar in Pakistan in view of the limited scope of the program and the huge amounts of economic aid flowing from the West to India. Pakistanis had often argued that economic aid enabled India to divert resources to defense, and was therefore essentially not different from military assistance.

The United States seriously tried to take these objections into account when it decided to provide arms to India; and the Harriman and Sandys missions sent to New Delhi in November 1962 to assess Indian needs did persuade Nehru to reopen negotiations on the Kashmir issue. But to convince Pakistan that its status as an ally provided it with many benefits that India did not receive was extremely difficult. American officials argued that Pakistan was receiving sophisticated equipment, such as tanks and jet aircraft, which was not being sent to India. Pakistani officials brushed aside the distinctions, saying they were too subtle for their populace. Reminders that Pakistan was receiving more economic assistance than India on a per capita basis were similarly brushed aside.

Ayub's objections to American arms for India were magnified by three attendant circumstances or considerations. He was angered by Washington's failure to consult with him, as promised, before providing arms to India. This still rankled several years later when Ayub underscored that "the United States government had ignored two very important points, that their decision to give arms aid to India was arrived at *without prior consultation* with Pakistan; and it was communicated to India *before* it was communicated to Pakistan."[4] The United States had simply informed Pakistan of its intention to grant military aid to India, which was not consultation at all, however understandable it may have been given the urgency of the circumstances. (However, Ayub made himself unavailable to the U.S. ambassador at a crucial interval by going on a hunting trip, which suggests that he was not eager for—or saw no hope in—serious discussions.) The United States felt that by informing Ayub of its plans and allowing him to register his objections before a public decision was announced, it had fulfilled its part of the bargain. Consultation to Ayub meant allowing him a near-veto power over any proposed move; consultation to the United States meant quite a different thing.

Apart from the issue of consultation, and much more important in the long run, were the quite different American and Pakistani assessments of the Chinese threat to South Asia. Ayub felt that the United States misread the extent of the Chinese military threat to the subcontinent (if it did not deliberately exaggerate it in order to draw India into its efforts to contain China). The Chinese pullback in the northeast confirmed him in his view that the Chinese aims had been limited to what was essentially a border problem.[5]

Third, Ayub was suspicious of certain American activities in Pakistan. Periodically he was annoyed by U.S. attempts to influence his government to do more for East Pakistan. Ayub also suspected, although not as strongly as some of his colleagues, that the United States was in touch with, if not encouraging, the political opposition throughout Pakistan.[6]

Underlying these considerations were highly emotional feelings in each country concerning the behavior of the other. Pakistanis felt betrayed by their Western allies, and the press and public did not disguise their outrage. The United States had officially proclaimed many times that it considered Pakistan an ally against the Communist nations, not against India, but this qualification had been disregarded by the Pakistanis. Policy is not merely what governments proclaim officially at the top level. Close ties between many U.S. and Pakistani officials had inflated their expectations of what the alliance would yield, and made the awakening all the more bitter. At the same time, the United States was also irritated by what seemed to be a Pakistani inability or unwillingness to take a broad view of the issues. Had not Pakistan signed up as a member of an anti-Communist alliance? Now it was objecting to measures to oppose the extension of Communist power in the area. Even if some of its arguments had merit, Pakistan's irate contentions that anything done for India in a time of peril was a Western betrayal of the alliance created more irritation than sympathy.

As the military balance on the subcontinent was shifting in India's favor, Pakistan concluded that a measure of its security had been lost in that the United States was less likely to restrain India or to deter it once there was a stake in its defense build-up. Just as India had maintained earlier that the United States could not control the use of arms given to Pakistan, so Pakistan was now using the same argument. Pakistan held that arms for defense against China could be used against itself, even though the United States provided arms chiefly for mountain operations rather than tanks or aircraft. This was no reassurance, however, for Pakistani and Indian troops faced each other in the mountains of Kashmir. As Ayub wrote, "It should also be noted that any army meant for China would by the nature of things be so positioned as to be able to wheel round swiftly and attack East Pakistan."[7]

Pakistanis may also have feared that the United States now intended to make India its chosen instrument in South Asia, consequently providing few if any arms to Pakistan rather than trying to become the principal arms supplier to both. Pakistanis probably also assumed that India was likely to receive more arms than the United States either intended to give or actually did give.

The decision of President Kennedy and Prime Minister Macmillan in December 1962 on a second installment of $120 million worth of arms for India, the joint U.S.-U.K.-Indian air defense exercise in 1963, and the long-term agreement to supply arms when Defense Minister Chavan visited the United States in April 1964 confirmed Pakistani leaders in their earlier fears regarding a major shift in American policy and the decline in Pakistan's influence on the United States. In response, Pakistan's policy now moved along several lines. It began to explore the possibility of forging links to China, to court Afro-Asian states, and to put additional pressure on India to come to a settlement. But it is important to recognize two things that Pakistan might have done but did not do: Pakistan did not try to match the Indian defense buildup nor did it seriously try to diversify its military procurement program. Pakistan's armed forces were stable at roughly 225,000 men between 1960 and 1965, and its defense outlay rose by only 30 per cent; Indian forces increased from 535,000 to 869,000 men and defense spending roughly tripled in this period.

Nor did Pakistan immediately try to cultivate the U.S.S.R.; to make headway with the Soviets and Chinese simultaneously seemed improbable. Peking looked like the best bet, for the Soviets appeared too closely tied to India. There were also the special U.S. facilities in West Pakistan, directed against the U.S.S.R., which circumscribed Ayub's maneuverability with Moscow. Ayub may still have been concerned over Soviet designs in Afghanistan. Thus it was not until April 1965, after the fall of Khrushchev, that Ayub made an official visit to the U.S.S.R. and relations began to improve.[8]

Ayub's efforts to improve relations with China and to put pressure on India were to be undertaken without cutting Pakistan's ties to the United States, as distinct from playing a less active or even a perfunctory role in SEATO and CENTO. Pakistan was still dependent on the United States for surplus agricultural products, for economic aid, and for arms. Moreover, European economic assistance was largely predicated on a high level of American assistance. Consequently, when Ayub made his secret speech on Pakistan's foreign policy before the National Assembly in December 1962, he took a cautious line. While admitting that changes would be explored and probably would be necessary, he cautioned his listeners that their country had few friends in the world and could not lightly disregard those it had. Accordingly, he moved step by step as events evolved and as it became absolutely clear that U.S. assistance to India was a long-term proposition.[9]

Sino-Pakistani Relations

The prospects for establishing a beneficial relationship with China while maintaining useful ties with the United States could hardly have seemed promising to Pakistan in view of U.S.-Chinese hostility. Fortunately for Pakistan, its relations with China, while never extensive or close, had not deteriorated much when Pakistan became an ally of the United States. Pakistan's actions in the years just after it entered the alliance, such as voting to uphold the moratorium on Chinese membership in the United Nations, were taken calmly by Peking. According to Chou En-lai, Pakistani Prime Minister Mohammad Ali at the Bandung Conference "told me that although Pakistan was a party to a military treaty, Pakistan was not against China. Pakistan had no fear China would commit aggression against her. As a result of that, we achieved a mutual understanding although we are still against military treaties."[10] Chou added that Peking was still interested in friendly relations.

Upon exchanging state visits in 1956, Prime Minister Suhrawardy and Chou En-lai stressed that, despite different political systems and divergent views on many problems, they had no real conflict of interest and wanted to strengthen the ties of friendship. Pakistan's occasional words of warmth toward China created little concern in the West. U.S. officials probably thought they were largely said for domestic political considerations and that nothing important would develop from them.

Thus when the United States and India began to move closer

together after the fall of 1962, there was no residue of hostility in Sino-Pakistani relations. In the years of friendly relations with New Delhi, Peking had never endorsed the Indian position that Kashmir was a part of India, and even Ayub's call for joint defense of the subcontinent in 1959 after the Sino-Indian border dispute became public occasioned only brief criticism by Peking.

China saw its opportunity to take advantage of the Indo-Pakistani quarrel, for making a friend of the enemy of your enemy is almost an automatic response in such a situation. Friendly relationships with India's neighbors were one way of isolating India as much as possible, as well as a useful demonstration that China was a reasonable and friendly nation. It would demonstrate to the Soviet leaders that a strategy of using India to counter China had drawbacks. In addition, it was a relatively cheap policy for China, for it did not demand that China take over the burden of supplying Pakistan's external needs. China was willing to broaden relations without demanding that Pakistan cut its ties with the United States. Perhaps Peking thought that either ally would become so annoyed with the actions of the other that a break would result in any case.

But old problems had to be settled before new links could be formed. Chinese and Pakistani maps showed both countries claiming the same small areas along the frontier between Pakistani-controlled Kashmir and the Chinese province of Sinkiang. Negotiations had been underway since May 1962, and on December 26, a Sino-Pakistani communiqué announced that complete agreement in principle had been reached on the border alignment. Details were ironed out in February 1963 and an agreement signed on March 2.

These moves infuriated India, which claimed that since all of Kashmir was legally Indian, Pakistan had no boundary with China. New Delhi also charged that Pakistan had surrendered some 2,500 square miles of Kashmiri territory to China. Pakistan answered the first charge by pointing out that the agreement was provisional until there was a final settlement of the Kashmir dispute. Pakistan also maintained that it surrendered no territory it actually held, but gained 750 square miles of territory previously under Chinese control.

The U.S. government, still hoping that India and Pakistan would see their major interest as reaching an accommodation, was dismayed that Pakistan should announce the agreement in the midst of negotiations with India. But when the actual alignment specified was examined, Pakistan had clearly bargained well.

During the next two years there was a proliferation of Sino-Pakistani contacts and activities.[11] An air agreement was negotiated whereby Pakistan International Airways could fly into China, and the Chinese airline into Pakistan. Frequent visits between high Chinese and Pakistani officials were supplemented by numerous visits of lower officials, cultural organizations, trade missions, and other bodies. In 1964 Peking extended a $60 million credit to Pakistan for the purchase of Chinese goods. And the Pakistan press began to exult in Pakistan's new-found friend, with praise for things Chinese on a level similar to that which had characterized the heyday of Sino-Indian friendship. Pakistani leaders probably were apprehensive late in 1964 when Peking attempted—after Khrushchev's downfall—to reopen border talks with India, but New Delhi's dismissal of the offer eased Pakistani concerns.

India's real apprehension, however, was not about cultural missions or air agreements. New Delhi feared that Pakistan and China had formed a secret military alliance, a fear that Pakistani officials—especially Foreign Minister Bhutto—cultivated, both for domestic political reasons and to increase India's apprehension and caution. Speaking in the Pakistan Assembly on July 17, 1963, Bhutto said, "Any attack by India on Pakistan would no longer confine the stakes to the independence and territorial integrity of Pakistan. An attack by India on Pakistan would also involve the security and territorial integrity of the largest state in Asia."[12]

It seems unlikely that Pakistan, still uncertain about Chinese motivations and reliability and moving cautiously lest it alienate the United States, had gone beyond a general understanding with China to keep in close touch regarding South Asian developments. But in Indian eyes the vastly different nature of the Pakistani and Chinese governments—one a radical Communist regime and the other a conservative Muslim one—appeared less important than bitter hostility of both toward India. Thus India became more convinced than ever that it needed military forces capable of holding off Pakistan and China simultaneously.

Pakistan Rejoins the Afro-Asian World

Pakistan had felt it necessary to accept an unpopular status among the Afro-Asian neutralist nations in order to win U.S. assistance in the 1950s, but this necessity was much resented. Once Ayub had consolidated his political position, he began systematically to broaden Pakistan's international ties. He traveled to Burma, Indonesia, and Japan in December 1960, and initiated contacts with other Afro-Asian leaders. Pakistan's major opportunity came in 1962, upon noting that most of the radical Afro-Asian nations did not rally to India's support in its struggle with China and that its military set-backs severely damaged Indian prestige. Efforts to develop ties with these countries seemed worthwhile. Difficult as the policy would be in view of Pakistan's continued membership in SEATO and CENTO, the substantive changes in policy and the growing ties with China gave Pakistani leaders some hope. Cultivation of the Afro-Asian countries offered several advantages. It would provide domestic popularity for a government that was uncertain of its support at home; it might be useful in winning support when the Kashmir issue came up in the United Nations; and it could gain prestige and influence for Pakistan in world affairs.

Pakistan and Indonesia moved closer together out of shared dislike of India, despite many differences and the contrasting styles of Ayub and Sukarno. Ayub and Foreign Minister Bhutto, a fiery advocate of closer ties with China and the Afro-Asian world, exchanged visits with the leaders of many Afro-Asian countries and gradually closer rela-tions developed. Pakistan urged that the next conference on Asia be of the Bandung type, including all Asians, rather than a conference of the nonaligned as had taken place in Belgrade in 1961. Symbolic of the shifting emphasis of Pakistan's foreign policy was Bhutto's bypassing the annual SEATO meeting in Manila in April 1964, to attend the Preparatory Ministerial Meeting of the Second Afro-Asian Conference in Jakarta. Special attention was paid to expand-ing relations with India's neighbors. A boundary agreement was reached with Burma, and Ayub visited Ceylon and Nepal in 1963. Nepal, he found, was willing to extend its links with Pakistan in order to lessen its dependence on India. Pakistan also induced Turkey and Iran to join with it in setting up an organization called Regional Cooperation for Development (RCD). Although the RCD, lacking access to outside funds, marshalled only limited strength, it did enable the three nations to cooperate outside the CENTO frame-work.

Despite its failure in some of these efforts—for example, the U.A.R. remained much closer to India than to Pakistan—Pakistan managed to win the acceptance of some radical Afro-Asian states while maintaining its ties with the pro-Western Asian states. Friendship with China, and Chinese praise of Pakistan's "unremitting struggles" against foreign pressure were distinct assets for a nation seeking status in the Afro-Asian world.

"Leaning on India"

India emerged from the war with China a scarred nation. Military equipment could be replaced; most of the territory lost in battle was recovered when the Chinese retreated; and the willingness of the West and the U.S.S.R. to provide aid of all types allowed India to hold fast to its policy of nonalignment. Yet the country's image of itself and its institutions, political as well as military, was shaken and its self-confidence undermined. Humiliation turned to frustration as it became clear that India would be unable to regain the rest of the disputed territory despite its ambitious and expensive defense buildup.

But this was not the extent of India's troubles. The country's economic momentum began to falter, and its government appeared to be buffeted by events rather than dominating them. Agricultural production stagnated and then declined, the rate of industrial growth fell, inflation became serious, debt-repayment obligations steadily mounted, and the balance of payments continued to deteriorate despite large sums of aid. The malaise and chronic factionalism of the Congress party became worse as Nehru's health failed, and the politicians were busy maneuvering for position in the impending succession.

Perhaps most serious of all, because it was so difficult to control, was the ominous growth of communal violence. Once the subcontinent had settled down after partition, communal violence between Hindus and Muslims had been infrequent and generally on a small scale. Beginning in the early 1960s, the scale and frequency of Hindu-Muslim clashes increased. It is still not wholly clear why communal relations became more brittle at this time, although the expulsion of Muslims from Assam by India, which claimed that many of them were Pakistani citizens who had entered India illegally, played a part.

At the same time, political and therefore communal tensions inside Kashmir were growing. India had ruled the state with an iron hand through Bakshi Ghulam Mohammed since the imprisonment of Sheikh Abdullah in 1953. Elections had been held but were rigidly controlled and much resented by many Kashmiris. The Bakshi regime was both oppressive and corrupt, and the fact that it was imposed on the Muslim population by New Delhi offset Kashmiri appreciation for the Indian-sponsored social reforms and economic development.

Late in 1963 New Delhi, concerned over the growing resentment at the Bakshi regime, forced it out of office. In this atmosphere the theft of a sacred Muslim relic in Srinigar late in 1963 set off widespread riots throughout the Vale of Kashmir.[13] Indian police and troops put down the riots firmly, but the outbursts convinced an already worried Indian government that there was a limit to how much even the meek Kashmiris would accept.

Although he had suffered a stroke just as the riots occurred and his health was failing, Nehru moved quickly to try to get the situation under control. He brought Lal Bahadur Shastri back into the government as Minister Without Portfolio and, in effect, deputy prime minister, giving him the assignment of working out a Kashmiri settlement, which, according to some reports, was to involve internal autonomy for Kashmir as well as a link with Pakistan.[14] A new regime was installed in the state headed by G. M. Sadiq, and a better deal promised the Kashmiris. Sheikh Abdullah was released from prison in hopes that the still immensely popular leader would help to negotiate a way out of the impasse, and Abdullah visited Ayub shortly after his initial talks with Nehru.

While the riots in Kashmir stimulated Indian action, they also sparked new communal outbreaks elsewhere, which limited New Delhi's freedom of action in Kashmir. Muslim violence in East Pakistan, in reaction to the events in Kashmir and to the expulsion of Muslims from Assam, made refugees of thousands of East Pakistani Hindus. The stories of horror they told in turn stimulated Hindus in eastern India to attack local Muslims. Concerned and frightened, both governments worked (especially at the top levels) to halt the violence, but each accused the other of not taking firm enough action against the instigators of the outbursts.

This was the situation in May 1964 when Nehru died after seventeen years as India's leader. The smooth election of Prime Minister Shastri was perhaps the best tribute to Nehru's memory and his labors to implant democratic institutions in India. But the country Nehru had led was also troubled and in a difficult situation. Shastri spoke at once of the need for Indo-Pakistani reconciliation so that the two countries could address the many problems facing them.

Ayub, as noted above, had decided that friendship was less likely than pressure to induce India to compromise on Kashmir. He had also been encouraged by the restiveness in Kashmir, taking this as an indication that the Kashmiris were no longer willing to accept Indian rule meekly. He had therefore embarked on a policy of "leaning on India."

Part of Ayub's policy of "leaning on India" was using Pakistan's new ties with China and Afro-Asian states to pressure India. But its most direct and dangerous aspect was Pakistan's resumption of more aggressive patrolling along the cease-fire line in Kashmir. There had always been sporadic small-scale incidents between patrols, often the result of farmers crossing the line to retrieve animals straying across the line or gather fruit in orchards. The presence of the United Nations forces and the disinclination of either India or Pakistan to challenge the *status quo* by force had kept the trouble limited. After the Sino-Indian war, clashes occurred more often, involving more soldiers, because of the stepped-up Pakistani activity; India, in turn, pursued a more active policy.

Shastri's talk of reconciliation created a temporary change in this atmosphere. He emphasized the need for time to get on top of the situation in India before meaningful moves could be made toward Pakistan. Ayub, acknowledging the reasonableness of this position, reduced his pressure, and tension eased for several months. Ayub and Shastri met in Karachi in October 1964, and the lack of measurable progress did not dampen the hopes of those in favor of a reconciliation.

But Shastri was under pressure from right-wing Hindu elements, who were growing stronger and demanding Indian hegemony rather than reconciliation with Pakistan. He was also faced with various domestic troubles, and Indians generally remained resentful of Pakistan's growing friendship with China. The Indian government, apparently concluding that a tough line was the only way to deal with the Kashmiris, announced in December 1964 that the state would be more closely integrated into India. In January 1965 the ruling party in Kashmir, the National Conference, merged completely with the Congress party. These moves infuriated Pakistan. Indians in turn were roused by Ayub's visits to Peking in March and to Moscow in April. They also saw Pakistani machinations behind Sheikh Abdullah's meeting with Chou En-lai in Algiers in January, and rearrested Abdullah as soon as he returned to India in April.

Ayub resumed his policy of "leaning on India," and tensions

mounted. In the first five months of 1965, for example, the United Nations Military Observer Group for India and Pakistan (UNMOGIP) reported 2,231 complaints by India and Pakistan. UNMOGIP confirmed 377 violations during this period, 218 of which were committed by Pakistan and 159 by India.[15]

America's Dilemma

The trend of events in the subcontinent was making it increasingly difficult for the West to maintain satisfactory ties with India and Pakistan while countering Chinese and Soviet influence in South Asia. Some American and British officials believed that the arguments for military aid to India were not as strong as they had once thought. The Chinese military danger seemed to be declining; those who had hoped to draw India into a closer relation as a means of containing Chinese power in Asia saw less chance of this. (India had long been dubious about U.S. policies in Southeast Asia; and while it was worried about Chinese activities there, it was unwilling to cooperate with the United States on an anti-Communist policy that would bring dissension with the U.S.S.R.) Furthermore, the aim of limiting the Soviet role in the Indian military picture was not being satisfactorily realized. Western officials had hoped that Indian armed forces would retain their Western orientation, but increasing amounts of Soviet arms were flowing into India.

These concerns paralleled earlier doubts in some quarters about the validity of the reasons for the alliance with Pakistan. The United States concluded that there was little choice but to continue moderate arms aid to both countries, trying as best it could to balance its interests in South Asia despite the renewed hostility. Neither the officials favoring India nor those urging a higher priority for Pakistan were able to carry the day, each group being more successful in blocking the other's proposals than in advancing its own policies.

The American government became increasingly unhappy as Pakistan expanded its ties with China and began its policy of leaning on India. According to its assessment, Pakistan should have pursued exactly the opposite course, trying to settle its quarrels with India and keeping its distance from China. In Pakistan's view, of course, the United States should have made its military and even economic assistance to India conditional on India's willingness to agree to what Pakistan regarded as a fair settlement on Kashmir.

With these divergent views, neither Pakistan's interpretation of its interests nor the American interpretation was convincing to the other party. American arguments that the 1964 agreement to provide long-term arms assistance was made in part to keep India from importing large amounts of arms from the U.S.S.R., and that such aid also enabled the United States to influence India against spending even larger sums for defense, were of no avail in Pakistan. The ominous Indian defense buildup was being aided by the West, and arguments that halting aid would harm Pakistan in the long run seemed ludicrous as well as self-serving to Pakistanis.

Nor was either ally able, or willing, to exert adequate pressure to cause the other to change its course. The United States expressed its displeasure and hinted that it might curtail its assistance if Pakistan went "too far." But it was difficult to say just what "too far" was, although clearly a Pakistani-Chinese military alliance would have fallen under this heading. Occasionally the United States did hold back on a particular aid project long enough to create new irritations but not enough to change Pakistan's course. When the United States threatened a major aid reduction by holding off from making its annual commitment at the July 1965 meeting of the aid-Pakistan consortium, other Western donors were annoyed with the United States, which limited the impact of the American move.

Pakistan had certain assets in this contest. It had the U.S. special facilities in its country, and was aware of the American hesitancy to take any action that might cause Pakistan to demand the removal of these installations. Pakistan was still a member of the Western military alliance system, and while Washington was no longer enamored with these alliances, it thought their break-up would be worse than having them quietly continue. Moreover, Pakistan retained the friendship and goodwill of many in Congress, the press, the military, and the intelligence services. The personal rapport that had been established between Presidents Johnson and Ayub was another asset, although a diminishing one.

Thus an uneasy compromise developed, which was periodically upset by specific acts or words on the part of one country or the other. In particular, Foreign Minister Bhutto and the Pakistani press created considerable annoyance for some U.S. officials. President Ayub's visit to China early in 1965 and some of his remarks there were also viewed with concern in Washington, although Ayub was careful in the course he followed on the Vietnam issue. In April 1965 the United

States cancelled an invitation to President Ayub to visit Washington
—officially it only postponed the visit, but the effect was much the
same. Since the United States did not feel it could receive Shastri
after cancelling Ayub's invitation, Shastri's visit was postponed too,
which annoyed the Indians even more than the Pakistanis.

Indo-American understanding and cooperation were also encountering more difficulties. The period when the U.S. Congress could refuse
to honor the administration's tentative commitment to aid in building
the giant Bokaro steel plant and India could back away from its agreement to allow the Voice of America to build a transmitter in India
without basically undermining U.S.-Indian relations was drawing to a
close. Washington was getting out of touch with leaders of both
countries at a time when their mutual hostility had reached a kindling
point.

The Rann of Kutch Incident

Tensions turned to shooting with the clash that took place in the
Rann of Kutch. It started on a small scale on April 8, 1965, over a
disputed border claim that the two countries had been unable to
settle during the 1959 negotiations; soon several thousand troops were
involved in the largest battle since 1949. The clash put the United
States in a difficult position and cast growing doubts (especially in
Congress) on the wisdom of providing military aid to two hostile
neighbors.

Kutch, formerly a princely state, was part of Gujerat State by
1965. It is located on the Arabian Sea about 350 miles northwest of
Bombay and 250 miles southeast of Karachi. The northern part of this
territory, known as the Rann (or marsh) of Kutch, is largely desert
during the dry season; but during the monsoon it is flooded, except for
a few points of high ground. The Rann was practically uninhabited
and of little value, although patrols of the two countries occasionally
made their way across it.

Since 1947, India had claimed the entire marsh. It maintained
that Pakistani territory did not extend beyond the higher ground that
lay to the north, which was the boundary between Kutch and the
Province of Sind during British times. Pakistan had not accepted
India's interpretation, insisting that since it was a body of water part
of the year, the boundary ran along the middle of the Rann or approximately along the 24th parallel. Some 3,500 square miles of ter-

ritory were in dispute. Outside observers believed that India's claims were basically correct, although not airtight.

In 1965 both countries were moving their forces forward to make good on their border claims, and each naturally blamed the other for the initial clash. Ayub quickly recognized the inherent advantages Pakistan enjoyed in the situation, and a strong stand fitted in with his general policy of "leaning on India." Pakistani forces outmaneuvered and outfought Indian troops during the next several weeks in battles involving artillery and tanks as well as infantry. With the onset of the summer monsoon India's position would become untenable as its forces would have to retreat many miles to the south while the Pakistani forces need pull back only a short distance to the higher ground in the north.

As the full extent of Pakistan's advantage was brought home to Indian officials and the public, some people began to talk about hitting Pakistan elsewhere. To be defeated by China was one thing; to be outfought (even on a small scale) by Pakistan was something else, which many Indians were determined not to accept. There was fear in the West and throughout the subcontinent that the conflict would get out of hand and might lead to full-scale war between the two countries. "It was barely credible, in 1962," commented *The Economist*, "that two great countries should be at the brink of full-scale war, as China and India were, over an almost inaccessible stretch of barren and snow-bound track. It is no more credible today that India and Pakistan should fight over a piece of barren land that spends half its life under water; yet it has happened."[16]

Widespread Indian indignation left the Prime Minister with little room for maneuver. The few voices urging caution, such as *The Times of India* and *The Hindustan Times*, were for a time drowned out by more chauvinistic clamor. At the outset, Shastri had told Parliament that India would not "allow" Pakistan to retain the position it had won, and that if there were cease-fire talks India would insist on a Pakistani withdrawal as the first order of business. Pakistan, always sensitive to what it felt was India's bullying tendency, rejected talks under such conditions. It suggested both sides pull back from the disputed area. New Delhi would have no part of that proposal; it would be an admission that there was a border dispute, and India insisted that the location of the border was clear and no dispute existed. But the Indian army was careful not to send units into areas where they could have been cut off and destroyed, and the absence of any dramatic Indian defeats kept public opinion from demanding even more vigorous and dangerous measures.

The predictability of Peking's support for Pakistan's position did not temper an irate Indian reaction. Many Indians feared that concerted Chinese and Pakistani moves were likely, since the Rann of Kutch fighting followed so closely upon Ayub's visit to Peking and visits by Chou En-lai and Foreign Minister Chen Yi to Pakistan. Equally worrisome was Moscow's expressed hope that India and Pakistan would exercise restraint and settle the dispute in a manner safeguarding the interests of both sides. The Soviet position not only seemed to equate the two countries—something India always resented when done by the West—but raised doubts about India's ability to retain Soviet support on Kashmir.

The United States did not escape India's censure during this period. As soon as the fighting began, charges were made that the Pakistani forces were using American equipment, of which India soon claimed to have photographic evidence. Some Western observers who managed to get close to the fighting apparently agreed. Opposition leaders cited the U.S. assurances that Pakistan would not use the arms supplied by America against India, and now the United States apparently was unwilling even to reprimand Pakistan immediately and publicly, much less prevent or take positive steps to halt the Pakistani action.[17] The Indian government was caught in the middle; it obviously wanted the United States to reprimand or restrain Pakistan, but saw much danger and little value in its critics' suggestions that it denounce the United States as an enemy.

Indian anger over Pakistan's use of American arms and the U.S. unwillingness to restrain Pakistan came just after the postponement of Shastri's visit to Washington, and his domestic opponents argued that this showed how little stature and influence he had in the United States. The whole affair brought to the surface once again the underlying Indian annoyance at being equated with Pakistan.

Even though American inaction was damaging relations with India, Washington believed there were strong reasons for hesitation. First of all, it was far from clear who was to blame for the fighting. Second, Washington wanted clear evidence that the Pakistani forces were using U.S. equipment before taking a stand on the issue. More important, the United States wanted to avoid choosing between India and Pakistan in view of its extensive interests in each country. The administration was also running into more trouble with Congress. Many members were irritated that two recipients of U.S. military aid were now fighting each other, and so the administration postponed deliveries of key items to Pakistan. Finally, the administration did not want to disrupt the efforts then under way for cease-fire talks.

Shortly after the fighting began, Britain had called for a cease-fire with restoration of the positions occupied by the two countries on January 1, 1965. Initially both countries took tough public stands on the procedural as well as substantive issues in dispute. Intense negotiations went on between London, New Delhi, and Karachi, with Washington content to let Prime Minister Wilson play the leading role. As the weeks passed with no agreement, Indian troops were sent to the border in the Punjab, putting additional pressure on Pakistan to agree to a settlement. This complicated the negotiations, for Pakistan wanted these Indian troops pulled back as part of the agreement. It also wanted to link settlement of the Rann of Kutch dispute with a Kashmir settlement, something India adamantly opposed. It was not until May 11 that both countries agreed in principle to a cease-fire, although one had been operating *de facto* for a week or two before that. It took until June 30 before both countries agreed on the terms of a cease-fire: a mutual withdrawal of forces, direct negotiations to settle the dispute, and arbitration in the event direct negotiations were not fruitful.

As India had always refused to submit the Kashmir dispute to international arbitration, there was considerable surprise when Prime Minister Shastri agreed to arbitration for the Rann of Kutch. This was not without precedent, for in 1959 both countries had agreed to arbitrate certain minor issues if they could not settle them directly. The areas in dispute then involved only a few miles here and there. Now India had gone considerably further, and Pakistanis began to wonder if it might not be possible to get India to follow such a procedure on Kashmir.

The War

The outcome of the Rann of Kutch episode left Pakistan dangerously overconfident and India dangerously frustrated. Public pressures within India to take a stronger line with Pakistan were mounting, and a growing body of opinion felt it would be wrong to go to any great lengths to avoid a conflict. The Kashmir dispute had inevitably become an active issue during Ayub's campaign for re-election early in 1965, and he was under some pressure to react to India's moves to merge Kashmir more tightly into India. Convinced that his policy of "leaning on India" was working, Ayub made the fateful decision to play for larger stakes by sending Pakistani-trained guerrillas into Kashmir.

The move may have seemed desirable to Ayub and his colleagues on several grounds. Perhaps the guerrillas could trigger a large-scale uprising and greatly weaken if not completely undermine Indian control of Kashmir. If this happened, India might feel forced to negotiate a settlement. In any case, disruption in Kashmir would bring the issue to world attention and concern, whereas leaving it quiescent would make world acceptance of India's control more likely.

The time also seemed appropriate to execute such a strategy. Over the long term, India's defense buildup would leave Pakistan in a weaker position on the subcontinent, and few Pakistanis thought India would deal fairly from a position of strength. Indeed, as India's indigenous defense production capability grew and as it acquired the capacity to produce nuclear weapons, New Delhi would be even less susceptible to the influence of the world community. Moreover, Indian leadership looked weak and uncertain to the Pakistanis. Ayub had never been an admirer of Nehru, but he recognized him as a leader of stature; it is unlikely that he regarded the diminutive Shastri as a dangerous opponent. Ayub probably believed that if India did respond militarily, Pakistan could at least defend itself—and this too might bring outside powers into the dispute. Finally, Ayub probably calculated that Indian fear of China would deter it from a vigorous move against Pakistan.

Yet if such carefully calculated considerations were in Ayub's mind, Pakistan's actions were also materially affected by overconfidence on Ayub's part. He had a record of almost unbroken successes since 1951, when he became the first Pakistani commander-in-chief of the army. He had negotiated the arms agreement with the United States, which enabled him to build up the armed forces. After the politicians had demonstrated their failure to govern, he had taken power and given Pakistan its first effective government. Under his leadership the country launched its first successful economic development program. He had not, of course, been able to prevent the United States from giving military assistance to India after 1962, but he had adjusted to this reverse by establishing closer relations with China and by winning a new standing in the Afro-Asian world. This long record of achievements must have bred great self-confidence in Ayub. But success stimu-

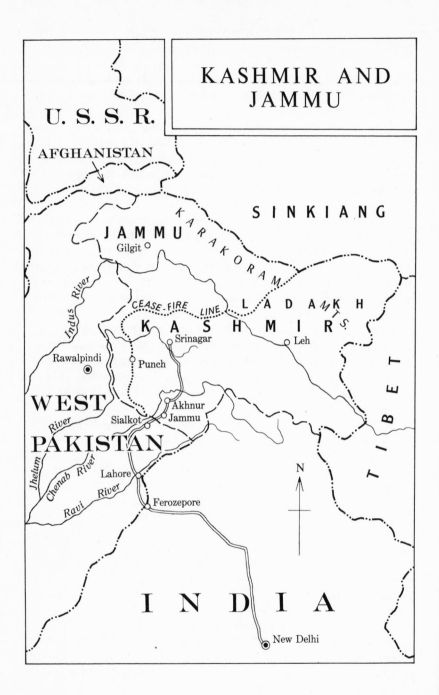

KASHMIR AND JAMMU

U.S.S.R.

AFGHANISTAN

SINKIANG

JAMMU

Gilgit

KARAKORAM

CEASE-FIRE LINE

LADAKH MTS.

KASHMIR

Srinagar

Leh

Indus River

Rawalpindi

Punch

WEST

River

Akhnur

Jammu

Sialkot

TIBET

PAKISTAN

Jhelum

Chenab River

Lahore

Ravi River

Ferozepore

N

INDIA

New Delhi

lates ambition, and for the first time in his career Ayub badly over-reached himself.

Several thousand Pakistani guerrillas were sent across the cease-fire line in Kashmir early in August. Many were picked up by Indian troops or police in the mountains, but others reached the Vale of Kashmir and even Srinigar. Some managed to blow up bridges and buildings, although the damage was not great. The guerrillas had little success in stirring up active opposition to Indian rule; traditional Kashmiri timidity and stern Indian measures against the infiltrators and their sympathizers—whether real or suspected—alike worked against the guerrillas.

Nonetheless, India was not content merely to round up the infiltrators after they entered Indian-controlled territory. New Delhi sent several thousand troops across the cease-fire line on August 25 to capture the Uri-Punch area, a bulge of about one hundred square miles that juts into Indian-held Kashmir, and the Haji Pir Pass to the west through which most of the infiltrators had come.

Indian seizure of these areas faced Ayub with an extremely difficult choice, for it was hardly possible to sustain a guerrilla campaign in Kashmir with the key passes in Indian hands. Pakistan had to back down or to raise the stakes. Raising the ante would risk a dangerous expansion of the fighting, for India had always insisted that if Pakistan tried to take Kashmir by force, India would attack across the Punjab plains. Backing down would be politically difficult for Ayub in the face of India's success in closing the passes and seizing Pakistani-held territory. It would in effect have acknowledged that India would control Kashmir for the foreseeable future. That course must have seemed even less appealing to the Pakistani government than raising the stakes.

On September 1 a Pakistani armored column crossed the cease-fire line in southern Kashmir. The column at first made good progress and drove back the Indian forces. Rather than limit the penetration to a tactical crossing to offset the Indian thrust to the north, however, the column continued to advance eastward until it took Akhnur and threatened the vital road over the mountains linking Srinigar with the plains of India. If Pakistan captured this road, Indian forces in Kashmir and in Ladakh would be cut off. Thus India was now left with the choice of yielding to Pakistan or expanding the war.

India's response was quick in coming. On September 5 its troops invaded West Pakistan on a wide front. The Indian government claimed that this attack was made only because they had information that Pakistan was about to attack India—a claim which hardly anyone believed. The major Indian thrust by several divisions was directed toward Lahore, only twenty miles from the border. A second thrust was launched from the Jammu area toward Sialkot, and a third attack originated from the area of Ferozpore. The air forces of both countries attacked along and behind the combat zone. Cities were blacked out at night, although they were largely spared from attack. Naval forces also were involved in a rather haphazard way, and many of the merchant ships of each country quickly put into friendly ports.

The two armies were the key to the unfolding drama, however, and in contrast to its previous record the Indian army gave a fair account of itself. Its larger forces were effectively utilized to wear down the Pakistani army. Despite more modern armor and greater mobility, the Pakistani forces were unable to break through the Indian lines and advance on India's cities as they had confidently assumed.[18] In fact, in a number of encounters the Pakistani armored units were outmaneuvered and outfought. This was a stunning reversal of the situation in the Rann of Kutch, and it shook the confidence of the Pakistani military in themselves and their leaders. It was also a surprise to most Western observers, who had rated the army's capabilities highly. After the initial Indian advances the battlelines remained relatively stationary, with neither side able to make much headway against the other.

The atmosphere in both countries was an intense and explosive mixture of self-righteousness and hatred. Indians were outraged that Pakistan had resorted to force to contest Indian control of Kashmir; Pakistanis were indignant that India thought the Pakistani guerrillas in Kashmir gave India a right to attack across an international border. Despite the emotional frenzy, the Muslim minority in India and the Hindu minority in Pakistan were well protected—something few observers would have predicted in such a situation.

Both directed their bitterness at the United States and the United Kingdom as well as at each other. Having argued that arms for its neighbor would someday be used against itself each now felt that its judgment had proven right and that the United States was wrong in thinking it could prevent a recipient from using the arms aggressively. Pakistanis were furious that the United States not only refused to support an ally after the Indian attack, but cut off all arms shipments to the subcontinent as well. This move obviously hurt Pakistan, almost entirely dependent upon U.S. arms, much more than

India, which received its arms from many sources. India, recognizing its advantages from the embargo, nevertheless berated the U.S. failure to condemn Pakistan for having started the affair, and thought Pakistan's status as an ally merited no consideration in view of its initiation of the fighting and its close relations with China.

The outbreak of war signaled an important failure of U.S. policy in the subcontinent. Even those U.S. officials to whom the goal of Indo-Pakistan reconciliation had seemed too ambitious to be realistic had predicated aid to each country on the belief that the two would not go to war. Some diversion of effort and resources had been accepted as inevitable because of the mutual antagonism, but their willingness to fight raised fundamental questions about the seriousness of their interest in development and defense of the subcontinent, and about the U.S. interest and ability to help them. In telling the Senate Appropriations Committee on September 8 that the United States had suspended military aid to both, Secretary Rusk said no new commitments of economic assistance were being made, and only those shipments already underway under past agreements were allowed to go forward:

> Now this will not be well received either in Pakistan or in India but we cannot be in a position of financing a war of these countries against each other. Nor can we be in a position of using aid under circumstances where the purpose of the aid is frustrated by the fighting itself. . . .
>
> Our problem has been, and obviously we have not succeeded, to pursue policies with Pakistan and India related to matters outside of the subcontinent and at the same time try not to contribute to the clash between the two within the subcontinent. This is still the shape of the present problem.[19]

Such basic issues could hardly be resolved until the implications of the war became clear, and these would depend on its scope and duration. Thus the immediate task for the United States and the United Kingdom, and for the world community generally, was to try to limit the war to the areas involved and to bring about a cease-fire as soon as possible.[20] Yet the anger of both countries at the United States limited its ability to exercise much influence. In contrast to the Rann of Kutch episode, the United Kingdom was unable to exercise much influence either, for Prime Minister Wilson's criticism of India for extending the war beyond Kashmir infuriated New Delhi. The aroused emotions in both countries also made the initial attempts of the United Nations to obtain a cease-fire unsuccessful. On his trip to the subcontinent early in September, Secretary-General U Thant found their positions inflexible.

Once the fighting began, the likely behavior of China posed a particular worry, for which Peking soon gave ample reason. A Chinese statement on September 7 pledged full support for Pakistan and condemned India for "criminal aggression," stating that it probably believed it could bully its neighbors because it had U.S. and Soviet support. China also sent notes to New Delhi on August 27 and September 8, charging India with border violations. On September 17 Peking issued another statement which accused India of many offenses, including intruding into Chinese territory from Sikkim and erecting fortifications on Chinese territory; it demanded that India pull back within three days or face "grave consequences." This ultimatum raised fears throughout the world that another Chinese military intervention was about to take place. Rumors of Chinese troop movements were common.

Both the United States and the U.S.S.R. publicly warned against any Chinese intervention, and these warnings probably were supplemented by private messages. Peking reacted furiously to the U.S. and Soviet moves. It accused the two countries of adding fuel to the flames and of collusion in their support of India and opposition to China, an obvious effort in Peking's general campaign to depict Moscow as a revisionist power hand-in-glove with Washington.

The Chinese stand placed the U.S.S.R. in a delicate position. If China attacked India in force and the West came to India's aid, Moscow would have had to do the same or see the position it had worked so hard to establish in India vanish. Moscow's position was also complicated by its desire to expand its ties with Pakistan, both to take advantage of Pakistan's alienation from the United States and to limit Chinese influence in the country. On August 24 *Pravda* had published a commentary which, after brushing aside the question of whether Indian or Pakistani versions of the situation were correct, made clear that Moscow did not intend to let its ties with India prevent it from expanding its relations with Pakistan:

Strengthening the ties between the U.S.S.R. and Pakistan must be regarded as a part of a general policy aimed at ensuring peace in Asia and throughout the world. We would like Soviet-Pakistani relations, like our traditional friendship with India, to be a stabilizing factor in the situation in Asia and to contribute to the normalization of relations between Pakistan and India.[21]

The only course that held any promise for Moscow was to work for a halt to the fighting. The Soviet government issued several calls for a cease-fire, and supported U.N. efforts to bring one about. Soviet concern grew as the fighting intensified, and on September 7 Moscow issued a statement calling on both sides to halt military operations and effect a mutual withdrawal at once; it even offered its good offices to help bring this about.[22] Thus the world was treated to the unusual spectacle of a Communist nation working to ameliorate rather than exacerbate a conflict between two bourgeois nations.

India responded to the Chinese ultimatum skillfully despite the tensions and fears prevailing in New Delhi that a wider conflict might be in store. (The presence of Foreign Minister Chen Yi in Pakistan early in September, following upon his visit just before the Rann of Kutch episode, heightened Indian concern about Sino-Pakistani collaboration.) The Indian government's reply was neither belligerent nor apologetic. Shastri denied most of the Chinese accusations and promised to investigate the remainder. He also hinted at a willingness to make certain minor concessions but made clear that India had no intention of bowing before Chinese pressure.

There was a widespread suspicion that Pakistan and China were coordinating their moves, possibly even planning concerted military action. Pakistan clearly wanted to capitalize on New Delhi's fear of a war on two fronts, and Chinese propaganda reinforced the impression of Sino-Pakistani collusion. While China's hostility toward India (and perhaps its private words to Pakistani leaders) may have contributed to Pakistan's decision to strike at India, the course of events suggests that China undertook only to make threats and move troops in order to tie down Indian forces along the Chinese border.

The first indication that Peking was hesitant about taking serious risks came on September 19, when China extended its ultimatum for another three days. Pakistan's poor military performance, India's careful response, and Soviet and American warnings probably all influenced China's decision. The general caution shown by Peking, unless its security interests were directly involved, no doubt was also a factor.

It also seems likely that Pakistan was dubious about military action by China and urged Peking to limit its involvement to threats and troop movements. Minor border harassments would have been of limited help to Pakistan, and a Chinese attack on the scale of the 1962 conflict would have been a desperate gamble for Pakistan. Ayub was aware that Pakistan was already in deep trouble as a result of his actions. While a Chinese attack would have greatly improved Pakistan's short-run military position if the United States and the U.S.S.R. had limited themselves to diplomatic protests, Ayub may have found it hard to believe that Washington and Moscow would stop there. He probably feared that both the United States and the U.S.S.R. would become strongly hostile to Pakistan and that his country would find itself without either major power as a supporter, hardly an appealing prospect.

In any case, potential Chinese involvement spurred both the Soviets and the West to new efforts in the Security Council to bring about a cease-fire. But during the early weeks of the conflict, as mentioned, neither country was inclined to pay much heed to unanimous Security Council calls for a cease-fire. Pakistan resisted any resolution that did not also provide for negotiations on Kashmir.

As the fighting continued, however, first India and then Pakistan became more amenable to a cease-fire. Pakistan was unsuccessful in obtaining either British or U.S. support for moves outside the Security Council. Moreover, its military position was becoming steadily weaker; its forces were unable to break through the Indian lines, and supplies were dwindling. The United States had never provided Pakistan with enough military supplies for an extended conflict, and shortages were beginning to affect operations.

Indians likewise began to see more reason for a cease-fire. If they continued to wear down Pakistan and take additional Pakistani territory with its Muslim population they would create serious complications for themselves. Yet to give back territory won at the cost of Indian blood would be politically difficult. India's leaders were also feeling international pressure to show some flexibility on Kashmir, and could not be confident that China would allow Pakistan to go down to complete defeat.

Despite the growing receptivity toward U.N. efforts to arrange a cease-fire the process of working one out was not easy. But the United States, Britain and the Soviet Union all insisted that stopping the fighting was the first order of business and cooperated in working out acceptable terms. By mid-September the Security Council succeeded in drawing up a resolution that was clear on the call for a cease-fire but vague enough on what was to follow so that India and Pakistan could each interpret it to suit themselves. India accepted on September 20 and Pakistan two days later. The fighting was over, but the work of the peacemakers had only begun.

10

Tashkent and After

The war was over, but the two armies still faced each other, occupying some territory belonging to the other country. Emotions remained at fever pitch, and there was an urgent need for military disengagement and for passions to subside.

The next step would not be easy, however, for the two nations interpreted the implications of the war and of the Security Council resolution quite differently. Most Indians were satisfied with their country's performance. They believed they had won the war, dealt firmly with Peking's threats, and protected the Muslim minority within India. Both secular and Hindu nationalists viewed the performance with pride, and it temporarily restored the loss of self-confidence suffered at the hands of the Chinese in 1962. New Delhi, convinced that its position was strong and its cause just, was in no mood to be flexible or accommodating.

The Pakistani public also appeared convinced they had done well in the war. Although it had not gained control of Kashmir or won any striking victories in the Punjab fighting, the army had valiantly held off the larger Indian forces. Many Pakistanis saw the acceptance of a cease-fire resolution as an opportunity to accomplish by diplomacy and negotiation what arms had failed to gain. The government's propaganda claims were largely responsible for this distorted picture, although a tendency to ignore unpalatable facts contributed to the public illusions.

Thus the next step after the cease-fire was beyond the capacity of the two countries acting alone, for in the prevailing tense atmosphere they could not themselves initiate the unpalatable compromises that were necessary. This step was also far more difficult for the Security Council. Neither the United States nor the United Kingdom was in a position to influence both India and Pakistan at this juncture; but an opening was there if the Soviet Union wanted to seize it.

The Tashkent Meeting

The groundwork had already been prepared for a Soviet initiative. On September 4 Premier Kosygin, in a move unprecedented for the Soviet Union, offered its good offices to help negotiate a settlement. Moscow renewed its offer on September 19 after the Chinese ultimatum and again publicized it to indicate the seriousness of its intentions. Both governments accepted the Soviet offer in principle, but neither was eager for an early meeting. As the following two months brought no progress toward disengagement, the Soviet offer was repeated in mid-November and the U.S.S.R. could soon inform Shastri that Ayub was willing to meet him on Soviet territory. Shastri told Parliament on November 23 that he had accepted and declared his willingness to go to Tashkent to have talks on the over-all Indo-Pakistani relationship, but he ruled out negotiating on the Kashmir issue itself.

The decision of the U.S.S.R. to sponsor the meeting was in itself a signal that Moscow would press both countries to reach a compromise. There may have been some officials in Moscow who felt that the Soviet Union would benefit more by following Khrushchev's policy of strong support for India; perhaps the ideologues were also dubious about cooperating with a nation created because of religious factors. But the new Soviet leaders thought otherwise, apparently fearing that a continued conflict would benefit either the West or China. They probably also believed that India's need for Soviet support was great enough to give Moscow some room to maneuver in trying to become the mediator if not the arbiter of the affairs of the subcontinent.

Despite its acceptance, India went to Tashkent with a notable lack of enthusiasm. Soviet leaders probably gave private assurances they would not abandon India, but a certain unease was nonetheless apparent in New Delhi. Pakistan's acceptance also was a delicate matter, for Peking did not approve the Soviet move. Yet while Peking denounced the Tashkent meeting as a joint U.S.-Soviet plot to support the Indian reactionaries, it did not attack Pakistan for attending—one of the few examples of Chinese verbal restraint in those years. There was, however, a sharp rise in Sino-Indian tensions in November when Chinese border troops began to patrol more aggressively along the Northeast Frontier Agency and on the Tibetan-Sikkimese border. Several clashes occurred, and there was fear that Peking was trying to torpedo the Tashkent meeting. The clashes soon ended, and Ayub and Shastri proceeded to Tashkent early in January. The comment of *The Times* (London) on January 3 was appropriately ironical: "How strange and intolerable it would have seemed to Curzon that the affairs of the subcontinent he ruled should be taken to Tashkent to be discussed under the patronage of a Russian."

The negotiations went forward by fits and starts, with Ayub and Shastri sometimes dealing directly and sometimes through Kosygin. Having committed Soviet prestige, Kosygin worked hard and long to persuade them to reach an agreement. He became more and more the mediator, stepping into the middle of the talks to break the deadlock on whether Kashmir should be on the agenda. Kashmir was not the only contentious issue; the issue of troop withdrawals also posed serious difficulties. Shastri was under heavy domestic pressure not to relinquish the control India had won of the Kashmir mountain passes used by Pakistani infiltrators. When negotiations bogged down in an impasse over the final communiqué, Kosygin re-entered the talks to salvage something from the stalemate. Through skillful use of pressure and persuasion he won the agreement of both leaders on January 10.

The communiqué illustrates that the agreement did not solve the basic problem dividing the two countries; it merely represented a willingness to move toward the *status quo ante*.[1] The Kashmir issue received only the briefest mention—the minimum that Pakistan could have accepted—with the phrasing that "each of the sides set forth its respective position" on the Kashmir question. Nor did the communiqué allude to the no-war pact that India wanted, although the document included a reaffirmation of the obligations of the two countries under the U.N. Charter to settle their disputes peacefully.

The most important point was the agreement of the two to withdraw their forces to positions held before the 1965 fighting, although the two leaders also pledged to discourage hostile propaganda and to work for friendly ties.

Both India and Pakistan hailed the pact as an important step to improving their relations, although some elements in India, both in the Congress party and among the opposition, denounced it because of the clause on troop withdrawal. Yet Shastri's untimely death at Tashkent made it certain that India would not repudiate his last official act. Indira Gandhi, upon becoming prime minister, quickly announced that India would honor the Tashkent agreement. In Pakistan there was much greater anguish and criticism of Ayub's agreement to return to the *status quo ante* without any tangible prospects for progress on the Kashmir issue.

The Tashkent agreement was a triumph for the Soviet Union, and for Kosygin personally. As Edward Crankshaw commented during the meetings:

> Mr. Kosygin, whose ideology demands the fostering of chaos and disruption in non-Communist lands, finds himself doing his level best to calm down a Hindu under direct threat from China and a Muslim supposed to be on friendly terms with Peking, embroiled in a quarrel over the possession of the mountain playground of the late British Raj.
> And, except for China, nobody minds.[2]

Indeed, the British and American governments were pleased if vaguely uneasy with the Russian initiative and the outcome of the meeting. The United States knew it was in no position to wield decisive influence in the subcontinent. Progress toward reducing tensions was so important to Western interests that the West gained if the U.S.S.R. succeeded, and Western leaders expressed their satisfaction publicly when agreement was reached at Tashkent.

Ayub's Triple Tightrope

President Ayub faced a host of problems as a result of the war and the Tashkent agreement. The most immediate and pressing was widespread domestic discontent with his government. The people had been fed a diet of illusions as to the progress of the war and the attitudes of the major powers. To a people whose emotions were at white heat,

Ayub's acceptance of a return to the *status quo ante* was incomprehensible. Opposition leaders in West Pakistan saw an opening and tried to exploit it.[3] Antigovernment riots broke out in several areas in West Pakistan, and all schools and universities were closed for a time. "If we were winning the war," people asked, "why did we accept a cease-fire and return to the *status quo?* If we weren't winning it, why did we get involved in the first place?" Ayub really had no satisfactory answers to these questions; he wanted to prevent the issues from being posed in this manner. He defended his actions as the only realistic course in speeches and broadcasts, exercised tighter control of the press, and arrested several opposition politicians. Rumors of dissatisfaction in the army gave hope to Ayub's opponents, but proved illusory or at least unexploitable.

Dissatisfaction also manifested itself in East Pakistan over the government's willingness to risk war with India while leaving its eastern wing practically defenseless. Sensing a rising tide of antagonism toward West Pakistani control, opposition politicians came forth with new demands for regional autonomy, which looked like secession to Ayub and his colleagues. Ayub countered by stressing the danger for East Pakistan if it had to face India alone. The government maintained its control in the East, but the issue of West Pakistani domination rose nearer the surface than it had for many years. In 1966 the government arrested thirty-five Bengalis including the leader of an opposition party, Sheikh Mujibur Rahman, later charging them with plotting to set up an independent East Pakistan. As one observer commented: "The fact that Sheikh Mujibur has been held in jail for nearly two years with no charge before the conspiracy was uncovered leads opponents of the Ayub regime here to the conclusion that the Sheikh himself has been the victim of an official conspiracy."[4]

Ayub was also faced with the need to reorient Pakistan's foreign policy, and here too public opinion presented problems. The articulate public in West Pakistan wanted no part of an accommodation with India unless it was based upon Indian concessions on Kashmir. But there was no chance that India would yield by diplomacy what it had held by fighting. Both East and West Pakistan wanted greater military forces for their protection. The government accorded top priority to larger and better equipped forces, but those officials responsible for economic affairs were concerned lest development be seriously retarded.

The Pakistani public's satisfaction with China's support and displeasure with the U.S. performance also posed dangers for Ayub. Pakistan, he felt, still needed to maintain useful relations with *both* countries. China, the only major power that had supported Pakistan, was willing to provide arms to replace those lost in battle. If the United States was not at present supplying arms, or did not renew its military aid program, its willingness to provide spare parts for the almost totally U.S.-equipped armed forces was still crucial. Moreover, if the promising economic development was to continue, it was important to obtain an assured flow of American economic assistance. Ayub did not publicly admit the extent of this dependence on the United States; indeed he tried to improve his bargaining position by repeatedly emphasizing that Pakistan's interest in U.S. aid was not a controlling determinant of its foreign policy. Nonetheless, he was pleased by his December 1965 visit to Washington. He and President Johnson apparently re-established a measure of the personal rapport they had enjoyed in the past. The freeze in relations between the two governments began to thaw, although public animosity toward the United States remained high in Pakistan.

Pakistan's relationship with China grew steadily closer throughout 1965 and the first half of 1966. On March 26, 1966, President Liu Shao-chi and Foreign Minister Chen Yi arrived for a state visit to Pakistan and were accorded one of the most lavish welcomes Pakistan had ever provided.[5] Crowds shouted anti-U.S. slogans and cheered the Chinese leaders. A few Chinese MIG-19 aircraft and tanks were displayed in a military parade, and the Pakistanis hinted that many more had been received. The Indian government claimed at the end of 1965 that China had granted $67.5 million in credits for arms and that Pakistani pilots were being trained in China.[6] On August 8, 1966, Indian Defense Minister Chavan told Parliament that China had supplied Pakistan with 200 tanks, enough equipment for two divisions, two squadrons of MIG-19's, and possibly some bombers.[7] Other sources thought that Pakistan was promised this much equipment, but that it would be delivered over a period of several years.

Relations expanded throughout 1966: "almost every month planeloads of Chinese and Pakistani delegations of various descriptions descend on the other country," *The Economist* commented. Sino-Pakistani cultural organizations were active in Pakistan. Trade between the two countries grew rapidly—from $13.5 million in 1961 to $68 million in 1967—but still accounted for only 4 per cent of Pakistan's total trade. China agreed in June 1966 to supply machinery for a heavy industrial complex, and a maritime agreement was signed in October 1966. A number of Chinese-aided installations were opened during the following years.

The Sino-Pakistani relationship did not expand indefinitely; even at its euphoric height—the period of Liu's visit in March 1966—Pakistani leaders spoke publicly of the limitations as well as the importance of the link with Peking. As Ayub said at the time, "the guiding principle of our foreign policy is that differences among other countries should not interfere with our relations with them. Consequently, alongside our ties of sincere friendship with China, we are developing friendly relations with the United States on the one hand, and the U.S.S.R. on the other."[8] And during Liu's visit Foreign Minister Bhutto told newsmen that Pakistan "will do nothing to endanger our relations with the United States in our relations with other countries, including China."[9] Liu frequently and fervently denounced the imperialists, but the concluding communiqué was mild and did not even mention Vietnam.

Peking's interest in the relationship declined as China became caught up in the Great Cultural Revolution after mid-1966, although Pakistan was the one Asian country that was never antagonized during this episode. This upheaval, as well as awareness that relations with China were not of unlimited importance, gradually tempered Pakistani enthusiasm. The dismissal of Foreign Minister Bhutto in June 1966, while related to domestic politics, was an indicator that Pakistan's relationship with China would be kept in check. Although the link with Peking had always been Ayub's policy, Bhutto's association with it in the public mind invested his departure with both a symbolic and real importance.

If neither the United States nor China was willing or able to supply all the needed military equipment, then Pakistan would obviously have to look elsewhere. Ayub was determined to diversify the sources of supply so that Pakistan would never again be so heavily dependent upon one supplier. Pakistan sought military equipment from a number of European sources, sometimes purchasing directly and sometimes through intermediaries. *Mirage* jet aircraft and submarines were obtained from France and F-86 Sabrejets from West Germany via Iran. Military spending increased from $265 million to $459 million between 1965 and 1968. The army added two new divisions as well as additional smaller units, the navy remained approximately the same size, and the air force cut its personnel while increasing its combat aircraft.

The one new development encouraging to Pakistan in the 1965 war was Moscow's refusal to side openly with India. This clearly called for Pakistan to see whether the Soviet Union could be enticed into moving beyond its diplomatic neutrality to the provision of military and economic support. The Soviet response was cautious in view of its ties to India and Pakistan's links to the United States and China. Increased trade created no problems, and between 1962 and 1967 Pakistan's trade with the U.S.S.R. rose from $8.3 million to $51 million. Also in 1966, the Soviet bloc made its first large economic aid commitments to Pakistan, $112 million, of which the Soviet Union supplied $84 million.

But these were matters of secondary concern. Pakistan found its principal goal with the U.S.S.R. was difficult to achieve, for the Soviet leaders were reluctant to curtail military assistance to India or provide significant amounts of military equipment to Pakistan. In 1966 a small number of army jeeps and trucks were obtained, and in 1967 the U.S.S.R. supplied a few helicopters. These items were not what the Pakistanis had hoped for when the chief of the air force visited Moscow in 1966 or when Ayub made his second visit in October 1967.[10] This disappointment seemed to persist through Kosygin's trip to Pakistan in April 1968, the first visit of a Soviet premier. Kosygin promised to provide economic assistance for a steel plant and a nuclear power station, but Pakistan apparently gained little satisfaction on military or political matters involving India.

Behind the scenes more serious negotiations may have taken place, for on May 20 Pakistan's foreign minister announced that his government would not extend the American lease on the communications and intelligence facility at Peshawar when it expired in July 1969. Peshawar was a powerful bargaining tool in Pakistan's hands, and its denial to the United States was probably worth something to the U.S.S.R., although the matter may not have directly arisen in whatever negotiations took place. Yet suspicions that something was afoot were further aroused when a Pakistani mission headed by the army commander went to Moscow in June, and in July a Soviet-Pakistan arms agreement was announced. Whether this success would be more meaningful for Pakistani foreign policy than its earlier successes with the United States and China remained uncertain.[11]

India Turns Inward

India came out of the war with Pakistan with a measure of the self-confidence it had lost in 1962 restored. Some of the leading Congress politicians wanted to hold national elections immediately while popular support of the government was strong. The confidence was short-lived, however, for the country was soon facing the most serious domestic problems it had encountered since just after independence.

Two poor monsoons in succession caused a sharp decline in agricultural output. Food grain production fell off by nearly 20 per cent between 1964–65 and 1965–66, and increased only slightly the following year.[12] With agriculture accounting for nearly half the national income and living standards so low, the effect of the poor harvests inevitably extended to the rest of the economy. Soaring food prices reduced buying power for other goods, and India experienced its first significant recession since independence. Moreover, the impact of India's extensive foreign borrowing over the years was now being felt more heavily. Debt repayments reached a level of nearly one-fifth of the country's exports and were scheduled to rise even higher. In the circumstances the defense buildup became more burdensome. These factors combined to dislocate the Third Five-Year Plan (1961–1966), forced India to devalue its currency, and made it impossible to start the Fourth Plan on schedule. Top priority had to be given to securing foodgrain from abroad and to formulating an agricultural development program that would prevent a recurrence of the country's current agony in the future.

India's troubles were not solely economic. The rapidly expanded educational system, particularly at the college level, began creaking at the seams. Disruption in the universities became increasingly common. Because of a general increase in violence and periodic breakdowns in public order, thoughtful citizens wondered about its future.

At first the domestic troubles seemed to have only a limited repercussion on the political scene. The opposition parties seemed unable to profit from the lack of drive and unity of the Congress party, and the latter continued to do well in the periodic by-elections. As India's troubles mounted throughout 1966, however, they took a heavier political toll; flaccidity and factionalism within the Congress party at the federal and state levels and rising popular dissatisfaction with its rule became ever more serious and obvious. The opposition parties took new hope and stepped up their agitation, which in turn spurred the tendency to resort to violent protest. The Delhi correspondent of *The Times* (London) wrote a series of articles, which stated without equivocation that "the great experiment of developing India within a democratic framework has failed" and predicted this would be "the fourth—and surely last—general election."[13] *The Economist*, while not going nearly so far, was obviously worried. Nonetheless, most observers thought that in the February 1967 national elections the party would be returned to office at the national level and in nearly all the states with only moderately reduced majorities.

But disunity within the Congress led many members who were not named as candidates to run as independents, and in many areas the opposition party showed a surprising ability to work out no-contest agreements. In a campaign waged over "grievances, not issues," a moderate decline in the popular vote won by the Congress party—41 per cent compared to 45 per cent in 1962—led to a stunning electoral setback.[14] Congress won only 288 out of 520 seats in Parliament; it had held 360 out of 508 seats before the election. Even more upsetting was its showing in the states. It lost its majority in eight of India's fifteen states, and its position in several others was extremely shaky. But only in a few states did any opposition party gain sufficiently to form an effective government, for Congress lost to a diverse amalgam of parties on both the right and the left. The defeat shook the confidence of the Congress leaders (several of whom lost their positions) and disrupted established relationships, forcing them to devote more of their time and energies to political maneuvering at both the national and state levels.

The inability of certain states to form governments that could maintain their legislative majorities led to several mid-term elections, but the varying results indicated no significant progress toward stability. The immobility of the central cabinet, caused by personal and regional rivalries and differing views on whether the government should move to the left or the right (or remain on dead center), became paralyzing. Finally, in mid-1969 Prime Minister Gandhi, seeking to consolidate her personal power and move to the left, forced the issue. The Congress party formally split into two groups.

Mrs. Gandhi, who demonstrated great skill at political maneuvering, remained in office as the head of a minority government pledged to pursue the more egalitarian policies increasingly demanded by India's millions as their horizons broadened and their impatience grew. Yet Mrs. Gandhi had to move with care, for her government was dependent on the support of regional or leftist parties (including some of the Communists) or on the abstention of the minority Congress group.

Because of the central government's problems, many observers forecast a speed-up in the flow of power from the center to the states, a subject of widespread comment as the Nehru era drew to a close. The British had always claimed that if they left, the religious, regional, linguistic, and caste divisions would fragment the country. The charge was indignantly denied by the nationalists, who claimed that an underlying unity had long existed and would provide the necessary cohesive force. After independence, Indians recognized that the British argument had some validity and attempted to devise a federal system that provided for adequate central power while allowing the states to play a larger role. Reorganization of the states along linguistic lines in 1956 was the major attempt to satisfy the strong popular desires for more regional autonomy. As long as the giant figure of Nehru dominated New Delhi, most of the power appeared to remain in the central government. Actually, it was far more complex, even when Nehru's influence was at its height, for many of the key decisions were always made at the state level.

Still, in the years after Nehru's death the primary threat to the unity of India came not from any of the main regions of the country but from the border peoples. New Delhi was unable to win more than sullen Kashmiri acquiescence to Indian rule. The release of Sheikh Abdullah in January 1968—an act requiring considerable political courage on Mrs. Gandhi's part—indicated New Delhi's awareness that it had failed to win Kashmiri support. Also disturbing was the failure of the establishment of Nagaland as a separate state to satisfy the rebel Naga tribesmen in the northeastern mountains, some of whom held out for complete independence even after the moderates ended their rebellion in 1969. Concern over the border areas was heightened by the revolt of nearby Mizo tribesmen in 1966 and the agitation of other hill tribes for political autonomy if not independence. These tribes had only minimal cultural links to India proper, and their peoples felt themselves different from and discriminated against by Indians. By 1967 the available evidence convinced many Indians and outside observers that China was arming and training guerrillas so that they could erode India's already tenuous authority along these frontiers.[15]

New Delhi's worries were also heightened by Chinese statements urging disaffected groups in India to revolt. The existence of an anti-Congress coalition government in West Bengal—in which the strongest element was the leftist and pro-Chinese Communist Party of India (Marxist), which had broken away from the Soviet-oriented Communist Party of India in 1964—intensified New Delhi's concern. Industrial strife spread rapidly in West Bengal when workers found they could seize factories without fear of police reprisals. Peasant riots were sparked by the activities of ultra-left-wing communists, who in 1969 established a third splinter party, the Communist Party of India (Marxist-Leninist), because of the dissatisfaction of many younger members with the party's policies.[16] Beginning in 1966, Chinese broadcasts became more incendiary. Peking proclaimed that "a new revolutionary storm is about to begin in India" based upon "the guidance of Mao Tse-tung's thought," and attacked even the CPI (Marxist). Mounting tensions brought on violent demonstrations at the Indian embassy in Peking and the Chinese embassy in New Delhi, and pressures to break diplomatic relations flared up dramatically if briefly.[17]

Despite the turmoil inside China during the Great Cultural Revolution, concern over the Chinese threat did not diminish. In fact, New Delhi's anxieties were increased by Nepal's insistence in 1969 that India withdraw its military liaison mission and its radio operators stationed along Nepal's border with China.[18] If the threat seemed less imminent it also became more far-ranging, for it now encompassed (1) the attempt to incite revolts within India and to subvert the border tribes in the northeast, (2) the conventional military threat, and (3) the nuclear threat. Each was seen to require a different response, ranging from political sophistication and counter-insurgency capability through conventional military force to, as some argued, an Indian nuclear force.

By the mid-1960s India had developed an impressive nuclear research development capability under the patronage of Nehru and the direction of the ambitious and dynamic Dr. Homi Bhabba. Nehru had always insisted that India would never produce nuclear weapons; but when China acquired a nuclear capability, officials emphasized India's ability to do the same. With each of the first several Chinese test explosions there was a new demand by some Indians that their country produce similar weapons. The demands often seemed as much concerned with Indian prestige as with security. At one point nearly 100 members of Parliament signed a manifesto calling on the government to develop nuclear weapons. Yet the amorphous grouping of those favoring such a move, their lack of support from any recognized national leader, and the costs—for a delivery system as well as weapons—enabled the government to contain the pressure.

As the Chinese nuclear tests continued, however, concern over that threat led India to explore the possibilities of guarantees from the two superpowers as an alternative to producing its own weapons. Indians insisted that such guarantees had to come from *both* Russia and the United States, however, lest their nonalignment be compromised by accepting a guarantee from only one country. In fact, many Indians objected to the idea of a joint guarantee, arguing that India could not rely on the vague promises that were the most that could be expected from any guarantors.[19]

The call for an Indian nuclear force also reflected a mood that the country should depend more on itself and less on outsiders. That mood stemmed partly from the growing resentment at being continually a supplicant for assistance from other nations and, consequently, having to listen to enormous amounts of advice from foreigners and accept more of it than India liked. Yet the new mood constantly clashed with the realities of the situation. India did not have the resources to maintain armed forces large enough to face Pakistan and China simultaneously while spending ever-increasing sums on economic development. Nuclear weapons would only intensify the dilemma.

India was fortunate in that there was little threat from Pakistan during these years. Since Rawalpindi was disposed neither to challenge nor to accommodate New Delhi, most Indian leaders were willing to ignore Pakistan insofar as possible and let relations remain in the state of quiet antagonism. Occasional public outbursts, such as occurred in February 1968 when a three-man arbitration commission awarded Pakistan about one-tenth of the disputed Rann of Kutch, soon quieted down.[20] However, India's construction of a dam across the Ganges at Farakka a few miles upstream from East Pakistan, which would divert water from East Pakistan, remained an issue that could explode at any time.

Even the Soviet decision to provide arms to Pakistan in mid-1968 provoked only a short-lived public outburst against Moscow and a moderately heightened concern about Pakistan. It did lead the Indian government to make one interesting and potentially important move. In August 1968 and again in January 1969 Prime Minister Gandhi indicated that India would be willing to discuss its border disputes with China. Mrs. Gandhi's willingness to enter into discussions without requiring that Peking meet India's former preconditions represented a shift in the Indian position. It was attacked by those in favor of continuing the hard line toward China; but with no Chinese response, the issue remained on the periphery of India's concerns.

At a time when the Soviet Union was moving to some extent away from India and toward Pakistan, and the United States was reducing its involvement in the region, the Indian government apparently wanted to see if it could increase its maneuverability and reduce its vulnerability in having both major neighbors as enemies. Lacking any sign of Chinese interest, there was little New Delhi could do but maintain its border claims and await a different Chinese response.

The American Disengagement

The war in Kashmir and the Tashkent meeting marked a turning point in American attitudes and involvement in the subcontinent. The most dramatic and immediate action was the halt in military aid, but the further effects were much wider. A declining number of American officials regarded Pakistan as an ally against any of the Communist powers, although few saw any reason to ask it to leave SEATO or CENTO. Similarly, India's domestic problems and regional struggles seemingly diminished its potential international role. But beyond these trends, a lessened concern with the subcontinent became noticeable. In part this reflected the American preoccupation with Vietnam, but it was also due to a realization that if India and Pakistan were going to focus on their animosities, it made little sense for the United States to pour in resources for the defense of the subcontinent. Furthermore, many Americans came to believe that the danger of communism winning these countries was not so great, at least in the short run. The local communist parties seemed far from seizing power, and the U.S.S.R. and China had experienced enough setbacks in the Afro-Asian world to make their gains in South Asia seem less ominous.

A key fact of political life in the United States during the mid-

1960s was the growing doubt in Congress and among the public that military aid was a useful instrument of American foreign policy. Doubt had turned to opposition in some quarters even before Vietnam caused growing numbers of Americans to question many of the aims and instrumentalities of U.S. foreign policy. Some critics took the readiness of Greece and Turkey to go to the brink of war over Cyprus in 1964 as evidence that other countries no longer felt constrained to hold their local quarrels in check because of an overriding fear of the Communist powers. U.S. military aid—even to NATO members like Greece and Turkey—would be contributing to local arms races rather than strengthening the security of the non-Communist world, criticism especially applicable to providing arms for India and Pakistan. There was a determined push in the Senate to halt military aid to both countries after the Rann of Kutch affair early in 1965, and only a strong effort by key administration officials was able to block the move. After the 1965 war the mood of opposition to arms aid mushroomed and would have made the political cost of gaining congressional approval for continued military assistance disproportionate to the benefits.

There were, of course, some officials who pressed hard for renewed arms aid. Those who favored Pakistan lobbied for continued support because Pakistan was an ally, but its links with China called this into question. A more persuasive argument was that U.S. arms had become an informal payment for the important Peshawar communications and intelligence facility, which continued in operation even though Pakistan had closed several smaller U.S. installations during the war with India. Yet to provide aid to Pakistan alone would alienate India, which made little sense if China was the enemy the administration's proclamations made it out to be.

Those officials who felt that India should be the focus of U.S. efforts claimed that as the bulwark against Communist China it should receive arms. But Moscow was liberally supplying arms, and India, it was soon apparent, did not lack weapons for defense against China. Thus U.S. arms assistance to India—aside from further alienating Pakistan—would really be an attempt to limit Indian reliance on Soviet weapons.

Military assistance to India or Pakistan, or to both, faced strong opposition. Consequently, the administration adopted a wait-and-see policy. President Johnson indicated on November 29, 1965, that neither military nor economic aid would be resumed until several conditions were met. Among his stipulations were that India and Pakistan work out a basis for living in peace, and that Pakistan's ties to Peking remain limited.[21] Further, he wanted the two governments to show some appreciation of American efforts to defend Southeast Asia from communism. Tashkent had provided a reasonable indication of the first point, and private talks and the slackening of Sino-Pakistani ties eventually took care of the second.

However, the third condition was inherently vague and subject to widely differing interpretations. If it meant endorsing the U.S. assessment of the Chinese threat, it was unacceptable to Pakistan. As the administration moved toward making the suspension of military assistance permanent, it lowered its sights regarding an acceptable Indian and Pakistani stance on Southeast Asia that would permit a renewal of economic assistance. An absence of active opposition to U.S. policy, rather than positive support of it, became the test, and both countries were circumspect in this regard. Thus the United States, still concerned about economic development in the subcontinent, once again began providing economic aid to the two nations in 1966.

By April 1967, after long and vigorous debate within the U.S. government, Washington edged back into the military picture by announcing that it would henceforth be willing to sell spare parts for the American arms the two countries already possessed, but that no new arms would be given or sold to either country.[22] (The U.S. had sold some "non-lethal" items such as trucks and radios to both since March 1966.) India complained that this move favored Pakistan, which had received much more equipment over the years. Pakistan was disgruntled with the U.S. refusal to supply such items as new tanks and aircraft. India's friends in the United States echoed the Indian complaint, while Pakistan's friends felt that providing only spare parts would not secure the U.S. interest there for long. It was a decision that satisfied no one; but satisfying either one fully would have alienated the other.

Declining fear of Communist aggression and falling confidence in Indian and Pakistani leadership had led the United States to reduce substantially its involvement and concern for the defense of the subcontinent. No defense treaties or commitments were abandoned, but the trend of American thinking was nonetheless clear: India and Pakistan were too concerned with their mutual quarrel to make military assistance to either a sound proposition.

This disengagement, however, was not easy to reconcile with the U.S. policy of discouraging nuclear proliferation. The nature of the Indian nuclear program led many Western officials to suspect that India was determined to develop its capability to produce nuclear weapons—a suspicion which its refusal to sign the nonproliferation treaty strengthened. Any American attempt to persuade India not to produce nuclear weapons left the United States open to the obvious Indian question: What will you do to help us if China threatens us—or actually attacks us—with nuclear bombs? President Johnson had said in October 1964, just after China's first nuclear explosion, that the United States would not stand idly by if China subjected India to nuclear blackmail. This vague assurance was hardly satisfactory. The United States was reluctant to provide anything approaching an ironclad nuclear guarantee, which could have left the initiative in Indian as well as Chinese hands, and this reluctance grew as the opposition to U.S. involvement in Asian wars increased. On June 17, 1968, the United States, the United Kingdom, and the U.S.S.R. declared that any non-nuclear country that signed the nuclear proliferation treaty and was then threatened with nuclear attack would have the support of the three powers through the U.N. Security Council. Two days later they supported a Security Council resolution to this effect.[23] But this was not enough to induce India to sign the treaty, although New Delhi continued to affirm its policy against developing nuclear weapons.

In contrast to military aid, the United States continued to provide extensive economic assistance. In fiscal years 1967 and 1968, its aid commitments (including surplus agricultural commodities) amounted to $583 million and $619 million for India and $230 million and $353 million for Pakistan.[24] Thereafter, however, foreign aid was encountering ever-increasing opposition in Congress and among the public. The amounts were reduced year by year, and new restrictions were written into the aid bills to try to prevent economic assistance from financing military build-ups.

The most dramatic aspect of U.S. aid to South Asia was the greatly increased shipment of surplus foodstuffs to avert famine and starvation. Two successive poor monsoons reduced food production precipitously in India and less sharply in Pakistan. Newspaper and television reports in the West portrayed an India on the verge of mass starvation. U.S. surplus foodstuffs had long supplied the major ports and other large cities, but now the relief had to be organized to

TABLE 1-A
India—Foreign Economic Aid, 1945–70
(U.S. $ million)

	United States		Other non-Communist countries[c]	International organizations[d]	U.S.S.R. and East Europe
	Commitments[a] (fiscal year)	Disbursements[b] (calendar year)	Disbursements (calendar year)	Commitments (fiscal year)	Commitments (calendar year from 1963 on)
Through 1960	2,349	1,791	e	604	808
1961	570	373	271	160	174f
1962	744	534	154	203	(174f)
1963	685	740	192	218	295f
1964	663	864	283	107	22
1965	697	854	329	231	639
1966	901	760	416	204	10
1967	583	838	379	268	0
1968	619	576	e	39	32
1969	442	466	e	221	0
1970	439	e	e	280	

Notes for Tables 1–A and 1–B:

a. Comprises A.I.D. and predecessor agencies, Food for Freedom, Peace Corps, Export-Import Bank long-term loans, and other official U.S. economic programs.

b. Net foreign assistance, after repayment of $580 million by India and $162 million by Pakistan over whole postwar period.

c. Comprises Australia, Austria, Belgium, Canada, Denmark, France, West Germany, Italy, Japan, Netherlands, Norway, Portugal, Sweden, Switzerland, U.K. Data represent total official bilateral flows, gross.

d. Includes IBRD, IDA, IFC, UNDP-SF, UNDP-TA, other U.N. programs; figures for Pakistan also include the Asian Development Bank.

e. No figures in the available sources.

f. Derived from subtracting yearly cumulative totals.

Pakistan—Foreign Economic Aid, 1945–70
(U.S. $ million)

	United States		Other non-Communist countries[c]	International organizations[d]	U.S.S.R. and East Europe	Communist China
	Commitments[a] (fiscal year)	Disbursements[b] (calendar year)	Disbursements (calendar year)	Commitments (fiscal year)	Commitments (calendar year from 1963 on)	Commitments (calendar year from 1963 on)
Through 1960	1,257	948	e	167	3	0
1961	168	218	35	109	30	0
1962	416	323	57	28	0f	0
1963	350	380	109	58	0f	0
1964	371	377	121	179	39f	60
1965	342	349	131	105	50	0
1966	142	220	131	92	112	0
1967	230	331	142	71	0	7
1968	353	278	e	52	67	42
1969	83	209	e	226	28	0
1970	213	e	e	104	10	200

Sources for Tables 1–A and 1–B:

U.S. and international organizations' commitments: Agency for International Development, *U.S. Overseas Loans and Grants and Assistance from International Organizations: Obligations and Loan Authorizations, July 1, 1945–June 30, 1967;* and *ibid., 1970.* [Special Reports Prepared for the House Foreign Affairs Committee].

U.S. disbursements: U.S. National Advisory Council on International Monetary and Financial Policies, *Annual Report to the President and to the Congress, July 1, 1969–June 30, 1970.* House Document No. 92-39. 92d Cong. 1st Sess., and earlier issues of this annual report.

Other non-Communist countries' disbursements: O.E.C.D., *Geographical Distribution of Financial Flows to Less Developed Countries, Disbursements, 1960–1964; 1965; 1966–1967.*

Soviet, East European, and Communist Chinese commitments: U.S. Department of State, Bureau of Intelligence and Research, annual reports on Communist aid to the less developed countries (title varies), No. 310, August 22, 1960; RSB-173, November 14, 1962; RSB-43, June 18, 1964; RSB-65, August 4, 1965; RSB-50, June 17, 1966; RSB-80, July 21, 1967; RSE-120, August 14, 1968; RSE-65, September 5, 1969; RECS-5, July 9, 1970; RECS-15, September 22, 1971; *The New York Times,* November 15, 1970.

reach rural areas as well. The Indian government concentrated on providing the distribution channels and the United States stepped up its shipments rapidly. By 1967 one-fourth of the U.S. wheat crop was going to India, in what must be ranked as one of the great cooperative efforts of the postwar world.

This episode shows neatly the interaction of humanitarian impulses and political imperatives. President Johnson insisted that the United States would not ship ever-increasing amounts of foodstuffs unless the recipient demonstrated determination to concentrate more on agriculture. In addition, he insisted that other countries supply a portion of the needs—either through foodstuffs or through providing fertilizers and other items. In making these stipulations the President was much influenced by the more demanding attitudes in Congress, which began to stiffen the terms of PL-480 and other laws governing distribution of surplus foodstuffs, especially to encourage the self-help efforts of the recipients. Pakistan had already moved substantially in the direction of the self-help requirements, placing more emphasis on agriculture during the early 1960s. The requirements rankled India, however, as did President Johnson's continual holding back of food supplies until he was convinced that India was doing all it should. Yet the policy was ultimately successful in contributing to India's giving greater priority to agriculture.

During these years the Vietnam issue also periodically strained U.S. ties with both India and Pakistan. Although both countries treated the U.S. intervention with a certain circumspection, they clearly were opposed to it—particularly the bombing of North Vietnam. Another issue causing difficulty was the outbreak of the Arab-Israeli war in June 1967. Both India and Pakistan strongly backed the Arab side while the United States supported Israel. The United States experienced considerable friction with India and Pakistan on the two issues, whose positions coincided closely with those of the Soviet Union.

The Soviet Advance

Developments in world affairs during the mid-1960s were not favoring the Soviets. The quarrel with China became increasingly open and bitter. The efforts of Kosygin and Brezhnev to work out a *modus vivendi* with Peking after they had ousted Khrushchev soon foundered on the rocks of Chinese obduracy. Soviet authority in Eastern Europe was weakened by nationalism in Rumania and later by liberalism in Czechoslovakia. In Africa and Asia the downfall of Nkrumah and Sukarno showed that the gains of many years' work could be wiped out overnight. Although NATO's cohesion was loosening, and the United States was bogged down in Vietnam, Moscow was finding it difficult to benefit from these opportunities. The limits of power were becoming visible to Soviets and Americans alike. Yet the Soviet leaders apparently concluded that they had little alternative to continued support of Afro-Asian governments unless they were willing to concede to the West (or perhaps to China) an open field.

In view of the setbacks the U.S.S.R. experienced elsewhere, the opportunities open to it in South Asia (and in the Middle East) must have seemed particularly appealing. Growing ideological concern about trends in India was not regarded as incompatible with expanded state-to-state relations.[25] The first Soviet move to capitalize on these opportunities was the sharp increase in arms shipments to India. Since 1964 the Soviet Union has agreed to provide nearly $1 billion worth of arms there, including submarines, jet aircraft, tanks, and artillery. India receives some 90 per cent of its imported arms from the U.S.S.R., whereas as late as 1962 this was only about 10 per cent.

Indo-Soviet economic ties also expanded. Moscow promised to provide approximately $1 billion in economic aid during India's Fourth Plan (1968–71), although about $200 million was aid that had been committed but not used during the Third Plan. Aid disbursements from the U.S.S.R. and the Eastern European Communist countries amounted to about $200 million a year by the mid-1960s, most of which was for state-owned projects in heavy industry. The general unwillingness of the United States to finance such projects had been clear to New Delhi after Congress refused to support the Kennedy administration's tentative commitment to build the giant Bokaro steel mill. Thus, in the judgment of many Indian planners and politicians, Soviet support was especially important to retain. Trade with the Communist countries roughly doubled between 1962 and 1969, increasing from about 10 per cent to 20 per cent of India's total world trade. Soviet agreement to supply petroleum (and help India prospect for it) enabled New Delhi to force down the price charged for oil imports by Western companies. But despite the Soviet agreement to buy some Indian manufactured goods, the basic pattern

TABLE 2-A
India—Foreign Trade, 1950, 1955, 1960–69

	Exports					Imports				
	Total	Communist countries[a]		Rest of world		Total	Communist countries[a]		Rest of world	
		U.S. $ million	per cent	U.S. $ million	per cent		U.S. $ million	per cent	U.S. $ million	per cent
1950	1171.9	5.4	0.5	1166.5	99.5	1137.0	9.3	0.8	1127.7	99.2
1955	1276.5	23.0	1.8	1253.5	98.2	1413.4	21.8	1.5	1391.6	98.5
1960	1332.3	119.9	9.0	1212.4	91.0	2123.6	74.5	3.5	2049.1	96.5
1961	1410.9	132.7	9.4	1278.2	90.6	2262.4	137.4	6.1	2125.0	93.9
1962	1414.9	171.1	12.1	1243.8	87.9	2360.6	224.5	9.5	2136.1	90.5
1963	1614.5	203.1	12.6	1411.4	87.4	2487.9	222.3	8.9	2265.6	91.1
1964	1731.6	271.9	15.7	1459.7	84.3	2703.2	279.8	10.4	2423.4	89.6
1965	1686.1	296.5	17.6	1389.6	82.4	2818.6	288.5	10.2	2530.1	89.8
1966	1607.2	296.2	18.4	1311.0	81.6	2750.0	280.7	10.2	2469.3	89.8
1967	1611.4	291.6	18.1	1319.8	81.9	2691.3	259.2	9.6	2432.1	90.4
1968	1748.1	319.4	18.3	1428.7	81.7	2509.5	303.8	12.1	2205.7	87.9
1969	1830.2	350.6	19.2	1479.6	80.8	2116.7	418.0	19.7	1698.7	80.3

Notes for Tables 2–A and 2–B:
a. Yugoslavia is not included; figures for 1950 include European Communist countries only.

TABLE 2–B
Pakistan—Foreign Trade, 1950, 1955, 1960–69

	Exports					Imports				
	Total	Communist countries[a]		Rest of world		Total	Communist countries[a]		Rest of world	
		U.S. $ million	per cent	U.S. $ million	per cent		U.S. $ million	per cent	U.S. $ million	per cent
1950	496.2	23.9	4.8	472.3	95.2	390.2	7.6	1.9	382.6	98.1
1955	400.7	5.1	1.3	395.6	98.7	289.1	.6	0.2	288.5	99.8
1960	392.5	32.8	8.4	359.7	91.6	644.0	14.7	2.3	629.3	97.7
1961	396.4	31.4	7.9	365.0	92.1	638.5	12.3	1.9	626.2	98.1
1962	420.8	15.9	3.8	404.9	96.2	734.2	16.8	2.3	717.4	97.7
1963	464.3	30.6	6.6	433.7	93.4	885.7	15.4	1.7	870.3	98.3
1964	493.5	57.9	11.7	435.6	88.3	994.6	36.6	3.7	958.0	96.3
1965	530.2	69.4	13.1	460.8	86.9	1042.0	49.8	4.8	992.2	95.2
1966	597.3	77.4	13.0	519.9	87.0	899.3	76.2	8.5	823.1	91.5
1967	596.5	84.5	14.2	512.0	85.8	1098.1	92.9	8.5	1005.2	91.5
1968	719.6	76.0	10.6	643.6	89.4	992.5	112.4	11.3	880.1	88.7
1969	682.2	102.5	15.0	579.7	85.0	1005.8	116.9	11.6	888.9	88.4

Sources for Tables 2–A and 2–B:
UN, IMF, IBRD: *Direction of International Trade*, Statistical Papers, Series T, Vol. V, No. 8, Annual Data for the Years 1938, 1948, and 1950–1953; *ibid.*, Vol. X, No. 8, Annual Data for the Years 1938, 1948, and 1955–1958.
IMF, IBRD: *Direction of Trade*, Annual, 1960–64; 1961–65; 1962–66; 1964–68; also March and April–June 1970.

of trade was the exchange of Soviet industrial goods for Indian raw materials and agricultural products—the standard pattern of trade between advanced nations and their colonies that Moscow has so often criticized.

At the time of Kosygin's visit to India in early 1968, there were reports that the U.S.S.R. had agreed to buy back the output of certain Soviet-built factories in India. Some observers saw this as the start of tying India into the Soviet economic orbit. Others felt it was merely a means to get Soviet experts into the plants, improve the quality of output, and thus enable India to repay its debts to Moscow. The failure to reach agreement on the much-discussed sale of Indian railway cars by 1970 because of stiff Soviet terms eased apprehensions on this score.

Yet it was easy to exaggerate the relative importance of the Soviet role, for India remained heavily dependent on the West for trade and economic aid. Overwhelmingly, Indian students still studied in the West when they went abroad, and cultural links with Europe and America were extensive. Moreover, the Soviet Union's changing policy toward Pakistan limited the political gains it could achieve from aid to India.

Extensive support of India had circumscribed the possibilities the U.S.S.R. saw in Pakistan's alienation from the United States immediately after 1965. In an exchange of state visits in 1967 and 1968, Pakistan tried to convince the U.S.S.R. not to supply India with so many arms. On both occasions the U.S.S.R. made clear its determination not to concede to Pakistan any influence on Soviet-Indian relations.

Moscow in time concluded that closer ties would reduce Pakistan's need to look to Peking, and also weaken the links to the United States, although it is unlikely that the U.S.S.R. wanted to replace the United States as a principal supplier of aid in view of Pakistan's heavy need. Closer relations with Pakistan might have the tactical benefit of demonstrating to the Indians that they could not take Soviet support for granted. True, such moves would annoy the Indians. But the U.S.S.R. took the anti-Soviet demonstrations in New Delhi after the news of its decision to sell arms to Pakistan calmly. Indeed, the move reflected a sound appraisal of India's dependence on the Soviet Union, for Mrs. Gandhi felt constrained by domestic and international considerations to play down the significance of the Soviet-Pakistani arms agreement despite her well-known efforts to prevent it.

The Advent of the Nixon Administration

The new Republican administration in January 1969 did not make any pronounced change in U.S. policy toward the subcontinent; the trend toward reduced involvement continued. Economic aid levels continued to decline, with President Nixon and the Congress in agreement that foreign aid should have a lower priority, given the many other demands on government resources. Pakistan fared better than India as these cuts were made, probably partly because of its better performance and perhaps partly because Nixon's warmer attitude toward Pakistan as Vice-President had not completely cooled during the intervening years. Moreover, Nixon found it easier to establish rapport with General Yahya Khan, Ayub's successor, than with Mrs. Gandhi, an important if unmeasurable element in U.S. policy.

Yet Nixon did not want to appear as the partisan of either country. During his visits in July and August 1969 he sought to convey an impression of even-handedness toward both countries. While he agreed to consider Pakistan's request for certain items of military equipment, he decided at first, after prolonged studies within the government, not to provide the arms. However, this decision was reversed in 1970 when the president personally decided to sell Pakistan twin-jet bombers, jet fighters, and armored personnel carriers with a reported value ranging from $15 million to $40 million.[26]

The U.S. intelligence installation at Peshawar was closed in July 1969, and for all practical purposes the U.S.-Pakistani alliance existed on paper only. The relationship became less close, but more soundly based for the long term because it rested upon more realistic appraisals by both countries of the interests and possibilities open to them. Obviously, the shift left some scars and bitterness, but once the need for change became apparent, both countries demonstrated political and diplomatic skill in making the shift with a minimum of the disruption that might have occurred in such a delicate operation.

The agitation that began late in 1968 and led to President Ayub's resignation caused Pakistan to turn inward, as India had done earlier. As the country attempted to establish a federal parliamentary system, it seemed likely that East Pakistan would have much greater influence in government affairs. The less hostile attitude of most East Pakistanis toward India offered some hope that relations between the two countries might improve.

The Nixon administration's low-profile policy, first set forth as the "Guam Doctrine" and enunciated more fully in the President's January 1970 message to Congress, elicited mixed reactions in India.[27] Although long-held fears of American domination of Asia were eased, there was worry that the United States would pull back so far it might fail to come to India's assistance in a future crisis. Moreover, with debt-repayment obligations increasing and demands for better living conditions mounting, the decline in U.S. economic resources flowing to India was disturbing.

Relations between India and the United States gradually became more distant. High-level official delegations would meet and have a useful exchange of views, but there were flare-ups when the United States agreed to sell arms to Pakistan and when India ordered the closing of several U.S. cultural centers in 1970 with vague accusations that they were engaged in improper activities. Even the flare-ups were low-keyed affairs, however, compared to some of the earlier squabbles.

The Soviet Union did not (with one exception, discussed below) make any quick dramatic moves to fill any "vacuum" resulting from the U.S. pullback. Among the possible reasons for this caution was the memory of the difficulties the United States had experienced when it assumed an activist role. Perhaps equally important, as one student of Soviet affairs put it, the U.S.S.R. "has come to understand something of the bleak realities of underdevelopment. During the past several years both its aid programme and its doctrine have been modified to correspond more closely with these realities."[28]

Moscow's short-term aims in Pakistan were apparently modest. It wanted to establish a presence and develop some ties and influence with the military establishment, and probably hoped to prevent Pakistan from becoming too dependent on China. The unexpected overthrow of Ayub indicated one difficulty in acquiring influence in a country where political forces can shift rapidly because power is concentrated in a few hands.

The U.S.S.R.'s policy toward India in these years appeared directed less toward a rapid expansion of Soviet influence than to deriving greater benefits from the activities it has long carried out. It attempted to drive hard bargains with India over the sale of Soviet commercial jetliners, the purchase of Indian railway wagons, and—according to some reports—requests for special access to Indian ports for the naval vessels sent into the Indian Ocean. Moscow had only limited success along these lines, although when it insisted that the Bokaro steel mill be constructed and operated according to its specifications, India reluctantly yielded. India opposed the U.S.S.R. on political issues: New Delhi did not sign the Nonproliferation Treaty despite Soviet criticism, it turned aside an attempt by Premier Kosygin to mediate a settlement of the Farakka dispute with Pakistan, and it forced the Soviet Union to halt construction of a cultural center undertaken without proper authorization. Moreover, the persistent Soviet practice of publishing maps of the subcontinent showing the Chinese version of the border was a periodic source of acrimony.

Yet if India generally adopted firm stands in dealings with Moscow, it did so carefully and usually looked for points of agreement that could be emphasized. Sympathy for the Soviet Union as a socialist country still existed among some prominent Indians. The Soviet invasion of Czechoslovakia in 1968 drew only mild criticism from Mrs. Gandhi, although others strongly attacked Moscow. The Soviet press and radio supported Mrs. Gandhi against the rival Congress party group, portraying the struggle as one between progressive "democratic forces" who want India to remain nonaligned and "right-wing" elements representing the forces of "reaction and imperialism."[29]

The single exception to the Soviet policy of caution was the proposal by Leonid Brezhnev, Secretary-General of the Communist party on June 7, 1969, that Asian countries form a collective security system. Brezhnev left no doubt that it was designed to contain China, and Peking's reaction was naturally sharp. Soviet leaders soon began to portray the proposal as less directly concerned with military security but rather as focused on increasing cooperation among Asian states.

Nonetheless, the proposal evoked negative reactions on the part of both India and Pakistan to any pact directed against China. Prime Minister Gandhi directly rejected the idea of any collective security pact, although she spoke of the desirability of a system of guaranties by the major powers to all the countries of Asia under United Nations auspices. Pakistan indicated it wanted to maintain friendly relations with China, thus effectively ruling out its participation. (Pakistan also rejected the associated Soviet proposals for greater economic cooperation with India and Afghanistan, and New Delhi was cool toward the idea.[30]) Because of the discouraging reaction the proposal received in India, Pakistan, and most other Asian countries, the Soviet leaders let the matter rest for a time. However, periodic references to the idea suggest Moscow believed it was useful as a sign of its intention to play a permanent role throughout the region and might someday gain favor.

The U.S.S.R. made extensive gains in the fifteen years following Khrushchev's and Bulganin's dramatic visit to several Asian countries in 1955. It became firmly entrenched as a major power in South Asia, perhaps even as *the* major power. At the same time, it learned that there are distinct limits to the influence of an outside power (at least in countries as large, complex, and mutually antagonistic as India and Pakistan), and that turning an impressive presence in these countries into major influence was much more difficult than establishing a presence in the first place.

11

India's Resurgence and Pakistan's Agony

While the events of early 1971 in India provided hope, those in Pakistan only provided discouragement; they also demonstrated anew the close links between domestic and foreign affairs and the perennial dilemmas facing outside powers. The outcome of the Indian national elections offered new hope for progress. But Pakistan's failure to establish a political system acceptable to its disparate peoples led to an upheaval beyond anything the subcontinent had experienced since the dismantling of the British Indian Empire. Hundreds of thousands of Pakistanis died and millions became refugees facing a grim future.

Nor was the tragedy confined to Pakistan. The immediate needs of the refugees inundating India stretched its capacity to the breaking point and dimmed its economic prospects. Moreover, their numbers threaten to cause communal upheavals in eastern India and to spark a new Indo-Pakistani war. Mrs. Gandhi's newly won mandate places her in a strong position to resist public clamor for action against Pakistan, but her control of events is by no means complete. The other countries involved in the subcontinent—the Soviet Union, China, and the major Western nations—are being forced to make difficult decisions about basic issues that will affect the area and their relations with it for years to come. These events and their longer run implications are discussed in some detail in Chapters 14 and 15, but a brief description will illustrate the hard choices required.

Mrs. Gandhi's Triumph

The drift and disarray that characterized Indian political life after the 1967 elections suggested that the stability and unity provided by the long dominance of the Congress party was a thing of the past. Mrs. Gandhi's adeptness at political maneuvering was acknowledged, but there was considerable skepticism about her ability to rebuild the Congress party and win adequate popular support to govern effectively. Most informed observers expected the 1972 general elections to demonstrate that political fragmentation was a fact of life in India and that coalition governments were the wave of the future.

By early 1971, however, Mrs. Gandhi felt confident enough of her prospects to call for new parliamentary elections a year earlier than necessary. Attuning her campaign to the growing popular demands for greater social justice and economic equality, Mrs. Gandhi kept conservative as well as leftist opposition forces on the defensive. The result was a stunning personal triumph in the March 1 poll: her wing of the Congress party increased its seats in Parliament from 228 to 350, and no other party held more than 25 seats. Power was clearly in her hands; whether it would be used intelligently and effectively was now the question.

Mrs. Gandhi's initial response provided little indication of how she would utilize her new opportunity to tackle India's many problems. She replaced some of the less qualified members of the cabinet with younger and more energetic men, and initiated programs to step up the pace of economic growth and provide more employment. But before any major efforts could be undertaken the outbreak of civil war in Pakistan created problems for India that immediately occupied center stage.

Pakistan's Perennial Dilemma

The upsurge of popular opposition which led to the enforced abdication of President Ayub early in 1969 reopened all the basic issues involving Pakistan's character as a nation. Pakistanis again began arguing and struggling over the course their country should pursue and, while most of the disputes were directly concerned with domestic affairs, the differences were so fundamental as to raise anew the possibility of a division of the country.

Prior to partition Hindu landowners, traders, and moneylenders had dominated Bengali Muslims, so the Hindu exodus provided new opportunities for East Pakistani Muslims. But experience with West Pakistani rule gradually convinced many of them that they had simply exchanged one alien exploiter for another. Such an attitude eroded the psychological unity of the country and intensified the East Pakistani movement for autonomy to the point where it took on the emotional characteristics of a drive against colonial rule.

The overthrow of the Ayub regime in 1969 grew out of opposition in West as well as East Pakistan, but East Pakistani grievances were especially sharp and difficult to resolve. General Yahya Khan, who succeeded Ayub, concluded that Pakistan could no longer avoid letting the people choose their government if chaos was to be avoided.[1] Yahya probably was sincere in this decision, but it could hardly have been made without misgivings in view of the military's low regard for Pakistani politicians. Moreover, Yahya probably expected elections to be inconclusive and lead to unstable coalitions, which could be influenced by the army.

Throughout 1969 and 1970 Pakistan made considerable progress in moving toward a democratically elected government. President Yahya and the country's leading politicians agreed that the new constitution would be parliamentary in character and based on a one-man one-vote principle, giving East Pakistan the dominant position in the central government. West Pakistan was divided into four provinces (they had been merged into one unit in 1955) in recognition of their regional aspirations. Yahya also indicated a willingness to accept a large measure of decentralization and provincial autonomy, provided the country's national integrity—as he saw it—was maintained. However, no agreement could be reached on the specifics of this issue in either the public or private discussions that took place prior to Pakistan's national elections in late 1970.

In contrast to the general repudiation of Ayub's domestic policies, officials holding power and politicians seeking to win it supported the broad outlines of his foreign policy of maintaining cordial relations with the United States, China, and the U.S.S.R. simultaneously. Some politicians wanted to shift the balance in one direction or the other, but most Pakistanis regarded the ability to obtain arms and economic assistance from these three countries as an achievement that should not lightly be put to risk.[2] The visits of President Yahya to Washington, Moscow, and Peking in 1970 demonstrated the continuity of policy; the U.S. agreement to sell arms, the Soviet promise to provide a one million ton steel mill, and the Chinese offer to make available about $200 million more in economic aid demonstrated its profitability. While Peking could hardly have been happy over Pakistan's receipt of Soviet and American arms, it continued to supply military equipment.

As the country moved to establish a new political system it seemed likely that East Pakistan would have greater influence in government affairs. The less hostile attitude of most East Pakistanis toward India offered some hope that relations would gradually improve. However, India's construction of a dam (the Farakka Barrage) to divert water from the Ganges River just before it enters East Pakistan was a stumbling block. Moreover, reports that China was building roads linking Sinkiang to the Pakistani-controlled part of Kashmir and establishing arms depots there periodically aroused Indian suspicions and fears; the opening of an all weather road in February 1971 was particularly worrisome to India.[3]

Pakistan's first national elections in December 1970 went smoothly, but they failed to provide a means to bridge the gap between the country's two wings. The overwhelming victory of Sheikh Mujibar Rahman's Awami League (which won all but two seats in East Pakistan, but none in the West) on a platform calling for a central government with power only for national defense and foreign affairs, indicated the intensity of the Bengalis' determination to control their own destiny. But Mujib's insistence that this required complete provincial control of foreign trade, foreign aid, and all powers of taxation appeared to the great majority of West Pakistanis as a demand for Mujib independence in all but name. When he refused to dilute his demands in negotiations with West Pakistani leaders, Yahya postponed the opening of the constituent assembly. Mujib and his followers reacted defiantly, staging a general strike and taking *de facto* control of East Pakistan for several weeks. Last-minute negotiations between Yahya and Mujib had little chance of overcoming such basic differences. The atmosphere in Dacca, tense and emotion-laden, was stimulating Bengali demands for complete independence. Yahya ordered the West-Pakistani-dominated army to seize control of East Pakistan on March 25, a task it undertook with brutal efficiency. The poorly organized and largely unarmed Bengalis soon lost control of the cities and towns, but managed to retain their authority in much of the countryside for a time. Within a few months it became apparent that the struggle would be prolonged as well as brutal.

Contrasting International Responses

The upheaval also had a powerful impact abroad, and nowhere more immediately and dramatically than in India. New Delhi had expected that a government led by East Pakistanis would open a new era in Indo-Pakistani relations. Frustrated in that hope, appalled by reports of attacks on defenseless civilians, and pressed by an inflamed public opinion—particularly in West Bengal—the Indian government reacted quickly but cautiously. Parliament unanimously proclaimed its sympathy for and support of the East Bengalis, and Mrs. Gandhi called on other nations to do the same. But New Delhi did not grant the newly proclaimed government of Bangla Desh diplomatic recognition. Its ability to hold any territory was uncertain, the conflict was legally an internal Pakistani affair (although the refugees in fact involved India), and there was the fear that an independent East Bengal might lead to secessionist demands in an already radicalized West Bengal. In fact, on several occasions Mrs. Gandhi said that it might be best for the subcontinent if East and West Pakistan retained some links. Nonetheless, Indo-Pakistani relations deteriorated sharply, raising fears of a new war.

As the refugees continued to pour into India (and as they were predominantly Hindu) the Indian government was forced to grapple with the interrelated problems of coping with their many needs and working out a policy to deal with the new situation in the subcontinent. Their immediate needs—food, medicine, and shelter—placed a severe strain on Indian resources. Rough calculations indicated that several hundred million dollars would be required even if they remained only six months, a burden which could undermine the opportunity for more rapid economic growth offered by India's newly-won political stability. Moreover, the refugees overwhelmed the small Indian border states and contributed to the downfall of the fragile West Bengal government; friction between them and the local populace posed a constant threat of further upheavals. Mrs. Gandhi warned her countrymen that "We will have to go through hell to meet this situation." But she added that the refugees were an international problem:

"We are looking after the refugees on a temporary basis. We have no intention of allowing them to settle here. Neither have we any intention of asking them to go back merely to be butchered."[4]

Yet no promising alternatives to such unacceptable choices were in sight. New Delhi exerted a major effort to get the international community to assume the economic costs of the refugees, while trying to move some of them away from the areas surrounding East Pakistan. It had limited success in the former, but no Indian state wanted hundreds of thousands of disease-ridden and impoverished newcomers. Furthermore, moving them away from the border seemed to imply accepting them on a permanent basis.

Thus India's long-term aim was to foster conditions in East Pakistan which would permit the refugees to return. To New Delhi this meant a political settlement between Yahya Khan and Mujib's forces, but it was difficult to formulate policies and priorities. It could not calmly contemplate an indefinite West Pakistani occupation of the East, for that would enable Pakistan to create new trouble in the already unstable eastern part of the subcontinent whenever it chose to do so. At the same time, any attempt on India's part to affect the situation directly posed dangers. Providing sanctuary and assistance to the rebel forces increased their ability to harass the army and its local collaborators, and gave India some ability to keep extreme leftists from gaining ascendancy. But continued turmoil and fighting could mean a continued flow of refugees, and would not provide conditions conducive to the return of the eight million already in India. Suggestions that the government impose a naval quarantine to prevent Pakistani troops and military supplies from reaching there or, more dramatically, seize enough of East Pakistan to resettle the refugees, held the danger of a full-scale war. While India was confident it could win such a conflict, it feared the disruptions that would result. New Delhi apparently decided to direct its major political effort into persuading other governments not to aid Pakistan, so as to force it to make a political accommodation. But India made clear that its restraint was not unlimited; by July responsible voices were suggesting that war with Pakistan would be a lesser burden than absorbing some ten million refugees—the number New Delhi expected to have arrived by the end of 1971.[5]

These developments also posed difficult choices for the major powers involved in South Asia. The Soviet Union, which since Tashkent had been moderately successful in expanding its influence in Pakistan without alienating India, spoke out against the army's action. President Podgorny, in an April 3 letter to Yahya which Moscow promptly publicized, urged him to end the "bloodshed and repression" and settle the issue by peaceful negotiations with East Pakistani representatives. Although Podgorny took no formal position on the substance of the issues in dispute, he spoke of the Awami League leaders as having "received such convincing support by the overwhelming majority" in the elections.[6] This was a clear rebuke to the Pakistani government, and apparently jolted it. Yahya replied by defending his action but assured Moscow that he would hold discussions with "rational representative elements" in East Pakistan as soon as possible.[7] Soviet concern that the struggle might lead to a new Indo-Pakistani conflict probably was a major reason for its involvement, which later included quiet diplomacy to restrain both nations. Moscow apparently did not halt its economic aid program to Pakistan, but Indian Foreign Minister Singh announced that the Soviet ambassador had assured him no arms were being shipped.[8]

Indo-Soviet ties were dramatically reaffirmed when Soviet Foreign Minister Gromyko signed a twenty year treaty of friendship and cooperation in New Delhi on August 9.[9] This was not a mutual security pact, but each party did agree to refrain from aiding a third party engaged in armed conflict with the other, and to cooperate with each other in the event of such a war. India probably saw such an agreement as serving several functions: It would solidify its ties with the U.S.S.R., and it was a useful warning to Pakistan—and China—that India would have a powerful friend if a new war came; it may have also felt that a dramatic move was required to jolt the United States and force it to reexamine its attempt to maintain some links with Pakistan. Moreover, India had been disappointed and angered that most Afro-Asian states supported the Pakistan government or remained silent, and this increased its feeling of isolation. New Delhi emphasized that it had not compromised its policy of nonalignment, remaining free to follow its own dictates. Mrs. Gandhi's overtures to Peking for a renewed dialogue, combined with her plans to visit the United States as well as the U.S.S.R., demonstrated her point.

The Soviet Union probably saw the agreement as formalizing the links that had developed between the two countries without committing it to any more specific course of action than the logic of its position already did; Moscow may also have hoped that the agreement would enable it to exercise restraint on New Delhi more effectively if that became necessary. The agreement, which was widely hailed in India, represented a Soviet advance there. But it represented a corresponding setback for Moscow's attempts to expand its influence in Pakistan, although Moscow went to some length to demonstrate that it was not committed to the cause of an independent East Bengal.

China also faced a difficult choice, and its course of action provides an interesting perspective on its thinking. Peking could encourage the East Pakistanis in their struggle against a conservative national government, hoping to turn an ethnic and cultural struggle into a people's war of national liberation. Or it could support the West Pakistanis because their traditional antagonism against India made them eager to have good relations with China. Peking chose the latter course, citing with apparent approval on April 4 Yahya's protests against Indian interference.[10] Chou En-lai spoke out more strongly in a note to Yahya on April 11, supporting Pakistan's moves to maintain the country's national integrity, and attacking India, the Soviet Union, and the United States for interfering in Pakistani affairs. China said that "should the Indian expansionists dare to launch aggression against Pakistan, the Chinese government and people will, as always, firmly support the Pakistan government and people in their just struggle to safeguard state sovereignty and national independence."[11] Peking apparently offered Pakistan an additional $20 million loan in May. However, it then said little more on the subject, evidently wanting to assess the course of events before committing itself further. Peking's long silence on the Indo-Soviet treaty was further evidence of its uncertainty, though Chou En-lai's August 30 remarks about China's determination to liberate the subcontinent suggested China intended to persist in its course.

The Western dilemma was clear: Either support of the attempt to hold East Pakistan by force, or encouragement of the latter's desire for independence, had major drawbacks. Most Western nations initially restricted themselves to urging Pakistan to work out a peaceful settlement, and offered to participate in international attempts to relieve the suffering. But they could not hope to remain uninvolved indefinitely. As Pakistan's major source of economic assistance, their aid would be an important factor in providing the resources the government required to hold the East and to maintain its position in the West. The press and public opinion in Western countries were appalled by the carnage wrought by the army and pressed their governments not to provide aid in the absence of a political settlement. (The report of the World Bank mission to Pakistan painted a gloomy picture of the situation in East Pakistan, and one which contradicted the Pakistani government's assertions that normalcy was returning.[12]) The World Bank and most members of the Aid-Pakistan Consortium favored this course, partly because development prospects did not justify new aid under such conditions and partly because of revulsion over the government's actions. The United Kingdom made its position along these lines particularly clear, which led to bitter Pakistani denunciations.

The outbreak of the civil war and the flood of refugees entering India presented the United States with difficult choices. (One of the reasons for this dilemma surfaced when it became known that Pakistan had helped lay the groundwork for Henry Kissinger's trip to Peking.) Early in April the government announcement that no more arms were to be sold to Pakistan gave the impression that an embargo had been imposed. It became clear in June that Washington, while issuing no new export licenses and not renewing old licenses as they expired, had not revoked those previously issued; this permitted several million dollars' worth of military items and spare parts to be exported. The American public and press, which were almost unanimous in condemnation of Pakistan's repression of the Bengalis, were enraged at the shipments and at what was felt to be another example of government deception. Moreover, the U.S. policy on economic assistance for Pakistan was confusing. The government gave the impression it would not make aid conditional on a political settlement —at least not publicly—but it in fact extended no new assistance other than supplies for relief and rehabilitation. In this atmosphere the Nixon administration suffered a major defeat when the House of Representatives voted to withhold U.S. aid for Pakistan (except for relief) until the refugees could return and political stability had been restored.[13]

U.S. policy apparently was based on the belief that, if it resorted to public condemnation or halted all arms shipments, it would have no chance of influencing Yahya Khan's regime. And if a new Indo-Pakistani war was to be prevented, this would, at a minimum, require a halt to the refugee flow. This in turn would depend on the prevention of famine in East Pakistan lest starvation cause more millions to flee to India, and on some progress toward a political accommodation between the Pakistan government and the people of Bengal. Since only the Pakistan government could undertake the necessary actions to see that foodstuffs were imported and distributed, this meant working together. By August there were indications that the United States was having some success in persuading Pakistan to agree to a relief effort under international auspices despite its reluctance to have outside officials observe its actions in East Pakistan.[14] Whether enough could be done to prevent widespread starvation remained to be seen. There was, however, no indication of any progress toward a political settlement; the cabinet appointed for East Pakistan was made up of men from parties rejected by the Bengali electorate. Yahya Khan appeared determined to make no significant concessions even to moderate Bengali opinion. Moreover, his decision to try Mujib as a traitor, with the verdict a foregone conclusion, threatened to cut off one of the few remaining paths to a political settlement.

The American refusal to embargo all arms shipments and to denounce Yahya's actions also provoked a crisis in Indo-U.S. relations.[15] Indian leaders believed they had been assured that no arms were being sent, and felt betrayed when the shipments were revealed. The United States was denounced by high Indian officials for "intervention on the side of the military rulers" and as contributing to genocide in East Pakistan. Indians were also incensed at U.S. calls for restraint by *both* India and Pakistan, and vigorously opposed U.S. suggestions that international officials be stationed on both sides of the border. To be equated with Pakistan at such a time was regarded as outrageous; nor did New Delhi want outsiders to observe the help it was providing for the guerrilla forces.

With the news that Kissinger's trip to Peking had been made from Pakistan, Indian apprehension increased further. At first New Delhi officially welcomed the prospect of any U.S.-China rapprochement that pointed toward Peking's admission to the United Nations and improved prospects for peace in Vietnam. But it soon became obvious that India was worried that Washington's desire to improve relations with Peking and its reliance on Pakistan as a link would lead it to pay little heed to India's interests. Foreign Minister Singh told Parliament that "while we welcome a rapprochement between Peking and Washington, we cannot look upon it with equanimity if it means domination of the two countries over this region."[16] Pro-Soviet groups in India attacked the planned visit in particularly harsh terms, with the Communist Party of India calling it a move "to isolate the Soviet Union, and if possible, to provoke a war between China and the Soviet Union."[17]

U.S. assistance to India to cope with the refugees, while greater than that supplied by any other nation, was regarded in New Delhi as woefully inadequate and addressed to the symptom rather than the cause of the trouble. Many Indians were convinced of two things: "If they [other countries] wish to they can force President Yahya Khan to bring about a political settlement in East Bengal, the only kind, which will enable the refugees to go back without a shot being fired. . . ." and, that "relief for refugees is a small part of the problem; the greater part is restoration of the democratic rights of the people of East Bengal."[18]

But the United States placed its major effort on preventing famine in East Pakistan, although it apparently privately urged Yahya to come to an accommodation with representative East Bengali opinion. Providing foodstuffs would not in itself be sufficient to prevent a new Indo-Pakistani war, for Pakistan was continuing to drive the Hindus out of East Pakistan and to rely on terror to suppress the Bengalis who remained. India continued to assert it would not permit Pakistan to solve its problems at India's expense; its efforts to train and supply the guerrilla forces gave them an increased capability for sabotage. India's provision of covering fire along the border and Pakistan's attacks on Indian border posts and staging areas steadily increased tensions. By July, Yahya was asserting that he would go to war if New Delhi's aid to the rebel forces allowed them to seize and hold any East Pakistani territory. U.N. Secretary-General U Thant issued an outspoken statement on August 2, when he warned in a memorandum to the Security Council that a major conflict could break out between India and Pakistan which "could all too easily expand."[19] All of the major powers had their reasons to try to prevent a new war, but all had other interests to protect as well. The environment was such that the specter of war, with China supporting Pakistan and the U.S.S.R. lined up with India, continued to haunt all major capitals by the autumn of 1971.

12

The Policies of the Past

Before turning to an examination of the likely course of events in the future, and the choices open to the United States, it would be useful to appraise how appropriate or inappropriate America's actions have been between the early 1950s and the outbreak of Pakistani civil war in 1971, in terms of realizing its objectives. (U.S. policies during the course of the civil war will be discussed in Part IV.) Such an exercise may provide some insights and guidelines. Any attempt to take a detached and long-range view at a time when passions are aroused over the present upheaval in Bengal is particularly difficult, but nonetheless necessary if the United States is to recognize its successes and failures so as to improve its performance in the future.

An appraisal of the performance of the United States in furthering its goals in South Asia between the early 1950s and 1971 reveals a mixed record of achievements and disappointments. Neither the worst fears nor the fondest hopes had materialized, though this probably was due as much to their unrealism as to the wisdom or errors of American policies. India and Pakistan had not been overrun by Soviet or Chinese armies, nor had they become hostile toward the West. The two countries had held together and made moderate economic progress, but Pakistan was undergoing its most critical test as a nation.

Each country had come to cooperate with one or both of the major Communist powers. We view this as less of a danger than we did fifteen years ago, for India and Pakistan have demonstrated their ability to have rather extensive relations with outside powers, without allowing them much influence over their own foreign or domestic policies. Although there had been substantial changes in the relationships among India, Pakistan and outside powers, the contest of the external powers for influence in South Asia had on the whole been a stand-off.[1] This conclusion holds despite the greater Soviet activity in the area, for the efforts of any one power are not easily translated into significant and sustained influence, especially when other outside powers remain involved.

Any attempt to evaluate U.S. performance must, however, try to answer the questions whether a shift in emphasis in certain policies or a different set of policies altogether would have served better. No definitive answers can be given, for history does not tell us the outcome of actions that were not taken. Nor would it be worthwhile to examine the likely consequences of all the different combinations of programs that could have been pursued or the extent to which policies were well or poorly executed. Yet some useful tentative judgments can be made about the likely results of certain alternate policies if the right questions are asked and the answers reflect the knowledge gained from the experiences of recent decades.

Was there any course of action open to the United States—doing something different or refraining from doing something it did—that would have basically altered Indo-Pakistani hostility and led the two countries to become good neighbors if not good friends? Specifically, could the United States have brought about a Kashmir settlement? My own conviction is that nothing the United States did or could have done would have changed the character of the relationship between the two countries. The relationship grew out of the beliefs, historical experiences, and deep-seated attitudes of the two peoples, and such attitudes are rarely if ever susceptible to fundamental changes by outside powers. (Chapter 15, on the future of Indo-Pakistani relations, discusses these attitudes in more detail.)

To conclude that an outside power could not basically alter Indo-Pakistani hostility does not mean that U.S. actions never lessened or exacerbated it. The clearest example of a potential crisis averted occurred in 1960, when the willingness of the United States and other Western nations to support the World Bank made the Indus

River settlement possible. Moreover, outside powers and the United Nations played useful roles in halting both wars over Kashmir.

On the other hand, provision of U.S. arms to Pakistan in 1954 and to India in 1962 demonstrably heightened tensions between the two nations. A few observers have argued that before the 1954 decision to supply arms to Pakistan the two countries were moving toward a Kashmir settlement, and our action was a challenge to India, causing it to abandon its pledge to hold and abide by a plebiscite in Kashmir. I believe that this view represents a misreading of developments at that time, and specifically of Indian intentions. India had not only insisted that a plebiscite be carried out essentially under its auspices—which no Pakistan government could have accepted—but Nehru had also stated publicly that India would not give up Kashmir. U.N. efforts to find an approach acceptable to both parties had been unsuccessful, and Nehru took the occasion to pull back from a politically embarrassing commitment. U.S. arms aid raised Pakistan's hopes of acquiring Kashmir, but it persisted in its Kashmir policy after U.S. arms aid was terminated.

Similarly, a refusal of U.S. arms to India in 1962 would not have been sufficient to promote a Kashmir settlement. Shaken as India was by its defeat and dependent as it was on outside aid, the war ended too quickly for American inaction to have led to a settlement. India, fearful after its defeat by China, probably would have stood firm against such pressure rather than accept the further humiliation of yielding a substantial part of Kashmir. New Delhi's action under such circumstances would have been based on the hope—which soon proved well-founded—that the U.S.S.R. would not have left it standing alone for long.

Another matter to consider in this evaluation is whether U.S. arms assistance first to Pakistan alone and later to both countries was responsible for their war in 1965. The U.S. arms program for Pakistan clearly altered the balance of power within the subcontinent, and India claimed that Pakistan would eventually use these arms against India rather than against the Communists. Similarly, Pakistan claimed that India's military buildup after 1962 would eventually bring New Delhi to use the arms against Pakistan rather than against China. In a way both were right, for Pakistan clearly initiated the 1965 conflict, although India expanded its scope. Thus U.S. efforts to allocate arms within the subcontinent in a manner which would prevent a war between the two countries obviously failed.

Yet the question of the extent of American responsibility for the war remains. The two countries fought over Kashmir in 1948 before the United States gave arms to either of them. During the 1954–62 period, when the United States was providing arms only to Pakistan, the Indo-Pakistani relationship was quite stable. It was only when the United States (and the U.S.S.R.) began to provide arms to India and the balance of power began to shift against Pakistan that instability and, in time, a new war, resulted. But would either of the alternate courses available to the United States after the Sino-Indian war have led to a different outcome? Abandoning the arms programs in Pakistan when the United States began to supply India could well have led Pakistan to seek closer ties with China and pushed it toward a military move against India before 1965. On the other hand, a decision against supplying any significant amount of U.S. arms to India would not have substantially slowed down its military buildup. One can argue that Pakistan would have felt more secure if the United States had remained firmly in its corner—difficult as it is to imagine the United States refusing India's requests for weapons after the Chinese attack. Nonetheless, my own judgment is that once India undertook a major buildup, the risk of a Pakistani move was high no matter what the United States did.

Another important question is whether the economic assistance that the United States furnished to India and Pakistan—over $9 billion to the former and over $4 billion to the latter—was a worthwhile use of American resources. I believe that it was, although it would be foolish to claim that U.S. aid programs have been as successful as it was hoped they would be. (Such aid, it should be noted, amounted to only a few dollars a year per capita for these populous countries.) Nonetheless, India and Pakistan made moderate economic progress after a long period of virtual stagnation. The responsibility for their record rests mainly with the two peoples themselves. But without outside economic assistance—and particularly aid from the United States, the major source of such support—the two countries would have been markedly less successful. (For example, aid to India and Pakistan in the early 1960s amounted to approximately 25 per cent and 40 per cent, respectively, of their total development expenditures.) Both countries made mistakes in their domestic programs, and the U.S. aid programs could have been better conceived and carried out. In an historical view, however, their record is a creditable one. Likewise, given America's lack of experience in promoting economic development in Asia, its aid programs made fewer mistakes than might have been expected.

Finally, and perhaps most important of all, was it wise to provide arms and form a military alliance with Pakistan? Or would a policy that placed greater emphasis on economic assistance to both countries have been more appropriate?

The alliance with Pakistan was based upon certain misconceptions by both parties as to the interests and goals of the other. Each country was primarily concerned with a different threat: the United States with the Soviet Union; Pakistan with India. Pakistan's fear of the Soviet Union (and to a lesser extent, China) was a secondary matter, although Ayub's proposal in 1959 for joint defense of the subcontinent indicates that such concern was real. The United States did not want India to threaten Pakistan's security, but regarded Pakistan's fears as excessive. Both allies knew that the other saw the world in a different light, but neither realized just how different their respective outlooks were. Despite these viewpoints, relations were quite close for many years. This reflected Pakistani awareness that U.S. military and economic assistance was a key factor in its survival as a nation, and American recognition that Pakistan was one of the main Asian countries willing to cooperate closely with the West. In time, however, changing conditions led to changes in U.S. policy that gave a higher priority to India. Pakistan's reaction to these shifts ended whatever prospects there were for the alliance by revealing the divergence of policies was too great to be contained within the alliance framework.

The alliance did bring important benefits to the United States in the field of military intelligence. The U-2 flights from Pakistan provided extremely important information about Soviet military affairs. Until it was closed in 1969, the communications facility at Peshawar enabled the United States to learn much about Soviet missile developments. The atomic detection stations supplied useful if less critical information about Soviet and perhaps Chinese nuclear tests.

Two difficulties of evaluation are involved here. The military intelligence was linked to the most vital security concerns of the United States, but it is not clear precisely how much the facilities in Pakistan contributed to information of Soviet military matters, and how much the knowledge contributed to actions which enhanced U.S. security.[2] Nor is there any satisfactory way to weigh the gains and losses involved. How does one compare the value of particular knowledge of Soviet military affairs with the political costs of obtaining it?

The policy of arming Pakistan stimulated a modest arms race in the subcontinent, causing a rise in the Indian defense budget from $410 million to nearly $600 million in the four years after 1954. But this increase in India's defense spending was small compared to the drastic jump that came with the Sino-Indian dispute. Arming Pakistan antagonized India, which, for a time, probably opposed U.S. policies in Asia and the world generally more vigorously than it would otherwise have done. Moreover, the Baghdad Pact, in which Pakistan participated principally at American urging, helped the Soviet Union to gain a foothold in the Arab states.[3]

The American alliance also enhanced the status of the military within Pakistan. Many Pakistanis came to regard the armed forces as one of their few capable institutions. This attitude probably was a factor behind the decision of the military to seize power in 1958 (although coups occurred in neutralist as well as allied nations, and the military played an important role in Pakistan before the U.S. became involved) and the willingness of the population to accept the take-over. It should be noted, however, that the Pakistani military did not move until the politicians of the 1950s had demonstrated their inability to foster either democracy or progress. In the short run this probably was beneficial to Pakistan and the United States, for Ayub's government stimulated considerable economic progress and was better for Pakistan than its predecessors. But it, too, failed to create a viable political system, and Pakistan is now suffering from its failure.

While the alliance strengthened the army relative to the politicians and West Pakistan relative to East Pakistan, American responsibility for the army's desperate attempt to hold the East by force is difficult to measure. One can argue, but hardly prove, that Pakistan would have worked out a political system acceptable to both wings if the politicians had remained in power; one can also argue that the country would have been shattered earlier, although in a different and less bloody manner, under the rule of the politicians. Moreover, Pakistan has received only modest amounts of U.S. arms since 1965 while its defense spending increased sharply.

In any case, it is clear that the events of 1971 constitute a serious setback for U.S. policy and, more importantly, a human tragedy of immense proportions. U.S. military support for Pakistan contributed only indirectly to these events, which resulted largely from forces at work inside Pakistan. But in view of the modest benefits that flowed from the alliance, the damage it did to U.S. relations with India, and the magnitude of the present upheaval in Bengal, on even the off chance that a different American policy would have resulted in a less tragic course, must lead one to conclude that the alliance policy was, on balance, a failure.

Finally, a shift in emphasis from military assistance would have had a beneficial effect on the economic progress of the two countries, but the extent is difficult to judge. Before Ayub took power, the government was little interested in economic development; soon after Ayub was in office and Pakistan became serious about development, the amount of foreign aid extended to it increased significantly. Only after the United States halted its arms assistance was Pakistan short of the amounts of economic aid it was capable of utilizing effectively.

The situation regarding India is more complex. In view of India's much greater size, a shifting of even a sizable portion of Pakistan's aid—say, one-third—to India would have been of only modest help. However, a U.S. view that the internal development of the two countries should have received higher priority *might* have led to an increase in the total volume of aid, which would have been at least marginally helpful. For countries with rapid population growth, living on the margin, even small differences in the rate of economic growth can be important, particularly since they have a cumulative effect over time.

To summarize briefly, a greater emphasis on economic development and a more flexible and more modest arms-supply program would have served U.S. interests—as well as those of India and Pakistan— somewhat better than the policies actually pursued. This conclusion is rather undramatic at a time when many if not most judgments on recent U.S. foreign policy either condemn it or, less frequently of late, praise it wholesale. It is tempting to believe that if only the United States had done things differently the situation would have turned out quite differently; the illusion of American omnipotence—whether for good or bad—dies hard. I have no inherent objections to strong praise or condemnation; but whatever may be the case regarding U.S. policy toward other areas, neither of such judgments is valid as far as South Asia is concerned.

PART FOUR

America's Role in South Asia

13

U.S. Interests in the Subcontinent

The great debate that began with the Vietnam war has raised, but far from answered, many basic questions concerning American foreign policy and its relationship to domestic policies. One of the few confident predictions that can be made in these rapidly changing times is that the United States will not quickly or easily find a new set of principles to guide its foreign policy in the years just ahead.

In part the reason is that it will be some time before the Vietnam war's myriad effects on the United States, on Asia, and on the world generally can be ascertained with any degree of precision. But there is a more basic reason why the present is a time of confusion regarding American foreign policy. We seldom recognize one unique aspect of America's experience in world affairs—its lack of involvement except when confronted with an acute threat to its security. After a hundred years of isolation the United States was drawn into the vortex of world politics three times in this century—during the First World War, the Second, and then the cold war. On each occasion the country displayed a great degree of consensus that there was a threat to national security and that the task at hand was to defeat or contain it. From 1941 until approximately 1965 the United States was mobilized psychologically as well as militarily against external threats, which enhanced internal social cohesion.

Today the dangers are less clear and the tasks correspondingly confused. The Sino-Soviet conflict, the Soviet Union's troubles in Eastern Europe, China's erratic course, and the revival of Western Europe and Japan have greatly altered the world scene. There is cooperation with the U.S.S.R. on some matters and competition on others. The U.S.-Soviet arms race, as is being recognized, can bring less rather than more security, and it devours huge sums of money badly needed for pressing domestic concerns. The dangers of war in the Middle East make obvious the need for at least that measure of Soviet-U.S. cooperation necessary to prevent the two superpowers from being dragged into direct military conflict. And the Chinese and American overtures in 1971 to establish a new relationship provide further uncertainties regarding U.S. relations with Asia and with the U.S.S.R.

At the same time, it would be foolish to conclude that Soviet or Chinese hostility is simply evaporating or will do so in the foreseeable future. The Soviet Union has been building up its conventional and strategic forces quite rapidly so that it can bring its military power to bear in distant areas. It is playing an increasing role in the area from North Africa through the Indian subcontinent; its navy is expanding operations in the Mediterranean, the Persian Gulf, and the Indian Ocean; its pilots are flying missions from Egyptian airfields. Yet the meaning of these developments is far from obvious. An active Soviet role throughout most of the area can be viewed as not only practically inevitable for a nearby superpower but also as a trend which will reach certain natural limits and create problems as well as opportunities for Moscow. Moreover, the Soviet desire to contain China —and vice versa—could have some beneficial effects for the United States. But there is no certainty that such a reassuring interpretation will turn out to be correct. The U.S.S.R. could, in the absence of any countervailing Western role, become the predominant external power in the entire area. Even if military power is more difficult to translate into political influence today than formerly (by no means yet a universal limiting condition), a sharp expansion of Soviet power is hardly a desirable situation for the United States.

Partly as a result of the profound changes that have occurred and of changed perceptions of the dangers facing us, but even more as a result of the frustration and bitterness growing out of the Vietnam war, there is a widespread American conviction that the country is over-involved in world affairs in general and in Asia in particular.

The most numerous adherents of this view generally stress the limits of American interests and power, some arguing that the United States has become an indiscriminate interventionist power.[1] They tend to see the underdeveloped world as inevitably marked by so much turmoil, violence and upheaval that the United States should be extremely careful and selective about where and how it gets involved. Many believe that any type of involvement brings pressures for further intervention because of considerations of prestige if the initial efforts to help are unsuccessful. They also believe that external dangers have diminished enough so that the country can and must devote less attention and resources to military and international affairs and more to dealing with such domestic problems as poverty, racial injustice, the alienation of youth, and the inescapable need to deal with the effects of a rapidly changing technology.

To complicate an already complex situation, there are also many Americans who believe that focusing our foreign policy on the containment of Communist power has been both unnecessary and wrong. Unnecessary, because neither the Soviets nor the Chinese were or are really aggressive powers—or at least not nearly as aggressive as most Americans have believed. Wrong, because the policy of containment has led us to support corrupt and reactionary regimes simply because they were anti-Communist rather than to support—or at least not oppose—those forces working for justice and reform in the underdeveloped countries. This group of critics is not as large as the first group, but its protests are heard because many in it are active publicists for their views.

Though both groups of critics score telling points on particular issues, they generally tend to overstate their cases—understatement being another casualty of the Vietnam war. The United States has intervened in only a small minority of the local conflagrations of the past two decades, although some of the interventions were unwise. Similarly, the United States has at times backed reform-minded governments in preference to more conservative regimes, although it has too often supported reactionary regimes against radical reformers when the latter were, sometimes incorrectly, identified with the Communists. Nonetheless, in the present Vietnam-drenched atmosphere the charges of the critics have sufficient validity to have a significant impact on a nation weary of its role abroad and worried about its domestic problems.

Together with the increasing desire for disengagement abroad there is growing recognition that the nations of the world are ever more interdependent. Interdependence is largely the effect of modern technology, especially modern means of communication and transportation that make the people everywhere more aware of conditions elsewhere and bind together national economies.[2] (Much of the activity is in the private sector—travel, business firms, publications, movies, educational exchange, foundation activities—proving that international relations are not determined solely by government policy.) Some observers even go so far as to maintain that a single world civilization is developing from the diffusion of modern technology and ideas, with national boundaries losing their meaning.

Even if such results are the eventual outcome of present trends, they are unlikely to emerge soon or, more importantly, at anything like an even pace throughout the world. Interdependence is occurring much more rapidly among the advanced nations, and probably will in the foreseeable future. Even among them, national loyalties remain strong, however much international cooperation is seen as valuable and essential. In the relations between the rich and poor nations the situation is far more complicated. To be sure, they are being drawn together by the forces mentioned above; yet, in respect to the growing disparity in wealth, they are drifting farther apart. The meaning of these disparate developments for U.S. foreign policy is certainly not clear, and the difficulties of restructuring a foreign policy in such complex situations and with such wide divergencies in trends and public opinion are obvious.

In considering future policies, the broad interests of the United States in India and Pakistan are relatively easy to discern: the political and economic development of the two countries, abatement of their mutual hostility, their security from external attack, and reasonably friendly relations with both. Reaching a judgment on the importance of these interests to the United States, their interrelationship, and the policies likely to further them is a more difficult process. In some cases the interests of the United States coincide with those of India and Pakistan; in others its interests are different from those of one or both countries, at least as these interests are perceived. Even on such matters as economic development, where interests are broadly similar, disagreements have often arisen over the particular strategy most likely to foster development, because of the different social and political impact of various policies. Since American influence is obviously limited in dealing with India and Pakistan, the United States will hardly be able to reach all its goals, and so will be forced either to neglect certain ones or settle for only a partial achievement of most of them. It will also be faced with difficult choices between immediate requirements (such as how to respond to the political turmoil in Pakistan) and long-run goals (the promotion of economic development) in compromises that will be unsatisfying and frustrating.

A certain *de facto* downgrading of American involvement has occurred. The United States did not provide significant amounts of military equipment to either country between 1965 and 1970 despite the willingness of the U.S.S.R. to send arms to both and China's willingness to supply to Pakistan. Even the 1970 agreement to sell arms to Pakistan was quite small by comparison to the quantity furnished in earlier years. New commitments of economic assistance to the two countries have also declined. In short there has been a substantial, though by no means total, withdrawal of the United States from the affairs of the subcontinent at the same time that the Soviet Union is expanding its activities and China is continuing its involvement.

The inclination of the United States to play a reduced role in the subcontinent while the Communist powers remain deeply involved represents—to the extent that it is a calculated decision rather than one taken by default as a result of concerns elsewhere—a judgment that India and Pakistan are less important than was once thought, less threatened by external aggression, and more capable of dealing with the Communist countries without conceding them much influence over internal affairs or foreign policy. In addition, cuts in U.S. economic aid have probably been motivated in part by declining confidence in the ability of the underdeveloped countries generally to progress at a rate regarded as satisfactory. But the declining confidence in the potential for growth is partially based on inaccurate views of the actual record, for the underdeveloped countries have by and large met the 5 per cent annual growth rate set as a target for the 1960s, despite the failures of the advanced countries to meet the goal of extending 1 per cent of their GNP as aid. But India is one of the countries whose record during the 1960s was disappointing.

The internal situations in India and Pakistan became less stable in the late 1960s. Since the development process we seek to help requires many changes, a rigid stability can hardly be our goal. Nonetheless, instability and turmoil can become so great as to undermine the efforts at modernization. There is now reason to think that the trend toward instability has been reversed in India, but the situation in Pakistan has deteriorated dramatically.

Moreover, as the events of early 1971 indicate, several of the key relationships and situations that will affect the interrelations of India, Pakistan, and the great powers are subject to rapid change in the future just as they have changed abruptly in the past. Pakistan's ability to remain united is uncertain; and either continued West Pakistani suppression of the eastern wing or a division of the country would pose serious problems for all concerned in ways that will be discussed shortly.

The course of Sino-Soviet relations will have important ramifications and, as they have fluctuated sharply, are difficult to predict with confidence. Both countries massed troops along their frontier in 1969, and Moscow hinted at a possible military move against China. Then the two nations opened negotiations over their border disputes. Yet in 1970 they celebrated the centennial of Lenin's birth by trading charges of unprecedented vituperation: Peking compared the Soviet leaders to Hitler, and Moscow replied by accusing Mao of abandoning his first wife to death at the hands of the Kuomintang and probably murdering his eldest son. After the U.S. move into Cambodia, however, the two governments temporarily muted their hostility, but no basic improvement took place. And each country believes the other is conspiring with the United States against it. All things considered, the Soviet-Chinese relationship seems likely to remain one of hostile coexistence, but neither war nor a substantial improvement in relations is beyond the realm of possibility.

Both the trend of events in the subcontinent and in great-power relations suggests that the United States should place a high value on maintaining flexibility in its policies. This cannot be an absolute standard, for it will sometimes be necessary to make a firm commitment to reach a particular goal. Nevertheless, the United States should be careful not to lock itself into rigid policies at a time when so much is in flux.

* * *

Just how important to the United States is the subcontinent? Is it vital to national security that the subcontinent not be hostile toward the United States? Or, at the other end of the spectrum, is such a development really a matter of indifference? Or does the answer lie somewhere in between, namely, that the area is important, at least in certain respects? If so, why and in what respects is it important?[3] Should we treat India and Pakistan differently (perhaps even "choosing" one or the other); or is their future linked to such an extent that we are impelled to treat them similarly?

Unfortunately there is no way of answering such questions with great precision. This is partly because of the nature of the area. Whereas one can say with confidence that it is vital that all of Europe not be hostile or that Paraguay or Uganda are relatively unimportant to our security, India and Pakistan obviously fall somewhere in between. Furthermore, the importance of South Asia depends partly on conditions elsewhere in the world. For example, the hostility of India and Pakistan would be unpleasant but not a threat to national security if the United States enjoyed friendly relations with the Soviet Union and China. The situation would be quite different if, at the other extreme, all four countries combined against the United States.

The fact that precision about the importance of the subcontinent is impossible does not mean that no judgment can be reached on the matter. Governments must make such judgments—implicitly if not explicitly—as a basis for their policies. The foregoing words of caution are set forth simply as a reminder that there is a limit as to how exact a statement can be made.

The view that India and Pakistan are vital to American security was succinctly set forth by Secretary of Defense McNamara in March 1966:

> [South Asia] has become, through a combination of circumstances and geography, a vital strategic area in the present contest between the expansionist and nonexpansionist power centers. In friendly hands or as nonaligned states, South Asia can be a bridge between Europe and the Far East and a major physical barrier to the southward expansion of Red China and the U.S.S.R.; in hostile hands, it would seal the long-term hope of building a free Asian coalition able to provide adequate counterweight to an expansionist China.[4]

That judgment, I think, overstates the importance of South Asia. American interests are partially a function of the interests and activities of other countries. It seems unlikely that either the Soviet Union or China has the capability—or the intention—of taking over the subcontinent directly and so organizing the area that it would make a positive contribution to Soviet or Chinese power rather than be a drain on their energies and resources. A somewhat more likely eventuality, although one that now seems remote in view of the splintering of the Communist movement in India and its extreme weakness in Pakistan, would be for local Communists to win control in South Asia and to ally themselves with either the U.S.S.R. or China, or both if the two countries settled their quarrels.

Before becoming too anxious over such (on the whole unlikely) developments, we should look at what is required for the formation of a Sino-Soviet–South Asia axis hostile to the West. It would require the settlement of the Sino-Soviet, the Sino-Indian, and the Indo-Pakistani disputes, plus rapid enough economic progress in South Asia so that the two countries would contribute substantively to such a grouping. Such developments cannot be completely excluded, and if they occurred they would have seriously adverse repercussions on the Middle East and Southeast Asia. However, they seem so unlikely as to make it extremely unwise to base American policies on preventing them.

As far as is known, South Asia contains no natural resources that are truly vital to the West. Nor is it really vital in terms of communication routes. The Middle East can be reached from Europe and the Mediterranean, and Southeast Asia from Australia and the Pacific. Even if India and Pakistan were actively hostile to the West, they could not prevent Western vessels from crossing the Indian Ocean. This is not to say that South Asia is unimportant in these respects and that its antagonism would not make life considerably more difficult for the United States, but only to argue that it is not vital.

McNamara's statement, made in arguing for congressional acceptance of the administration's foreign aid request, also reflects the habit U.S. officials have developed, sometimes unconsciously, of overstating American interests in various areas and issues in order to gain support for their policies. To argue that South Asia is literally *vital* to us means that we could not survive as a nation if it became friendly to our enemies and hostile to us, and it logically follows that we must do anything that is required to prevent such a development from taking place.

While it would be misleading and possibly foolhardy to regard South Asia as vital to American national security, I think that it would be an equally serious mistake to regard the area as being of little or no concern. Just as in the past we tended to overstate the importance of the underdeveloped countries to American security, there is now a danger of understating it. Nations have few vital interests, but are constantly engaged in the business of trying to advance interests or prevent adverse developments of greater or lesser importance by the commitment of larger or smaller amounts of resources and national prestige. The nature of our interests (or our perception of them) can change, and present neglect may jeopardize a future position. The future of the Western position in Southeast Asia and in the Middle East (especially the Arab lands) is not bright, which increases the importance of South Asia. Finally, the fact that it is extremely hard to evaluate the importance of American interests in developments elsewhere in the world relative to the urgency of specific domestic problems does not mean that all but the most vital foreign concerns can be ignored until the domestic problems are solved.

The issue of communism in South Asia is more difficult to evaluate than it was at the height of the cold war. Many Americans believe that it remains vital to contain communism around the world, while others believe that the cold war is over and we can be relatively unconcerned about the spread of communism. In my view it is important that South Asia not become Communist. Since the local Communist parties are weak in Pakistan and fragmented in India (and both Moscow and Peking give first consideration to advancing their own interests rather than aiding local parties), this is a long-range rather than an acute problem, but one worth being concerned about nonetheless.

Despite the divisions within what was once a unified Communist bloc, and the various types of communism that are evolving, it seems likely that it will be many years before any real change in the natural inclination of Communist states to oppose the United States occurs. India and Pakistan have, over the years, opposed the United States on some issues and cooperated with the Soviet Union or China (or both) on other matters. Yet neither has been generally hostile to the West or to the United States, and each has demonstrated the limited nature of its cooperation with the Communist powers—something the Indo-Soviet treaty by itself is unlikely to change.

If the two countries were to become Communist, it seems likely that they would become actively hostile toward the United States and more cooperative with one—though probably not both—of the major Communist powers. It could even be argued that the main effect would be to increase the troubles within the Communist world, and that therefore the West need not be concerned about communism in South Asia. In my opinion, however, the trouble created for the West by their increased hostility would more than offset any benefits to be gained from greater antagonism with the Communist world. In fact, such antagonism probably is beneficial to the non-Communist world only so long as it is limited; a Sino-Soviet war, for example, is undesirable from any standpoint.

Or it might happen that one nation goes Communist and the other responds by becoming actively anti-Communist and seeking closer ties with the United States. This situation would hardly be a favorable one. The United States could rush in to help the anti-Communist nation, but the intense involvement necessary for success is something America should avoid wherever possible. If, on the other hand, the United States stood aside or rendered only minimal aid to the anti-Communist nation, it surely would come under very heavy pressure from two if not three of its major neighbors. In short, the rise of one or two additional Communist powers in South Asia would shift the balance of power in an adverse manner. Even in the worst of circumstances the West could maintain its basic national security in a nuclear age, but the result would nonetheless be an adverse one.

Finally, the freedom and progress of the Indian and Pakistani people would not be served if they were to live under Communist regimes. The record of the Indian government since independence, like that of all non-Communist governments, leaves much to be desired; and the carnage wrought by the present Pakistani regime in the name of national integrity is a tragedy for the subcontinent. But exchanging one type of repression for another would represent no advance, and the records of Communist and non-Communist countries (especially those divided countries, like Korea or Germany, where direct comparisons are most instructive) generally indicate that the several varieties of Communist systems fail to serve their citizens as well as most of the diverse non-Communist systems do.

None of these considerations means that the United States has an imperative and overriding mission to prevent the area from becoming Communist and should do whatever is necessary (including the dispatch of troops) to prevent it. Neither its interests nor capabilities are that great. But recognition that concern over communism should not be the alpha and omega of American foreign policy does not imply that we should ignore the issue. Rather, we should try to see it in clearer perspective than we have in the past.

Another possible development seriously adverse to our interests would be if South Asia were to descend into chaos or near-chaos as the result of internal upheavals due to frustration over the lack of domestic progress, to political strife or insurgency, or because of new and perhaps more serious conflicts between India and Pakistan.[5] Violent change and intense national rivalries stimulate outside intervention. Since the policies of the great powers are still influenced by their view that geographical dominion and territorial political control are the keys to power and even survival, a chaotic situation in South Asia could lead to deeper involvement or intervention by outside powers. Indeed, one or the other of the local forces in such struggles probably would attempt to draw in external support to improve its prospects. That the actions of each outside power might be motivated as much by a desire to keep other powers from improving their position as by a desire to enhance its own position, would not lessen the dangers inherent in such development. No U.S. government would lightly intervene in such circumstances in the near future as a result of the experience in Vietnam; but if such developments seemed to pose a serious threat some years hence, intervention cannot be ruled out. One need not overdramatize the dangers of such a series of events to conclude that it is worth trying to forestall chaos and avoid intervention.

The same considerations suggest that the traditional American view that it is in the U.S. interest that India and Pakistan retain their national identity and territorial integrity was correct. Even if one had believed that South Asia would be better served if India and Pakistan were either reunited or divided into additional independent states, the likely turmoil made the value of such changes seem dubious at best. The struggle in East Pakistan provides a classic case as to how an attempted secession can lead to turmoil and open warfare, for any national government is likely to fight to maintain its country's territorial integrity against secessionist challenges. Nationalists and secessionists then attempt to draw in foreign support, thereby increasing the dangers of open confrontation.

The continuation of unity in India will depend, of course, overwhelmingly on India's own efforts, but the United States should be ready to make whatever contribution it can to furthering national cohesion. However, the failure of Pakistan's most recent attempt to create a political system acceptable to the people in both parts of the country raises the question as to whether the traditional U.S. view in favor of national unity, while good in the abstract, is still appropriate. This, of course, depends very largely on whether a truly voluntary association of East and West Pakistanis is possible any longer, for unity resting only on bayonets would eliminate both justice and the possibility of economic development and would not be tenable as a permanent solution. But the viability of such a solution may depend partly on the actions of outside powers. For example, if the central government can retain control of East Pakistan only by virtue of its receipt of external aid, what conditions should be attached to the aid by its donors? Humane treatment of East Pakistan? Allocation of most of the aid funds to it? If independence seems virtually inevitable, should outside powers attempt indirectly or even directly to help bring it about as painlessly as possible, or is this an unwise move and unwarranted interference in the affairs of another country? The questions are only posed at this point; a more detailed appraisal and an attempted answer and suggested course of action are set forth in Chapters 14 and 15.

There is also a growing, if still very imperfect, recognition that the rich nations of the world in general and the United States in particular have a very real stake in building a more just and less dangerous world community.[6] This is especially important when national interests over a period of a generation or two are considered. Political leaders often feel they cannot look that far ahead or act upon the basis of such long-range consideration. Yet such a period only corresponds to the lifetime of our children, and it is hardly soft-headed or sentimental to conclude that their future is of interest to us. As the Pearson Commission pointed out:

> We must not, in short, interpret national interest in a narrow and restricted sense. Indeed, the acceleration of history, which is largely the result of the bewildering impact of modern technology, has changed the whole concept of national interest. Who can now ask where his country will be in a few decades without asking where the world will be? If we wish that world to be secure and prosperous, we must show a common concern for the common problems of all peoples.[7]

It is especially important that the United States not take a narrow or short-term view of its national interest. If the largest and economically most advanced nation of the world follows such a course, smaller nations are likely to conclude that they lack any power to create a better world order and thus to look only to their immediate and narrow national interests. We shall all be the worse off if this occurs.[8] The United States would benefit in important though intangible respects if other nations were convinced that it was basically supporting the growing desire of peoples everywhere for economic progress and social justice. Moreover, if the present international system is to work successfully, the underdeveloped Asian countries as well as rich Western nations must share in its benefits. This is not to raise the specter of the poor of the world uniting in frustration and anger to overrun the rich nations. The organization and effort necessary for such an upsurge would be many times greater—and take fully as long to muster—as the task of transforming their poverty into wealth. They can, however, disrupt the present system to an unpleasant if not critical degree if they see no future for themselves as a part of it.

The interest in the world community is much broader than any interest the United States has in seeing the poor countries become richer so that they would be more important trading partners. This is not because trade is unimportant or because trade between rich and poor countries automatically results in exploitation of the poor nations, for trade generally helps development. But the present value of the profit to be gained over the years is likely to be much less than what would be expended on any meaningful aid program in countries such as India and Pakistan.

Another point to be examined is the American interest in the type of political and economic systems adopted by these countries. Does the United States have a national interest in a democratic political system and a private enterprise economic system? It does have an interest in a reasonable degree of political stability, and in our age, in Asia as elsewhere, this means a measure of popular participation in the political process. Yet it is difficult to demonstrate that a democracy will automatically concentrate on development, or that it will adopt a restrained policy toward its neighbors. Conversely, there are authoritarian regimes concentrating on development and the welfare of their citizens. The long-term prospects for democracy are not so bright in India or so hopeless in Pakistan—nor are our interests so closely connected with their political systems—to make this concern a dominant consideration in our policies.

Much the same can be said regarding the type of economic system they adopt. The issue here is often portrayed as sharper than it really is. Even if India and Pakistan move to the left in the next few years, neither country is going to put its private sector out of business or even prevent it from growing, and both governments will have to do certain things—such as owning and operating railroads, utilities, and some industrial establishments—that will differ from the American or European patterns.

Unquestionably, we derive psychological security from observing other nations operating under political and economic systems similar to our own, and surely the same is true of the Communists. But diversity is not an inherent ideological problem for us, nor should we make it one; the West has in fact (if not always in rhetoric) demonstrated it can work with many different types of governments. Although there are some countries with governments so inept or repressive as to make it unwise to support them, this is emphatically not true of India; whether it will be true of Pakistan in the future is considered in Chapters 14 and 15.

Finally, the United States has moral and humanitarian interests in the political, economic, and social progress of India and Pakistan. These considerations are related to our interest in a sound world order although the motivations are distinct. Many people are unwilling to accept the idea of moral and humanitarian interests because they see no clear way of applying them in practice. How does one decide the extent of such obligations and the way they are integrated with other foreign-policy goals or weighed against domestic responsibilities? Do we have an obligation to keep other peoples from starving, but no more? Do we have an obligation to help raise their standard of living? To what level? If a nation undermines our interests—or wastes its own resources beyond a "reasonable" degree—does this cancel the obligation? One could go on with such questions almost indefinitely; but once any obligation in this area is acknowledged, it cannot be evaded in policy decisions because of the attendant complexities.

There are two further general objections to concluding that moral and humanitarian considerations should affect our foreign policy. The first is that when they are combined with the traditional considerations of national interest, the result is such a hodge-podge of different elements that it is impossible to sort them out and ascertain why different types of action are taken. But a desire for simplicity and neatness is hardly an adequate reason for excluding humanitarian considerations. There is, in addition, the hazard that a nation will try to deceive the world—and actually deceive itself—on the reasons for its actions, using the cloak of altruism to cover narrow self-interest.

Throughout history, man has attempted to ennoble his basest deeds in this manner, and the practice will not disappear. Yet it seems likely that if our actions are based more on humanitarian considerations, we will be better off than we have been in the past; for, in effect, our deeds will be brought more closely in line with our words.

The second objection rests on the assertion that nations can—or as some say, should—act only in accord with their national interests, which are taken to apply only to material or security considerations. This criticism is generally directed against foreign aid proposed on humanitarian or moral grounds rather than on specified political objectives. Strangely, many who hold this view find no inconsistency in supporting disaster relief for those suffering from natural calamities like floods or earthquakes. But it is difficult to see how disaster relief is different *in principle* from aid for economic development. Economic assistance is much more complex and the results more uncertain, but that is true also of military alliances, arms aid, diplomatic maneuvers, and nearly all the other instruments of foreign policy. Humanitarian considerations have long been a factor (though an unmeasurable one) in U.S. aid programs, as they are for the growing programs of certain European countries.

Nearly two decades ago Reinhold Niebuhr, a political realist as well as a moralist, stated the issue in a manner that has perennial relevance:

Every nation must come to terms with the fact that . . . the force of collective self-interest is so great, that national policy must be based upon it; yet also the sensitive conscience recognizes that the moral obligation of the individual transcends his particular community. Loyalty to the community is therefore morally tolerable only if it includes values wider than those of the community.[9]

Hans Morgenthau, the dean of political realists, made another pertinent point regarding morality and foreign policy when he wrote:

. . . the United States, in a unique sense, is being judged by other nations, and it is judged by itself in terms of its compliance with the moral standards which it has set for itself. . . .

We have noticed, not only from the Russian example but from our own experience . . . to what extent the real power of a nation consists not in the number of nuclear warheads it holds or the number of divisions or aircraft carriers, but of the moral image it presents—not only in words but, more particularly, in deeds—to the rest of the world. . . .

Thus the crisis of American foreign policy is, on the most fundamental level, a moral crisis, and this moral crisis is not limited to foreign policy.[10]

There is room for debate over what America's moral responsibilities in the world are; but when political realists like Professor Morgenthau criticize U.S. policy in Vietnam because it is immoral as well as against the national interest, it is hard to maintain that foreign policy and moral concerns are unrelated. A wealthy America cannot fulfill its moral obligations in the present age if it is unconcerned with the fate of those less fortunate as they struggle to achieve a better life.

* * *

U.S. policy toward another country or area can be approached in several ways. One is to determine the importance of the area, then decide the specific policies that are most likely to enable the United States to reach its goals there. Another is to begin by looking at the probable trends in the area and then decide how the United States should shape its policies to take advantage of them. A third approach is to look at the key issues that must be faced by the United States and, in deciding how to deal with them, set forth the framework of national policy. These approaches are not mutually exclusive, for any comprehensive policy statement will deal in some measure with the importance of the area to the United States, the probable trends, and the key issues.

I have discussed the general importance of India and Pakistan to the United States in this chapter, concentrating on underlying issues. The following three chapters are organized around an examination of the main issues that this country will have to consider in formulating its policies. At the same time, conclusions on how to deal with the issues will be heavily influenced by the analysis of present and probable trends in the area over the coming years. Chapters 14-16 deal, respectively, with (1) the role the United States should play in the economic development of India and Pakistan, (2) the policy it should adopt toward the important regional conflicts, and (3) the position the United States should take in regard to the defense of the subcontinent. All of these matters are interrelated, and the final chapter briefly summarizes the conclusions and discusses the future positions of the United States and the subcontinent in light of the policy recommendations.

14

Development Problems and Prospects

The termination of British rule in the subcontinent in 1947 marked the end of the struggle of more than one-seventh of the world's population to win freedom. It was also a beginning, for the two new countries faced the more difficult tasks of fashioning and operating political and economic systems that would enable them to develop national strength and create a decent life for the masses of people suffering from poverty and injustice. Much has changed in India and Pakistan since 1947. New institutions and industries have been created, and growing segments of both nations have shaken off the lethargy of centuries. At the same time, old problems have persisted and new ones have arisen, thus placing additional demands and strains on both countries.

The $13 billion in economic assistance that the United States has provided the two countries testifies to our belief that their domestic progress was important to us as well as to them. The more than $8 billion extended by other non-Communist countries and international organizations indicates a similar assessment. But while aid commitments by most other non-Communist countries are remaining stable or even rising, U.S. aid appropriations have been declining for several years. Many Americans have concluded that the United States should further reduce its aid, and some have even argued that external aid merely allows the ruling groups to postpone the drastic social and economic reforms that are necessary for ultimate success in the modernization process.

Thus, before discussing the role the United States might play in the development process in India and Pakistan, it is necessary to draw up a short balance sheet of their efforts to date, outline their problems and opportunities, and arrive at some conclusions about their prospects. This survey will of necessity be brief and selective, for this is not a book about the internal problems and prospects of India and Pakistan. Yet foreign and domestic policies are seldom as distinct as the two adjectives imply, and no sensible decisions on foreign aid can be made that ignore the present situation and possibilities.

India: The Long Road Ahead

India's achievements were many and varied during its first fifteen years of independence. It overcame the upheaval of partition, integrated hundreds of princely states, drew up a new constitution, held three nationwide general elections, and had an outstanding record of political stability. India also enacted a variety of economic and social reforms and rapidly—perhaps even too rapidly—expanded educational opportunities. Under Nehru's guidance India gave high priority to an economic development program that focused the aspirations and energies of a growing number of Indians on modernization. During the first two Five-Year Plans, from 1951 to 1961, the economy expanded by about 3 to 4 per cent a year, having grown almost imperceptibly since the beginning of this century.[1] Foodgrain production rose by about 40 per cent, or nearly twice as fast as population, and industrial output rose by 85 per cent. The level of investment climbed steadily, and India's merchants gradually began to acquire some of the characteristics of industrialists.

These achievements were based on a combination of factors almost unique in the underdeveloped world. India had outstanding leadership and a strong political party which was able to work out policies that satisfied a large proportion of the country's modern-minded citizens while retaining the support of most of those with a traditional outlook. India also had an effective civil service (at least for the traditional functions of government) and a nonpolitical army loyal to the established authority and able to step in to assure internal security when such action was necessary. India's achievements provided hope that, despite the many obstacles, the country would gradually overcome its backwardness. If India received the rising level of foreign aid it required, its prospects would be encouraging.[2]

The 1960s were, however, a disappointing time in India. It proved impossible to step up the pace of development as planned. Foodgrain production stagnated at about 80 million tons annually from 1960 to 1964, jumped to 88 million tons the next year, and then fell precipitously to 72 million tons and 75 million tons in 1966 and 1967. With population increasing rapidly, huge imports were required. Agricultural setbacks and the increased defense spending caused by the wars with China in 1962 and Pakistan in 1965 brought on a recession. These troubles made it impossible for India to complete its Third Five-Year Plan (1961–66) successfully or to begin its Fourth Plan in 1966 as originally intended, despite the high levels of economic assistance it received.[3]

India's political system also was subjected to serious strains in the latter half of the 1960s. The Congress government made the transition from Nehru to Shastri and from Shastri to Mrs. Gandhi smoothly, but in the 1967 general election the Congress party lost

TABLE 3

Indian Parliamentary Election Results

Party	Seats					
	1971	1970[b]	1967	1962	1957	1952
Congress (R)	350	228	288	358	371	354
Congress (O)	16	65	—	—	—	—
Swatantra	8	35	43	18	—	—
CPI	23	24	23	29	27	26
CPI (M)	25	19	19	—	—	—
JS	22	33	35	14	4	3
PSP	2	15	13	12	19	20
SSP	3	17	23	—	—	—
Others and Independents	66	83	76	60	73	83
Totals	515[a]	519	520	491	494	486

Notes:

a. Three seats undeclared.

b. No election was held in 1970, but this was the distribution of seats after the Congress party split.

Source: India News (Washington, D.C.: Embassy of India), February 26, 1971; March 19, 1971.

control of nearly half of the state governments and barely managed to retain its majority in Parliament. This dramatic setback was as much due to defections of dissident Congressmen and to the ability of opposition parties to work together against the Congress party as to the latter's loss of popular votes—which declined from 44.7 per cent in the 1962 parliamentary elections to 40.7 per cent in 1967. Nonetheless, the setback to the Congress party ushered in a period of political uncertainty and instability. This was especially noticeable at the level of the states, which were enlarging their already substantial powers. In some states a variety of parties and individuals, with little in common beyond a desire for power, formed and reformed coalition governments—a few of which were dominated by one or the other of India's Communist parties. The weakened Congress leadership at the center could do little to prevent this.[4] As a result, the opinions of informed observers shifted from hope and some confidence to fear over India's future.

The shift in opinion was most dramatically illustrated by the publication of Gunnar Myrdal's *Asian Drama* in 1968.[5] This monumental work is as comprehensive as it is pessimistic about the future of India and most of the other countries of South Asia. Unimpressed by the progress made since independence, the study dwells upon the negative effects of the social systems (especially in India with its caste, linguistic, and religious attitudes which hinder modernization), the weak resource bases, unfavorable climates, corruption, misdirected educational policies, and the large and rapidly growing populations. Myrdal is convinced that the modern industrial sector in these economies remains largely isolated from the traditional sectors and thus does not stimulate them or assure the spread of more productive attitudes. He also lays great stress on the general lack of social discipline in these "soft states" (which leads to lax enforcement of the laws and regulations enacted) and on the futility of basing economic plans on Western concepts in the conditions of South Asia, which are so different from conditions where the economic theories arose. Myrdal's pessimism is reinforced by his conviction that a revolutionary change in social and economic relationships and in personal values is essential to rapid progress, but that because of the failure to carry out such a revolution at the time of independence, the strategic opportunity was missed. Now, power is firmly in the hands of those who have no intention of permitting thoroughgoing change. The study ends on the depressing note that the outlook for modernization is quite bleak.

Further losses suffered by the Congress party in several state elections early in 1969 and, later in the year, the dramatic split at the national level between Mrs. Gandhi's supporters and the more conservative party elements intensified the pessimism. The country's only nationwide political party was in disarray, and the central government was dependent on the support of other parties for the first time since independence. Political standards were declining (especially at the state level where sordid bargaining for votes and aisle-crossing became increasingly common); and because of the periodic inability of some states to form governments, the center imposed Presidents' rule for varying periods of time.[6] Was Indian democracy disintegrating, and an authoritarian government about to assume power? Even if an unstable democracy continued, how could it effectively deal with the great difficulties India faced in its development effort?

There were several arguments against a pessimistic response to these questions. The Indian political process was becoming more responsive to groups formerly excluded from a significant role in political life. This was producing turmoil as well as greater participation; and such a transformation could hardly take place smoothly. The India of 1970 was not the India of 1950: it was more educated, more urbanized, more politically aware, and more demanding—especially toward the Congress party, which had raised its hopes and expectations. But India's federal system is able to absorb a considerable amount of shock in one state and then in another without endangering the entire country. This limits the potential of extremist movements on the right or left. Both Hindu traditionalists and the Indian Communists have thus far demonstrated strength only in selected areas—and both movements have tended to fragment over time as they attempted to expand their constituencies.

India's size and diversity are so overwhelming that one wonders whether any but a federal democratic system would be flexible enough to provide effective government for long. The problems of governing such a large and heterogeneous population would give any potential strongman pause. These circumstances provide no absolute assurance that democracy will survive—or that an authoritarian government would be a disaster. If the parliamentary system broke down, it seems unlikely that the Indian military establishment (which apparently is still basically nonpolitical) would stand idle while the nation disintegrated. Military leaders probably would work with other groups with a national outlook and a desire for development to provide a functioning government. But they also know they would face many difficulties, and this knowledge is one asset of Indian democracy.

Mrs. Gandhi apparently spent little time worrying about such matters; instead she worked diligently to increase her party's strength and popularity. She proved adept at political maneuvering, much to the dismay of the old guard who originally placed her in the Prime Ministership only to see her cut them off from power. Her moves to nationalize banks and end the special privileges of the princes, as symbols of her expressed determination to pursue a more radical policy, gradually won her increased popularity.

By early 1971 she was ready for her next dramatic move—the dissolution of Parliament and the holding of new elections a year ahead of schedule. The old guard Congress party forged electoral agreements in many areas with the conservative Swatantra party, the Hindu Jan Sangh, and one of the socialist parties whose animosity toward Mrs. Gandhi overshadowed all else in its considerations. Yet it soon became apparent to the people that these parties had no positive program, and in the early March election Mrs. Gandhi's Congress party won a dramatic victory by increasing its seats from 228 to 350, or better than a two-thirds majority. The conservative opposition was reduced to insignificance, and nearly all of the regionally based parties suffered a similar fate. Only the two Communist parties held out against the tide, but they remained small and their strength was limited to a few areas. (Unfortunately, the left-wing Communists won additional seats in the important state of West Bengal; their strength, the activities of ultra-left-wing Maoist terrorists, and the refugee influx portend continued turmoil there.) Mrs. Gandhi's political position in parliament and the country was much enhanced, at least for the next several years.

There is, moreover, reason to believe that India's economic prospects are not as gloomy as some observers proclaim. The thesis that basic changes in the social system and personal attitudes of the South Asian peoples must precede significant economic progress is open to challenge. It is equally plausible that if the opportunities for advancement are present, people—including many with traditional outlooks—will respond to them, although not in precisely the same way people elsewhere would, and their responses will produce new attitudes.[7] This is demonstrated by an extremely important change in the past few years that provides a basis for at least cautious optimism regarding one of India's major problems: It is the series of developments that has come to be called the Green Revolution—and it has largely occurred since the publication of *Asian Drama*.[8]

The new strains of wheat and rice, which are becoming more widely available, have already demonstrated that crop yields can be increased severalfold when the seeds are properly combined with irrigation and water control, fertilizer, and pesticides, and when grain prices are sufficiently attractive to the farmers. Carrying out the Green Revolution, however, demands well-coordinated programs. Moreover, it offers greater prospective gains to regions with ample supplies of water and to the more prosperous peasants who can take advantage of the new opportunities. This has already exacerbated social tensions and led to outbreaks of violence in India and scattered attempts by poorer peasants to seize land, situations which are likely to recur.[9]

The potential gains are so large and so important that India (and Pakistan) have little choice but to push ahead with the necessary programs, facing the unfortunate side-effects as best they can. Considerable progress has already been made: for example, wheat production in 1968–69 was more than 50 per cent above the previous record crop. Still, the progress to date is only a start, for outside scattered pockets there have been as yet no dramatic increases in the important rice crop. Nevertheless, the potential exists to provide a much improved diet for India's burgeoning millions, while buying some time to cope with the explosive population problem.

Foodgrains are only part of the picture, of course, and the long-term outlook for the country depends upon the interaction of many distinct elements: the quality of political leadership, the development of the attitudes and institutions necessary for modernization, the rate of economic progress, population growth, and India's relations with its neighbors and the great powers, to name only the more prominent factors. Progress in coping with these difficult problems will rest upon the performance of the Indians themselves, although outside powers can by their acts or inaction have an effect in some areas.

What are the chances of India making at least satisfactory progress? It is, of course, impossible to define satisfactory progress in any very precise way, such as a particular rate of economic growth. Basically, however, it would mean doing well enough for an accepted and reasonably effective political system to continue, for national unity to prevail, for economic and social injustice to decline, for living standards to rise and, in time, for the economy to become self-sustaining.

Perhaps, given the role of the government in Indian life, the most important domestic factor in determining India's progress over the next few years will be the quality of the leadership Mrs. Gandhi and her colleagues provide. Her victory could be the first step toward revital-izing a tired party and refurbishing its image, which had been steadily becoming one of self-seeking politicians who did little but reiterate worn-out slogans. But Mrs. Gandhi must demonstrate that her gov-ernment is capable of dealing with at least some of India's pressing problems in a manner that is meaningful to the people. This will re-quire a combination of real progress and of politically appealing sym-bols; for while slow gains in economic growth (the only kind pos-sible) are necessary, they are less likely to win popular acclaim and elections than dramatic moves such as Mrs. Gandhi's nationalization of the banks.

One perennial danger is that the government will adopt politically appealing measures that have an adverse economic effect, such as pil-ing new controls on an already overregulated economy. Another is that it will inflate expectations by pushing through new laws which, while commendable in themselves, cannot be implemented because of political opposition within the governing party or lack of adequate administrative resources and flexibility. Moreover, many of Mrs. Gandhi's supporters are by no means oriented toward reforms—espe-cially land reform—but have lined up behind her because they think she will win out over the old guard and thus be the one to distribute patronage and other favors. While these conservatives and moderates will at times provide a check on Mrs. Gandhi's impulsive tendencies, by that very fact they will also limit the government's ability to move. Finally, the government may not be willing to impose the sacrifices on the people necessary to move the economy ahead rapidly.

These dangers are clearly illustrated in India's Fourth Five-Year Plan (1969–74), which aims at stepping up the growth rate to 5.5 per cent annually. The plan (as revised in 1970) calls for the expendi-ture of $32.2 billion, with just over two-thirds in the public sector and the rest in the private sector. It is more than twice as large as the Third Plan in terms of current rupee prices, but because of inflation it is only about 50 per cent larger in real terms. The pattern of outlays is basically similar to the Third Plan, but it recognizes the necessity to expand agriculture rapidly and to move quickly in the crucial task of lowering the birth rate. Special programs to aid agriculture are to be undertaken outside the plan, and there is to be a sharp increase in family-planning activities.

Success in carrying out the plan will depend on raising the necessary domestic resources, securing the required foreign exchange through exports and foreign aid, and implementing the many projects on schedule. These general requirements apply to both the public and private sectors, although in somewhat different ways. For example, the private sector probably has the managerial capacity to carry out its part of the plan, but its ability to raise the necessary resources will be heavily influenced by the economic and tax policies of the national and state governments. The government, on the other hand, has the means to mobilize domestic resources if it has the will to do so, but it may lack the managerial skills to implement on schedule some of the projects it undertakes.

There is reason for serious doubt about raising all the required domestic resources. Political pressures on both the federal and the state governments to provide expanded current services will make it hard to hold the growth of expenditures for such services to planned levels. Moreover, Mrs. Gandhi's pledges to pursue a socialist course and to reduce income disparities may lead the government to take steps that will reduce the funds available to the private sector, although thus far it has generally acted so as to minimize this danger. In addition, it is doubtful that the public-sector enterprises, which at least until recently have been operating at a deficit, can generate the roughly $2 billion in profits that are to help finance the plan. It is possible, of course, for the federal and state governments to make up these shortages by increased taxation and by higher charges for services it presently provides. But, such measures are already scheduled to provide an additional $3.5 billion. This in itself will be extremely difficult in view of the political costs involved, and it would be unrealistic to expect new taxes to make up for large shortfalls in other areas of resource mobilization. Increased deficit financing probably can take up some, but only some, of the slack. While it would be a mistake to focus only on these problems, given India's past record of mobilizing large sums for its plans, a shortfall of at least modest proportions seems likely.

In turning to India's foreign-exchange requirements, several points should be specially noted. Exports must grow by 7 per cent annually to reach target levels. This is considerably above the long-term trend, but less out of line with the record of recent years when India has worked hard to expand exports.

The plan projections for foreign aid are less ambitious. During most of the 1960s India received net foreign assistance of approximately $1 billion a year. Gross aid rose from about $1.2 billion a year to $1.6 billion, but repayment obligations also rose from about $200 million to nearly $500 million. The Fourth Plan, however, calls for only half the total net foreign assistance received during the Third Plan—that is, only about $2.5 billion. This is partly because the expanded machine-building capacity developed over the years makes India less dependent on capital imports, partly because of a political desire to be less dependent on outside powers, but particularly because of a judgment that aid levels are in fact likely to decline. Meanwhile, repayment obligations continue to rise, and India must secure gross aid of about $5 billion since debt repayments will require some $2.5 billion.

Even if India gets the specified amounts of foreign exchange from exports and aid receipts, it will face difficulties in securing adequate imports of raw materials, spare parts, and various semi-processed goods to keep the economy moving ahead without spending more for such imports than scheduled. The government has traditionally underestimated the amount of maintenance imports needed when the economy was expanding, and one suspects this tendency has not ended.

To summarize, the Fourth Plan aims at stepping up the rate of growth from about 3 per cent to 5.5 per cent annually while net foreign aid declines by about 50 per cent. This is to be accomplished by a greater reliance on domestic savings and investment. The economy expanded by 5–6 per cent during the first two years of the plan, but more difficult tests lie ahead. Despite the potential of the Green Revolution and the existence of much under-utilized industrial capacity— imports have been held down in order to build up foreign-exchange reserves—it seems doubtful that India can substantially increase its rate of growth at the same time it receives only about half of the net foreign aid of recent years. Indeed, unless the added burden of caring for the refugees from East Pakistan can be eased, India's economy is likely to suffer significantly.

Pakistan: The Disintegration of a Nation?

Pakistan's first decade as a nation demonstrated two points: its remarkable ability to create a government and survive despite the upheavals that attended its birth, and its inability to establish the basic institutions necessary to enable the country to progress politically or economically. The once dominant Muslim League, oriented almost entirely toward winning partition, had no positive social or economic program, and its popular support steadily diminished. The appeal of other Pakistani political parties seldom reached beyond particular regions or groups. Moreover, civil servants and military officers began in the early 1950s to play an active political role, though for the most part they did so behind the scenes. Pakistan never held general elections, took years to prepare a constitution which was never fully put into effect, and made no real attempt to embark upon an economic development program. The division of the country into east and west wings and the attempt to create a state based upon Islamic principles presented additional complications.

Many of these problems receded into the background after the 1958 military coup of Ayub and his colleagues, a take-over that was originally supported by many and accepted by nearly everyone. Ayub was convinced that the divisions among the country's various regions, religious sects, political parties, and economic interest groups were so fundamental that purposeful and effective national leadership was impossible under a parliamentary system. Only a centralized government with a strong president offered any hope of stability and progress.

Gradually the regime gained confidence and effectiveness. It shifted its efforts from keeping the streets clean and curtailing corruption to working out a political structure and an economic development program. The government drafted a constitution, which was adopted in 1962 and which allowed a measure of popular participation while preserving Ayub's authority unimpaired. Ayub dominated and played off his rivals while keeping the ultimate source of his power, the armed forces, in the background; and his victory in the 1965 presidential election seemed to confirm his judgment as to the type of government Pakistan needed. The political system attracted attention as a possible middle way between dictatorship and parliamentary democracy.

In addition to establishing an apparently effective political system, the Ayub government also sponsored Pakistan's first serious economic development program. During its first decade Pakistan's rate of economic growth was only about 2.5 per cent annually, or about equal to the rate of population growth. The only bright spot was the rapid development of light industry—principally cotton and jute textiles. This, however, was offset by the failure of agriculture to keep up with population growth, which in time ended the country's self-sufficiency in food production. Pakistan was slow to establish a planning apparatus, and its First Five-Year Plan was not even published until 1957, two years after it was to have begun.

The most important contribution Ayub's government made toward economic development was simply to give it a high priority and sustained attention. The government, confident it would be in power for many years, was able to draw up and implement long-term programs. During the Second Five-Year Plan (1960–65) more funds—partly from taxation and partly from increased foreign aid—were devoted to economic development. Industry continued to expand rapidly, the rate of growth of the key agricultural sector rose significantly, and gross national product increased by about 5.5 per cent annually.[10]

The economy continued to grow at about the same rate during the Third Five-Year Plan (1965–70), and Pakistan attracted international attention as one of the success stories among the underdeveloped countries.[11] But grave problems were forming beneath the surface. Sharply increased defense spending in the wake of the war with India, a severe drought early in the plan period, and less foreign aid than anticipated made it impossible for Pakistan to realize its ambitious investment targets and its goal of an annual GNP growth rate of 7 per cent. In fact, only by cutting back on planned social welfare outlays was the growth rate held above 5 per cent.

Although Ayub overcame the immediate domestic political repercussions of the war with India, the conflict was, in retrospect, the beginning of the end for him. The war exacerbated the East Pakistani feeling against rule by the West Pakistanis and led numerous politicians in the eastern wing to press demands for a degree of autonomy that seemed to Ayub to foreshadow eventual secession. He resorted more and more to political repression of his opponents in both wings. This appeared to work for a time, but repression led to disaffection. The officially sponsored adulation of Ayub continued until it became laughable to some and irritating to even more Pakistanis, and in this atmosphere Ayub lost touch with popular opinion. Nepotism and corruption were on the increase, and after Ayub's illness in 1967 the question of a successor naturally became an issue. Prices rose rapidly, and the principal beneficiaries of Pakistan's economic growth were the small number of industrialists and the wealthier peasants, which created much dissatisfaction among other groups. Finally, although the rate of growth increased in East as well as West Pakistan, the really dramatic advances were made in the western wing, which received about two-thirds of the total investment during the 1960s.[12] The more numerous East Pakistanis, who had long provided over half of the country's exports, regarded this as a new form of colonial exploitation.

As the vulnerability of Ayub's regime became more evident during 1968, opposition leaders and aggrieved groups took the offensive. Ayub's alternating attempts to repress the agitation and to play off his rivals by offering selective concessions no longer worked; even former supporters began to attack him. The spreading demonstrations became increasingly violent, and government authority appeared to be collapsing. Ayub's announcement that he would not stand for re-election in 1970 could not stem the tide, nor could his promise of direct elections and the return to a parliamentary system.[13] Ultimately the army under General Yahya Khan felt compelled to intervene to prevent a violent social and political upheaval. Pakistan had succumbed to the inherent weakness of any country ruled by one man; the political institutions created by Ayub, having no real life of their own, were essentially a means of cloaking his personal rule and that of the steadily narrowing spectrum of groups he represented.

Thus Pakistan once again set out to construct a political system combining effective government with an adequate measure of popular participation—or at least popular acceptance. President Yahya's strategy was to grant enough of the demands of the aggrieved groups to encourage moderation and a willingness to reach compromise agreements. Late in 1969 he announced that on October 5, 1970, Pakistan would hold the first national elections in its history in order to elect a constituent assembly. As consensus developed on certain issues, President Yahya stipulated that the new constitution should conform to these ideas. The new government was to be parliamentary rather than presidential, thus satisfying those committed to democracy and fearful of the re-establishment of an Ayub-type regime. Representation in the parliament was to be on the basis of "one man, one vote" rather than parity between the two wings of the country, which he hoped would ease the fears of the more numerous East Pakistanis that West Pakistan would continue its domination. Yahya also set in motion the division of West Pakistan into four smaller provinces, reverting to the situation before their merger into one unit in 1955, thus satisfying the peoples of the less populous regions of West Pakistan who resented the dominant position of the Punjab.

Yet it became apparent that the interim government could not settle certain intractable issues over which the country was so deeply divided that only an elected government could resolve them—if they could be settled at all. The most important issue was the division of authority between the provinces and the central government, with many Pakistanis (especially in the east) determined that virtually all authority reside in the provinces and others convinced that such an outcome would soon lead to national disintegration. The extent to which Islamic principles and law were to be incorporated into the constitution and policies of the nation was another matter about which there was much disagreement. Pakistan had uneasily compromised this issue in the past, but the tendency of some politicians and parties to claim they were the true defenders of Islam and brand their opponents as anti-Islamic portended trouble. The power of the president as head of state—and possibly as the "representative" of the powerful civil-military bureaucracy that has directly or indirectly ruled the nation during most of its existence—was also an important issue, although one usually referred to obliquely rather than directly. President Yahya's insistence that any new constitution adopted by the constituent assembly must be approved by him—an approval contingent on the constitution's maintaining the integrity of Pakistan—was the specific expression of this issue and the source of much dispute.

The election was postponed until December 1970 because of disruptions caused by floods earlier in the year, and in November nature again intervened. East Pakistan suffered one of the worst natural disasters of the century in the cyclone and tidal wave which killed several hundred thousand people. The government's lethargic response added fuel to Bengali anger, and intensified their conviction that provincial autonomy was essential—an attitude that benefited the Awami League. The elections, held in this atmosphere indicated that Pakistan was basically two separate polities. Sheikh Mujibar Rahman's Awami League, which won a dramatic victory by capturing all but two of East Pakistan's seats, had run on his platform of provincial autonomy, moderate socialism, and, less openly, a normalization of relations with India. Z. A. Bhutto's newly formed Pakistan's People's Party, which won over 60 per cent of the seats in the western wing (almost entirely in the Punjab and Sind) campaigned for a stronger central government, extensive socialization, and a harsh anti-Indian line. Neither party won any seats in the other wing of the country.

The East Pakistani demand for complete provincial autonomy quickly became the central political and constitutional issue facing the country. The nature of Sheik Mujib's "six-point" autonomy program illustrates the extent of the Bengali demands. The central government was to be responsible only for foreign affairs and defense, while the provinces were to be in complete control of economic affairs, including foreign trade and foreign aid. All taxes were to be levied by the provinces, which would provide funds to the central government for the military and foreign services.

Negotiations among the country's political leaders and President Yahya in the early months of 1971 soon demonstrated that all concerned were caught up in the politics of intransigence rather than of compromise. Yahya and the military were determined that the armed forces be assured an adequate budget, and to them this probably meant a central government with the power to tax. Bhutto (and most of the other politicians from the western wing) insisted that the government could not control foreign affairs unless it controlled foreign trade and aid; his ambition for a prominent role in the central government was also involved. Most West Pakistanis felt that their willingness to give the Bengalis a majority in the national assembly and moderate provincial autonomy demonstrated their good faith. The Awami League demands looked dangerously like secession in all but name.

Sheikh Mujib's sweeping victory placed him in a position of great strength, but it also limited his room for maneuver. The Bengalis were strongly behind him, and, because his party had won an absolute majority of seats, they expected him to hold to his demands in substance if not in detail. Extreme leftists led by Maulana Bhashani pressed him hard to take a tough line. And Mujib himself showed little desire for compromise. Heading a central government with some role in taxation and economic affairs, thus making possible the transfer of resources from the west to the east, held less interest for him and his colleagues than completely controlling East Pakistan.

By late February it was clear that no basic understanding could be resolved before the constituent assembly was due to meet on March 3, and Bhutto announced that his party would not attend the sessions unless Mujib indicated a willingness to compromise. Yahya, perplexed, frustrated, and dubious about proceeding in the face of such a boycott, yielded to Bhutto's blackmail and on March 1 postponed the opening session indefinitely.

Yahya's action was a tragic miscalculation, for it set in motion a series of events that led to civil war. The Awami League responded with defiance; it called a general strike and then took control of East

Pakistan. Mujib began issuing orders to government officials there, who soon demonstrated that their allegiance was to him rather than to President Yahya. It was the most successful non-cooperation movement the subcontinent had ever seen. As ominous as the defiance of martial law were the rising popular emotions and growing demands for independence rather than autonomy. The Pakistan flag was replaced with the emblem of Bangla Desh (Bengali homeland), and Bengalis began to harass the army and non-Bengalis living in the province, who as refugees from India supported a strong national government.[14] Mujib succeeded in controlling some of these activities, but could not prevent them all.

Such actions were humiliating to Yahya who was already under considerable pressure from some military colleagues to assert the regime's authority by forceful moves. At the same time he was impressed by the extent of Bengali solidarity, and on March 6 reversed himself and called for the assembly to convene on March 25. But Mujib insisted on an end to martial law and the transfer of power to elected representatives before the assembly met, conditions Yahya refused to accept. He had already begun to send reinforcements to the East, although it is not clear whether these were to enable the government to prevent a secessionist effort or to crush an autonomy movement. Similarly, Yahya's mid-March trip to Dacca can be interpreted either as reflecting a desperate desire to find some basis for accommodation, or as a means of buying time until the army had been reinforced. But the arrival of more West Pakistani troops increased Bengali suspicions and led to new and bigger clashes.

The record of the final negotiations between Yahya, Mujib, and Bhutto is confusing and their motivations and intentions are unclear. What is clear is that Yahya's postponement of the assembly confirmed Bengali suspicions that West Pakistanis did not intend to abide by the results of a free election if its outcome displeased them; continued domination and exploitation appeared to be their portion. The Bengali reaction intensified West Pakistani suspicions that Pakistan was about to be destroyed and stimulated their apprehensions of having to face an India ten times the size of West Pakistan. Moreover, Mujib seemed to Yahya—and to some outside observers—to be playing a devious game. In this atmosphere Yahya, probably pushed by hawks within his ranks, could not bring himself to take the risk of trusting Mujib and his colleagues, and on March 25 took the greater risk of trying to solve the country's political problem by a resort to arms.

A government that has lost its moral authority can rule millions of hostile people with an army of some 50,000 only by terrorizing them into submission. The action of the military demonstrated this fact, for from the beginning they were ruthless. Within a few months several hundred thousand Bengalis apparently were dead and several million (mostly Hindu) had fled to India. In addition to calculated terror there was widespread indiscriminate killing, partly due to old animosities between Punjabis and Bengalis and partly due to the frenzied blood lust that often overtakes men let loose under such circumstances. Moreover, thousands of Muslim Biharis who had settled in East Pakistan after partition were slaughtered by Bengalis jealous of their modest prosperity, and convinced that they were working with the military.

The military demonstrated efficiency as well as ruthlessness. They quickly scattered the ill-organized Bengali forces (perhaps 20,000 Bengalis from the military and border guards, as well as thousands of police, joined the rebellion) and gained control of the key locations before the monsoon struck in June. But, if the government won the first round and retains certain important advantages in the struggle, a brief survey of its problems indicates that its long-term position is unenviable.

Yahya's regime must accomplish four things in order to hold East Pakistan. It must (1) put down the resistance movement; (2) revive the administration in the East; (3) find East Pakistani politicians loyal to Pakistan and acceptable to the Bengalis; and (4) maintain a firm base of power in West Pakistan. Each will be difficult, and together they may well be impossible.

The regime's most important assets in dealing with these problems are, in addition to its military strength, the determination of its leaders and its ability to punish those who refuse to cooperate with it and reward those who do. It can not only imprison suspected enemies, but it can take away their property and offer it, as well as the lands and other property left behind by the refugees, to those East Pakistanis willing to support the regime. Such power weighs heavily in an area where widespread poverty forces many people to concentrate on sheer survival.

The government has demonstrated that it can control any area it sends its troops into, but they cannot be everywhere at once. (It has already reduced its forces in West Pakistan somewhat, and probably will be reluctant to cut them further out of fear of an Indian attack.) Transport facilities in the East have been badly damaged, and government mobility during the monsoons and in times of flood will be hampered.

The resistance forces in the East are still poorly armed and organized. Although their capabilities are gradually increasing, strong guerrilla movements take time to develop even when the political environment is favorable and outside help is available. The resistance apparently consists of three groups: the leaders and members of the Awami League who escaped arrest, but who evidently made little preparation for the situation they now face; Bengali soldiers, border guards, and policemen, who have done most of the fighting; and extreme leftist forces of various hues and orientations. The conventional wisdom suggests that the leftists should be better organized and, as extremists rather than moderates, better able to take advantage of a chaotic situation than the middle class lawyers, teachers, and businessmen of the Awami League. Yet the leftists are also led by middle class elements and have a long history of factional infighting, a characteristic of Bengali politics that even war is unlikely to erase. Under these circumstances the second group may play the key role, and they probably have no political orientation as yet beyond a populist Bengali nationalism. Although further resistance carries the threat of continued turmoil, reprisals, and suffering, so many have suffered so much in the recent bloodbath that many Bengalis probably are convinced that they can only win a decent future through independence. Thus while the government's control of key areas is probably secure, at least for a time, it will not be able to prevent continuing sabotage and harassment.

But the regime must do more than maintain a tenuous order in the province; its shattered administration must be rebuilt if it is to prevent famine and epidemics and get the economy operating again.[15] It must collect taxes and revive exports to pay for the costs of its military operations as well as the normal expenses of government. But the administration has been shattered; relying on West Pakistanis, Biharis, and Bengali collaborators to staff it will further antagonize most Bengalis, but their hostility will make it difficult to trust many of them. (Few West Pakistanis or Biharis will want to serve beyond the reach of the army's protection, which does not encompass the province's thousands of villages.) The regime has offered most civil servants (as well as police and soldiers) amnesty on the ground that they were misled. Sheer necessity will force some to accept, but slowdowns and passive resistance will be problems. In short, a weak administration at best.

Even if the regime is moderately successful in dealing with these issues, it must find political leaders loyal to it who are not obvious puppets. Yahya still asserts that he wants to turn power over to "responsible" political leaders. But where can he find such people when he has banned the Awami League (and arrested and charged its leader with treason) just after it won 75 per cent of the vote? The government's appeals for political collaborators have received little response; hatred of West Pakistanis and fear of reprisals by resistance forces apparently are keeping most politicians with any support from cooperating. Yahya may hold "elections" for the seats of those Awami League officials under arrest, or in India, in order to replace them with regime supporters, but it will be difficult to make any political arrangements that depend on such men amount to more than a façade.

Perhaps most important of all, the regime's long-term position in the western wing is far from secure. Its actions have so far won considerable public support there, for its claim that its action was necessary to prevent separatists (supported by India) from destroying Pakistan has been generally accepted. Despite the government's use of the widespread fear of India, this support will be difficult to maintain as the costs become more apparent. Students, workers, and middle class elements who overthrew Ayub did not do so to open the way for another military regime. The politicians who won the elections want power. Bhutto in particular appears concerned that his control over his hastily organized party will not survive a long period of martial law. Yet the government can hardly turn over power to civilians in the west until it reaches some sort of a political accommodation with the east. Yahya is casting around for a constitutional structure which gives the politicians some power while retaining ultimate control through continued martial law, but any such arrangements are unlikely to be more than stop-gaps.

The economic costs of the government's policy are likely to be the most directly felt burdens, however, and they have already begun to pinch. Pakistan's economy was in difficulty when the fighting began, and the war intensified all its problems—exports are down, tax revenues are off, and foreign exchange reserves are nearly exhausted. The market for West Pakistani textiles in the East has dried up, which costs workers their jobs and farmers their cotton markets. Imports have already been cut back sharply, and further cuts in consumption and social welfare seem likely. Military spending is rising, for top priority must be given to keeping the military machine operating. Finally, Pakistan normally receives about $450 million annually in resources from Western countries, who see little chance of economic development until a political settlement is reached. Pakistan has defaulted on some of its foreign debt obligations, but these are not large enough to prevent further import cuts with much more dramatic impact on the economy of West as well as East Pakistan. It is easy to overestimate the short-run political impact of economic troubles, or the dependence of under-developed countries on outside resources, but Pakistan's economy is vulnerable to such factors over time. West Pakistani willingness to sacrifice in order to hold the country together gives the government some room for maneuver, but continued austerity is seldom a popular policy.

Thus the classic conditions for a stalemate exist. The Bengalis are likely to remain unreconciled to West Pakistani rule but unable to end it, at least in the near future. The government has little chance of re-storing a voluntary acceptance of its authority, but is convinced that giving East Pakistan autonomy would soon lead to Pakistan's destruc-tion, something no leader can contemplate. A compromise involving genuine but limited autonomy may become possible if the stalemate continues and wears down each side, but its terms are difficult to see.[16] Indeed, the army's actions have probably convinced many Bengalis that their lives will never be secure until West Pakistani troops leave the East, but such a demand would be seen by West Pakistan as remov-ing the only instrument by which it can maintain the integrity of the country.

America's Choices in South Asia

American policy-makers have long debated whether the United States should give top priority to its relations with India or Pakistan or try to balance its relations with the two countries by following a similar policy toward each. During the 1950s the United States clearly favored Pakistan, a policy which gradually shifted during the 1960s until it was abandoned after the 1965 war. The events in the sub-continent during 1971 have raised that issue again with new urgency: Can the United States treat two countries in such different circum-stances in the same manner, or should it adopt quite different policies toward them? Is it even possible to have a long-range policy toward Pakistan at the present time, when its future as a nation is so un-certain?

I would argue that because the nature of American interests in the subcontinent is fundamentally linked to their development as healthy societies, and because it is so difficult to see one country falling into chaos without ultimately damaging the other, the United States should follow as broadly similar policies toward each as their circumstances permit. This does not mean equating the two countries. India, as the larger one, will obviously require more economic assistance if the United States continues to be involved in its development efforts. But it does mean that differences in American policies toward them should grow out of differences in their efforts to advance and their prospects as countries.

If Pakistan had resolved its basic political problem in either of two ways—establishing a constitutional and political system acceptable to East and West Pakistanis alike, or agreeing to a peaceful separation —then the United States and other involved nations could have treated the countries similarly. But the Pakistani civil war changes all that. The most pressing task is to deal with the issue in such a way as to minimize the risks of its leading to a new Indo-Pakistani war and to maximize the chances of a political settlement inside Pakistan that will enable the country to turn to economic development. These matters will be determined largely by the governments and peoples of the two countries, for on issues of war and peace and national integrity, outside powers have only limited influence. Yet it is clear that the United States already is involved in these matters to the point that even a decision to do nothing would have major repercussions.

The first issue facing the United States and other Western countries is how to prevent famine from the upheavals in East Pakistan, a problem that will continue for some time. This probably is the simplest of the issues, for there is widespread agreement that the Western nations should continue to supply foodstuffs and medicines to those in need, whether they be the refugees in India or the destitute in East Pakistan. Beyond this, the United States should be willing to provide assistance to overcome the ravages of war. Although such measures might provide some indirect assistance to the regime's ability to continue a policy of repression, the main beneficiary would be the people in the east.

The next stage would be a difficult one, for if order is restored and the worst of the war damage overcome, the issue of whether or not to provide large-scale economic development assistance will arise. Here the aid suppliers should be forthcoming in their willingness to help, but firmly insistent that such assistance is conditioned on a political settlement and on a willingness to allow the refugees to return to their homes. (Decisions in this area will become increasingly complex and difficult if the government makes substantial, but not sufficient concessions to Bengali demands—a policy it has so far spurned.) The government will object strongly that this is attaching political strings to aid; that it is interfering in Pakistan's domestic affairs; that the absence of large-scale fighting (and perhaps the presence of certain Bengalis in the government) is proof the people there accept the situation; and that if the Western nations do not aid Pakistan, it will have no choice but to turn to China. Even if the United States accepts all these assertions, it should hold firm on the ground that as the prospects for development are poor unless there is a genuine settlement with the eastern wing, Pakistan does not deserve the allocation of scarce aid resources. Moreover, the United States should make plain —at least in private—that it is interested in a rough measure of social and economic justice as well as in economic development, and a government that fails to provide this hardly merits support. In taking this stance the United States should avoid self-righteousness or moralizing: The Vietnam experience should reduce these temptations. Its purpose should not be to give vent to indignation or to punish the Pakistani government, but only to help all concerned take the painful steps necessary to deal with their agonizing problems.

Even if U.S. officials demonstrate considerable diplomatic skill in dealing with Pakistan, the problem will remain a thorny one, for the root issues involved are the locus of power within Pakistan and the preservation of the nation. Pakistani leaders will find it difficult to give up power after having failed to turn over power to the elected representatives of the people in March 1971; it will be even more difficult to do so if such a course seems to mean the end of Pakistan. The United States can sympathize with all concerned but should be firm that, while it has no desire to see Pakistan dissolved, it cannot assist the government to hold the eastern wing at bayonet point. When and if this crucial issue is settled, either by an agreement providing for continued links or by the establishment of separate countries, U.S. policy should be guided by the broad considerations set forth below.

Turning to India, there are two sets of questions that should be asked before reaching any conclusions about U.S. economic policy toward the subcontinent:

1. Are the prospects for India such that aid from the United States and other Western countries will give it a reasonable chance to make satisfactory economic progress? What is the likely result, both in the subcontinent and its relationships with the major powers, if aid is reduced to minimal levels?
2. If the United States decides to provide more than minimal assistance, how much should be provided? What should be the terms of the aid extended and what conditions should be attached? Which areas should receive priority in aid allotments? What should our trade policies be?

India's dependence on substantial imports of raw materials and industrial goods beyond what it can earn through exports indicates that a continued decline in U.S. aid—say, to about $100-125 million annually—would be distinctly adverse to the country and our relations with it. Even if other Western governments maintained their aid programs, the total amount of aid would not greatly exceed scheduled debt repayment obligations—and it is not at all certain that other governments would continue their programs if the chances of economic progress in the subcontinent appeared bleak. It could be argued that a sharp curtailment of aid would shock India into working harder and making the social and economic reforms that would foster more rapid development. But it seems more likely that curtailing aid would bring a prolonged decline in the rate of economic growth. The reduced resources available to the central government would weaken one of the major factors making for national unity. The fading hope that their country would succeed in modernizing would make the struggle for political power and control of resources increasingly bitter, and in time could lead to growing violence, the disintegration of public order, and perhaps to the rise of extremists of the right or left. The short-term reaction probably would be greater reliance on coercion by the present power structures, but in time the chances of violent upheavals or rule by a harsh and narrowly nationalistic regime would rise and the prospects for democratic or even relatively benign authoritarian government would decline.

A curtailment in aid would not only create new resentment against the United States but also result in a marked increase in Soviet influence and present new opportunities to the local Communist parties. Moscow would not be without its problems in this situation. Probably it much prefers a gradual rather than a rapid Western withdrawal from the area to avoid coming under heavy Indian pressure to step up Soviet aid faster than it is prepared to. It would encounter problems in gaining greater influence in India without antagonizing Pakistan, and vice versa, especially as it would also be trying to limit the influence of China and the local Communists favorable to Peking. Yet these are problems resulting from success rather than from failure —or more accurately, from Western failure. While local nationalism and the above-mentioned pressures would make a direct Soviet "take-over" unlikely, the U.S.S.R. would almost certainly become the predominant external power in South Asia, as it is already in most of the Arab lands.

Equally important, the reduced prospects for achieving even barely tolerable living standards for more than a half billion people would also diminish the chances of building a better world community. In view of the wider awareness in the developed world of conditions in other lands, this could have adverse repercussions on our own basic attitudes and outlook.

How far these trends would go and how they would interact would depend upon so many events within the subcontinent and in world affairs as to make prediction impossible. But, at some point in the process, there would be more than a minor danger that the United States would see the trend of events as dangerous to its security and be drawn into a struggle in circumstances that could hardly be propitious. Because of the widespread revulsion against the involvement in Vietnam and hesitancy to become militarily involved in Asia again, such action would be taken only with great reluctance and probably not before the memory and bitterness of Vietnam had faded. In any case, it is a situation worth trying to avoid.

If the results of a continued reduction in aid levels are likely to be adverse, it does not automatically follow that the United States should substantially increase its aid. It would be idle to pretend that India is assured of making rapid enough economic progress to satisfy its citizens even if it receives large-scale U.S. aid—perhaps $750 million to India (exclusive of surplus agricultural products) annually. For years U.S. officials and citizens concerned with foreign affairs made claims for the likely results of foreign aid that were not fully borne out by events. These claims reflected several distorting conditions: (1) the success of the Marshall Plan and insufficient awareness of the differences between economic recovery and economic development; (2) the lack of experience in and knowledge of Asia and other underdeveloped areas; and (3) the fact that part of what was said about the effect of aid was rhetoric to sway Congress and the public to support administration requests rather than careful analysis of its probable impact. But we should not overlook the number of success stories in economic development and the many others for which the outcome is still inconclusive.

India still hangs in the balance. Substantial progress has been made in many fields, and the prospects are reasonably good in a number of others. The biggest uncertainties are the likely quality of the political leadership (especially its success in changing outmoded attitudes and in developing appropriate new institutions) and the progress made in lowering birth rates. They will require political leadership that is at least moderately effective in focusing sufficient energy and effort on economic development and in seeing that the scarce resources available are directed insofar as possible to constructive and productive uses. The chances are fairly good that Mrs. Gandhi and her supporters will retain sufficient support to provide relatively stable government. Adopting and implementing effective policies will be difficult, and the temptation will be great to substitute sloganeering and popular but irrelevant policies rather than to face the task of revitalizing the government and the administration. Yet Mrs. Gandhi's increased efforts to promote land reform and provide rural employment opportunities through an expanded public works program offer hope, if not assurance, of progress in these critical areas.

The population prospects of the subcontinent are discouraging. Populations are growing by about 2.5 per cent a year in India and Pakistan; a continuation of these rates would bring their populations to about 900 million and 200 million by 1990. Difficult as it would be to feed such huge populations, food might not be the greatest problem, for low levels of productivity and the availability of better techniques indicate that improving food production by 3 per cent annually is a goal they can achieve. The truly critical problems would be providing schools and housing, creating employment opportunities, and coping with the further surge of urbanization that would result. Spiraling unemployment in great urban complexes lacking even the minimum amenities could spell continual turmoil.

Despite the crucial importance of this matter, there is relatively little that outside powers can do directly. Given present techniques of birth control, the key factors are education, motivation, and effective administration of programs that reach the masses. (The major contribution the West could make would be the discovery of a cheaper and more effective type of birth control for uneducated peasants.) Some experts believe that significant progress in reducing the birth rate is likely in the next decade or two, and point to certain small countries as well as a few areas in the subcontinent where progress is noticeable.[17] Whether or not such progress will be rapid and widespread enough in view of the great numbers now reaching childbearing age is still uncertain. Awareness of the problem is growing, but India has yet to make the all-out commitment to population control that is necessary.

Thus, however much one would like to come forth with a ringing assertion that if the West provides substantial aid, India will make rapid economic progress, it is impossible to do so—at least for this author. It could happen, but in my judgment the chances are not that bright. At the same time, because of the progress they have already made and promising developments like the Green Revolution, it would be equally misleading to rate the prospects as dismal or hopeless. Instead, it would seem India has a fair chance to progress if aid commitments increase substantially from their presently declining levels. Given the importance of India and the probable consequences if it fails to make satisfactory progress, the United States should reverse the trend toward lower aid levels and provide, in conjunction with other advanced nations, the substantial flow of resources so necessary to make more rapid economic progress.

It is neither appropriate nor necessary to go into great detail about the particular policies that the United States should follow in fostering economic development. It is inappropriate, because this is not a book about economic development strategy or U.S. foreign economic policy. It is unnecessary, because the basic question is one of will rather than of methods. To be sure, the methods and techniques adopted are important, but the crucial element is the decision to make a major effort to provide large-scale assistance.

There is already considerable agreement among those who have studied the matter on the particular policies that can and should be adopted. The program will have to be a long-term one to be successful, for there is little chance of India achieving self-sustaining growth in the years immediately ahead. As any prospects for repayment lie far in the future, present debt repayments must be rescheduled, loan terms eased, and the proportion of aid that must be used for the direct purchase of U.S. goods gradually decreased. Exports should also be allowed easier access to the U.S. markets, possibly through preferential treatment as President Nixon has suggested. Even with increased access to the markets of advanced countries (which would provide a stimulus to efficiency for Indian firms), aid will be necessary for a long period before greater export and import substitution make it possible for assistance to decline significantly.

The United States should also gradually increase the proportion of aid that goes through multilateral channels so as to insulate it, as far as possible, from the short-term vicissitudes of its political relationships. Moreover, the performance standards set by international organizations create somewhat less resentment because they can be set on a uniform basis that is largely free of narrow political considerations. Yet we would be deluding ourselves in thinking that aid could be both increased and dramatically shifted to multilateral channels, for these organizations labor under many problems that limit their ability to take on much larger responsibilities. The Pearson Commission, which was very favorable to the multilateral approach, concluded that an increase from 10 to 20 percent was all the aid that could be effectively handled by multilateral organizations.[18] Similarly, the report by Sir Robert Jackson on the capacity of the numerous United Nations organizations engaged in development work states quite bluntly that until an improved system of organization and management is installed, these bodies cannot effectively utilize substantially more funds.[19] Consequently, the major U.S. efforts should be toward greater multilateral coordination among the aid donors through consortia already operating.

Another important issue involves the conditions attached to aid. Three broad choices are available. The first is to attach practically no conditions beyond use of the money for the purpose specified. This is relatively simple if the aid is for specific projects, and can—at least in theory—be done even if the aid is for general economic development programs. But this becomes more difficult as the size of a foreign aid program increases and its impact spreads.

The second choice is to condition aid on the economic performance of the recipient, as measured by the latter's rate of savings, level of investment, rate of economic growth, or willingness to follow certain policies. Most economic development experts favor this course, although with many differences of opinion about the appropriate way, and the proper time-span, to measure performance. Advocacy of such conditions reflects not only the view that they are politically necessary to obtain funds from rich countries but also the conviction that aid is useful because it provides influence or "leverage" over the recipient's economic policies as well as a transfer of resources.

The third choice is to require the recipient to meet certain social, political or military conditions: make certain social or economic reforms, pursue a "pro-American" foreign policy, join an alliance, refrain from acquiring certain types of weapons or from spending more than a certain amount for defense. While such conditions are often popular in the donor country, they are so strongly resented by recipients that they sometimes refuse aid under these circumstances, especially if the conditions are explicit.

While the underdeveloped countries would obviously prefer the first course, they would be astounded if it actually occurred, for it is inconceivable that donor countries will supply billions of dollars annually, even as loans, without requiring anything more than that the money be spent for the general purpose of economic development. Since the essential requirement of any foreign aid policy is that Congress provide some aid to dispense, a complete abandonment of all conditions lies in the realm of fantasy rather than policy.

It is, however, essential that aid be conditioned on the economic performance of the recipients, especially if the United States is to provide the sizable resources to India I have suggested. The question is what standard of economic performance should be used as a measuring rod. Those who believe that the recipient countries will develop more rapidly if they are required, as part of the aid bargain, to accept certain policy judgments of outside advisers (whether from individual foreign countries or from multilateral institutions) urge that recipient governments reach agreement with the donors on some if not all of the basic economic policies to be followed. This is the general position adopted by the Pearson Commission, although it emphasized that the agreement should result from a close and continuing exchange of views and mutual give-and-take. Whether the Commission reached this conclusion because it believed that the donors possessed greater wisdom about development policies or because it felt that such a position was necessary for adequate sums of aid to be forthcoming is difficult to tell. Probably both reasons were behind its conclusion.

Yet there are major liabilities in making aid conditional upon specific economic policies—cutting consumption and increasing savings, relying more on private enterprise (domestic or foreign) or the market mechanism, devoting more or less resources to industry relative to agriculture, or adopting certain fiscal and monetary policies—at least in the cases of India and Pakistan. The liabilities spring partly from the fact that both countries have many well-trained officials with growing experience in the development process, and it is far from certain that the *typical* foreign adviser, who often serves only a few years in a country, is more knowledgeable about its problems. The foreign adviser may be quick to note some policies that obviously should be changed, but the local official may be just as aware of the need for change and far more aware of the political and social reasons behind the policies or of the inherent obstacles to change.

The potential as well as the danger involved in using aid to influence another country's economic policy was demonstrated when India devalued the rupee in 1966. The arguments of the Western donors (and international agencies) and the leverage their aid had gained, as well as a recognition by some Indian leaders that the rupee was overvalued, were behind the move. But the failure of the United States to supply the amount of aid planned in conjunction with the devaluation meant that India was unable to reap the expected benefits. Conditions might have been worse if India had not devalued. This, however, was of little consolation to Indian leaders who had carried out the move at the urging and insistence of foreign officials and reaped domestic political attacks without any offsetting improvement in economic conditions.

The insistence of donor governments on the adoption of a set of policies will often create such political problems for the local government (since the new policies are sure to hurt certain groups) that, unless its leaders are substantially convinced the policies are correct, they will only half-heartedly implement them—perhaps pleading that conditions have changed since the agreements were made or that not all of the aid was received in the manner and period promised. Hirschman and Bird have strongly criticized the whole concept of program aid on these grounds, and although the problem is real, it is not my impression that it is as critical as they conclude.[20]

On the third choice, there is growing awareness and agreement that requiring recipient countries to meet direct military or political conditions which have no clear relationship to economic development (such as joining an alliance, or pursuing a pro-Western foreign policy) in return for economic aid is not only counterproductive but unnecessary.[21] Western Europe and Japan, having lost their political and military power and responsibilities in nearly all underdeveloped countries, have recognized this more clearly than we have in recent years, although the United States is generally much less concerned about direct political and military *quid pro quos* than it was ten or even five years ago.

A more difficult dilemma is whether aid should be conditioned in any way upon carrying out social or economic reforms, limiting defense spending, or settling disputes with neighbors. The aim of American policy should be to produce more rapid aggregate economic growth *and* to help develop a society characterized by personal and political freedom and by social and economic justice. Such reforms clearly are of concern to us. Some observers believe that the poor countries *must* adopt certain measures—land reforms, educational reforms, or change customs like protecting India's unproductive cows —or they will be unlikely to achieve either economic development or any economic or social justice. Similarly, the Kashmir dispute has clearly limited what could have been profitable economic cooperation between India and Pakistan and led them to spend money on arms that could have been used for development.

The most important factors in reaching any decisions about aid conditions are a sense of proportion and perspective. There are countries whose economic policies are so counterproductive that they do not merit aid, especially when it is in short supply generally. This is not the case with India, however much we might think its performance would be improved by certain changes in policy. Similarly, there probably will be situations where aggregate growth rates are satisfactory but certain groups or regions are so exploited as to raise doubts whether aid should be continued.

But if we consider what is involved in conditioning aid on noneconomic factors, we probably should draw back in all but the most extreme cases. For if we insist on certain broad economic policies and on forcing changes in systems of education, land tenure, or social relationships, we are not only requiring those in power to give it up but we are also not far from exercising the effective power of government in the recipient country. Since aid, even if increased severalfold, would still be a small (though important) part of the resources available to the local government, its opposition to remaking their society to U.S. specifications would range from fierce to unyielding. Similar responses would prevail regarding the settlement of territorial disputes with neighbors or the general level of defense spending and, to a lesser degree, to the types of weapons procured.[22]

All things considered, it would be the wisest course to condition U.S. aid on performance, primarily as measured by the rate of economic growth. Some agreement on general economic policies is necessary, but the United States should avoid as much as possible going into detail on these matters. A policy of offering more aid if India achieves satisfactory growth would have distinct advantages. It would provide an indirect incentive for improving relations and for holding down defense expenditures, while leaving the ultimate decisions on these matters where they must rest, namely in the hands of those directly involved. It would similarly provide an incentive to utilize private foreign investment, without taking away the power of decision on this sensitive issue. Such a policy would also make it clear that the United States is not attempting to dictate the policies of other countries. Ironically, once they become convinced of this, it probably would be possible to have a freer and more productive dialogue about their economic policies.

15

Regional Conflicts and the Great Powers

Probably nothing has been as important in determining international political relationships in South Asia as the regional conflicts involving the subcontinent itself. These conflicts have created both opportunities and dilemmas for India and Pakistan and for the outside powers attempting to advance their own interests and gain influence in South Asia. While anticolonialism, the desire for close relations with other Asian countries, and the need for economic and military assistance have been and will remain important concerns for India and Pakistan, their mutual hostility and the Sino-Indian dispute have played crucial roles in the evolution of their foreign policies.

Compared to these two quarrels, the disputes between either India or Pakistan and their smaller South Asian neighbors have thus far been of minor importance in international politics. India's relations with Nepal have been close but uneasy. Nepal's importance to the defense of the subcontinent makes it impossible for India to be indifferent to Nepal's relations with China, or even to what goes on inside Nepal. At the same time, India's pervasive cultural influence and Nepal's dependence on India for most of its trade and for access to the outside world (which the new road from Kathmandu to Lhasa will not do much to change) make Indian attempts to influence Nepalese policy an extremely sensitive issue. As a result, Nepal has gradually reduced the special privileges that India inherited from the British. New Delhi has reluctantly acquiesced, calculating that it has little choice but to seek the best relations possible with whatever government is in power in Kathmandu in order to limit as much as possible Nepal's relations with China. Thus far, King Mahendra has shown consistent diplomatic skill in enhancing Nepal's freedom generally and maintaining a nonaligned posture between India and China—the supreme accomplishment of his policy.[1] American policy has been based on the recognition that assistance to Nepal should be independent of but generally complementary to India's effort; this is the only sensible course open to the United States. China has been content to attempt to expand its influence gradually, and no dramatic shifts in policy seem likely.

As for Bhutan and Sikkim, India has special and comprehensive treaty relationships with these strategically located ministates. In consequence, the U.S. role in these areas will continue to be minimal even with Bhutan in the United Nations. The quarrel between Pakistan and Afghanistan over Pushtunistan (see Chapter 4) has waxed and waned for twenty years, never quite breaking out into open warfare and never quite being abandoned. Since 1964, however, the issue has been largely dormant. Afghanistan's leaders, preoccupied with domestic affairs, seem to have concluded that there is little they can do to influence developments across the Durand line, although upheavals in Pakistan might lead them to reassess their judgment. Under these circumstances, the United States can only play a limited role, since its influence in either country is not great at this point. Unless the dispute shows signs of flaring into a much bigger conflict than has occurred in the past, the United States should largely stand aside.

Convinced that their location makes friendly relations with the U.S.S.R. a necessity, Afghan leaders have taken pains not to antagonize Moscow. They have demonstrated their ability to deal with the Soviet Union and maintain control of Afghanistan's affairs. If Moscow ever attempts to use Afghanistan's dependence on it to exercise a dominant influence in the country, the United States should be prepared to ease the task of reorienting Afghanistan's trade by helping it to find markets abroad. This would not be too large a task in view of the modest volume of Afghanistan's trade, though it would require the cooperation of Pakistan or Iran or both. Finally, as its political system loosens up and develops, Afghanistan's susceptibility to outside influence may gradually increase, but this is unlikely to be a critical problem for many years.

The Perennial Hostility

Few disputes have been as tragic as the prolonged conflict between India and Pakistan, whose progress is so important to the welfare of Asia. Both countries have immense obstacles to overcome in the process of modernization, yet both are burdened by a quarrel that diverts resources and energies from development to defense and adds to the insecurity of the Hindu and Muslim minorities. Britain, the United Nations, the United States, and, more recently, the Soviet Union have invested much effort and prestige in attempting to ameliorate or settle this quarrel. Occasionally they have succeeded on a particular issue, but the basic elements of the conflict have remained recalcitrant to their good offices. Trouble can flare up abruptly, as it did in March 1971, threatening a third Indo-Pakistani war and forcing hard choices on external powers.

The tragic nature of the quarrel is recognized by many Indians

TABLE 4

India and Pakistan: Defense Expenditures, 1955, 1960, and 1965
Through 1970[a]
(million rupees)[b]

	India[c]	Pakistan[d]
1955	1,979	683
1960	2,670	960
1965	8,058	1,263
1966	8,848	2,855
1967	9,086	2,294
1968	9,684	2,187
1969	10,332	2,427
1970	11,047[e]	2,761[e]

Notes:
a. These figures do not include the value of military assistance received from abroad for either country.
b. The rate of exchange of the Indian rupee was 4.76 to $1.00 until 1966, when it was devalued to 7.5; the Pakistani rupee has remained at 4.76 throughout the period covered.
c. Year ends 31 March.
d. Year ends 30 June (from 1959 on).
e. Revised estimate.

Sources:
United Nations, *Statistical Yearbook 1957; 1964; 1970.*

and Pakistanis. Their leaders have periodically emphasized, publicly and privately, their desire for better relations; yet far more character-istic have been the charges and countercharges of politicians, the press and radio of both countries over the past twenty-odd years. Citizens of each country base their judgments upon the worst possible interpretations of the words and actions of the other side, and the national heroes of one country are despised in the other.[2]

Most Pakistanis have long argued that India's refusal to accept the two-nation theory and its implications (i.e., yielding the Muslim state of Kashmir) and Indian statements expressing a desire for a reunited subcontinent indicate that India has never truly accepted partition. Hence they conclude that India intends to seize their country when the opportunity arises. India's failure to attack when Pakistan was extremely weak in the years just after partition and its willingness to agree to a cease-fire in 1965 when the tide of battle was going in its favor are facts that have no discernible impact on Pakistani thinking —at least in the western wing. Indian support of the East Pakistanis during 1971 has only intensified West Pakistani convictions that India's basic aim remains the destruction of Pakistan.

There have, of course, been important differences in the attitudes of East and West Pakistanis toward India.[3] While the East Paki-stanis have had no desire to be dominated by Hindus as they were before partition, they have never been as concerned about Kashmir as the West Pakistanis, and have seen value to themselves in normal relations with India. Moreover, with civil war, West Pakistanis rather than Indians have come to be regarded by many Bengalis as the enemy; indeed, India is now regarded as a friend by many—though hardly all—East Pakistanis.

Similarly, Indians are convinced that the anti-Hindu animus and fears that brought Pakistan into being sustain it even today, and that specific Indian concessions would not lead to an alteration in Paki-stan's hostility. Neither set of fears—Indian or Pakistani—is entirely irrational although both are much exaggerated. Because of the his-toric antagonisms and current disputes, these anxieties will fade slowly at best. The leaders, moreover, have seldom seen much chance of resolving the key disputes through negotiation, for domestic political pressures in each country force an uncompromising if not a belligerent stand toward the other.

Until 1971, the Kashmir dispute was the focal point of these an-tagonisms, and now the question of the future of East Pakistan has added new complexities and burdens to the relationship between India and the two wings of Pakistan. The antagonism between West Pakistanis and Indians remains the key element in the situation, but hostility between Hindus and the Bengali Muslims has by no means disappeared. A consideration of the Kashmir issue indicates the difficulty of bringing about better Indo-Pakistani relations; analysis of their policies in the upheaval in East Pakistan demonstrates the hazard of new conflict.

The civil war in East Pakistan has demonstrated that, while religious differences brought about partition in 1947, religious unity is not by itself an adequate basis for nationhood. In the atmosphere of the 1940s, when the struggle for the mantle of the British Raj was between Hindus and Muslims, the Muslims of what became East and West Pakistan were drawn together in fear of the larger Hindu community. For many years thereafter neither the struggle for power between the peoples of Pakistan's two wings nor the many differences between them—language, culture, environment, and ways of life—led to a challenge to the idea of a united Pakistan. To Bengalis as well as the various people in West Pakistan, Hindus and Muslims were two separate peoples who required two nations in the subcontinent. But the trend of events in the 1960s, culminating in the 1971 upheaval in Bengal, have led many Bengalis to see the West Pakistanis as their oppressors rather than their protectors against India. If Pakistan survives, it probably will be either on the basis of West Pakistani military domination or with only a nominal and face-saving link. Indeed, their experiences may have led the Bengalis beyond the point of willingness to accept anything less than complete independence. Most wars of secession do not succeed, and the vanquished continue to live with the victors. But most states are not composed of areas over a thousand miles apart.

West Pakistanis saw the situation quite differently; to them the Hindus of East Pakistan (who voted overwhelmingly for the Awami League) and the Indians were the cause of the trouble and the heart of the problem. This attitude, and the Indian reaction, indicates how little either have ever really understood the hopes and fears of the other. Muslims have typically regarded Hindus as devious, untrustworthy and hypocritical; most Hindus have reciprocated with a mixture of contempt and fear of Muslims, looking upon them as intolerant and brutal. Such stereotypes surfaced in 1971, and demonstrated anew the centrality of communalism in the political life of the subcontinent. As Selig Harrison has commented:

What happened in March 25 was not the inexplicable behavior of madmen or sadists. It reflected the frankly stated fear that a sovereign East Pakistan would inevitably link up with India to create a new balance of power in the subcontinent. The excesses committed by the Pakistani Army leaders are only partly to be explained in terms of their vindictive racial contempt for the Bengalis. Basically, their policy of repression demonstrated the deep sense of insecurity they felt when they belatedly realized the extent and strength of Bengali separatism.

Pakistan never fully recovered from the traumatic shock inflicted by the Indo-Pakistan war of September 1965. . . . Tashkent marked the start of a painful psychological deflation which had not yet run its course when the Awami League election sweep in East Pakistan last December brought the long-simmering Bengal crisis to a head. Having just come to terms with the fact that they presided over a country one fourth as big as India, West Pakistani leaders reacted in desperation to a prospect of a secession that might reduce them to the position of a country one tenth as big.[4]

But having chosen the course they did, Yahya and his associates seemed to have little idea of what political moves to make to win over any substantial body of Bengali opinion. Indeed, their strategy seems to hinge upon convincing the Bengalis they cannot win and must therefore accept a unified Pakistan. But Indian support of the guerrillas makes this difficult, and Yahya's threats to attack India if New Delhi's support enables the guerrillas seriously to threaten continued military control are clearly designed to deter India from a more active role. Some observers believe the threats must be taken at face value despite their seeming unreality in view of Pakistan's desperate position. The military leaders, they reason, could never accept defeat at the hands of Bengali irregulars. Such an event would not only be unbearably humiliating but would threaten the position of the military establishment in Pakistani life; better to move against India, perhaps by attacking Kashmir. The world community might move in and stop the war and India's support of the guerrillas. Even if it did not, and India won and East Pakistan became independent, the ensuing anti-Indian emotions in West Pakistan would restrain those West Pakistanis (such as the Baluchis and Pathans), who resent Punjabi domination, from trying to go their own way. While it seems unlikely that the military leaders formulated any such clear strategy, they might react along these lines if cornered.

Yahya has, however, made a deliberate effort to portray the struggle as one between India and Pakistan. He has played upon worldwide fears of a new war by emphasizing India's support of the guerrillas, and offered to meet Mrs. Gandhi to reduce the danger of war. India energetically strove to counter this effort. Foreign Minister Singh's July 21 statement succinctly set forth the basic Indian approach:

> Pakistan has been trying for some time to mislead the world into thinking that the situation in Bangla Desh is a matter between Pakistan and India whereas in fact it is a matter between the military rulers of West Pakistan and the people of Bangla Desh. It is the Pakistan regime's own actions, and the brutalities committed by the Pakistan Army in Bangla Desh, that have landed Pakistan in a morass in Bangla Desh. Only a settlement with the already elected representatives of the people of Bangla Desh will enable the military rulers of Pakistan to extricate themselves from this morass.[5]

But if India insisted that the basic issue was between the Pakistani government and the elected representatives of the people of East Pakistan, it remained hesitant about recognizing the newly-proclaimed Bangla Desh government. This hesitation suggests that India is not eager to see Pakistan divided, much less to undo partition and reabsorb it. Some Indians do have these aims, and nearly all want to keep Pakistan militarily weak. However, government leaders probably are dubious about the benefits India would derive from having a potentially unstable independent East Pakistan in an already unstable area.[6] India's record in attempting to integrate the various hill tribes along the Chinese and Burmese borders has been uneven; and trouble is chronic in West Bengal, where the more radical of India's two major Communist parties as well as an ultra-leftist peasant guerrilla force have won growing support in recent years. Under the circumstances, the idea of adding direct responsibility for over 70 million Bengalis— 60 million of them Muslim—to India's already difficult Bengali and Hindu-Muslim problems probably is appalling. Thus Mrs. Gandhi, under heavy pressure to recognize Bangla Desh, may have seen the Indo-Soviet treaty as not only useful in itself but as a way of deflecting such pressures.

But India's dilemma of trying to force a political settlement without risking war remained; if the guerrilla forces were unsuccessful Pakistan had little incentive to compromise with the Bengalis, but if guerrilla strength grew the danger of Pakistan striking at India increased. Thus New Delhi was forced to tread a narrow line. Soviet support reassured a worried and isolated India, but Moscow's principal concern in the upheaval seemed to prevent a new war. The Soviet Union's long-term geopolitical interests in West Pakistan were greater than its interests in East Pakistan. Thus it appeared dubious about any recognition of Bangla Desh.

The U.S. interests in the conflict are reasonably clear—the prevention of war or famine, and a political settlement by the contending forces within Pakistan that will not only permit the refugees to return but will establish a durable and representative political system. But the strength of passions has led many Americans to question whether an essentially moderate and pragmatic policy can succeed. Might it not be better to accept the inevitability of Pakistan's dissolution and work to mitigate the dangers involved in reaching such a result? How can the United States proclaim that the people should have the right to choose their government in Vietnam and refuse to support the elected representatives of the Bengalis?

Such a choice may become unavoidable if the Pakistani government continues to follow an intransigent policy, but there are powerful reasons for trying to avoid it. Working for, or actively acquiescing in, the destruction of another nation is one of the most momentous decisions any nation makes. The United States should be especially cautious about such a course when it involves an Asian nation whose effort to preserve its national unity has won widespread support among the Afro-Asian countries—a factor largely overlooked in Western discussions. Moreover, the dangers of war in such an event are substantial. One generally overlooked matter is the future of the so far unmolested half-million or so Bengalis living in West Pakistan and the million Biharis living in East Pakistan; the fate of each group is unpleasant to contemplate if the country is torn apart.

In these circumstances, the United States, acting in concert with other Western nations, should make no further arms shipments and should continue its present policy of withholding economic aid commitments. Furthermore, Washington should make clear that in the event Pakistan attacks India the United States will firmly and openly support India. There is no assurance that such a course would change Yahya's policy, but it might lead to a rethinking and a more flexible approach.

Such policy shifts, and the provision of much more assistance to India to deal with the refugee problem, should make it easier for Mrs. Gandhi to resist demands for military action. In this connection U.S. assistance should go largely to the Indian government, which wants to and is capable of, handling the problem. The disadvantages of U.N. refugee camps is clear from the case of the Palestine Arabs.

Even if the current crisis is resolved, India and Pakistan will still be confronted with the Kashmir dispute. There has always been considerable disagreement among Indians, Pakistanis, and outside observers on the importance of the Kashmir issue. Some think that a Kashmir settlement would greatly change the nature of Indo-Pakistani relations; others say it is more a reflection than a cause of their basic hostilities, which would remain even if a settlement were achieved.

Two observations are pertinent here. First, the legacy of antagonism lies heavily on both peoples and colors their attitudes toward each other, and a settlement of the Kashmir dispute would probably not lead to really close, cooperative relations, for many years at least. Second, in the event a settlement were reached and there would be a significant improvement in relations, the dangers of war would be reduced, energy and resources could be devoted to other pressing matters, and outside powers would be less able to exploit their differences.

Over the years, Pakistan has tried almost every strategy it could think of to acquire Kashmir. While none has succeeded, West Pakistanis remain unreconciled to the present situation and unwilling to concede defeat, fearing they would thereby formally accept second-class status on the subcontinent. The Indians, essentially satisfied with the *status quo*, have tried to keep both the Kashmir issue dormant and outside powers from playing any role in it. They have always stressed that the issue should be settled through bilateral negotiations—if, indeed, anything were to be done about the matter—and New Delhi has always stressed the desirability of settling other differences between India and Pakistan first to establish the proper atmosphere for negotiations on Kashmir.

Yet the Indian government has won only the sullen acquiescence of the Kashmiris in their present political condition. Communal tensions have remained high, and some Kashmiris have become more open in their opposition.[7] While India's military and police controls probably will remain strong enough to prevent an uprising or to suppress one if it occurs, it is having increasing difficulty finding Kashmir politicians who are able, popular, and loyal. The arrest in January 1971 of several hundred members of the Plebiscite Front (which advocates self-determination for Kashmir and was banned in 1971 for such advocacy) and New Delhi's refusal to permit Sheikh Abdullah to reenter the state lest trouble occur during the elections demonstrate the fragility of the political scene. New Delhi might be willing to give Kashmir greater autonomy if it thought this would satisfy rather than stimulate local demands; but in the absence of any indication to the contrary, present policies will probably continue.

It is difficult to see any settlement during the next few years, a conclusion that seems inescapable upon examining what would be required for a solution. The first possibility would involve substantial Indian concessions accompanied by a Pakistani willingness to accept only part of its claims in Kashmir. New Delhi would have to give up at least a significant portion of the Vale of Kashmir. This would seem to be the absolute minimum that any Pakistani government could accept and still survive politically.

Pakistan's willingness to accept such a compromise is really academic, however, for there is practically no chance of India giving up part of the Vale in the foreseeable future. Those nationalists with a basically secular outlook have never willingly accepted Jinnah's theory that Hindus and Muslims were in fact two separate nations. Though compelled to accept partition because they believed it was the only way to gain independence without a civil war, they are unwilling to see the theory applied any more broadly than it was in the initial partition of the subcontinent. Some of them feel that Kashmir offers India the opportunity to prove that the two-nation theory is invalid by demonstrating that Hindus and Muslims can live and work together. Those Indians who are more appropriately described as Hindu nationalists are equally opposed to yielding anything, partly because they resist concessions of any kind to Muslims and partly because they consider Kashmir a part of sacred Indian soil.

Indian spokesmen have often expressed their belief that a plebiscite in the state would be fought basically along communal lines since the only thing Pakistan has to offer to the Kashmiris is Islam. They have privately expressed the fear that a plebiscite would heighten Hindu-Muslim tensions within India and that, if the Kashmiris opted for Pakistan, it would be difficult if not impossible to prevent enraged Hindus from slaughtering large numbers of Indian Muslims. But India's achievement in providing for the safety of its Muslim citizens during the 1965 fighting with Pakistan casts some doubt on the argument.

There are other domestic considerations behind India's stand. Many Indians fear that yielding would encourage other groups to demand separation from the Indian union. Moreover, if they acknowledge that Pakistan has any legitimate interest in Kashmir—an interest which they believe can only be based on Islam—they would indirectly be admitting that Pakistan has a legitimate interest in the status and welfare of Indian Muslims. Pakistan's official disclaimers on this point carry little weight, for whenever there is a communal riot in India, Pakistanis are obviously concerned.

There are also strategic considerations. Yielding Kashmir would weaken India's strategic position vis-à-vis Pakistan. Furthermore, if India gave up the Vale of Kashmir, through which its troops must pass to reach the Chinese frontier, it would be impossible to defend Ladakh. India would be unwilling to be dependent on transit rights for its troops, even if guaranteed, particularly in view of Pakistan's co-operation with Communist China in recent years.

Finally, there is the simple desire of any country to hold the territory it possesses, a resolve that has been hardened in India's case by Pakistan's attempt to wrest Kashmir by force in 1965. It is well to remember here that any Indian politician contemplating concessions on Kashmir would have to take into account the fact that the losses would be immediate and tangible while the gains would be nebulous and long term. These factors frustrated the hopes that arose (in 1952–53, 1959–60, and 1964) when the two nations seemed to be moving closer to a settlement.

Could external pressure force India to give up a substantial part of what it now holds in Kashmir, and force Pakistan to accept less than it thinks it should get? Both countries are, after all, dependent upon external assistance for economic aid and military equipment. But the dispute touches the deepest emotions and the strongest convictions of the people and leaders of both countries, and it seems unlikely that pressure by any single external power could force either or both disputants to modify their positions significantly. It is theoretically possible, of course, to envision the Western countries and the U.S.S.R. jointly bringing pressure on India and Pakistan. Yet such pressure would be so open and blatant as to arouse the most dogged determination on the part of both countries to stand firm. The pressure would have to last for a considerable time, and moreover, the West and the U.S.S.R. would have to agree on a specific plan and stick with it despite temptations to undercut each other—or to attempt to offset any moves China might make. Such a development is extremely unlikely.

Third, the prospect for settling the dispute on any basis other than a clear territorial division is equally bleak. Joint rule or condominium requires an extraordinary degree of trust and identity of purpose between the two ruling governments. Suggestions have also been made for a solution on the basis of special rights for the nonsovereign power, involving a special economic status for Kashmir with the state linked in some manner to both India and Pakistan; transit rights for the nonsovereign power; joint defense of the state; and joint citizenship for Kashmiris in both India and Pakistan. These proposals might supplement rather than substitute for a territorial settlement. By themselves they are simply not adequate to meet the needs of either India or Pakistan.

Independence has also been suggested as a possible solution. This probably would appeal to the Kashmiris, for whom the ideal solution would be an independent Kashmir trading with and providing tourist services for India and Pakistan and receiving aid from all the major powers. Pakistani leaders might accept such a solution, but India seems unlikely to agree, its leaders probably fearing that in the subsequent struggle for influence in the area with Pakistan and Communist China, India would be in a less advantageous position than it is at present.

Under these circumstances the United States should basically take a hands-off position in the Kashmir dispute unless the situation threatens to lead to a new conflict or the prospects for a settlement go up considerably. If the issue is brought to the United Nations again, the United States should quietly support any feasible proposal without expecting much to result from its efforts. The time may arrive when the two countries, recognizing that they are pursuing foreign-policy ambitions beyond their means, demonstrate a willingness to compromise on Kashmir. Reaching a solution would, of course still be extremely difficult. However, as indicated above, this is all far in the future, and there is little that the United States or indeed any outside power can do to induce a change in attitudes. It would be a serious disservice to mislead any Pakistanis who still believe the United States has the power to force a settlement of the dispute. A frank admission of inability to play a determining role is likely to lead to a better understanding than a periodic raising and dashing of hopes.

Thus far the Soviet Union has not shown much interest in working with the West on any of these questions, as distinct from working along a parallel course at times. However, if its attitude should change, the United States should not hesitate to cooperate, for even in terms of a narrowly conceived national interest the benefits from seeing agreements reached and in preventing a new war outweigh any advantages Moscow would obtain from its role in such efforts.

Sino-Indian Hostility: A Reappraisal

It has long been the conviction of American officials that regional conflicts between non-Communist nations have been damaging to U.S. efforts to contain Communist power. At the same time, they have generally believed that quarrels between Communist and non-Communist countries brought benefits as well as dangers to the United States. They were both worried and annoyed by Sino-Indian friendship in the Panch Sheel era, and reacted to the emerging border dispute between India and China with quiet satisfaction, thinking that it would awaken India to the dangers of communism and the need to cooperate with the West. Some Western officials also saw additional benefits. The border dispute, they felt, would strengthen Indian nationalism, thus offsetting the many divisive tendencies within the country, and would undermine the position of the then united Communist Party of India. In addition, the inherent dangers of the dispute might bring India and Pakistan closer together, and the United States might benefit from the trouble it created between the U.S.S.R. and China.

India's initial unwillingness even to consider joint defense of the subcontinent was discouraging, although the effort to settle many of the outstanding disputes with Pakistan in the years 1959 and 1960 was a hopeful sign. But there was no significant progress on Kashmir. India won the support of the United States and the United Kingdom, and the neutrality of the U.S.S.R., in its quarrel with Communist China and held Soviet support against Pakistan for many years, all of which made it unwilling to make any substantial concessions to gain a settlement of either the Kashmir issue or the border dispute with China.

It is time to reappraise whether the Sino-Indian dispute still is—if it ever was—in the U.S. interest. Observers have expressed widely divergent views on the nature of the dispute. Those who see it primarily as a conflict over boundaries call attention to China's willingness to settle its border disputes with its other neighbors and stress China's limited ability to carry out any ambitious policy in the subcontinent. Others, while agreeing that boundaries are important in the Sino-

Indian dispute, see it as much more than this. They stress Peking's worldwide revolutionary aims, and generally give greater weight to Peking's words relative to its deeds as an indication of Chinese intentions than does the first group. They point to China's willingness to provide Pakistan with scarce military equipment as another indication of the high priority it assigns to South Asia.

Yet China's interests in the subcontinent are secondary. Conflict with the Soviet Union, the struggle with the United States, Taiwan, Japan, and China's many interests in Southeast Asia—all are basically more important to Peking than its relations with India and Pakistan. Clearly, if only because of proximity, India and Pakistan are of greater interest than the Middle East, Africa, or Latin America, but China's real interests in the two South Asian countries, at least for the foreseeable future, are quite limited.

Obviously Peking considers the border dispute important, and is unwilling to sacrifice territory it regards as its own to maintain good relations with India. This may, however, represent a judgment that India—in league with the West and the U.S.S.R.—has used the border question to undermine Chinese influence in Tibet and weaken China generally. Peking, however, apparently does not view India by itself as sufficiently strong or dynamic to be a serious competitor in Asia. This conclusion, while my personal judgment, would rule out the thesis advanced by some that China's actions along the Sino-Indian frontier, and its efforts to cultivate Nepal and Pakistan, derive primarily from a strategy of keeping India preoccupied in the subcontinent so that it cannot compete in Southeast Asia.

The general Indian view tends to be quite different. For years New Delhi could not believe that Peking would press its border demands at the price of India's friendship. Yet the evasive manner in which Chinese leaders dealt with the boundary question during the 1950s—and especially the expansion of their earlier claims in the Aksai Chin area in 1960—eventually convinced Indian leaders that the border claims were but one step toward a more ominous if indefinable goal. The 1962 war and China's subsequent links to Pakistan reinforced these fears. China's suggestions for a compromise settlement in 1960, its restraint in not sending troops beyond its border claims in 1962, and its early withdrawal from NEFA have never been considered by Indians as evidence that China may have more limited goals. Most Indians have become convinced that China is, in Nehru's words, "a country with profoundly inimical intentions toward our independence and institutions" and that the border dispute is part of an effort to pressure India "to follow the Chinese line, both in her domestic and external policies, or risk disintegration in the process of resisting that pressure." China's later calls for Maoist revolution in India and its aid to tribal rebels in the Himalayas are seen not as a shift from an earlier policy but as an indication of what Peking's true goals have always been.

There is another possible explanation of China's motives, at least before the outbreak of the Great Cultural Revolution. The direct routes from western China to Tibet pass through extremely difficult terrain and are sometimes impassable in winter. A less direct but more dependable route is through Sinkiang into Tibet from the northwest, which has to pass through the disputed Aksai Chin territory to avoid the rugged terrain to its north. Possession of this area is of great importance to China if its position in Tibet is to be secure. India's unwillingness in 1960 to accept a compromise border settlement recognizing this area as Chinese was probably interpreted in Peking as demonstrating that India did not really accept Chinese control of Tibet, but was following the old British policy of seeking to make it a buffer state. The outrage expressed by the Indian press, the public, and some members of Parliament over suppression of the Tibetan revolt in 1959 had already made China suspicious.

Similarly, India's forward movement of its troops in Ladakh in 1961 and 1962 gave China the choice of losing important territory or responding with military force. The advance was successful enough so that Nehru could tell Parliament in August 1962 that India had recovered 2,500 square miles of its territory. Furthermore, Peking apparently felt under extreme pressure from all sides at this time. It was convinced that the Soviet Union was trying to undermine its control of Sinkiang, and that the Chinese Nationalists were planning a major military move. Having concluded that a military response was necessary, Peking apparently designed its attack to achieve its territorial objectives, forcing India to accept Chinese terms for a settlement, humiliating it in the eyes of other nations, and demonstrating to other countries that China would strike out hard if pressed. (Calling attention to the Indian advance does not imply that India was the aggressor, for the territory was in dispute and China had moved in earlier. It does imply that the Chinese attack was not unprovoked, although it was clearly disproportionate to the Indian move.)

This interpretation does not mean that the Sino-Indian dispute is no more than a border quarrel. A certain degree of rivalry is almost inherent in the relationship of the two most populous nations of Asia, each having different political and economic systems. Moreover, Peking's suspicions that New Delhi is a tool of U.S. and Soviet efforts to encircle China (and perhaps detach Tibet) and Indian worries that Peking is committed to fomenting revolution in India will cause both to be hesitant about the possibility and value of normalizing relations as distinct from muting their hostility. Yet perceptions and policies do change over time, especially between countries whose vital interests are not conflicting.

If this assessment is correct, is there any basis for a settlement of the border dispute that would meet the needs of the two nations and permit a lessening of hostility? The Indian government naturally argues that its boundary claims in both the northeast and Ladakh, as well as the few small disputed areas between Ladakh and Nepal, are entirely valid, and most Indians take the same position. As one commentator has expressed the Indian conviction:

> The report of the Indian and Chinese officials on the Boundary Question . . . provides conclusive evidence in support of the Indian border alignment in each sector by detailed reference to geography, tradition, treaties and administration. It also exposes the total failure of the Chinese to substantiate any part of a single one of their extravagant territorial claims.[8]

New Delhi asserts that these areas are legally part of India and have long been recognized as such.[9] The conviction that it has a good legal case is one reason for India's firm stand, and was behind Nehru's 1962 comment that India might be willing to refer the dispute to the International Court of Justice.

The legal aspects of the Indian and Chinese claims are nevertheless both complex and unclear. Each side relies on tenuous arguments on certain points. Western scholars who have examined the matter in detail generally agree that India's claims to nearly all of NEFA are notably stronger than China's, but there is a division of opinion as to whether either side has a strong claim to the disputed Aksai Chin.

Alastair Lamb has concluded:

> A study of the Sino-Indian boundary, at least from the standpoint of its historical evolution up to 1947, suggests that the Chinese, either in their own right or as the masters of Tibet, have legitimate claims to a few

small tracts of territory south of the McMahon Line and, perhaps (if there are such things as legitimate claims over desert country), to the northern part of Aksai Chin through which runs their road. All this amounts to about 7,000 square miles of territory out of a total Chinese claim of more than 45,000 square miles. For the remaining 38,000 or so square miles the Chinese case, on grounds of history, tradition, treaty, and administration is nowhere particularly good or worthy of the attention of a Great Power.[10]

Turning from the legal aspects of the dispute, the Himalayas are India's natural defense line on its northeastern frontier. If China were to acquire the southern slopes, India's ability to defend itself would be seriously jeopardized. On the other hand, the portion of the Aksai Chin that New Delhi claims as Indian territory is not strategically important for the defense of India. India's natural defense line in this area is the Karakoram Mountains, which run south of the Aksai Chin from northwest to southeast. Therefore an agreement which recognized Indian claims along the northeastern frontier and those of China to the Aksai Chin would meet the strategic requirements of both countries.

Such an agreement would offer several advantages to India. It would lessen the chances of another war between the two countries. It would reduce the upward pressure on Indian defense spending (which more than trebled in the 1960s and exerts a heavy drag on the economy), and might in time make some cutbacks possible. By lowering tensions, it might also ease India's sense of need for nuclear weapons. Finally, it would weaken if not undermine the Sino-Pakistani relationship. Thus India's defense burdens and dependence on the superpowers would both be decreased.

These also are good reasons for concluding that the Sino-Indian conflict is against U.S. interests and that a border settlement is desirable. India did not, and will not, seek a rapprochement with Pakistan in order to strengthen its position vis-à-vis China. Indeed, instead of leading to better relations, the Sino-Indian conflict led to greater Indo-Pakistani hostility as the United States and Britain moved to aid India and as Pakistan and China drew closer together in response. Interestingly, too, it does not seem to have much weakened the position of the Indian Communists; and while it was a factor in splitting the movement, it was not the major cause of division.[11]

One could reasonably remark that the U.S. interest in easing Sino-Indian hostility was, at least until recently, somewhat academic. If there was ever a dispute the United States could influence less, it would be hard to find: its influence is obviously limited with India and still practically nonexistent with China. Yet U.S. policy should do nothing that makes an eventual settlement more difficult, such as encouraging India to view China as more of a threat than it is. Indeed, in view of President Nixon's overtures to China in 1971, there is a need to assure India that U.S. moves to normalize relations with China are designed to create a less dangerous situation in East Asia, rather than to work with Peking against New Delhi in South Asia. Until that Indian concern is dealt with, even quiet suggestions by the United States that settlement of the border dispute was desirable would arouse new concern on the part of Indian leaders. In time, however, it may be possible to make this view known in a constructive manner.

There are possible dangers in such a policy. India might come to fear that the United States was no longer concerned about its security vis-à-vis China, and decide that it had no choice but to rely more heavily on the Soviet Union. But the danger of a major shift in relationships is limited as long as the United States does not withdraw from the area.

At present, Moscow is probably more aware of the opportunities than the dangers in the Sino-Indian dispute but, depending upon the state of its relations with Peking, might at some point see some benefits in a border settlement. India would be cautious about moving toward a rapprochement with China unless there were signs China were similarly inclined. Such an Indian move could alienate the U.S.S.R. However, if Sino-Indian relations were to improve, India would have less need for Soviet support. In any case, Moscow's desire to maintain its position in India would limit its willingness to penalize New Delhi for such a move. Pakistan's links with China did not prevent Moscow from providing it with assistance, which further suggests that New Delhi has room for maneuver.

Indeed, as the memories of 1962 become less vivid some Indians are beginning to take a new look at the situation and may conclude that neither the great friendship of the Panch Sheel era nor the bitter animosity of recent years is a normal or desirable type of relationship. They may in time decide that a compromise settlement—the Aksai Chin remaining with China and NEFA remaining with India— would represent a sensible arrangement. Although it claims all of Kashmir is legally Indian, New Delhi has at times offered to settle for the *status quo* with Pakistan. A settlement along the same lines with

China would seem eminently sensible, although it would be politically difficult for India; New Delhi's problem would be eased if Peking recognized India's special position in the Himalayan border States. At the same time, New Delhi will need to convince Peking that India and the U.S.S.R. are not working together to undermine China's position in Tibet and Sinkiang.

Such a settlement, it should be emphasized, is clearly dependent on a major shift in Chinese attitudes and foreign policy in the direction of normalizing relations with its neighbors. Peking's failure to respond to Mrs. Gandhi's hints in 1968 and 1969 that India would welcome new discussions indicate that Peking was not ready for such a departure. Few if any Chinese leaders are likely to want to help India, but Peking may try to reduce the number of its enemies. There are advantages in being prepared for such a change without, of course, abandoning the preparedness necessary in case Peking decides to follow a more dangerous course.

16

Defense of the Subcontinent

Concern over the security of Asia in the wake of the Korean War brought on America's heavy involvement in South Asian affairs. From the signing of the U.S.-Pakistani military aid agreement in 1954 until the Indo-Pakistani war in 1965, the United States supplied its ally with arms worth between $700 and $800 million.[1] It sold India a modest amount of military equipment before 1962, and gave India arms worth about $85 million between the 1962 conflict with China and the 1965 war with Pakistan. The attempt to bolster the defensive position of the two hostile neighbors against possible attack from outside the subcontinent forced the United States constantly to consider the impact of its military aid on the regional balance of power. But the rationale for supplying arms to India and Pakistan lost its appeal as the political costs of the policy became too high after the 1965 war. To preclude the Soviet Union and China from becoming major arms suppliers seemed both impossible and unnecessary, for the American experience demonstrated the limits of the influence that could be obtained by such means.

Yet the foregoing remarks may imply a greater American military involvement in South Asian affairs than was actually the case. The amount of arms supplied, especially to India, has been much less than that given to some smaller nations in the Middle East or the Far East, and the U.S. government has seldom if ever seriously considered the use of its military forces in South Asia. This reflects the fact that—except for a short period during and just after the 1962 Sino-Indian war—the United States has regarded India and Pakistan as less in danger of external attack than the areas to the east or west.

Of several reasons for this, the geography of the subcontinent is probably the most important. South Asia is relatively isolated. Although the mountain ranges separating the subcontinent from the U.S.S.R. and China are not impassable, they make major aggression from the north extremely difficult. Furthermore, the main centers of Soviet and Chinese power are far distant from South Asia. Because national power tends to follow the routes of least geographical resistance, the chances of the major powers clashing are greater in other, more accessible regions. China's naval forces are small and are unlikely to assume any role of importance in the Indian Ocean in the foreseeable future. The Soviet Navy, now the world's second largest, is increasing its activities in the Persian Gulf and Indian Ocean, but this is a gradual process and probably will remain so even if the Suez Canal is reopened.

The United States has only a few vessels in the area, although it is planning to build jointly with Britain an air and communications base on the small island of Diego Garcia, about 1,200 miles south of India. As long as the United States maintains a strong naval position in the Pacific, it need not become unduly excited about the effect on India and Pakistan of Soviet vessels operating in the Indian Ocean— although cruises by units of the Pacific fleet to demonstrate American interests and capabilities there are in order.[2]

A second reason is the size of the two countries and of their armed forces. It would take a relatively large and well-supplied military force to cross the mountains and defeat the local forces. It is possible, of course, for a defending army to get chewed up on the mountains as a result of poor strategy and inept operations, as happened to India in 1962, and thus leave the country open to invasion. Yet, having won a victory in the Himalayas, what does the invader do next? Occupying such large nations would be unprofitable even if possible.

In addition, South Asia contains no great industrial complexes, and no important natural resources, such as the petroleum deposits of the Middle East. Its strategic importance would have been greater if the United States or Britain had obtained major military installations in the subcontinent, but for a variety of reasons this never occurred.

TABLE 5

India and Pakistan: Size and Composition of Armed Forces,
1960 and 1965–70

	India				Pakistan			
	Total	Army[a]	Navy	Air force	Total	Army	Navy	Air force
1960	535,200	500,000	8,800	26,400	223,000	200,740	7,260	15,000
1965	869,000	825,000	16,000	28,000	233,000	205,000	8,000	20,000
1966	879,000	807,000	17,000	55,000	278,350	250,000	8,350	20,000
1967	977,000	900,000	17,000	60,000	323,000	300,000	9,000	14,000
1968	1,033,000	950,000	25,000	58,000	324,000	300,000	9,000	15,000
1969[b]	925,000	848,000	20,000	57,000	324,000	300,000	9,000	15,000
1970	930,000	800,000	40,000	90,000	324,500	300,000	9,500	15,000

Notes:
a. Includes approximately 25,000 Azad Kashmir troops.
b. Published figures indicating that the Indian army was reduced substantially
and the navy and air force expanded sharply since 1969 should be regarded
skeptically in view of trends in defense expenditures and Indian defense policy.

Sources:
   The Statesman's Year Book 1960 (London: Macmillan & Co. Ltd., 1960);
H. Roberts Coward, "Military Technology in Developing Countries" (Cambridge, Mass.: Center for International Studies, 1964); The Military Balance
1965–1966; 1966–1967; 1967–1968; 1968–1969; 1969–1970; 1970–1971 (London: The Institute for Strategic Studies).

Just as the location and size of the countries of South Asia have
largely accounted for the relatively low priority accorded the defense
of the subcontinent in U.S. planning, so their internal geography has
precluded any thought of military involvement in local quarrels. (The
situation is quite different in the Eastern Mediterranean where the
U.S. Sixth Fleet still partially shields the area from Soviet power
and has on occasion been used to restrain local conflicts, as when
King Hussein was threatened in 1957 and 1970.) The principal con-
centrations of Indian and Pakistani forces are in the north, where
the clashes of 1962 and 1965 occurred, hundreds of miles from the
seaports. Even if the United States were inclined to intervene, it
would be extremely difficult to bring in its ground forces; its air power
could be brought to bear more quickly, but any large-scale deploy-
ment would require a logistical buildup, which takes time.

   Given these circumstances and the growing American opposition
to military engagement in Asia, does it make sense to consider
whether the United States should even be concerned about the se-

curity of India and Pakistan? I believe that it not only makes sense but is essential to any general survey of the U.S. role in the area. While current American attitudes, which are so largely a reaction to the Vietnam experience, should not be ignored, they should not be regarded as a straitjacket for the indefinite future. The United States is still in an alliance relationship with Pakistan (nominal though it is) and is selling some military equipment to India and Pakistan. In addition, it wants India to sign the nonproliferation treaty or, even without formally committing itself, not to produce nuclear weapons. Finally, India and Pakistan are intensely concerned with their security problems. The considerations set forth in the preceding pages limit the dangers of any major invasion by an external power; but Indo-Pakistani hostility, the Sino-Indian border conflict, and the need to maintain domestic order, combined with their poverty, make India and Pakistan dependent on outside support and thus subject to external influence.

Soviet Military Posture

As the publication of captured Soviet-Nazi documents by the U.S. government after World War II showed, the Soviet government shared the old Czarist interest in the Persian Gulf–Indian Ocean area.[3] Yet in the years before and after World War II, Soviet interest in South Asia was much less than in Europe, the Far East, or the Middle East.

Few students of Soviet foreign policy would hold that there is a direct Soviet military threat to the area today, whatever might be the case if there were no countervailing Western military power in the world. Indeed, the very phrase, "the Soviet military threat to South Asia," has a certain anachronistic ring to it. So far as can be ascertained, Soviet military doctrine has no interest in an offensive thrust in South Asia, which would frighten countries from North Africa through Southeast Asia at a time when Moscow is making steady progress in expanding its role by less dangerous means. Ideology assures the Soviet leaders that in time communism will triumph in this part of the world, basically because of the underlying social and economic forces. The U.S.S.R. will work to increase its influence, helping those forces congenial to it when it seems feasible and compatible with Soviet interests. However, Soviet leaders appear to regard fundamental changes in this area as far in the future, although it seems that there are some differences among them about the prospects.

At present their extensive military aid program probably reflects not only the traditional Soviet desire to reduce the Western role in the area but a policy of building up Indian strength vis-à-vis China.

It is possible, of course, that this assessment is unduly influenced by the present national mood and that it underestimates the danger of the Soviet military threat simply because we do not want to prepare to deal with it. Nonetheless, if it underestimates the danger, it probably does not do so by very much. If Soviet policy does take a more militant turn, it seems unlikely to shift so rapidly as to make it impossible for the United States to revise its judgment and take whatever steps are appropriate.

The Chinese Military Threat

A judgment of the nature and extent of the various types of threat —ranging from subversion and guerrilla war through conventional warfare to nuclear attack—posed by Communist China is more difficult to make with confidence for several reasons.[4]

India's natural defense line at its northeastern frontier runs along the ridge of the Himalayas, which the McMahon Line largely follows. If China were to acquire the southern slopes, India's ability to defend itself would be seriously undermined. Along the central sector of its frontier India is not free to act as it wishes. Nepal is fully independent, and Bhutan is now virtually independent. Only in Sikkim, where Indian troops are stationed, is New Delhi basically in control of the security situation.

Peking has made plain that it does not recognize any special Indian rights in these areas and has gradually expanded its role in Nepal over the years. Its activities in Bhutan have apparently been minimal, but as long as China and India are at odds any Chinese interest in Bhutan or Sikkim will make New Delhi nervous. Peking seems likely to continue with a cautious, low-risk policy, but its rejection of India's claim to a special status in the border states and its willingness to trade with them and to provide assistance improves their bargaining position with India. At the same time, as the leaders of the border states are aware of the fate of the Tibetans and recognize their economic dependence on India, they will move cautiously in trying to loosen their ties to India. In short, no basic change in the situation is likely, but India's defense problem will continue to be complicated by its lack of military freedom in the area.

There are also indications that the Chinese have supplied arms and training for rebel groups—especially the Nagas—within India, and the border peoples have been the targets of Chinese propaganda.[5] With such a policy Peking can cause trouble for New Delhi at little cost or risk to itself. But in some areas the people are so primitive they are hard to reach with political appeals. Some of the more advanced groups are ethnically and culturally akin to the Tibetans, and their awareness of the treatment of the Tibetans limits the appeal of the Chinese. Moreover, the various groups in the Himalayas are often antagonistic toward each other as well as toward the Indians. All of this suggests that Chinese influence will be difficult to establish and expand, although some groups will accept Chinese assistance in order to strengthen their bargaining positions with India. Thus while a well-planned and executed Chinese program of propaganda and subversion could increase India's troubles, India would have to do a poor job indeed before it lost control of any of the territories. India's policy of offering aid and autonomy to many of these groups has been at least partially successful, as in Nagaland where the revolt is largely ended. In any case, India's desire to handle these matters on its own is as strong as is America's reluctance to become involved.

Another point is worth emphasizing. Even if everything went wrong for India and anti-Indian and pro-Chinese groups gained effective control of some territory, these borderlands would not be good bases for an Indian Communist guerrilla movement aiming to take over India. The goal of the hill people is autonomy or independence, not control of lands beyond their own. If Indian Communists based themselves in these areas and cooperated with these groups, they might well weaken their appeal in the rest of India, whose people have no desire to see any part of their country lost.

Peking's strong propaganda support (possibly supplemented by some arms) for Communist rebels in West Bengal also needs to be considered in this connection. This state, torn by political turmoil and violence in recent years, has spawned a third and ultra-radical Communist party (the Marxist-Leninist faction) oriented to and praised by Peking. While the state is periodically governed directly from New Delhi under President's rule, the combination of deteriorating economic and social conditions and the terrorist tradition in Bengal make it difficult to control the violence. But it is local conditions rather than Chinese activities that give rise to the new terrorists, and their fate will depend on what India does or fails to do in the area.

All these factors—the existence of independent Himalayan border states, dissatisfied hill tribes, and political violence in West Bengal —pose serious political problems for India, either by restricting its military freedom or requiring the diversion of troops to maintain control of Indian territory. But they are ultimately political rather than military problems, however necessary it is to have and use military force to deal with them until political solutions can be worked out.

China's ability to conduct conventional military operations poses a potentially serious threat to India even though the cutoff of Soviet military supplies has held down its military capabilities. The Chinese have stockpiled supplies in Tibet and Sinkiang, and have built an extensive network of roads along their side of the frontier. The Indian Defense Ministry in 1970 estimated that China had 130,000–150,000 troops in Tibet. Still, Chinese forces are at the end of a supply line some 2,000 miles long, and would find it extremely difficult to support a sizable and prolonged military operation against India.

While China's military capabilities have remained about the same, India's have increased as its defense expenditures and the size of its armed forces have expanded rapidly (see Tables 4 and 5). The armed forces have received about $1 billion worth of military equipment from abroad since 1962 (chiefly from the U.S.S.R.), and Indian defense plants are turning out modern equipment in growing volume.[6] However, Indian equipment is still far from standardized, which increases its training and maintenance problems.

The improvement in India's position has not eliminated several serious weaknesses. If India's supply lines are shorter, they are nevertheless more difficult than those of the Chinese. The rise from the Gangetic plain to the Himalayan crests in northeastern India is over 25,000 feet, whereas these crests are only a few thousand feet above the Tibetan plateau. Moreover, in the northeast the supply line must pass through the narrow gap between the Himalayan border states and East Pakistan, a point which must be held if Indian troops in Assam and NEFA are not to be cut off. The situation is equally difficult in Ladakh. Supplies from India proper must pass over the mountains to Kashmir, and then be hauled either over the narrow and winding road through Leh to the frontier or be air-dropped.

Finally, the Indian forces performed poorly against the Chinese in 1962 and were only moderately effective against Pakistan in 1965.

They are clearly better equipped than in the past and undoubtedly have learned some lessons from their battle experiences. However, rapid growth probably has lowered former standards of military skill at some levels in the services.

Thus it is difficult to judge the relative military capabilities of India and China along their Himalayan frontier. About the only conclusion one can set forth with confidence is that it probably is impossible for India to hold all the territory it now occupies in the event of a major Chinese attack. The initial advantages of terrain would be too heavily with the Chinese for the Indians to hold the crestline. At the same time, if India yields some ground in the fighting, keeping its main forces near the Himalayan foothills in NEFA or behind the Karakoram Range in Ladakh, China's logistical problems will increase and India's will decrease to a point which should make it possible to withstand a sizable attack. Having had its forces overwhelmed in 1962 in part because they were posted too far forward, India now appears to be following a less ambitious but also less risky strategy.

An examination of Chinese capabilities as distinct from intentions indicates that there are three general types of policy that might be followed. The first would be for the Chinese to pursue an essentially defensive or *status quo* policy designed to hold the areas presently under their control. The second would be to attempt at some point to seize all the territory they claim. This would precipitate a conflict of at least the magnitude of the 1962 fighting and could be considerably larger and longer because of the growth of India's military forces. The third and most ambitious policy would involve a major Chinese assault to defeat India's military forces and move into the Assam plains in the northeast and into Indian-held Ladakh or even Kashmir itself. (It could also involve an attack on one or more of the Himalayan border states. That India has not stationed large-scale forces along the border with Nepal or Bhutan suggests it does not anticipate an attack here, regarding its task as primarily that of limiting Chinese political influence.) Conflict could result either from a coldly calculated decision before the fighting started or from the escalation of smaller-scale skirmishes, or—though it seems unlikely—from a Chinese decision to intervene in an Indo-Pakistani war.

Assuming that India continues its present policy of attempting to keep the border quiet, which of these policies is the most likely Chinese course of action? Since policy is a function of the instruments available as well as the interests and goals of a nation, the third possibility probably is beyond Chinese capabilities. Moreover, it is important to keep in mind the limited nature of Chinese interests in South Asia, referred to above, and to remember that China has not resorted to all-out action in the past. China's leaders have been extravagant of word but cautious of deed.

As between an essentially defensive policy and an effort to take the territory it claims, the choice will depend upon the interplay of power factors and political relations among the major countries involved. China seems content with the present *de facto* boundaries, and has made no attempt to move across them. When its troops had defeated the Indian army in 1962, it did not attempt to hold on to NEFA but retreated to about the position it now holds, which suggests that China does not believe it has to control all the areas it claims. Finally, it is unlikely that China has the military capability to seize and hold all of NEFA—at least without a major and prolonged buildup in Tibet.

Chinese intentions toward India are not independent of Peking's other problems. Despite its recent diplomatic moves, China faces enemies on almost all sides—the U.S.S.R. in the north and west, the United States, Japan and Taiwan in the east, and India in the southwest. Thus it is forced to keep major forces deployed to deal with a range of dangers, and must wonder whether a new conflict with India would not bring either the United States or the U.S.S.R., or both, to India's assistance at some point. If Peking today is less worried about the United States in view of America's obvious reluctance to remain militarily engaged in Asia, it probably is more worried about what Moscow might do. While India also faces more than one enemy, with about half of its military strength deployed against Pakistan, this does not seem a sufficient condition for China to adopt an adventuresome course in South Asia.

Even if such a judgment about the likelihood of a new Sino-Indian clash is correct, it depends upon India maintaining an adequate military capability vis-à-vis China, and thus raises the question of the desirability of supplying some U.S. arms to India. In considering this matter it is important to be quite clear on one point: India is building up its domestic arms industry and is receiving large amounts of military equipment from the Soviet Union, and while much of this is for the forces facing Pakistan it enhances India's military posture against China as well. Any large-scale supply of U.S. arms would in effect be designed less for defense against China than to preclude the U.S.S.R. from maintaining its position as virtually the sole external supplier of the Indian armed forces.

There is no reason for the United States to change its basic policy of not becoming a major arms supplier to India and Pakistan. The external threats do not warrant such a change, and the influence either the U.S.S.R. or China gains by supplying arms is likely to stop well short of any danger point. To be sure, the peace and security of the two countries is partially dependent on the balance of power within the subcontinent, but the liabilities of trying to maintain such a balance in a situation complicated by several regional quarrels and competing arms suppliers would considerably outweigh any advantages. If a new conflict develops with China, the United States should be prepared to provide India with an emergency supply of arms but without making any long-term commitments until the new political and strategic situation growing out of such a war can be carefully assessed.

At the same time, the policy of not selling any "lethal" weapons to either country, which the United States followed from 1965 to 1970, was unduly rigid for the long run. This is partly because there are circumstances when supplying particular items is advantageous—particularly if the choice is between agreeing to our European allies selling some used equipment they received through our aid program or seeing India and Pakistan buying much more expensive equipment. The United States has been moving to reduce its involvement in Asian military and political affairs, and further moves in this direction are probable. The shift is not only basically sound but overdue. At the same time, the Asian countries are uncertain as to the extent of our pullback and its implications for their security. The interests of the United States as well as of India are best served if the latter is not overwhelmingly dependent on a single outside source of arms, and if the United States demonstrates in a modest way that it is not disinterested in the security concerns of the subcontinent. There is no reason to correct past overinvolvement in these matters by future underinvolvement. Yet a shift from a policy of trying to control the balance of power within the subcontinent and to provide India and Pakistan with arms for defense against external threats to a policy of complete noninvolvement would represent precisely the kind of overcorrection that should be avoided.

Selling arms to India occasionally may create pressures to do so continually—and certainly will lead to complaints from Pakistan. Frank and open explanations of the reasons behind American actions can only mitigate the latter problem, but keeping the amount of such sales small and excluding the newest and most sophisticated weapons will minimize the former dangers. The danger of such sales—say, $20–25 million a year—contributing significantly to an arms race is slight, for the amount is but a small fraction of the Indian defense budget.

But if the United States should be willing to sell arms to India occasionally, the same does not hold true for Pakistan when the major concern of its government is maintaining its hold on East Pakistan. Just as in the case of economic development assistance, the United States should refrain from supplying any military equipment until a political system is established that is acceptable to both wings of the country. Although there is a U.S. interest in preventing the fragmentation of the subcontinent, it is not an interest that overrides all other considerations.

The Indian Nuclear Issue

The extent of the Chinese nuclear threat to India, what India can and should do about it, and what policy the United States should pursue with respect to these matters forms one of the most complex military issues involving South Asia. Chinese nuclear explosions and missile firings in recent years have generated mounting pressure for the development of nuclear weapons despite the Indian government's long-standing public opposition both to nuclear weapons in general and to Indian possession of such weapons. Thus far, government leaders have been publicly united in this position. Moreover, military leaders apparently have little interest in acquiring nuclear weapons, preferring to concentrate the available funds on conventional forces. Yet India has a nuclear program which provides the option to produce weapons, and the program is designed to keep this option open.

The Canada-India research reactor is capable of producing enough uranium for about two small bombs a year, and India also has a chemical separation plant. It has built up an impressive nuclear research establishment, which apparently has the necessary skills for weapons design and production. New Delhi has invested several hundred million dollars in its nuclear facilities, and the investment is rising rapidly with the construction of several large nuclear power reactors. When these reactors are completed, India probably will be able to produce a few dozen small bombs a year.

Those in favor of an Indian nuclear weapons program argue partly on grounds of status and prestige, but their major point is that without such weapons India would be subject to nuclear threats and blackmail and have no satisfactory way of responding. In such vital matters as national security, they argue, one country cannot depend completely on others and that in any case no one is offering an ironclad guarantee to come to India's defense in the event of a nuclear attack.[7] Some proponents may also believe that the chances of drawing the major nuclear powers into a conflict with China would increase if India possessed nuclear bombs. In any case, it would give India a voice in Asian security matters that it would not otherwise have.

While India has signed the test-ban treaty, it has made plain that it will not sign the nonproliferation treaty despite Soviet and American urging, and it has shown considerable unease and resentment at indications of any convergence of American and Soviet policies.[8] India has demonstrated only sporadic interest in guarantees by the nuclear powers. Many Indians do not believe that the U.S.-U.K.-U.S.S.R. statement that the three countries would take action through the U.N. Security Council against a nuclear aggressor offers adequate protection. Moreover, most politically conscious Indians derive psychological satisfaction from their country's stance of independence and nonalignment in foreign affairs and believe that this policy has enhanced its international stature and increased its political bargaining power. Many of them feel that self-reliance rather than single or multiple guarantees are the proper course for India to follow.

Those Indians objecting to nuclear weapons point to a number of obstacles. They cite the traditional Indian opposition to nuclear weapons as increasing the risks and dangers of war in general. They emphasize that India has committed itself not to use the reactors it has acquired for any but peaceful purposes, and would suffer if it broke its word. They stress, of course, the very heavy cost of any significant nuclear weapons program, pointing out that this would add a further burden to India's economic development effort. Some also believe that the Chinese nuclear weapons program is designed chiefly to deter an attack on China itself by the superpowers rather than to threaten its neighbors. Beyond this, they argue that in any case India by itself cannot hope to build a significant nuclear weapons arsenal and an adequate delivery system to deter China, but must either formally or informally rely upon protection by the superpowers. Finally, they argue that an Indian decision to produce nuclear weapons would have a very serious effect on Pakistan, and might even drive it into much closer cooperation with China.

Clearly, even a moderate-sized nuclear weapons program would be expensive for India, but more because of the cost of a delivery system than because of the cost of the weapons themselves. There is a growing recognition that India would have to rely on missiles to have an effective delivery system—one that could reach the major centers of China. Leonard Beaton suggested several years ago that acquiring first the scientific and industrial facilities and then a missile force capable of reaching the key Chinese targets more than 2,000 miles away would require an outlay of $2 to $3 billion over a ten-year period—the higher figure if hydrogen weapons were produced.[9] This program would add a minimum of $200 to $300 million a year to the Indian defense budget. James R. Schlesinger, on the other hand, has expressed the view that the costs would be five times as great, which would require a 50 to 75 per cent increase in defense spending.[10] While some Indians still talk of building a useful deterrent for about $1 billion, the government and informed opinion have also become increasingly aware of the magnitude of the costs. Moreover, the inability of the United Kingdom to absorb the costs of a meaningful delivery system has given some Indians pause.

Defense Minister Swaran Singh has cited a U.N. study indicating the cost of creating a modest capability would be $7.6 billion over a ten-year period, while an unofficial estimate by an Indian research organization holds that the costs would amount to $10-15 billion over a ten-year period.[11] In view of the tendency of the costs of such programs everywhere to outrun estimates, one wonders if $20 billion (which would require a doubling of the defense budget) would not turn out to be closer to the actual costs. Moreover, the time involved could also be significantly longer than planned because of technological complexities.

Thus the debate goes on in India with renewed demands for nuclear weapons and ballistic missiles whenever the Chinese make a new advance, as with the orbiting of a satellite in April 1970. The Indians are obviously in a dilemma, and their choice becomes increasingly difficult as the Chinese forge ahead on the one hand while the cost estimates of a meaningful program steadily mount on the other. Pre-

dicting Indian policy in these circumstances is especially problematical. There is a fair chance that within a few years domestic political
pressures will lead the government to undertake a token weapons program, which would give India the status of a nuclear power. (This
might be rationalized by claiming that India was developing tactical
weapons for use in the Himalayan passes, thus playing down the
costs.) A more likely possibility, however, is that India will concentrate on developing its options to the maximum extent possible while
refraining from any positive decision to go nuclear. This would involve additional expenditures, especially in the missile field, but India
is already moving to speed up the development of missiles and a
further step-up is likely.[12] In any case, India's capabilities and security
problems make it a prime candidate to join the nuclear club and thus
a matter of concern to the United States.[13]

The United States has always opposed an Indian nuclear weapons
program as part of its general policy against nuclear proliferation, and
there are several reasons for concluding that this position is sound.
Such a program would be an added burden on the Indian economy,
and one that could grow considerably over the years. A program of
any significance would divert a disproportionate share of India's limited supply of scientific and technical talent. India's development
efforts are crucial to its future and leave little room for any large-
scale diversion of resources, material or human. Thus a major nuclear
weapons program would deal a blow to India's development effort
and should not be undertaken unless the Chinese nuclear threat is seen
to be more clearly and specifically directed against India than seems
to be the case now.

An equally dramatic and unfavorable effect of a nuclear weapons
program would be its impact on Pakistan. There would seem to be
four choices open to Pakistan in such an event, all of them extremely
poor ones: (1) accept Indian hegemony on the subcontinent; (2)
turn back to the United States and the United Kingdom and try to
get a firm guarantee against India; (3) move closer to China, hoping
to acquire a measure of nuclear protection from Peking; (4) begin
the long and arduous task of developing its own nuclear weapons.
The first would seem intolerable and the second impossible, so relying
partly on the third alternative and in time on the fourth seem to be
the most likely courses of action, unsatisfactory though they be.

Finally, one need not adopt the extreme view that if India went
nuclear other countries would inevitably follow (the domino theory

of nuclear proliferation) to conclude that an Indian nuclear weapons program would reduce the inhibitions on other countries. Countries which go nuclear do so because of a strong conviction that their basic security position requires them to have nuclear weapons. Yet nations, like individuals, are influenced by what others do as well as by careful consideration of their own needs, and India's policy probably will have some influence on the policies of others. Nor need one be an alarmist to conclude that the dangers of nuclear conflict probably increase as nuclear weapons come to be possessed by more countries.

Unfortunately, the prospects are not bright for influencing Indian policy on this matter much beyond what is possible by quiet persuasion and making New Delhi fully aware of the heavy costs involved. The United States should periodically reiterate its past assurances that India will not stand alone if China threatens it with nuclear weapons, in order to strengthen the position of those Indians who argue that the best—though not ideal—course for India is to rely as much as possible on implicit superpower guarantees. Such assertions would carry little weight in the present climate, but may be more useful when and if Indo-American relations improve. Even then, India would not want to sacrifice its freedom of action by accepting a commitment only from the United States. It would be unwise, as well as politically impossible for the United States to offer an ironclad guarantee committing it to use nuclear weapons in situations almost completely outside its control. The United States should reduce its assistance to India's general nuclear and missile development effort if it produces nuclear weapons, but India probably will hold off any affirmative decision until it no longer needs outside aid or can get it elsewhere. The United States could also, of course, resort to threats or curtailment of economic aid. Such measures probably would have some impact, although the impact could be just the opposite of what was intended if the matter became a prominent political dispute. Even if such action were to have an influence, it probably would limit the size of the weapons program rather than prevent it altogether if New Delhi had decided national security required it. Moreover, it seems doubtful that the American interest in nonproliferation is great enough to carry through on such threats, especially as they seem unlikely to succeed.[14]

The U.S.S.R. has criticized nations unwilling to sign the nonproliferation treaty, but its desire for good relations with India to counter China seems to have a higher priority than its opposition to Indian acquisition of nuclear weapons. Thus its position seems to have become less firm in the past year or so, and it seems doubtful that it would take any strong action if India began to produce nuclear weapons.

A South Asian Military Role Outside the Subcontinent?

It is also germane to consider the role India and Pakistan might play in the security of other parts of Asia. American interest in the military strength of the two countries has not been solely concerned with their ability to defend the subcontinent. Originally, the Pakistanis were regarded as potential partners in the containment of Russian and Chinese power. The idea of strengthening Pakistan so that it could help contain Communist power in the Middle East and Southeast Asia, it is now clear, never had more than limited validity in view of its quarrel with India. Even if Pakistan were to overcome its present crisis, there is no prospect of its playing such a role unless there were a dramatic improvement in Indo-Pakistani relations. (Even in such an event, the interest of Pakistan in assuming such a role is dubious.)

The present alliance relationship with Pakistan is in reality moribund. President Yahya Khan has called CENTO a "dead letter," and Pakistan's view of SEATO is the same. The question of Pakistan's membership in both alliances cannot be considered apart from the desires of the other members and the basic issue of the future of the alliances themselves. Quietly dismantling our ties might cause some trouble, but it would put the relationship on a more realistic basis than allowing them to continue. The principal drawback to continuing the formal U.S. alliance relationship with Pakistan is that it perpetuates an anachronistic and meaningless relationship, which is hardly a desirable course of action at a time when we are trying to set forth the extent and limitations of our foreign commitments more clearly. Moreover, there is an advantage in demonstrating an ability to abandon outworn policies. It should not be done in any spirit of hostility toward Pakistan but simply as a means of bringing the formal relationship into line with the actual relationship.

If few any longer believe that Pakistan can play a role in the defense of other parts of Asia, the idea that India—perhaps together with Japan and Indonesia—has an important role in containing Chinese power in Southeast Asia is still heard. (Ironically, it apparently has become an element in Soviet thinking as well.) Advocates of this course think in terms of informal cooperation rather than a formal alliance. They believe that such an arrangement would be more flexible and less offensive to Asian sensitivities than an alliance like SEATO. Britain is pulling back from the area, and the United States will shoulder a diminishing share of the burden of containing China. The Asian countries themselves should learn to work together and assume primary responsibility.

There seems much to be said for relying on India and Japan working with the Southeast Asian countries to contain China when one looks at the map. The population and resources of all these countries more than match China's. Japan has great economic power and could be strong militarily, and India has great reserves of manpower and is a potential major power over the longer term. There are also cultural ties of many centuries' duration between India and Southeast Asia, and all of these countries have some broad common interests, such as the desire to remain independent and not be dominated by China.

From the American point of view, there are certain apparent advantages in such a development, provided it did not occur in such a manner as to provoke the very Chinese actions it sought to deter. The United States would be relieved of part of its burden, and its political liabilities would be reduced. But the prospects for such cooperation, at least over the next decade, seem so poor that it would be unwise to put much effort into it or reliance upon it. India, Japan, and the countries in Southeast Asia have practically no history of political cooperation and have shown only a limited inclination to move in that direction. Historic or modern political antagonisms have so far been an important source of discord within Southeast Asia, and attitudes on these issues will change only slowly. In particular, the Japanese are still thought of as former invaders rather than future protectors, and if the Southeast Asian countries do not fear Indian power neither do they respect it. India probably will remain preoccupied with its disputes with Pakistan and with Communist China; even if Pakistan disintegrates and India establishes its hegemony over the subcontinent, its domestic problems will severely limit India's ability to project its power beyond South Asia. The Japanese have little regard for Indian capabilities and even less desire to use their self-defense forces overseas.

Alastair Buchan has stated the problems of such an approach in the following passage, worth quoting at length.

In the first place, Indian military power is only just adequate for India's own security, and her position is bedevilled by the Indo-Pakistan dispute; India has no spare resources to contribute to the general security of Southern Asia. Indonesia is internally very weak and presumably can only acquire internal strength and cohesion very gradually, and she is distrusted by her neighbours because of the history of the Sukarno era. Japan . . . has still not lived down entirely the hostility generated by the war. In any case she is still unwilling to undertake any general international commitments. . . .

In the second place there is no sense of identity of interest between Delhi, Tokyo, and Jakarta. There is no tradition of co-operation between them; true, there has been some very modest co-operation between Indonesia and India, and between Japan and India, but my own experience from running two conferences two years ago—one in Delhi, one in Tokyo—on Asian security problems with a mixed group of Asians, Europeans, Americans and Australians, was not reassuring. We found in those two capitals two wholly different definitions of Asia; to the Indian, Asia begins at the Nile and ends at some indeterminate point on the far side of Mandalay; whereas to the Japanese Asia is a Pacific conception, the states that border the Pacific. So the prospects of serious Indo-Japanese co-operation seem to me pretty poor for the immediate future.[15]

Examination of the dangers facing non-Communist Asia today and the contribution India or Japan could make toward meeting those dangers indicates that neither country has more than a minor military role to play. The primary danger to Southeast Asia is not the threat of direct Chinese military aggression, but that local revolutionaries (perhaps Communist and perhaps aided by China or North Vietnam) will seize upon grievances, legitimate or illegitimate, of the local peoples and organize guerrilla warfare to topple the governments in power. It is difficult if not impossible to see either India or Japan making much of a contribution to dealing with this sort of threat. India's experience in trying to cope with the Naga rebels certainly will not incline it to seek involvement in such operations abroad.

India's policy in Southeast Asia has tended more toward conciliation and amelioration of disputes and reliance on local nationalism than toward direct containment of Chinese or North Vietnamese power. In view of India's determination to maintain good relations with the U.S.S.R., Indian policy is unlikely to change much in this regard. Finally, and perhaps most important of all, its ability to play a growing role will at best develop very slowly.

Thus, the attempt to have India, Japan, and the other free countries of Asia cooperate closely in the containment of Chinese power is not only unrealistic but would be seen by Peking as a U.S.-Soviet effort to use Japan and India as proxies. Indeed, any American effort to encourage such moves while seeking a rapprochement with China would tend to undermine the latter effort. This does not mean that the United States should not encourage the closer cooperation that some observers see developing among these Asian countries.[16] However, we should recognize that such cooperation has little to do with directly containing the Chinese, and is more to be thought of as encouraging the growth of a healthy Asian political climate. We should also recognize that this cooperation will be more meaningful and more enduring if Asian countries take the lead, as they are beginning to do. Discreet support for such efforts by the United States, Britain, Japan, and India will be useful; direct sponsorship will be counterproductive.

17

America and the Future of India and Pakistan

Americans, bitterly divided by the Vietnam experience, are more uncertain about their country's role in the world than they have been
for a generation. For some, the first principle of foreign policy is
simply "No more Vietnams," while other issues involving Asia can
await consideration at some indefinite point in the future. At the
other extreme, an indeterminate but declining number still cling to a
basic if modified cold war outlook, hoping that the country has the
will to continue to fulfill what they regard as America's international
responsibilities. Nearly all are convinced that greater attention should
be given to domestic concerns.

No useful evaluation of the fundamental issues in U.S.–South
Asian relations can be made without considering the major trends in
world affairs, for they will profoundly influence not only what the
United States does on the subcontinent but also how Americans view
their role and responsibilities in the world. The perennial problem
here is to escape from the temptation to view present and prospective
conditions only in light of today's hopes and fears. Failure to have

seen the Communist danger in context (especially as divisions occurred within the Communist world), to distinguish between the nature of the initial postwar Soviet challenge in Europe and the later Communist problems in Southeast Asia, and to give due weight to the great differences in importance between various regions, led the United States to convert a generally successful containment of Soviet and Chinese power into a Southeast Asian policy that failed, and went far to discredit the basic posture of U.S. foreign policy.

Today the temptation for the United States is a different one. Preoccupied with Vietnam and its deleterious impact at home and abroad, many Americans are becoming convinced that Communist control of Vietnam, while undesirable, would not imperil any vital American interest. But acceptance of this view, combined with the widespread determination to avoid future Vietnams, often leads toward another and potentially dangerous pair of conclusions: that what happens in underdeveloped areas is of little or no concern to the United States; and that either Soviet and Chinese aims in these areas are relatively benign or their efforts are unlikely to suceed. While we should not take an alarmist attitude toward Soviet and Chinese aims and activities in India and Pakistan—despite the Indo-Soviet treaty—it would be a serious mistake to ignore them in formulating our policy. Though the cold war has been muted, the U.S.S.R. and China remain adversaries of the United States and the West, and their efforts to expand their influence will persist.

The late summer of 1971 is hardly an auspicious time to complete a study on U.S. policy toward a subcontinent torn by strife and facing the danger of war. If war comes it will, of course, be necessary to reappraise and modify American policies. At the same time, certain underlying elements will continue to be relevant. Accordingly, the emphasis in this concluding chapter is on the long-run issues rather than on responses to immediate crises.

Two of the major determinants of the pattern of international relations involving the subcontinent are the Indo-Pakistani quarrel in its several manifestations, and Sino-Indian hostility. Compromise settlements of specific points at issue would be beneficial to those directly concerned and to the Western nations interested in the progress of the subcontinent. Yet the beginning of wisdom is to recognize our limited ability to affect what other countries regard as their vital interests, whether or not such interests seem vital to us.

The Indo-Pakistani dispute grows out of the most basic attitudes of the two peoples, attitudes that have intensified over several hundred years. That such hostility can eventually decline is clear both from other examples of previously antagonistic neighbors settling their quarrels and from the general fact that no relationship is immune to change over a long period. Yet if such a change is to come, it can only result from new Indian and Pakistani perceptions of what their national interests are, and there is little the United States can do to foster such perceptions. It can hardly do more than reduce the chances of war amidst the present upheaval.

The Sino-Indian dispute presents a somewhat different picture, for the elements of a compromise border settlement that would protect the interests of both parties is apparent and was described in Chapter 15. Moreover, the hostility between the two countries, being relatively recent, is a less deeply rooted sentiment. Yet China's continued support of Pakistan and India's determination to offset its earlier humiliation probably mean that any border settlement lies some distance in the future, and even then the relationship between the two countries probably would remain uneasy and suspicious. The United States can do little in this situation, but at the appropriate moment what little it can do could be of some importance. The United States should make it clear that while the basic decisions are naturally for the two countries to make, it sees no reason why India and China should not work toward a normalization of relations.

The military concern of the United States with the subcontinent (as set forth in Chapter 16) suggests that it can take a relatively detached position on these matters. Neither country is likely to be overrun by forces from outside the subcontinent, and there is no reason for the United States to attempt to renew its military aid programs to either country. At the same time, two changes in U.S. policy would be useful. One would be to encourage Pakistan to withdraw from SEATO, regardless of the organization's future, for Pakistan's presence is now more of an anomaly and an embarrassment than a contribution. The other Asian members might object to a Pakistani withdrawal at a time when the United States is trying to disengage from Vietnam, but it should not be impossible to convince them that losing what is in effect a nonparticipating member would not detract from whatever strength SEATO possesses. The same principle applies to Pakistan's membership in CENTO. In this case, however, it probably would be best to let the organization expire, because the Regional Cooperation for Development is already in existence, and

Turkey, Pakistan, and Iran can simply let it replace the largely defunct CENTO. To demonstrate its continued interest, the United States can rely on Turkish membership in NATO and on good bilateral relations with Iran. (The termination of CENTO would end Britain's involvement; as it withdraws from Asia, its membership becomes steadily less meaningful in any case.) One additional benefit from such changes would be to convince people at home and abroad that the United States is not determined to cling to outmoded instruments and recognizes the difference between shadow and substance in power relationships.

With the shift in stance toward these alliances, it would be useful to make one change in U.S. military supply policy. The United States sells "nonlethal" military items to India and Pakistan, and spare parts for U.S. weapons already in their possession, and in 1970 it agreed to a "one-time" sale of certain weapons to Pakistan. All sales of weapons to Pakistan should be suspended during the course of its civil war. When and if it establishes a political system acceptable to both wings, or if it divides into two nations, the suspension should be reviewed. As regards India, the United States should be willing to sell, on occasion, a particular weapons system if it is appropriate for India's needs. This should be done sparingly, and the United States should not try to maintain any particular balance of power between India and Pakistan as in the past. During a period of pulling back from over-involvement in Asian military affairs, it is important to make clear that the United States is not completely uninterested in Asian security problems.

But if the United States should limit its direct involvement in South Asian military affairs and, to the extent possible, its political quarrels, it does not follow that it should similarly play only a minor role in the economic development efforts of the two countries. In this area American policy has been moving in the wrong direction, as aid levels have steadily declined in recent years. Appropriations for the Agency for International Development (AID), which are the heart of the U.S. aid program and account for about half of the total aid provided for all countries, have declined from nearly $3 billion a few years ago to just under $1.5 billion in 1969 and 1970.[1] New AID commitments to India (exclusive of surplus foodstuffs) have declined from about $466 million in 1962 to $159 million in 1970, and aid to Pakistan from $240 million to $119 million in the same period. These reduced commitments have only recently affected the amount of aid actually disbursed, because of the large amounts still in the pipeline, but the impact will soon intensify.

Nonetheless, weary with the economic, military, and psychological burdens it has borne since the beginning of World War II, and worried about the many unmet needs and desires of the American people, both the President and Congress are moving to cut back U.S. efforts to help the underdeveloped nations move away from poverty. Americans are discouraged by the slow pace of growth in many underdeveloped countries. This attitude often overlooks the fact that some countries (like Iran, South Korea, and Taiwan) have made impressive progress in the past decade or so.

The prevailing discouragement also reflects an earlier, unrealistic expectation regarding the difficulties involved and the time it would take for the largest and poorest countries, such as India and Pakistan, to demonstrate their ability to move from the inertia of centuries into the modern age. This is the task of at least two or three generations, and if one surveys the progress that has been made—in terms not only of expanded production but also of the expanding horizons of the people—there is reason for encouragement despite the current strife.

Recommendations for more aid for India and Pakistan (as well as other countries) have been made by every group that has examined the issue, for all have concluded that the poor countries need more aid and that the advanced countries can afford to provide it.[2] Yet the gap between such recommendations and the trend of U.S. policy grows wider year by year. The United States, always the leader in the total amount of foreign aid, is steadily falling behind more and more of the other developed but less wealthy nations, according to the various indices used to measure the common aid effort.

There is, of course, no assurance that U.S. aid—and the equally important aid of the other advanced nations—will enable India and Pakistan to be successful in their endeavors. This is a fact that must be faced forthrightly, for advocates of aid are now paying for the claims made in the past about the favorable short-run impact of aid programs. And it is an unpalatable fact, because an aid program must be large to be useful for countries the size of India and Pakistan. Thus America faces a difficult task in South Asia, for it must be willing to invest heavily with no guarantee that it will achieve its long-term goals.

Many people will regard the above policy recommendation as politically impractical because it calls for much in the way of economic resources, for which the United States would demand little in the way of military or even diplomatic support. Moreover, at first glance, the recommendation appears little concerned with balance-of-power considerations and checking Soviet and Chinese influences. Two important comments about the policy itself should be made.

First, I have tried to make clear that I do not think America can ignore Soviet and Chinese attempts to gain influence in the subcontinent, the levels of Indian and Pakistani defense spending (including a possible Indian nuclear weapons program), and the quarrels between the countries in the area. At the same time, I do not think it can do much about these matters directly. However much the United States finds it necessary to be involved in the political disputes and security concerns at certain times, the most promising way to attempt to deal with the subcontinent in the long-run is indirectly, by helping to build better societies. This is emotionally less satisfying than taking a "tough" line—particularly when other countries irritate us at times—but it is more likely to achieve long-term success. Even here the U.S. contribution, though large in terms of dollars (especially in relation to America's present aid program), would be marginal to the recipients' own efforts; but, for countries living on the margin, this contribution would be of great importance.

Second, America's strategy should not be particularly influenced by whether or not what is done for India would create problems in the U.S. relationship with Pakistan, and vice versa. Such matters are usually determined too much by the desire to maintain good relations in the short term. Rather, a special effort should be made to keep America's focus on its long-term interests and goals.

Is it politically practical to think in terms of a reversal, in the near future, of the declining levels of foreign aid? No shift in direction seems likely. Strong presidential leadership would be necessary, and in August 1971 President Nixon ordered an even greater cutback in foreign assistance. An effective political constituency would also be necessary to support an aid program commensurate with U.S. capabilities and responsibilities.[3] Yet if it is difficult to see this developing quickly, it is equally difficult to see Americans turning their backs on nations attempting to move away from abject poverty. This includes India and Pakistan, which are especially critical because of their size and location.

Finally, we should recognize that success is not assured in any case. Rapid economic growth will not automatically lead to stability, democracy, and peace in the subcontinent. But it is important not to think there is no cause and effect relationship whatsoever, for without economic progress it is impossible to see a decent future for these countries. And without this, there can be no adequate protection of basic U.S. interests in South Asia.

Notes

Chapter 1

1. It was also in 1947 that British power began to recede from the Middle East. London was unable to continue supporting Greece and Turkey, and turned the problem over to the United States. It also felt compelled to admit its inability to handle the Palestine situation, which it placed before the United Nations. Nonetheless, England was determined to maintain as much as possible of its position in the Arab world.

Chapter 2

1. Communalism is the term used in South Asia to describe the attitudes of insecurity and fear—or superiority and contempt—felt by members of a group and the actions taken to protect or advance their common interests. Such groups are usually religious, regional, or linguistic, but may be economic as well.
2. W. Norman Brown, *The United States and India and Pakistan*, Rev. and Enlarged Ed. (Cambridge, Mass.: Harvard University Press, 1963), p. 134.
3. *The New York Times*, November 8 and 9, 1966.
4. The Muslims of Bengal were mostly in the eastern part of the province, and transportation and communication facilities between Calcutta and eastern Bengal were poor.
5. Bengal then included the area that has since become the states of Bihar, Orissa, and Assam—an area that even then totalled about 80 million people.
6. See S. R. Mehrotra, "The Early Organization of the Indian National Con-

gress, 1885–1920," *India Quarterly*, Vol. XXII, No. 4, Oct.–Dec. 1966, pp. 329–52.

7. As early as 1858, when the British government took direct control of India from the East India Company following the Mutiny, Britain had stated as its goal that Indians be progressively associated with the administration. Following the Indian Councils Act of 1861, some Indians were appointed to the national and provincial legislative councils, though government officials comprised the bulk of the council's membership. However, the policy of advancing Indians was applied very cautiously. Throughout most of the nineteenth century those Indians who held office were advisers appointed by the government and had no real authority, and there were restrictions placed upon Indian civil servants when dealing with Europeans. It was not until 1892 that some of the nonofficial council members were chosen by a system of recommendation by lower bodies, which amounted to indirect election.

8. B. R. Ambedkar, *Pakistan, or Partition of India* Rev. Ed. (Bombay: Thacker and Co., 1945), p. 175.

9. Ian Stephens, *Pakistan* (New York: Frederick A. Praeger, 1963), p. 76.

10. W. Norman Brown, cited, pp. 127–28.

11. Maulana Abul Kalam Azad, *India Wins Freedom* (New York: Longmans, Green and Co., 1960), p. 26.

12. The rivalry between the two countries was so intense that Pakistan was unwilling to celebrate its independence on the same day India did. Thus Pakistan received its freedom on August 14, which it celebrates as Partition day, while India observes August 15 as Independence day.

13. See Wayne A. Wilcox, *Pakistan: The Consolidation of a Nation* (New York: Columbia University Press, 1963), for a discussion of Jinnah's policy toward the princely states.

14. The way these states were dealt with by India is described in V. P. Menon, *The Story of the Integration of the Indian States* (Calcutta: Orient Longmans, 1956).

15. This second group was the caste to which Nehru's family belonged; the family had left Kashmir early in the 18th century for service at the Mughal court.

16. Speech by Nehru in Parliament, in S. L. Poplai, *Select Documents on Asian Affairs, India 1947–1950*, Vol. I, *Internal Affairs* (London: Oxford University Press, 1959), p. 383.

17. See Michael Brecher, "Kashmir: A Case Study in United Nations Mediations," *Pacific Affairs*, Vol. XXVI, No. 3, September 1953, p. 195.

18. The United Nations observer teams that operated along the cease-fire line also helped to keep the frequency and scope of border incidents within tolerable limits for many years.

Chapter 3

1. J. Nehru, *An Autobiography* (London: John Lane, 1936), p. 591. Nehru goes on to say, however, that "still I incline more and more towards Communist philosophy."

2. J. Nehru, *The Discovery of India* (New York: The John Day Co., 1946), p. 528.

3. "The Pursuit of Peace," *Vital Speeches of the Day*, Vol. 16, No. 2, November 1, 1949, p. 48.

4. That a new nation like India should carry on as if it were possible to separate

power from politics appears less surprising when it is remembered that in these same years "power politics" was a dirty phrase in the United States, independent for over 150 years. For example, Roosevelt could tell Congress in 1945 that he hoped the agreements made at Yalta would "spell the end of the system of unilateral action, the exclusive alliances, the spheres of influence, the balances of power, and all the other expedients that have been tried for centuries—and have always failed."

5. J. Nehru, *India's Foreign Policy: Selected Speeches, September 1946–April 1961* (New Delhi: Government of India, Ministry of Information and Broadcasting, Publications Division, 1961), pp. 101–2. Hereafter cited as Nehru, *India's Foreign Policy.*

6. All-India Congress Committee, *The Background of India's Foreign Policy* (New Delhi, 1952), pp. 43–44.

7. See Lloyd I. Rudolph and Susanne Hoeber Rudolph, "Generals and Politicians in India," *Pacific Affairs*, Vol. XXXVII, No. 1, Spring 1964, pp. 5–19, for a study of how the Indian government handled these matters.

8. Bisheshwar Prasad, *Our Foreign Policy Legacy: A Study of British Indian Foreign Policy* (New Delhi: People's Publishing House, 1965), pp. 62–63.

9. Quoted in Josef Korbel, *Danger in Kashmir* (Princeton, N. J.: Princeton University Press, 1954), pp. 127–30. Such statements as this, combined with India's refusal to apply the two-nation theory to Kashmir and other harassments, convinced many Pakistanis that there was an Indian conspiracy to destroy Pakistan, despite other statements in which Nehru insisted India accepted partition as a fact of life.

10. Nirad C. Chaudhuri, *The Continent of Circe* (New York: Oxford University Press, 1966), p. 244.

11. Nehru, *India's Foreign Policy*, p. 145.

12. "Some people talk rather loosely, and, if I may say so, rather foolishly, of India becoming the leader of this or the leader of that or the leader of Asia. Now, I do not like that at all. It is a bad approach, this business of leadership. But it is true that, because of the various factors I have mentioned, a certain special responsibility is cast on India. India realizes it, and other countries realize it also. The responsibility is not necessarily for leadership, but for taking the initiative sometimes and helping others to cooperate." Nehru, *India's Foreign Policy*, p. 44.

13. Taya Zinkin, "Indian Foreign Policy: An Interpretation of Attitudes," *World Politics*, Vol. VII, No. 2, January 1955, p. 181.

14. There were, of course, differences among Indians in their attitudes toward the superpowers, the view of Indian Communists being only the most dramatic example. Yet there was enough similarity in outlook among politically important Indians to speak of a general outlook.

15. J. Nehru, *India's Foreign Policy*, p. 47.

16. Quoted in Ross N. Berkes and Mohinder S. Bedi, *The Diplomacy of India: Indian Foreign Policy in the United Nations* (Stanford, Calif.: Stanford University Press, 1958), p. 107. This book contains a perceptive study of India's policy regarding the Korean War on pp. 105–39.

17. *Same*, pp. 108–9.

18. As Dean Acheson states in his memoirs, the U.S. task at this time was not made easier by the British suggesting the admission of Communist China to the United Nations and that concessions be made to secure a cease-fire. *Present at the Creation* (New York: W. W. Norton & Co., 1969), pp. 416–20.

Chapter 4

1. There have also been disputes among West Pakistanis concerning the division of power within West Pakistan, but this involved internal West Pakistani politics and policies toward Afghanistan more than policy toward India.
2. West Pakistan had 33.8 million people in the 1951 census, while East Pakistan had 42.1 million.
3. For over ten years after partition the Pakistani government and press generally refused to refer to its neighbor as India lest it would seem to acknowledge that India (rather than the two countries jointly) was the successor of British India, or that India was anything other than a Hindu state. Thus the term Bharat, an old Indian term meaning Hindustan, was used until Ayub sensibly called a halt to such petty behavior after he took power in Pakistan.
4. This judgment, of course, is that of an outside observer, or perhaps of a Pakistani official or economist with a national outlook. The outlook of most Pakistanis varied according to their position: to the potential entrepreneur Pakistan was a land of challenge and opportunity; to the refugee without influence or connections it was a disappointment, though this feeling was partly offset by the fact that he no longer needed to fear communal violence.
5. Pakistan received only about 20 per cent of undivided India's foreign exchange reserves at the time of independence.
6. See Major General Fazal Muqeem Khan, *The Story of the Pakistan Army* (Karachi: Oxford University Press (Pakistan Branch), 1963), especially Chapters 3 and 4 for a description of the division of the British Indian army and the organization of the Pakistan army.
7. Quoted in V. P. Menon, *The Transfer of Power in India* (Princeton, N.J.: Princeton University Press, 1957), p. 384.
8. *Same*, p. 382.
9. John Connell, *Auchinleck* (London: Cassell & Co., 1959), p. 920.
10. K. Sarwar Hasan, "The Foreign Policy of Mr. Liaquat Ali Khan," *Pakistan Horizon*, Vol. IV, No. 4, December 1951, p. 193.
11. Keith Callard, *Pakistan's Foreign Policy: An Interpretation*, Rev. Ed., (New York: Institute of Pacific Relations, 1959), p. 7.
12. The Indian Independence Act provided that the arrangements between the Crown and the tribes living in Tribal Territory lapsed with independence. The tribes then affirmed their allegiance to Pakistan in a series of tribal assemblies.
13. The Afghanistan government had no desire to see the Pushtuns living on their side of the border exercise this right.
14. James W. Spain, "The Pathan Borderlands," *The Middle East Journal*, Vol. 15, No. 2, Spring 1961, p. 166.
15. Not until the Sino-Indian conflict became public in 1959 did India, whose case against China rested heavily upon the validity of the McMahon Line in the northeast, support Pakistan's claim that the Durand Line was the border between Pakistan and Afghanistan.

Chapter 5

1. X, "The Sources of Soviet Conduct," *Foreign Affairs*, Vol. 25, No. 4, July 1947, pp. 566–582.

2. George F. Kennan, *Memoirs: 1925–1950* (Boston: Atlantic-Little, Brown, 1967).

3. Nor did Israel (then preoccupied with domestic affairs and absorbing the flood of refugees) wish to antagonize the U.S.S.R., thus dashing any hope of securing Soviet agreement to permit Russian Jews to emigrate to Israel.

4. John C. Campbell, *Defense of the Middle East* (New York: Praeger for the Council on Foreign Relations, 1960), pp. 45–48.

5. The causes of these fluctuations are described in Norman D. Palmer, *South Asia and United States Policy* (Boston: Houghton Mifflin Co., 1966), pp. 13–16.

6. See Phillips Talbot and S. L. Poplai, *India and America: A Study of Their Relations* (New York: Harper and Brothers, 1958), for an analysis of the underlying reasons that India and the United States were so often on different sides of international issues despite the fact that they shared important interests and values.

7. Selig Harrison, "India, Pakistan, and the United States, Part I—Case History of a Mistake," *The New Republic*, August 10, 1959, pp. 10–17.

8. Sir Olaf originally had looked to India as the key nation in this scheme, but soon recognized that Indian nonalignment made that impossible.

9. United Kingdom officials were also divided over the wisdom of extending military assistance to Pakistan, with those officials oriented toward India dubious or critical of such a program despite the arguments of Sir Olaf Caroe and others who held similar views.

10. "Report on the Near East," Address by Secretary Dulles, *Department of State Bulletin*, Vol. XXVIII, No. 729, June 15, 1953, pp. 831–35.

11. U.S. House of Representatives, Committee on Foreign Affairs *Hearings, Mutual Security Act Extension*, 83rd Cong. 1st sess., 1953, pp. 720–21.

12. *The New York Times*, November 2, 1953.

13. See James W. Spain, "Military Assistance for Pakistan," *The American Political Science Review*, Vol. XLVIII, No. 3, September 1954, pp. 738–51 for a description of the inception of the arms aid program and the extent to which leaks to the press were utilized. Harrison also stresses this point in his study of the program.

14. *The New York Times*, November 12, 1953.

15. *The New York Times*, November 19, 1953.

16. *Department of State Bulletin*, Vol. XXX, No. 766, March 1, 1954, pp. 327–28.

17. Britain's attitude toward the U.S.-Pakistan arms agreement, which obviously reduced British influence in Pakistan, and toward the Northern Tier concept, had previously been lukewarm. Since British interests in the Middle East were largely in the Arab lands to the south, it thought in terms of a defense organization based upon its position there. However, late in 1954 it had bowed before the rising demands of Egyptian nationalism and agreed to evacuate the Suez base, and the Northern Tier approach then became more appealing.

18. Little seems to have been done in the way of prepositioning supplies for U.S. troops, nor was any serious attention ever given to the defense of East Pakistan.

19. Such views may have been influenced by the widespread response to the United Nations campaign in Korea. If Turkey could send a brigade 8,000 miles, might not Pakistan send troops to the Middle East or Southeast Asia?

20. See Khalid Bin Sayeed, "Pakistan's Foreign Policy: An Analysis of Pakistani

Fears and Interests," *Asian Survey,* Vol. IV, No. 3, March 1964, pp. 746–56, for a study of the reasons behind the changing Pakistani attitudes.

Chapter 6

1. See Walter Z. Laqueur, *The Soviet Union and the Middle East* (New York: Praeger, 1959), pp. 17–22, for a more extensive discussion of these issues.

2. The development of Indian communism and the relations between Moscow and the Communist party of India are traced in Gene D. Overstreet and Marshall Windmiller, *Communism in India* (Berkeley: University of California Press, 1959).

3. *Same,* p. 357.

4. Overstreet and Windmiller, cited, pp. 356–57. The figures given can only be regarded as estimates, for they come from party sources; Overstreet and Windmiller, however, did not regard them as grossly inflated but as reasonably accurate reflections of the party's growth.

5. A. M. Dyakov, *Indiya i Pakistan* (India and Pakistan) (Moscow: Pravda Publishing House, 1950), p. 8; cited in David J. Dallin, *Soviet Foreign Policy After Stalin* (Philadelphia: Lippincott, 1961), p. 292.

6. *Large Soviet Encyclopedia* (in Russian), 2nd Ed., Vol. 6 (1951), p. 316. Cited in Dallin, p. 291.

7. See Charles B. McLane, *Soviet Strategies in Southeast Asia: An Exploration of Eastern Policy under Lenin and Stalin* (Princeton, N. J.: Princeton University Press, 1966), pp. 351–60. McLane argues that while Soviet policy encouraged militant action, there is no evidence Moscow ordered such insurrections.

8. The Communist party in Andhra was dominated by wealthy peasants of the dominant Kamma caste, which made Maoist acceptance of wealthy peasants particularly attractive to them.

9. John H. Kautsky, *Moscow and the Communist Party of India* (New York: John Wiley & Sons, 1956). See Chapter 4, pp. 86–121, for a description of the shift to a neo-Maoist strategy.

10. "Mighty Advance of the National Liberation Movement in the Colonial and Dependent Countries," *For a Lasting Peace, For a People's Democracy!* No. 4 (64), Bucharest, January 27, 1950, p. 1.

11. See Kautsky, cited, pp. 199–202. Overstreet and Windmiller also provide many illustrations of ineffectual or nonexistent Soviet guidance; see pp. 260, 270–74, and 284.

12. In 1952 Stalin had said that "peaceful coexistence of capitalism and communism is fully possible," but by then Stalin's words were regarded with much skepticism. Richard P. Stebbins, *The United States in World Affairs, 1952* (New York: Harper & Brothers for the Council on Foreign Relations, 1953), p. 43, discusses this statement of Stalin.

13. "Ajoy Ghosh Answers Questions on Communist Policies," *New Age* (weekly) II, December 12, 1954, p. 13; cited in Overstreet and Windmiller, p. 317.

14. Nehru's statement in the Lok Sabha, March 20, 1956, quoted in Arthur Stein, "India's Relations with the U.S.S.R., 1953–1963," *Orbis,* Vol. VIII, No. 2, Summer 1964, pp. 361–62.

15. *Dawn,* Karachi, December 20, 1953.

16. "Report on the Near East," *Department of State Bulletin,* Vol. XXVIII, No. 729, June 15, 1953, pp. 831–35.

17. *The New York Times,* March 25, 1958.
18. Jawaharlal Nehru, "The Basic Approach," *AICC Economic Review,* Vol. X, No. 8–9, August 15, 1958, pp. 3–6.
19. P. Yudin, "Can We Accept Pandit Nehru's Approach?," *World Marxist Review,* Vol. 1, No. 4, December 1958, pp. 42–54.

Chapter 7

1. A. Doak Barnett, *Communist China and Asia* (New York: Harper & Brothers, 1960), p. 77.
2. Howard L. Boorman, "Sources of Chinese Communist Conduct," *The Virginia Quarterly Review,* Vol. 42, No. 4, Autumn 1966, p. 512.
3. Conrad Brandt, Benjamin Schwartz and John K. Fairbank, *A Documentary History of Chinese Communism* (Cambridge, Mass.: Harvard University Press, 1952), pp. 449–61.
4. A. N. Mukherjee, *Sino-Indian Relations and the Communists* (Calcutta: Institute of Political and Social Studies, 1960), p. 1.
5. "Mighty Advance in the National Liberation Movement in the Colonial and Dependent Countries," *For a Lasting Peace, for a People's Democracy!* cited, p. 1.
6. K. M. Panikkar, *In Two Chinas* (London; George Allen and Unwin, Ltd., 1955), p. 102.
7. Some influential voices in the West argued for recognition of Tibetan independence and support for it as a bulwark against communism. See *The Economist,* December 10, 1949. The journal qualified its remarks by pointing out that such a policy on the part of the United States and the United Kingdom would be possible only if India took a similar line.
8. On December 6, 1950, Nehru stated in Parliament: "Our interest in the internal conditions of Nepal has become still more acute and personal, because of the developments across our borders, to be frank, especially those in China and Tibet. . . . From time immemorial, the Himalayas have provided us with a magnificent frontier. . . . We cannot allow that barrier to be penetrated because it is also the principal barrier to India. Therefore, much as we appreciate the independence of Nepal, we cannot allow anything to go wrong in Nepal or permit that barrier to be crossed or weakened, because that would be a risk to our own security." *Jawaharlal Nehru's Speeches, 1949–1953* Vol. 2 (New Delhi: Government of India, Ministry of Information and Broadcasting, Publications Division, 1957), p. 177.
9. See Parushotam L. Mehra, "India, China and Tibet, 1950–54," *India Quarterly,* Vol. XII, No. 1, January–March 1956, pp. 3–22 for a comprehensive and cautiously favorable analysis of the treaty.
10. W. F. Van Eekelen, *Indian Foreign Policy and the Border Dispute with China* (The Hague: Martinus Nijhoff, 1964), p. 41. Chapter 3 of this book is an interesting study of the origin and nature of the five principles of peaceful coexistence.
11. Van Eekelen points out that an American note to Japan in 1941 suggested that the two nations agree to adopt four "fundamental principles" in a draft Mutual Declaration of Policy. These principles were virtually the same as Panch Sheel, but the idea was rejected by Japan. "It is one of the ironies of history that here we had America proposing a system of coexistence which was rejected by an Asian country. Thirteen years later the West would

be suspicious of a similar initiative by Asia, because of its assumed Communist connotations." Same, pp. 42–43.

12. See George McT. Kahin, *The Asian-African Conference: Bandung, Indonesia, April 1955* (Ithaca, N. Y.; Cornell University Press, 1956).

13. The attitude of the leaders of most pro-Western nations was one of satisfaction that the conference had not turned out to be basically anti-Western (or, more accurately, anti-those nations that had aligned themselves with the West) plus skepticism about the prospect of future cooperation.

14. One could argue from (1) U.S. nonrecognition of Communist China and continued recognition of Nationalist China as the rightful government of all of China and (2) earlier statements that Communist rule of China would not last, that the United States was not really interested in seeing the Peking regime accommodate its neighbors in this way. This may have been true for a time, but by the mid-1950s it appears that this no longer represented the actual as distinct from the proclaimed U.S. policy.

15. Japan had only begun its remarkable postwar economic growth. Moreover, it had no military power and little political appeal.

16. Control of foreign policy and the military establishments were the last elements of authority to be turned over to the local leaders by the colonial powers. Thus Nehru once said independence consisted "fundamentally and basically of foreign relations."

17. More extensive descriptions of this shift and the reasons for it can be found in A. Doak Barnett, *Communist China and Asia* (New York: Harper & Brothers, 1960), pp. 105–109; and Harold Hinton, *Communist China and World Politics* (Boston: Houghton Mifflin Company, 1966), pp. 33–42.

18. Some students of Asian affairs have speculated that Nehru's aim was broader than this, and that he was also trying to establish a gentleman's agreement that acknowledged Chinese predominance in Vietnam and Indian predominance in the rest of Southeast Asia. This cannot be disproved, and Nehru obviously would have been pleased by such an arrangement. Yet it is equally obvious that such a scheme would hardly have appealed to the Chinese.

19. India also noticed that Chou En-lai did not endorse India's position on Kashmir when he visited India late in 1956. Perhaps that was because he was to visit Pakistan as well, but this worried India nonetheless.

20. Ministry of External Affairs, Government of India, *Notes, Memoranda and Letters Exchanged and Agreements Signed Between The Governments of India and China* (White Paper, September 8, 1959), pp. 26–27. Hereinafter cited as White Paper No. I.

21. White Paper No. I, p. 28.

22. Same, pp. 48–51.

23. Same, pp. 52–54.

24. See George Ginsburgs and Michael Mathos, *Communist China and Tibet: The First Dozen Years* (The Hague: Martinus Nijhoff, 1964).

25. Text of the Dalai Lama's press conference appears in *The New York Times*, June 21, 1959.

26. White Paper No. I, pp. 60–62.

27. Same, pp. 63–65.

28. Secretariat of the National Council of the CPI, March 31, 1959, cited in Chanakya Sen, *Tibet Disappears* (Bombay: Asia Publishing House, 1960), p. 305.

29. There apparently was some uncertainty in Peking for a time, for on May 6, *Peoples Daily* published a long article on India which referred to Nehru in

friendly terms, although criticizing him for some aspects of his policy toward Tibet, and hinting at China's ability to stir up trouble inside India. See "The Revolution in Tibet and Nehru's Philosophy," in *Peking Review*, Vol. 2, No. 19, May 12, 1959, pp. 6–15.

30. White Paper No. I, pp. 73–76.

31. The Indian Constitution permits the central government to remove a state government and govern the state directly from New Delhi for a time under certain circumstances. Widespread opposition to the Communist regime developed in Kerala during 1959, and New Delhi imposed central rule in July on the ground that law and order were breaking down.

32. The radical elements in the party had always been dubious if not actually opposed to the CPI's moderate course during the mid-1950s. After the ouster of the Kerala government the radicals became more actively opposed to cooperation with the Nehru government, which it regarded as becoming increasingly reactionary and pro-Western. They argued that New Delhi would never let the CPI come to power, and so the party's "peaceful course" strategy formally adopted in 1958 was inappropriate. The controlling moderates continued to regard the Nehru government—and particularly Nehru himself—as progressive and thus regarded continued though limited cooperation as the corrective course. (In this they were generally in line with Soviet thinking.) It would be a mistake to see the positions of the CPI leaders as determined solely by policy differences, for personal ambitions, regional divisions, and factional conflicts have always been a key element influencing party decisions. With the continually shifting alignments within the party such designations as "moderates" and "radicals" were seldom clear-cut and can only be used with caution.

33. White Paper No. III, pp. 45–46.

34. Same, pp. 47–51.

35. See A. R. Field, "Bhutan, Kham and the Upper Assam Line," *Orbis*, Vol. III, No. 2, Summer 1959, pp. 180–92; and Leo E. Rose, "Sino-Indian Rivalry and the Himalayan Border States," *Orbis*, Vol. V, No. 2, Summer 1961, pp. 198–215 for discussion of these issues.

36. The officials met for three long sessions in 1960, but could not reach agreement on either facts or interpretations. Each side wrote a separate report, and both were published by India in February 1961.

37. *Pravda*, September 10, 1959; cited in *The Current Digest of the Soviet Press*, Vol. XI, No. 36, October 7, 1959, p. 14.

38. "The Truth about How the Leaders of the C.P.S.U. Have Allied Themselves With India Against China," *Peking Review*, No. 45, November 8, 1963, pp. 18–27.

39. Bhabani Sen Gupta, in *The Fulcrum of Asia; Relations among China, India Pakistan, and the U. S. S. R.* (New York: Pegasus, 1970), assigns ideological and power considerations involving India a central role—though not a dominant one—in the Sino-Soviet split. See pp. 163–78. While such an interpretation is possible, in my judgment it suggests greater and more persistent preoccupation with India on the part of Soviet and Chinese leaders than seems likely in view of the many weightier problems that concerned them.

40. For an extensive description of this problem and how it was solved see Aloys Arthur Michel, *The Indus Rivers: A Study of the Effects of Partition* (New Haven: Yale University Press, 1967).

41. However, the government was upset—and the public was angered—by Secre-

tary Herter's statement in the autumn of 1959 that the United States was uncertain of the merits of the Indian and Chinese border claims.

Chapter 8

1. John F. Kennedy, *The Strategy of Peace*, Allan Nevins, ed. (New York: Harper & Brothers, 1960), p. 142.
2. See Ian C. C. Graham, "The Indo-Soviet MIG Deal and Its International Repercussions," *Asian Survey*, Vol. IV, No. 5, May 1964, pp. 823–32, for a detailed description of this episode.
3. Actually, the U.S. government had considerable difficulty deciding how to view MIGs for India. Would the disadvantages that would result from having the U.S.S.R. become involved with the Indian air force be offset by the friction to Sino-Soviet relations that probably would result?
4. Kennedy had always been strongly in favor of economic assistance to Pakistan; it was military aid and political support that he was skeptical about, given his view of India's importance.
5. William S. White, *The Professional: Lyndon B. Johnson* (Boston: Houghton Mifflin Co., 1964), pp. 240–44.
6. Not without disputes, however, such as the one that occurred in mid-1961 over Pakistan's use of armed forces to repulse Afghan tribal raiders along the frontier. What seemed a legitimate measure of self-defense to Pakistan was seen in Washington as another regrettable regional quarrel that could drive Afghanistan closer to the U.S.S.R. Following this incident, Pakistan closed the frontier to the nomads from Afghanistan who traditionally wintered their flocks in Pakistan. The government claimed it did this because they brought disease and damaged Pakistani crops, but an attempt to pressure Afghanistan to call off the Pushtunistan campaign clearly was the major reason. Afghanistan reacted by breaking diplomatic relations and closing its border, and turned to the U.S.S.R. for trade and transshipment purposes. Washington was opposed on both humanitarian and political grounds, but to no avail, for Pakistan refused to change its course.
7. White Paper VI, pp. 1–2.
8. Same, pp. 3–4.
9. Same, p. 9.
10. Same, p. 10.
11. Same, p. 18.
12. Same, p. 43.
13. Same, p. 56.
14. *Peking Review*, Vol. V, No. 42, October 19, 1962, p. 6.
15. *Hindustan Times*, August 9, 1962, quoted in V. P. Dutt, "India and China: Betrayal, Humiliation, Reappraisal," in *Policies Toward China: Views from Six Continents*, A. M. Halpern, ed. (New York: McGraw-Hill for the Council on Foreign Relations, 1965), p. 217.
16. Several dozen notes were exchanged between India and China on this matter between late 1961 and October 1962. It seems unlikely that the Chinese charges were complete fabrications.
17. V. P. Dutt, cited, pp. 217–18.
18. C. N. Satyapalan, "The Sino-Indian Border Conflict," *Orbis*, Vol. VIII, No. 2, Summer 1964, p. 389.
19. Same, p. 388.

20. Jawaharlal Nehru, "Changing India," *Foreign Affairs*, Vol. 41, No. 3, April 1963, p. 458.
21. *Pravda*, October 25, 1962, in *Current Digest of the Soviet Press*, Vol. XIV, No. 43, November 21, 1962, p. 17.
22. D. R. Mankekar, *Indian Express*, November 1, 1962, cited in V. P. Dutt, p. 219.
23. For a time India paid the United States and the United Kingdom rupees for these arms, but the pretense that this meant they were being purchased was soon dropped and they were provided as grants.

Chapter 9

1. Wayne A. Wilcox, *India, Pakistan, and the Rise of China* (New York: Walker and Company, 1964), p. 75.
2. Mohammed Ayub Khan, *Friends Not Masters* (London: Oxford University Press, 1967), pp. 140–41.
3. Same. The text of the letters is on pp. 141–43.
4. Same, p. 145.
5. Possibly Ayub felt that the Indian military showing had been so poor that the United States was unwise to count on Indian cooperation as of much use in the containment of China. This view of the limited nature of the Chinese military threat, it should be noted, was quite different from Ayub's view in 1959 when he called for joint defense of the subcontinent.
6. Pakistan and the United States were already at odds over policy toward Afghanistan, with Pakistan taking a hard line and the United States fearing that such action would push Afghanistan closer to the Soviet Union.
7. Mohammed Ayub Khan, "The Pakistan-American Alliance: Stresses and Strains," *Foreign Affairs*, Vol. 42, No. 2, January 1964, p. 204.
8. Ayub's conversations with the Soviet leaders are discussed in *Friends Not Masters*, cited, pp. 168–74.
9. A perceptive analysis of Pakistani attitudes in this period is set forth in Khalid Bin Sayeed, "Pakistan's Foreign Policy: An Analysis of Pakistani Fears and Interests," *Asian Survey*, Vol. IV, No. 3, March 1964, pp. 746–56.
10. Cited in George McA. Kahin, *The Asian-African Conference, Bandung, Indonesia, April 1955* (Ithaca, N.Y.: Cornell University Press, 1956), p. 57.
11. Two articles which discuss the evolution of Sino-Pakistan relations in some detail are S. M. Burke, "Sino-Pakistani Relations," *Orbis*, Vol. VIII, No. 2, Summer 1964, pp. 391–404; and Khalid B. Sayeed, "Pakistan and China: The Scope and Limits of Convergent Policies," in A. M. Halpern, ed., *Policies Toward China: Views from Six Continents* (New York: McGraw Hill for the Council on Foreign Relations, 1965), pp. 229–61.
12. Cited in S. P. Seth, "China as a Factor in Indo-Pakistani Politics," *The World Today*, Vol. 25, No. 1, January 1969, p. 43.
13. Rumors circulated that the theft was the work of Bakshi's men, a charge never proved but widely believed in Kashmir.
14. Richard Critchfield, "Tortured Kashmir: Background to Conflict," *The Reporter*, November 4, 1965, pp. 28–30.
15. United Nations: Security Council, *Report by the Secretary General on the Current Situation in Kashmir with Particular Reference to the Cease-Fire Agreement, The Cease-Fire Line and the Functioning of UNMOGIP*, S/6651, 3 September 1965.

16. *The Economist*, May 1, 1965, pp. 502–03.
17. Pakistan also claimed that India was using U.S. equipment in the fighting, but the small amount of U.S. arms apparently used had been purchased by India in earlier years and not acquired through the aid program.
18. See Leo Heiman, "Lessons from the War in Kashmir," *Military Review*, February 1966, pp. 22–29, for a succinct description of the strategy and tactics of the two countries.
19. U.S. Senate, Committee on Appropriations, Hearings, *Foreign Assistance and Related Agencies Appropriations for 1966*, 89th Cong., 1st Sess., 1965, pp. 18–19.
20. Particular attention was devoted to preventing an outbreak of fighting involving East Pakistan, which Western governments felt would result in events getting completely out of control.
21. See *Current Digest of the Soviet Press*, Vol. XVII, No. 34, September 15, 1965, pp. 15–16.
22. Same, Vol XVII, No. 36, September 29, 1965, p. 12.

Chapter 10

1. The text of the Tashkent Declaration is in *The New York Times*, January 11, 1966.
2. *The London Observer*, January 9, 1966, p. 11.
3. The reaction in East Pakistan was just the opposite. The Tashkent agreement won wide support as reducing the danger of war; even the opposition political parties there supported the agreement.
4. Joseph Lelyveld, "35 in Dacca Face Conspiracy Charge," *The New York Times*, August 5, 1968.
5. The United States was host to Mrs. Gandhi while its ally Pakistan was honoring Lui, which was a further indication of the vanishing substance of the old relationships and the complexity of the new ones.
6. *The New York Times*, December 30, 1965.
7. *The Times* (London), August 9, 1966.
8. *The New York Times*, March 6, 1966.
9. *The New York Times*, March 30, 1966.
10. An interesting and illustrative fact was that while Ayub was in Moscow, one of his ministers was in Peking and another in the United States.
11. Soviet-Pakistani relations are discussed in detail in Zubeida Hasan, "Pakistan's Relations with the U.S.S.R. in the 1960s," *The World Today*, January 1969, pp. 26–35, and by S. P. Seth, "Russia's Role in Indo-Pak Politics," *Asian Survey*, August 1969, Vol. IX, No. 8, pp. 614–24.
12. Most Indian agricultural statistics are compiled on the basis of a crop year which runs from July 1 to June 30.
13. Neville Maxwell, "India's Disintegrating Democracy," *The Times* (London), January 27, 1967.
14. See Norman D. Palmer, "India's Fourth General Elections," *Asian Survey*, Vol. VII, No. 5, May 1967, pp. 275–91, for a analysis.
15. See Peter Hazelhurst, "Chinese Aid for Assam Rebels," *The Times* (London), June 17, 1968; "The Balkans of Asia," *The Economist*, June 29, 1968.
16. The origin and implications of these developments are discussed in Marcus F. Franda, "India's Third Communist Party," *Asian Survey*, Vol. IX, No. 11, November 1969, pp. 797–817.

17. Chinese policy in this period is discussed in Bhabani Sen Gupta, "A Maoist Line for India," *The China Quarterly*, No. 33, January–March 1968, pp. 3–16.
18. *The New York Times*, September 7, 1969.
19. India's rather disappointing efforts to secure nuclear guarantees during this period are traced by A. G. Noorani, "India's Quest For a Nuclear Guarantee," *Asian Survey*, Vol. VII, No. 7, July 1967, pp. 490–502.
20. *The New York Times*, February 20, 1968.
21. *The New York Times*, Nov. 30, 1965; *The Washington Post*, Nov. 30, 1965.
22. *The Washington Post*, April 13, 1967.
23. United Nations, Office of Public Information/372, *Treaty on the Non-Proliferation of Nuclear Weapons*, New York, 1969.
24. Agency for International Development, *U.S. Overseas Loans and Grants and Assistance From International Organizations: Obligations and Loan Authorizations, July 1, 1945–June 30, 1969.* April 24, 1970, pp. 15, 23.
25. For a discussion of these divergent trends see Bhabani Sen Gupta, *The Fulcrum of Asia* (New York: Pegasus, 1970) pp. 243–62.
26. *The New York Times*, October 11, 1970.
27. Richard M. Nixon, "United States Foreign Policy for the 1970s: A New Strategy for Peace," *Weekly Compilation of Presidential Documents*, Vol. 6, No. 8, February 23, 1970, pp. 194–239.
28. Robert S. Jaster, "Foreign Aid and Economic Development: The Shifting Soviet View," *International Affairs*, Vol. 45, No. 3, July 1969, pp. 452–64. The gradual revision of Soviet expectations that they would make rapid gains in the underdeveloped nations is also analyzed in an earlier article by Philip E. Mosely, "Communist Policy and the Third World," *The Review of Politics*, Vol. 28, No. 2, April 1966, pp. 210–37.
29. *Pravda*, November 14, 1969; in *The Current Digest of the Soviet Press*, Vol. XXI, No. 46, December 10, 1969, p. 15.
30. For a discussion of this issue see Hemen Ray, "Soviet Diplomacy in Asia," *Problems of Communism*, Vol. XIX, No. 2, March–April 1970, pp. 46–49.

Chapter 11

1. See Aziz Ahmad, "Pakistan Faces Democracy: A Provisional Nation," *The Round Table*, No. 242, April 1971, pp. 227–37, for a brief but comprehensive survey of Pakistan's various attempts to work out a satisfactory political system.
2. The key political parties called for Pakistan to leave CENTO and SEATO, but since Pakistan's alliances with the West were more nominal than real this would not have represented a major shift.
3. *The New York Times*, May 3, 1970; *Pakistan News Digest*, February 15, 1971.
4. *The Overseas Hindustan Times*, June 26, 1971.
5. Peter Hazelhurst discusses the reasoning of one prominent Indian advocate of a military solution in *The Times* (London), July 13, 1971.
6. *Current Digest of the Soviet Press*, Vol. XXIII, No. 14, May 4, 1971.
7. *The New York Times*, April 7, 1971.
8. Delhi Domestic Service, July 6, 1971, reported in *Foreign Broadcast Information Service: Daily Report: Middle East and Africa*, July 6, 1971.
9. *The New York Times*, August 10, 1971.
10. *Peking Review*, April 16, 1971.

11. Karachi Domestic Service, April 12, 1971, reported in *Foreign Broadcast Information Service: Middle East and Africa*, April 12, 1971.
12. *The New York Times*, July 13, 1971.
13. *The New York Times*, August 4, 1971.
14. *The New York Times*, August 1, 1971.
15. Sydney H. Schanberg, "U.S.-Indian Relations: A New Low" *The New York Times*, July 2, 1971.
16. Delhi Domestic Service, July 20, 1971, reported in *Foreign Broadcast Information Service*, July 21, 1971.
17. *Ibid.*
18. Pran Chopra, "The Treacherous Phase," *The Overseas Hindustan Times*, July 10, 1971.
19. *The New York Times*, August 3, 1971.

Chapter 12

1. India's success at balancing the United States and the U.S.S.R. has extracted a price, for India's security and maneuverability have declined substantially. See William J. Barnds, "India in Transition: Friends and Neighbors," *Foreign Affairs*, Vol. 46, No. 3, April 1968, pp. 548–61. See also Richard L. Siegal, "Evaluating the Results of Foreign Policy: Soviet and American Efforts in India," *The Social Science Foundation and Graduate School of International Studies Monograph Series in World Affairs*, University of Denver, Vol. 6, No. 4, 1969.
2. Those who believe that the United States has consistently spent too much on its military forces might argue that this is simply an example of according too high a priority to security considerations. It seems more likely, however, that in the absence of information about Soviet strategic capabilities the United States would have imagined them to be greater than they were and thus devoted more resources to military uses.
3. Moscow's opportunity to move into the area was also linked closely to the Arab search for great-power support against Israel and to the general anti-Western orientation of some Arab states.

Chapter 13

1. For an examination of this viewpoint see Charles Gati, "Another Grand Debate? The Limitationist Critique of American Foreign Policy," *World Politics*, Vol. XXI, No. 1, October 1968, pp. 133–51.
2. The effect of televised battle scenes on attitudes toward Vietnam is one of the more dramatic examples of the impact of modern communications, while the extremely close coordination between the major industrial nations in international financial matters is a striking example of economic interdependence.
3. The concept of the national interest poses certain analytical problems in view of the different interests—real or merely felt—of people within the nation, but it remains useful as a rough practical guide.
4. Testimony of March 30, 1966. *Foreign Assistance Act of 1966: Hearings Before the Committee on Foreign Affairs, House of Representatives*, p. 269.
5. Such troubles could also spring from incidents of communal violence in the subcontinent, which increased from 132 in 1966 to 346 in 1968 in

India, according to official statistics. See *The Economist*, London, September 27, 1969, p. 26. Even more ominous than their frequency is the size of some of these riots. Between 500 and 1,000 people were killed in communal riots in Ahmadabad in September 1969, and more than 150 in riots in the state of Maharashtra in May 1970.

6. This does not mean that the United States can or should try to make the world over in its image or make the world safe for democracy. Such grandiose goals are either undesirable or impossible and illustrate a periodic American tendency to adopt goals without relating them to the means the country has to reach them. Yet the reality of the U.S. interest in helping to foster a tolerable world community is most simply illustrated by trying to find someone who will agree to the proposition that the United States as a nation has *no* interest in the kind of world order of which it is a part.

7. Report of the Commission on International Development, *Partners in Development* (New York: Praeger, 1969), p. 9.

8. For example, the willingness of the United States to take the lead in negotiating liberal trade policies since World War II has encouraged others to adopt similar policies to the net benefit of all countries concerned. Without U.S. leadership such a development would not have occurred, and the trend may well be reversed if the United States begins imposing new trade barriers.

9. Reinhold Niebuhr, *The Irony of American History* (New York: Charles Scribner's Sons, 1952), pp. 36–37.

10. Hans Morgenthau, "The Present Tragedy of America," *Worldview*, Vol. 12, No. 9, September 1969, pp. 15–16.

Chapter 14

1. Economists who have examined Indian and Pakistani statistics closely have a low opinion of their accuracy. While careful use of the available statistics can provide a general impression of economic trends, their limitations should continually be kept in mind.

2. Despite its title, *Quiet Crisis in India: Economic Development and American Policy*, by John P. Lewis (Washington: The Brookings Institution, 1962) is basically an optimistic study of the past record and future possibilities at the time.

3. While the transfer of resources to India (and Pakistan) increased substantially, much of this transfer was in the form of loans, often at close to commercial terms. Moreover, rising prices and the practice of tying aid to purchases from the donor country reduced the stated amount of the transfers made.

4. See N. C. B. Ray, "The Politics of India's Coalitions," *The Political Quarterly*, Vol. 40, No. 3, July–September 1969, pp. 296–306.

5. Gunnar Myrdal, *Asian Drama: An Inquiry into the Poverty of Nations* (New York: Twentieth Century Fund, 1968).

6. Under the Indian constitution, New Delhi can take direct control of a state if law and order break down or if the state is unable to form a government.

7. See Lloyd and Susanne Rudolph, *The Modernity of Tradition: Political Development in India* (Chicago: University of Chicago Press, 1967), for an analysis of the way traditional institutions often adjust to new situations while appearing to remain the same.

8. Myrdal does take note of the Green Revolution in a later book, *The Challenge of World Poverty*. However, he stresses the problems it will create—which are serious—while giving much less weight to the opportunities it offers.

9. For a thorough examination of the implications of the Green Revolution, see Clifford R. Wharton, Jr., "The Green Revolution: Cornucopia or Pandora's Box?" *Foreign Affairs*, Vol. 47, No. 3, April 1969, pp. 464–76; Francine R. Frankel, "India's New Strategy of Agricultural Development: Political Costs of Agrarian Modernization," *The Journal of Asian Studies*, Vol. XXVIII, No. 4, August 1969; and Wolf Ladejinsky, "Ironies of India's Green Revolution," *Foreign Affairs*, Vol. 48, No. 4, July 1970, pp. 758–68.

10. A thorough examination of Pakistan's economic growth can be found in Gustav F. Papanek, *Pakistan's Development: Social Goals and Private Incentives* (Cambridge, Mass.: Harvard University Press, 1967).

11. Pakistan has a better record than India, which is attributed to greater reliance on the market mechanism and less administrative control, more emphasis on agriculture, and a larger volume of foreign aid relative to its population. Edward S. Mason, *Economic Development in India and Pakistan*, Harvard University Center for International Affairs, Occasional Paper No. 13, September 1966.

12. The statistical basis for determining income levels in the two wings is weak, but the disparity increased from a 9 per cent higher per capita income in West Pakistan in 1949–50 to a 40 per cent difference in 1964–65. Papanek, cited, p. 318.

13. One of the key political structures created by Ayub was the Basic Democracies system. The Basic Democrats were elected to provide a measure of local self-government; they also had the responsibility of electing the president. It was obviously easier for an incumbent president to win re-election by providing favors and intimidating a majority of the 80,000 Basic Democrats than by winning the support of a majority of the country's adult population.

14. See Peggy Durdin, "The Political Tidal Wave that Struck East Pakistan," *The New York Times Magazine*, May 2, 1971, for a good description of the situation in East Pakistan in March.

15. East Pakistan normally has a foodgrain deficit of nearly 2 million tons, which probably increased to over 3 million tons as a result of the cyclone and tidal wave. Moreover, the civil war has reduced plantings, and inadequate transportation will make it difficult to move supplies. Offsetting these factors to some degree is the loss of nearly 10 per cent of the population.

16. One long-range possibility suggested involves basic shifts toward looser links between East and West Pakistan, but linked to an Indian grant of autonomy to Kashmir as part of a major effort to create an Indo-Pakistani rapprochement. See Selig S. Harrison, "Nehru's Plan for Peace," *The New Republic*, June 19, 1971.

17. Frank N. Notestein, "The Population Crisis: Reasons for Hope," *Foreign Affairs*, Vol. 46, No. 1, October 1967, pp. 167–80; and Carl E. Taylor, "Population Trends in an Indian Village," *Scientific American*, Vol. 223, No. 1, July 1970, pp. 106–14.

18. This calculation, however, was on the basis of a substantial increase in total aid, so that the amount handled by multilateral bodies, chiefly the IBRD and IDA, would increase five-fold by 1975.

19. *United Nations: A Study of the Capacity of the United Nations Development System*, Geneva, 1969; DP/5; prepared by Sir Robert Jackson.
20. Albert O. Hirshman and Richard M. Bird, *Foreign Aid: A Critique and a Proposal*, Essays in International Finance, No. 69, Princeton University, July 1968.
21. The obvious exception involves a recipient country at war, but in those circumstances economic goals are (at least in the short term) subordinate to military and political considerations.
22. Moreover, the recipient countries are aware of the differences between donor countries as to what conditions to attach to aid and often exploit this bargaining position. The manner in which India has done this is described in P. J. Eldridge, *The Politics of Foreign Aid in India* (New York: Schocken Books, 1969).

Chapter 15

1. Leo E. Rose and Roger Dial, "Can a Ministate Find True Happiness in a World Dominated by Protagonist Powers?: The Nepal Case," *The Annals of the American Academy of Political and Social Science*, Vol. 386, Nov. 1969, pp. 89–101. The article gives an excellent description of the considerations influencing Nepalese foreign policy as it has evolved in the last twenty years.
2. Nor are the scholars of the two countries able to find common ground. For some typical Indian views, see the special issue "India's Relations with Pakistan" *International Studies*, Vol. 8, Nos. 1–2, July–October 1966; and for typical Pakistani views see "Pakistan's Relations with India—The Recent Phase" by the Editorial Staff of *Pakistan Horizon*, Vol. XII, No. 3, September 1959, pp. 263–75, and G. W. Choudhury, *Pakistan's Relations with India: 1947–1966* (New York: Praeger, 1968).
3. There is also less anti-Pakistan feeling in South India than in other parts of the country. But sentiment in this area has generally been passive rather than opposed to official policy.
4. Selig S. Harrison, "Nehru's Plan for Peace," *The New Republic*, June 19, 1971.
5. *Indian and Foreign Review* (New Delhi), August 1, 1971.
6. Pakistanis probably would find it almost impossible to believe that India has no clear policy on this issue. This represents the tendency of nations to believe that an antagonist has a hostile policy covering every contingency and to interpret all its actions in terms of such an assumed aim.
7. David E. Lockwood, "Sheikh Abdullah and the Politics of Kashmir," *Asian Survey*, Vol. IX, No. 5, May 1969.
8. B. G. Verghese, "A Reassessment of Indian Policy in Asia," *India Quarterly*, Vol. XVII, No. 2, April–June 1961, p. 103.
9. However, Harold Hinton points out that maps issued by the Government of India between 1947 and 1950 show no line for the Ladakh area of Kashmir but simply state "Boundary Undefined." Harold C. Hinton, *Communist China in World Politics* (Boston: Houghton Mifflin Company, 1966), p. 280.
10. Alastair Lamb, *The China-India Border: The Origins of the Disputed Boundaries* (London: Oxford University Press for the Royal Institute of

International Affairs, 1964), p. 175. A similar position is taken by W. F. Van Eekelen, *Indian Foreign Policy and the Border Dispute with China* (The Hague: Martinus Nijhoff, 1964), while a position quite similar to that of the Indian government is taken by Margaret W. Fisher, Leo E. Rose, and Robert A. Huttenback, *Himalayan Battleground: Sino-Indian Rivalry in Ladakh* (New York: Praeger, 1963).

11. It can be objected that such a policy means leaving China in control of Tibet and its people. That the Tibetans deserve a better fate is clear; but it is equally clear that they will gain autonomy or freedom only if Chinese authority disintegrates, and that neither India nor the United States can or should try to bring about that development.

Chapter 16

1. *The New York Times*, April 13, 1967. The U.S. government has never made public the amount of arms assistance provided to Pakistan, but an examination of the amount of U.S. arms furnished to other countries in the Middle East suggests this is about what Pakistan actually received. This does not include small grants of U.S. surplus arms.

2. Neither India nor Pakistan is sympathetic to Western naval operations in the Indian Ocean and they are unlikely to make naval facilities available to the West at a time of international tension. However, neither are likely to provide such facilities to the U.S.S.R. or to China. For a somewhat more concerned view of the situation see T. B. Millar, "The Indian and Pacific Oceans: Some Strategic Considerations," The Institute for Strategic Studies, London, Adelphi Paper No. 57, May 1969.

3. Following the conclusion of the Nazi-Soviet pact in August 1939, the Germans and Russians conducted negotiations during 1940 on apportioning future spheres of influence among Germany, Russia, Italy and Japan. Negotiations centered on the future of Eastern Europe, but the German draft agreement provided for a declaration by the U.S.S.R. "that its territorial aspirations center south of the national territory of the Soviet Union in the direction of the Indian Ocean." (*Nazi-Soviet Relations, 1939–1941: Documents from the Archives of the German Foreign Office*, Washington: Department of State, 1948, p. 257.) The Soviet leaders were not diverted from European matters by the German proposal, but neither did they ignore it: they simply demanded more. They said the draft was acceptable, provided several changes were made, including one specifying "that the area south of Batum and Baku in the general direction of the Persian Gulf is recognized as the center of the aspirations of the Soviet Union." (Same, p. 259.) These negotiations came to nothing because of the German attack on Russia. While it would be misleading to regard them as a blueprint for Soviet strategy, they do suggest that Soviet aspirations were not markedly different from those of the czars.

4. Two interesting Indian views of these defense problems are Major General D. Som Dutt "The Defence of India's Northern Borders," Adelphi Paper No. 25, Institute for Strategic Studies, London, January 1966, and Dilip Mukerjee, "India's Defence Perspectives," *International Affairs*, London, October 1968, Vol. 44, No. 4, pp. 666–76.

5. See *The Economist*, June 15, 1968; *The Times* (London) June 17, 1968; and *The New Statesman*, August 23, 1968.

6. For a description of India's defense and defense production build-up see K. Subrahmanyam, "The Challenge of the Seventies to India's Security," *India Quarterly*, Vol. XXVII, No. 2, April–June 1970, pp. 134–42.
7. For an example of conflicting Indian views on the acquisition of nuclear weapons see "The Indian Nuclear Debate," *Seminar*, No. 83, July 1966, pp. 392–402.
8. For an official Indian statement and an unofficial but representative American statement of Indian and U.S. views on the Nonproliferation Treaty see A. S. Gonsalves and Wayne Wilcox, "The Nuclear Nonproliferation Treaty: Indian and American Views," *Asia*, No. 15, Summer 1969, pp. 72–92.
9. Leonard Beaton, "Capabilities of Non-nuclear Powers," pp. 13–38, in *A World of Nuclear Powers?* Alastair Buchan, ed. (Englewood Cliffs, N. J.: Prentice-Hall for The American Assembly, 1966).
10. James R. Schlesinger, "Nuclear Spread," *The Yale Review*, Autumn 1967, Vol. LVII, No. 1, pp. 66-84.
11. "A Strategy for India for a Credible Posture Against a Nuclear Adversary," The Institute for Defence Studies and Analyses, New Delhi, November 1968, p. 6.
12. Dr. Vikram Sarabhai, Chairman of the Atomic Energy Commission, on May 25, 1970 announced a ten-year space program designed to enable India to launch satellites by 1980. *India News*, Vol. IX, No. 11, June 5, 1970.
13. See K. Subrahmanyam, "The Asian Balance of Power in the Seventies: An Indian View," The Institute for Defence Studies and Analyses, New Delhi, 1968, for a thoughtful statement of the Indian position.
14. See Shelton L. Williams, *The U.S., India, and the Bomb*, Studies in International Affairs, No. 12, The Johns Hopkins Press, Baltimore, 1969 for a detailed analysis of this problem and particularly the limitations on America's ability to influence Indian policy.
15. Alastair Buchan, "The Balance of Power in Asia after Vietnam," *Royal Central Asian Journal*, Vol. LVI, June 1969, Part II, pp. 138–39.
16. Werner Levi, "The Future of Southeast Asia," *Asian Survey*, Vol. X, No. 4, April 1970, pp. 348–57.

Chapter 17

1. The other major allocations go to the Food for Freedom program, various international agencies, and the Export-Import Bank.
2. See Willard L. Thorp, "Foreign Aid: A Report on the Reports," *Foreign Affairs*, Vol. 48, No. 3, April 1970, pp. 561–73.
3. For an interesting discussion about building a new constituency see Edward K. Hamilton, "Toward Public Confidence on Foreign Aid," *World Affairs*, Vol. 132, No. 4, March 1970, pp. 287–304.

Selected Bibliography

It is impossible to record in any systematic way the voluminous material which exists on the major countries dealt with in this study. But the following list of books and documents tries to point out those which have been of particular help to the author—for both facts and understanding in composing the present volume. In addition, the author has drawn upon information in such newspapers and weeklies as *The New York Times*, *The Times* (London), *The Washington Post*, *The Economist*, *Interwing* (Rawalpindi), *Current Digest of the Soviet Press*, *Peking Review*, and various Indian and Pakistani newspapers as well as the U.S. government's "Foreign Broadcast Information Service."

Among the periodicals which have been especially helpful the following should be mentioned: *Asian Survey* (Berkeley), *Foreign Affairs* (New York, *India Quarterly* (New Delhi), *International Affairs* (London), *International Affairs* (Moscow), *International Studies* (New Delhi), *Journal of Asian Studies* (Ann Arbor), *Orbis* (Philadelphia), *Pacific Affairs* (Vancouver), *Pakistan Horizon* (Karachi).

AMBEDKAR, B. R.   *Pakistan, or Partition of India.* Bombay: Thacker and Co., 1945, rev. ed.

AZAD, MAULANA ABUL KALAM.   *India Wins Freedom: An Autobiographical Narrative.* New York: Longmans, Green and Co., 1960.

BARNETT, A. DOAK.   *Communist China and Asia: Challenge to American Policy.* New York: Harper & Brothers, 1960.

BERKES, ROSS N. and MOHINDER S. BEDI.   *The Diplomacy of India: In-*
dian Foreign Policy in the United Nations. Stanford, California:
Stanford University Press, 1958.

BRECHER, MICHAEL.   *Nehru: A Political Biography.* London: Oxford
University Press, 1959.

BROWN, W. NORMAN.   *The United States and India and Pakistan.* Cambridge, Massachusetts: Harvard University Press, 1963, rev. and
enlarged ed.

CALLARD, KEITH.   *Pakistan: A Political Study.* New York: Macmillan,
1957.

————.   *Pakistan's Foreign Policy: An Interpretation,* Second Edition
Revised and Enlarged. New York: Institute of Pacific Relations,
1959.

CAMPBELL, JOHN C.   *Defense of the Middle East: Problems of American*
Policy. New York: Praeger, 1960, rev. ed.

CHAUDHRI, M. A.   *Pakistan and the Great Powers.* Karachi: Council for
Pakistan Studies (in cooperation with the University of Karachi),
1970.

CHAUDHURI, NIRAD C.   *The Continent of Circe: Being an Essay on the*
Peoples of India. New York: Oxford University Press, 1966.

CHOUDHURY, G. W.   *Pakistan's Relations with India: 1947–1966.* New
York: Praeger, 1968.

DALLIN, DAVID J.   *Soviet Foreign Policy after Stalin.* Philadelphia: Lippincott, 1961.

DAS GUPTA, J. B.   *Indo-Pakistan Relations: 1947–1955.* Amsterdam:
Djambatan, 1958.

DUTT, D. SOM.   "The Defence of India's Northern Borders," *Adelphi*
Paper No. 25. London: Institute for Strategic Studies, January 1966.

DUTT, V. P.   *China and the World: An Analysis of Communist China's*
Foreign Policy. New York: Praeger, 1966.

ELDRIDGE, P. J.   *The Politics of Foreign Aid in India.* New York:
Schocken Books, 1969.

FISHER, MARGARET W., LEO E. ROSE, and ROBERT A. HUTTENBACK.
Himalayan Battleground: Sino-Indian Rivalry in Ladakh. New York:
Praeger, 1963.

GALBRAITH, JOHN KENNETH.   *Ambassador's Journal: A Personal Account*
of the Kennedy Years. Boston: Houghton Mifflin, 1969.

Government of India, Ministry of External Affairs.   *Notes, Memoranda*
and Letters Exchanged and Agreements Signed Between the Gov-
ernments of India and China (White Paper, September 8, 1959).
(Cited as White Paper No. I.) Also: White Papers Nos. II, III,
VI, VII.

Government of India, Ministry of Information and Broadcasting, Publications Division.   *J. Nehru, India's Foreign Policy: Selected*
Speeches, September 1946–April 1961. 1961.

————.   *Jawaharlal Nehru's Speeches.* Vol. 2, 1963.

GRIFFITH, WILLIAM E. *The Sino-Soviet Rift*. Cambridge, Massachusetts: The M.I.T. Press, 1964.

HALPERIN, A., ed. *Policies toward China: Views from Six Continents*. New York: McGraw-Hill, 1965.

HARRISON, SELIG. *India: The Most Dangerous Decades*. Princeton, New Jersey: Princeton University Press, 1960.

HINTON, HAROLD. *Communist China and World Politics*. Boston: Houghton Mifflin Company, 1966.

HODSON, H. V. *The Great Divide: Britain—India—Pakistan*. London: Hutchinson, 1969.

ISAACS, HAROLD. *Scratches on Our Minds: American Images of China and India*. New York: Day, 1958.

KAUTSKY, JOHN H. *Moscow and the Communist Party of India: A Study in the Postwar Evaluation of International Communist Strategy*. New York: John Wiley & Sons, 1956.

KAVIC, LORNE J. *India's Quest for Security: Defense Policies, 1947–1965*. Berkeley and Los Angeles: University of California Press, 1967.

KHAN, FAZAL MUQEEM. *The Story of the Pakistan Army*. Karachi: Oxford University Press (Pakistan Branch), 1963.

KHAN, MOHAMMED AYUB. *Friends Not Masters: A Political Autobiography*. London: Oxford University Press, 1967.

KORBEL, JOSEF. *Danger in Kashmir*. Princeton, New Jersey: Princeton University Press, 1954.

KOTHARI, RAJNI. *Politics in India*. Boston: Little Brown & Co., 1970.

LAMB, ALASTAIR. *The China-India Border: The Origins of the Disputed Boundaries*. London: Oxford University Press for the Royal Institute of International Affairs, 1964.

LAQUEUR, WALTER Z. *The Soviet Union and the Middle East*. New York: Praeger, 1959.

LEWIS, JOHN P. *Quiet Crisis in India: Economic Development and American Policy*. Washington: The Brookings Institution, 1962.

McLANE, CHARLES B. *Soviet Strategies in Southeast Asia: An Exploration of Eastern Policy under Lenin and Stalin*. Princeton, New Jersey: Princeton University Press, 1966.

MASON, EDWARD S. *Economic Development in India and Pakistan*. Harvard University Center for International Affairs, Occasional Paper No. 13, September 1966.

MAXWELL, NEVILLE. *India's China War*. New York: Pantheon Books, 1970.

MENON, V. P. *The Story of the Integration of the Indian States*. Calcutta: Orient Longmans, 1956.

———. *The Transfer of Power in India*. Princeton, New Jersey: Princeton University Press, 1957.

MILLAR, T. B. "The Indian and Pacific Oceans: Some Strategic Considerations." London: The Institute for Strategic Studies, Adelphi Paper No. 57, May 1969.

MUKERJEE, DILIP. "India's Defence Perspectives," *International Affairs*, (London), October 1968, Vol. 44, pp. 666–76.

MYRDAL, GUNNAR. *Asian Drama: An Inquiry into the Poverty of Nations*. New York: Twentieth Century Fund, 1968.

———. *The Challenge of World Poverty*. New York: Pantheon Books, 1970.

NEHRU, JAWAHARLAL. *The Discovery of India*. New York: The John Day Company, 1946.

———. *Jawaharlal Nehru: An Autobiography*. London: John Lane, 1936.

OVERSTREET, GENE D. and MARSHALL WINDMILLER. *Communism in India*. Berkeley: University of California Press, 1959.

PALMER, NORMAN D. *South Asia and United States Policy*. Boston: Houghton Mifflin Company, 1966.

PANIKKAR, K. M. *In Two Chinas: Memoirs of a Diplomat*. London: George Allen and Unwin, Ltd., 1955.

PAPANEK, GUSTAV F. *Pakistan's Development: Social Goals and Private Incentives*. Cambridge: Harvard University Press, 1967.

PRASAD, BISHESHWAR. *Our Foreign Policy Legacy: A Study of British Indian Foreign Policy*. New Delhi: People's Publishing House, 1965.

Report of the Commission on International Development. *Partners in Development*. New York: Praeger, 1969.

RUDOLPH, LLOYD I., and SUSANNE HOEBER RUDOLPH. *The Modernity of Tradition: Political Development in India*. Chicago: University of Chicago Press, 1967.

SEN GUPTA, BHABANI. *The Fulcrum of Asia: Relations Among China, India, Pakistan and the U.S.S.R.* New York: Pegasus, 1970.

SINGH, PATWANT. *India and the Future of Asia*. New York: Alfred A. Knopf, 1966.

STEIN, ARTHUR. *India and the Soviet Union*. Chicago: University of Chicago Press, 1969.

STEPHENS, IAN. *Pakistan*. New York: Frederick A. Praeger, 1963.

SUBRAHMANYAM, K. "The Asian Balance of Power in the Seventies: An Indian View." New Delhi: The Institute for Defence Studies and Analyses, 1968.

TALBOT, PHILLIPS and S. L. POPLAI. *India and America: A Study of Their Relations*. New York: Harper & Brothers, 1958.

TINKER, HUGH. *India and Pakistan: A Political Analysis*, rev. ed. New York: Praeger, 1968.

ULAM, ADAM B. *Expansion and Coexistence: The History of Soviet Foreign Policy, 1917–67*. New York: Praeger, 1968.

United Nations: *A Study of the Capacity of the United Nations Development System*. DP/5; prepared by Sir Robert Jackson. Geneva, 1969.

United Nations: Security Council, *Report by the Secretary General on the Current Situation in Kashmir with Particular Reference to the Cease-Fire Agreement, The Cease-Fire Line and the Functioning of UNMOGIP,* S/6651, 3 September 1965.

U.S. Congress
House. Committee on Foreign Affairs, *Hearings, Foreign Assistance Act of 1966,* 89th Congress, 2d Session; and subsequent hearings.
————. *Hearings, Mutual Security Act Extension,* 83rd Congress, 1st Session; and subsequent hearings.
Senate. Committee on Appropriations, *Hearings, Foreign Assistance and Related Agencies Appropriations for 1966,* 89th Congress, 1st Session; and subsequent hearings.

VAN EEKELEN, W. F. *Indian Foreign Policy and the Border Dispute with China.* The Hague: Martinus Nijhoff, 1964.

VON VORYS, KARL. *Political Development in Pakistan.* Princeton, New Jersey: Princeton University Press, 1965.

WEINER, MYRON. *The Politics of Scarcity: Public Pressure and Political Response in India.* Chicago: University of Chicago Press, 1962.

WILCOX, WAYNE A. *India, Pakistan, and the Rise of China.* New York: Walker and Company, 1964.

————. *Pakistan: The Consolidation of a Nation.* New York: Columbia University Press, 1963.

WILLIAMS, SHELTON L. *The U.S., India, and the Bomb,* Studies in International Affairs, No. 12. Baltimore: The Johns Hopkins Press, 1969.

ZAGORIA, DONALD S. *The Sino-Soviet Conflict 1956–1961.* Princeton, New Jersey: Princeton University Press, 1962.

Index

Abdul Ghafar Khan, 77
Abdullah, Sheikh of Kashmir, 39, 42–43, 192, 312–13; Chou En-lai meets with, 194; Liaquat on, 41; release from prison, 40, 193, 219
Acheson, Dean, 92
Afghan wars, 3, 18
Afghanistan, 3, 52, 78–79, 102, 115, 236; and Kashmir, 39; Khrushchev visit to, 119, 124; and Pakistan, 92, 94, 102; Pathans of, 78; Pushtunistan dispute, 45, 77–79, 305; and U.S.S.R., 124, 127, 187, 305–6; and U.S., 92, 94, 305–6
Africa, 76, 85, 138, 142; see also Afro-Asian nations
Afro-Asian nations, 1; growth rate of, 261; and national unity, 311; neutralism of, 138, 142, see also Nonalignment; and Pakistan, 190–92, 243; Preparatory Ministerial Meeting of the Second Afro-Asian Conference (Jakarta, 1964), 191; and Sino-Indian border war, 178; and U.S.S.R., 222, 229
Agency for International Development (AID), 345; see also Foreign aid

Ahmad Khan, 22
Akbar, Mogul Emperor, 79
Akhnur (Kashmir), 203
Aksai Chin (Kashmir), 147, 149, 150; Chinese claims to, 154, 317–20; Indian claims to, 142, 143; settlement for (proposed), 321; see also Kashmir dispute; Ladakh; Sino-Indian border war
All-India Congress Committee, 32, 72
Amritsar massacre (1919), 18–19, 20
Andhra, 112, 120
Anglo-Chinese border claims agreement (1846), 150
Anglo-Egyptian Sudan, 86
Anglo-Egyptian Treaty (1936), 87
Anglo-Iranian Oil Company, 86
Arab-Israeli war (1967), 228; see also Israel
Arabian Sea, 78
Arms race, 258; see also Nonproliferation treaty; Nuclear capability
Asia, 1–5, 84, 136, 140, 195–97; British in, 3, 5; and China, 140, 185–86, 261, 318, 319, 327–33; Communist threat to, 5, 59, 61, 89, 131, 222, 265–66, 326; defense of: 100, 139,

Asia (cont.):
323–41, proposals for, 235–36, 252; economic development, 268–70; food production, 80, 297, see also Green Revolution; geography of, 324, 325; military coups in, 142; military role of, 338–41; neutralism, 138, 142, see also Nonalignment; outside influences on, 249; political systems, 269, 270, see also Communism; private investment in, 303; regional conflicts, 267, 304–22; Regional Cooperation for Development, 344; and revolution, prospects for, 135; "solidarity," 59–60, 62, 76; Southeast, 265, 338–41; and U.S.S.R., 108–9, 206–8, 228–32, 318, 319, 326–27; and U.S.: 1–5, 140, 195–97; choices in, 292–303; disengagement, 8–9, 222–28, 234–35, 261, 332, 345; importance to, 257–72; policies toward, 248–54
Asian Drama, 276, 279
Asian Relations Conferences: (1947), 59; (1949), 60
Assam, 23, 73, 329, 330; and expulsion of Muslims, 192, 193; and partition, 29–30
Ataturk, Mustafa Kamal, 20
Atlee, Clement, 29
Auchinleck, Claude, 41, 72
Australasia, 84
Austrian Peace Treaty (1956), 120
Awami League, 240, 243, 308; general strike by, 286–88; outlawing of, 291; preparedness of, 290; see also Mujibar Rahman, Sheikh
Ayub Khan, 91, 201, 203, 212–16; and China, 187; domestic opposition to, 212–13; downfall of, 235, 238, 239, 284–85; foreign visits: to Afro-Asian nations, 190–91; to Peking, 194, 196, 199; to U.S.S.R., 194, 216; to U.S., 169, 197, 214; joint defense proposal, 252; "leaning on India" policy, 193–95, 198, see also Indo-Pakistani relations; overconfidence of, 201–3; and military establishment, 103–6; political stability under, 7, 9, 283; and President Johnson, 196, 214; and President Kennedy, on India, 184; on relations with great powers, 215; takeover by (1958), 158–59, 283; on

U.S. aid, 95, 185, see also Foreign aid
Azad, Maulana, 28, 31, 72
Azerbaijan (U.S.S.R.), 84

Baghdad Pact, 98–99, 114, 121, 252; British membership in, 127; and U.S.S.R., 123
Bandung Conference (1955), 138–39, 188; see also Panch Sheel period
Bangla Desh, 241, 288, 310–11; see also Bengal, East; Pakistan, East
Barnett, Doak, 129
Bay of Pigs, 167
Beaton, Leonard, 335
Bedi, Mohinder S., 66
Bengal, 23, 30, 33, 34; East, 28, 241, 290; West, 69, 220, 328; see also Bangla Desh; Pakistan, East
Berkes, Ross N., 66
Berlin blockade, 85
Berlin wall, 169
Bhabba, Homi, 220
"Bharat" (East Pakistan), 69
Bhashani, Maulana, 287
Bhutan, 52, 63, 143, 153, 330; Chinese interest in, 327; foreign relations of, 305; treaty with India, 134
Bhutto, Z. A., 190, 191, 215, 286, 287, 291
Bihar, 28
Bird, Richard M., 301
Bowles, Chester, 91, 92, 96, 161, 167
Brezhnev, Leonid, 228–29, 235–36
Britain, 3, 83, 84, 128, 339; and British Commonwealth, see Commonwealth; and communalism, 14–15; Communist Party of (CPGB), 109; Diego Garcia military base, 324; Himalayan frontier policy, 50–53; and India (post-independence), 24–25, 57–59, 204–5, 208, see also British India; and Iran, 87, 88, 99; and Kashmir, 39; Labour party of, 25, 75; and Middle East, 85; and Pakistan, 75, 184, 204–5, 208, 244; and Suez attack, 122; and Tibet, 133, 134
British India, 3–4, 8, 29; Amritsar massacre, 18–20; Army, 3, 25, 53, 70, 93; Cabinet Mission on Independence, 26–27; Communist party

of, 109, 110; constitution for (1935), 21; "Direct Action Day," 28; financial disputes, 34; foreign liabilities, 48–49; foreign policy tradition, 45–54; independence for, 4, 13, 21–32, 44, 45; irrigation system, 35; noncooperation movement, 19–20, 21; and NWFP, 29, 40, 70, 77; Pakistan's inheritance from, 78; Royal Air Force, 25, 53; Royal Navy, 3, 25, 53; and self-rule, 16–19, 21; and World War II, 24–25; *see also* India

Brown, W. Norman, 31

Buchan, Alastair, 339–40

Buddhism, 38

Bulganin, Nikolai, 118, 119, 124, 236

Bunker, Ellsworth, 126

Burma, 3, 4, 52, 75, 178; Ayub visit to, 191; border agreement with China, 151; civil war in, 112; Khrushchev visit to, 119; military takeover (1958), 152

Byroade, Henry A., 92

Callard, Keith, 74

Cambodia, 178, 262

Canada-India research reactor, 333

Caroe, Olaf, 91

Caste system, 14, 20, 39

CENTO (Central Treaty Organization), 181, 188, 222; dissolution of (proposed), 344–45; Pakistani membership in, 191, 338

Ceylon, 4, 75, 178, 191

Chavan, Y. B., 187, 214

Chen Yi, 199, 207, 214

Chiang Kai-shek, 61, 84; *see also* China, Nationalist

China: and Burmese border agreement, 151; Common Program of the Chinese People's Political Consultative Conference (1949), 137; Cultural Revolution, 215, 220, 318; economic progress and plans, 128, 135; foreign policy: (mid 1950s), 135–36, (late 1950s), 141–43; foreign relations, *see* Sino-Indian relations, Sino-Pakistani relations, Sino-Soviet Relations; and Great Leap Forward, 142, 145; Hundred Flowers Campaign in, 141; and India, *see* Sino-Indian relations; and Japan, 130; and Kashmir dispute,

206–8; and Korean War, 66–67; military capabilities of, 329–31; modernization in, 5; national unification of, 130–31; Nationalist, *see* China, Nationalist; Nepalese border agreement, 151; and Pakistan, *see* Sino-Pakistani relations; propaganda programs of, 328; road-building activities of, 234, 240; and Second National People's Congress (1959), 145; 1949 takeover of, 3, 130; and U.S.S.R., *see* Sino-Soviet relations; U.N. representation, *see* United Nations

China, Nationalist, 61, 126, 318; Kuomintang regime, 130, 131, 132; postwar position of, 83, 84; and Sino-Indian border dispute, 160; *see also* Taiwan

Chou En-lai, 66, 136, 188; and Afro-Asian neutrals, 142; at Bandung, 139; border solution proposal, 154–55; and Nehru, 151, 153–54, 156, 170; on Pakistani civil war, 244; and Sheikh Abdullah, 194; on Sino-Indian boundaries, 143; on Tibet, 144; and visits to India, 139–40; and visit to Pakistan, 199

Churchill, Winston, 24, 25, 57, 64

Coexistence, *see* Union of Soviet Socialist Republics, détente policies of

Cold war, 1, 7, 45, 342, 343; and India, 62–67, 96; and Pakistan, 79–80

Colombo Plan, 60

Colonialism, 1, 4; Asian fear of, 139–41; Indian policy toward, 59, 62, 67; and Pakistan and Muslim nations, 75–77; U.S. policy toward, 88–89, 93

Commonwealth of Nations (British), 67; and India, 57–59; multiracial nature of, 58–59; and Pakistan, 58, 74–75

Commonwealth Prime Ministers Conference (1951), 75

Communalism, 8, 21, 43, 69, 308–9; (in mid-1940s), 26, 29–31; (post-independence), 32–33, 54; as basis of antagonism, 13–15; in India, 192, 193; in Kashmir, 56–57, 192–94; in Punjab, 39–40; in West Pakistan, 94; *see also* Indo-Pakistani relations

Communism: and Asian defense organization, 100; ideological role of, 2, 108–9, 129, 131, 229; Nehru on, 46–47, 128; as threat to Asia, 5, 59, 61, 89, 222, 265–66, 326; U.S. policy of containment of, 84–85, 259, 265–66

Communist Party of India (CPI), 7, 24, 47, 64, 276, 316; and China, 131, 132; and "constitutional communism," 119–20; formation and early days of, 108–11; in Hyderabad, 112, 113; in Kerala, 128; and Nehru, 110–11, 113, 120; revolutionary attempts, 111–13; Second Congress (1948), 111; on Sino-American rapprochement, 246, 258; and Sino-Indian border war, 176; split in, 320; and Tibet, 145, 147

Communist Party of India (Marxist), 220

Communist Party of India (Marxist-Leninist), 220, 328

Congo, 167

Congress Party (India), 7, 21–22, 39, 235; and Communists, 119; elections (1971), 238, 275–78; factionalism of, 16, 192, 217, 218; foreign policy of, 45–46, 50; founding of, 15–16; Gandhi's transformation of, 20; independence plans, 26, 27, 28; and Muslim League, 15–21; outlawing of, 24–25, 110; and partition, 30–32, 71; and Princely states, 36; "Quit India" drive, 24, 110; and socialism, 117; and U.S. Arms to Pakistan, 96

Containment policy, see Communism, U.S. policy of containment of

Cooper, John Sherman, 161

Crankshaw, Edward, 212

Cripps, Stafford, 24, 110

Cripps mission (1942), 110

Cuban missile crisis, 175, 176, 178, 179

Currency problems, 56; Indian, 217, 301; Pakistani, 80

Curzon, Lord George, 16

Cyprus, 223

Czechoslovakia, 85, 124, 229, 235

Dalai Lama (Tibet), 144, 145

Diego-Garcia military base, 324

Dien Bien Phu, 97; see also Indochina

Dogra-Ladakh Agreement (1842), 150

Dogras (of Jammu), 39

Dulles, John Foster, 89, 103, 121; on aid to India, 125; on arms to Pakistan, 96; on Middle East defense organization, 92–93, 97; and Nehru, 121

Durand Line, 52–53, 78

Dyer, General, 18–19

Economist, The, 198, 214

Egypt, 87, 92, 99, 115; see also Suez base; Suez canal; United Arab Republic

Eisenhower, Dwight D., 80, 126, 142, 162; on arms to Pakistan, 95, 96–97; and NATO, 86; on U.S.-Indian relations, 116; and visit to India, 161

Eisenhower Doctrine, 126, 142

Farakka Barrage dispute, 221, 235, 240

Formosa Strait, 66

Foreign aid: aid consortia, 167, 244; arms aid, see below; conditions attached to, 299–303, 337; food aid, 225–28, 293, 345; humanitarian concerns and, 270–72; to India: 117, 184–85, food, 90–91, 161, projections for, 281–82, table (1945–70), 226, from U.S.S.R., 118, 157, 234, 235, from U.S., see below; multilateral, 299, 300; to Pakistan, 102, 184–85, table (1945–70), 227, see also U.S. economic aid, below

Arms aid: British, to India, 118, 168, 179, 180; Chinese, to Pakistan, 8, 214, 215; French, to India, 118, 168; to Middle East, 87; Soviet: to Afghanistan, 124, to Asia, 115, 116, 118, 182, to India, 168, 185, 187, 295–96, 331–32, to Pakistan, 162, 216, 232; U.S.: 89, 195, 196, 323–24, 345, cessation of, 222–25, 311, 345, future of, 344, 345, to India, 118, 179, 331–33, "non-lethal," 224, 332, 345, "one-time," 345, to Pakistan, see below; "spare parts," 224

U.S. economic aid: 6–9, 89, 166, 205, 251–52, 254, 347; cuts in, 261, 273–74; expansion in (proposed), 345–48; to India: 64–65, 125, 126, 197, (early 1960s), 128, 167, future of, 294–99, increase in, 229, 311–12, and nuclear weapons, 337, Pakistan's reaction to, 127; to Pakistan, 8, 188, 293–94; under President Johnson, 223–25; under President Nixon, 233; to Western Europe, 85, 86

U.S.-Pakistani military aid agreement (1954), 91–97, 136, 214, 252–54, 323, 332, 333; cessation of, 311, 345; and domestic Pakistani politics, 104; F-104 aircraft, 169–70; India's reaction to, 94–97, 103; questions and reflections on, 100–106; and shipments (1970), 245, 246; and U.S.S.R., 96, 103, 123

Foreign Affairs, 84

France, 4, 83, 84; and Dien Bien Phu, 97; in Indochina, 85, 86, 131, 135, 136; and Suez attack, 122, 127

Fulbright, J. William, 96

Galbraith, John Kenneth, 160–61, 167

Gandhi, Indira, 212; and Asian collective security system (proposed), 236; on China, 222, 322; egalitarian policies of, 218–19, 238, 278, 280, 281, 297; election victory (1971), 9, 237, 238; and Pakistani civil war, 237, 241–42; and President Nixon, 233; on Soviet-Pakistani arms agreement, 232; Soviet support of, 235, *see also* Indo-Soviet Treaty

Gandhi, Mohandas, 19–21, 31, 32

Geneva Conference (1954), 97, 117, 121

Germany, 47, 83, 119, 266

Ghana, 178

Ghosh, Ajoy, 120

Goa dispute, 119, 121

Gokhale, Gopal Krishna, 16

Gomal pass (Afghanistan), 79

Gracey, General, 41

Gulab Singh (of Jammu), 39

Great Britain, *see* Britain

Greece, 84, 85, 86, 223

Green Revolution, 278–79, 282, 298

Guam Doctrine, 234

Gujarat state, 197

Gurkhas (Nepal), 53

Haji-Pir pass (Kashmir), 203

Harriman and Sandys missions (1962), 181, 185

Harrison, Selig, 91, 308–9

Hasan, K. Sarwar, 73

Himalayan border states, 50–53, 219–20; Chinese threat to, 327–33; Indian efforts in, 153–55; *see also* individual country entries

Himalayan mountains, 3, 50–51, 67; defense function of, 320, 327; as Sino-Indian frontier, 51–53, 62, 148–50, map, 148

Hindu Kush mountains, 3, 52

Hindu Mahasabha party, 24, 31, 72

Hinduism, 13–15; *see also* Communalism

Hindustan Times, 147, 174, 198

Hirschman, Albert O., 301

Ho Chi Minh, 114

Hungary, 122, 127

Hussein, King of Jordan, 325

Hyderabad, 37–38; Indian takeover, 72; Telengana revolt, 112, 113

India, 48–49, 59–61, 71–72, 307, 338–41; All-India Committee, 32; Bokaro steel plant, 118, 197, 229, 234, 235; and border states, *see* Himalayan border states; Calcutta riots (1946), 28; caste system, 14, 20, 39; and China, *see* Sino-Indian relations; civil service, 274; Communist parties, *see* Communist Party of India; Congress party, *see* Congress Party; defense policies, *see below*; domestic political stability: (1947–67), 7, 9, (mid-1960s), 217–22, (late 1960s), 261–62; educational system, 217; elections: (1967), 275, (1971), 217–18, 278, table, 275, in Andhra state, 120; Farakka Barrage construction, 221, 235, 240; federal system, 219, 277–78; Five year plans: 274, 275, 2nd (1956–61), 117, 125, 126, 3rd (1961–66), 167, 217, 280, 282, 4th (1969–74), 217, 229, 280–81, 282, *see also* economic development, *below*; food grain production, 126, 217, 274, 275, *see also* Green Revolution; foreign policy, *see below*; guerrilla movements, 328; Harriman and Sandys missions, 181, 185; Hindu Mahasabha party, 24, 31, 72; land reform, 22, 297; League Against

India (cont.):

Imperialism, 46; military capabilities of, 329–32, see also Indian National Army; Mizo revolt (1966), 219; Naga rebellion, 328, 340; nationalism, 20–21, 109; nuclear capability, see Nuclear capability; population problems, 297–98; princely states, 35–38; public works programs, 297; "Quit India" movement, 24, 110; Swatantra party, 278; trade, see Trade; Unionist party, 29; United Provinces, 22; and U.S., see Indo-U.S. relations; wheat shipments to, 90, 91, 161; see also British India

defense policies: 180, 217, 252, 274; expenditures, 320, 329, 333, 347; table, 306; under Nehru, 152–53; nuclear weapons, see Nuclear capability; post-independence, 53; reliance on Britain, 58; suppliers, see Foreign aid, arms aid; U.S.-U.K. air exercises, 187; see also Indian National Army; Menon, Krishna

economic development: 48, 152, 260–61; Bokaro steel plant, see above; dependence of, on West, 142, 232; under Nehru, 274–82; and private investment, 48, 126; see also Five year plans, above

financial problems: debt repayments, 217, 234, 282, 295, 298; recession, 217; rupee devaluation, 217, 301

foreign policy: British legacy, 45–54; under Nehru, 44–48; see also Indo-Pakistani relations; Indo-Soviet relations; Indo-U.S. relations; Nonalignment

Indian Express, The, 147

Indian National Army (INA), 25, 29, 53, 274–75, 277–78; under Britain, 3, 25, 53, 70, 93; table, 325

Indian National Congress, see Congress Party

Indian Ocean, 51, 235; Chinese presence in, 324; Soviet presence in, 258, 324, 327; U.S. presence in, 324

Indian Union, 29, 39

Indo-American Conference (1957), 167

Indo-Bhutanese Treaty (1949), 134

Indo-Pakistani relations, 2, 6–8, 71–74; (post-independence), 33–35, 54–57, 69–70; (late 1950s), 127–28; (under Shastri), 193, 194; (late 1960s), 221–22; and Ayub's downfall, 284–85; and hostility to West, 6, 204–5, 208; Indira Gandhi on, 237; and Junagadh, 36–37; "leaning on India" policy, 192–95; and nuclear threat, 336; and Pakistani civil war, 241–42, 284; and Sino-Indian conflict, 320; and South Asian future, 343–44; U Thant and, 247; and U.S.S.R., 206–8; U.S. policy toward, 195–97, 199–200, 249–51, 347; see also Communalism; Minorities problem

Indo-Soviet relations, 2, 107–25, 216; (early 1950s), 64, 65; (post-Stalin), 116–18; (mid-1950s), 118–21; (late 1950s), 127–28, 155–62; (mid-1960s), 182, 210; (late 1960s), 228–32, 235–36; Nehru on, 46–47; and nuclear weapons, 337–38; and Pakistan, 158–62, 232; and sale of railway cars, 232–35; treaty of friendship and cooperation (1971), 243, 265, 310, 343; and U.S., 158–62

Indo-Soviet Treaty (1971), 243, 265, 310, 343

Indo-U.S. relations, 2, 234, 260–62; (postwar), 64–67; (early 1950s), 90, 116–18; (mid-1950s), 121; (late 1950s), 125–28; (under Kennedy), 167–68; (under Nixon), 233–36; future prospects, 342–48; Indian hostility toward, 6, 204–5, 208; and Pakistani civil war, 246; see also Foreign aid

Indochina, 89, 135; French presence in, 85, 86, 97, 131, 135, 136

Indonesia, 60, 75, 338; Ayub visit to, 191; civil war in, 112; and Prime Ministers Conference (1954), 138

Indus River agreement, 8, 249–50

Indus River system, 35, 78

International Bank for Reconstruction and Development, 159, 161, 167, 244, 249

International Court of Justice, 319

Iqbal, Sir Muhammad, 23

Iran, 84, 86, 345, 346; anti-Westernism of, 93; and Britain, 87, 88, 99;

and Regional Cooperation for Development (RCD), 191
Iraq, 99, 127
Irrigation systems, 35, 72
Iskander Mirza, 95
Islam, 13–15, 68, 71, 283, 286, 313, 314; see also Communalism
Islamic Economic Conference (1949), 76
Islamic socialism, 79
Israel, 61, 91, 115; invasion of Sinai by, 122; and Six-Day War (1967), 228; U.S. attitude toward, 93
Izvestia, 156–57

Jackson, Robert, 299
Jammu (India), 38–40, 204; see also Kasmir dispute
Jan Sangh, 278
Japan: 85, 110, 301; Ayub visit to, 190–91; role of, in Asia, 338–41; in war with China (1937), 130
Japanese Peace Treaty, 61, 91
Jernegan, John P., 94
Jinnah, Mohammed Ali, 17; death of, 80; "Direct Action Day," 28; and Kashmir, 39–41; as Muslim spokesman, 23, 25, 26; and partition, 23–24, 30–32; on princely states, 36; and two-nation theory, 55, 74, 307, 313
Johnson, Lyndon B.: on aid, 223–24, 228; Asian trip of (1961), 169; and Ayub, 196, 214; on nuclear blackmail, 225
Junagadh (India), 36–37, 42, 72; see also Kashmir dispute

Kalimpong (India), 144, 145, 147
Karakoram mountains, 154, 320, 330
Karakoram pass, 149
Kashmir, 52, 67, 121, 122; access to, 34, 234, 240; Azad Kashmir government, 40, 41; Brahmins, 39; communal violence, 56–57, 192–94; dispute, see Kashmir dispute; independence for (proposed), 315; Islamic interest in, 42, 313, 314; Maharaja of, 39, 40, 72–73; plebiscite (proposed), 43, 312, 313; political divisions, 38, 39; political parties, 194; Vale of, 38, 193, 313
Kashmir dispute, 8, 38–43, 189, 302;

American policy on: 64, 127, 128, 181–82, and pressure for settlement, 169, 170, 249, 250–51, 314, 315; and Britain, 181–82; cease-fires (1949), 42, (1965), 63, 207–9, 307; Chinese involvement in, 206–8, 234, 240; and Pakistan, 69, 74–75, 159–60, 189; second (1965), 200–208; settlement prospects, 96, 103, 169, 170, 200, 249–51, 312–15; and Sino-Pakistani border agreement (1962), 173, see also Ladakh; strategic value, 39, 314; and U.S.S.R., 8, 39, 118, 119, 124; and U.N., see United Nations
Kashmir National Conference, 39
Kathiawar Peninsula, 36–37
Kaul, B. M., 173
Kennan, George, 84–85, 92
Kennedy, John F., 165–67, 184, 187
Kerala, 128, 155
Khilafat movement (Turkey), 19, 20
Khrushchev, Nikita, 114, 118, 119, 124, 236; and "De-Stalinization," 120; détente policies, 113–16, 142, 157–58, 165; downfall of, 187, 190; on Sino-Indian dispute, 157; and visit to Burma (1955), 119; and visit to China, 151; and visit to India (1955), 118, 119; and visit to Kashmir, 124; and visit to U.S., 151
Khyber pass (Afghanistan), 79
Kissinger, Henry, 245, 246
Korea, 266, 346
Korean War, 4, 5, 6, 91, 113, 114, 323; armistice, 89, 136; and China, 132–33, 135; Indian attitude toward, 65–67; and U.N., 66, 80, 85; and U.S., 85–86
Kosygin, Aleksei; and China, 228–29; and Farakka dispute, 235; and Tashkent, 210–12; and visit to India (1968), 232; and visit to Pakistan (1968), 216
Kurdish tribes (Iraq), 99
Kurrum pass (Afghanistan), 79

Ladakh (Kashmir), 38, 142, 330; border clashes, 146, 151; boundary claims, 170, 318, 319; supply lines to, 329; see also Aksai Chin; Kashmir dispute

Lamb, Alastair, 319–20
League Against Imperialism (India), 46
Lebanon, 126
Lenin, V. I., 108, 109
Liaquat, Ali, 41; assassination of, 57, 80, 94; and Kashmir, 74–75; and minorities problem, 56; and visit to U.S. (1950), 79
Liu Shao-chi, 214
Lucknow Pact, 17–18, 21

McMahon Line, 136, 149, 172, 174, 327; Chou En-lai on, 143, 153; CPI on, 147; and Sino-Burmese Treaty, 151; and U.S.S.R., 178
Macmillan, Harold, 187
McNamara, Robert, 263, 264
Madras, 112
Mahendra, King of Nepal, 153, 305
Malakand pass (Afghanistan), 79
Malaya, 112
Malenkov, Georgi, 114
Manila Conference, 98
Mao Tse-tung, 141, 177; on CPI, 131; on Soviet détente policies, 157–58
Marshall Plan, 85, 296
Marx, Karl, 46; see also Communism
Menon, Krishna, 122, 138–39; as Defense Minister, 152–53, 168, 176
Middle East, 68, 76–77, 83, 258, 338; arms aid to, 87; British presence in, 85–88; and colonial rule, 60–61; and Northern Tier scheme, 93–94, 97; security organization for, 86–88, 92–93, 97; U.S.S.R. in, 229
Middle East Command (proposed), 87
Mikoyan, Anastas, 124
Minorities problem, 13, 29–30, 55–56; Hindus in Pakistan, 13, 289; and Kashmir war, 204, 209; Kurdish in Turkey, 99; Muslims in India, 13, 192, 193; post-partition migration and, 33–35; see also Communalism
Minto-Morley reforms, 17; see also British India, and self-rule
Mohammad, Bakshi Ghulam, 94, 95, 192
Mohammad Ali of Bogra, 94, 102, 188
Morgenthau, Hans, 271–72
Morley, Lord John, 17
Morocco, 85

Moscow-Peking axis, see Sino-Soviet relations
Mossadegh, Muhammad, 93, 99
Mountbatten, Lord, 75; and Kashmir, 40–41; and partition, 29–32
Mughal Empire, 17
Mujibar Rahman, Sheikh, 213, 240, 286–88; "six-point autonomy program," 286–87; trial of, 246
Muslim Conference (1950), 34, 40, 76
Muslim League, 21–22, 26, 27, 28, 94; estrangement of, from Congress party, 15–21; lack of program of, 282–83; and partition, 23–24, 30–32; and princely states, 36
Muslims, 75–77; Bengali, 239,–41; geographical distribution of, 13, 15, see also Communalism; Islam; Minorities problem
Mutual Security Act (1958), 167
Myrdal, Gunnar, 276, 279

Nagaland rebels (India), 328, 340
Nasser, Gamal Abdel, 126, 127
Nationalism: Arab, 126; Asian, 59–61, 108–9; Indian, 20–21, 109; Soviet exploitation of, 115–16
NATO, see North Atlantic Treaty Organization
Nazi-Soviet Pact, 46
Nehru, Jawarharlal, 56, 59, 139, 141; and Chou En-lai, 151, 153–54, 156, 170; on communism, 46–47, 128; and Communist China, 62, 140, 143; Communist view of, 120–21; and CPI, 110–11, 113; death of, 193; defense policies of, 152–53; domestic criticism of, 151–52; and Dulles, 121; on East-West détente, 117; and independence porposals, 27–28; on India's foreign policy, 44–48, see also Nonalignment; on Kashmir, 41, 159–60, 193; on Korean War, 65–66; meeting of, with President Kennedy, 168; on nonalignment, 49, 65, 156, see also Nonalignment; on Panch Sheel, 145; and partition, 25, 31, 32, 54–55; on Soviet troops in Hungary, 122, 123; and Tibet, 133, 134, 136, 144–47; and U.S.S.R., 46–47, 118–19, 137, see also Indo-Soviet rela-

tions; and U.S., 79, 90, 95–97, 126, *see also* Indo-U.S. relations

Nepal, 52, 63, 134, 153, 317, 319; Ayub's visit to, 191; and China, 142, 151, 304, 305, 327; Gurkhas, 53; and India, 220, 304–5; and U.S., 305

Netherlands, 4, 60

New York Times, The, 95, 96, 106

Niebuhr, Reinhold, 271

Nixon, Richard M., 96, 233–36; Guam Doctrine, 234; on Indian exports, 298–99; rapprochement with China, 246, 258, 321

Nizam (of Hyderabad), 37–38

Nkrumah, Kwame, 229

Nonalignment, 94, 102, 140–42; and Bandung conference, 138, 188; Belgrade Conference (1961), 191; and Sino-Indian war, 179; Soviet exploitation of, 114–15; U.S. support of, 166–67

Indian: 90, 92, 122, 156, 192; and cold war, 63–67; and Indo-U.S. friction, 90; Nehru on, 49, 65, 156; and nuclear weapons, 334; reassessment of, 179–82; and Soviet treaty of friendship, 243; and Tibetan border dispute, 146

Noncooperation movement (India), 19–21

Nonproliferation treaty, 225, 235, 334; *see also* Nuclear capability

North Atlantic Treaty, 85

North Atlantic Treaty Organization (NATO), 85, 86, 87, 98, 229

Northeast Frontier Agency (NEFA), 329, 330, 331; border clashes, 146; British annexation of, 52; Chinese withdrawal from, 317; Indian claims to, 154; Sino-Indian claims, 142, 149, 151, 154, 211; settlement for (proposed), 321; Thagla Ridge, 174

Northwest Frontier Province (NWFP), 29, 40, 70, 77; and Northern Tier scheme, 93–94, 97

Nuclear capability: British, 335; Chinese, 220, 252, 333, 336; Indian, 201, 220–21, 225, 320, 326, 333–38; nonproliferation of, 119, 225; Soviet, 86, 252; and Test-Ban Treaty, 334; U.S., 126, 165

Pakistan: agriculture, 283, 284; aid to, *see* Foreign aid; armed forces, table, 325; Army, 70, 80, 100; and Asia, 183, 338–39; beginnings of, as nation, 4, 44, 282–83; and British Commonwealth, 58, 74–75; and China, *see* Sino-Pakistani relations; and cold war, 79–80; Communist party of, 79; constitutions: (1962), 283, (1969), 285, 286; debt repayments, 292; decolonization and Muslim nations, 75–77; defense policies: 70, 187, 252, 284, 291; devaluation, 80; domestic stability, 7, 9, 158, 261–62, *see also* Pakistani civil war; East, *see* Pakistan, East; economic development: 214, 215, 254, 260–61, 283, burdens of, 291–92, Five Year plans, 70, 284, GNP growth, 284; elections: (1969), 285, 286, 288, (1970), 239, 240; expenditures, 347, (table), 306, and suppliers, 214–16, *see also* Foreign aid; federal parliamentary system, 239; food production, 80; foreign policy: (mid-1960s), 183–88, goals, 71, "Islamic" policy, 68; under Yahya, 239–40; general strike (1970), 286; "hierarchs," 94–95, 102–4; Islamic principles, 68, 71, 283, 286; Lahore riots (1953), 101; martial law, 289–91; military bases: 101, 123, Peshawar, 162, 216, 223, 233, 252; military establishment, 103–6, 152, 252–53, *see also* Army, defense policies, *above*; national unity, 54–55, 69, 267–68, 308, 311; natural disasters, 286; population, 283; Rawalpindi conspiracy, 94; Regional Cooperation for Development, 191; resource allocation, 69; trade, *see* Trade; and treaty with Turkey (1954), 97, 98; two-nation theory, 55, 74, 307, 313; and U.S.S.R., *see* Union of Soviet Socialist Republics, and Pakistan; U.N. admission for, 42, 77; West, *see* Pakistan, West; World Bank mission to, 244

Pakistan, East: 289–90; Army seizure of, 240; and attitude toward India, 69, 240, 307; and autonomy demands, 213, 239–41, 284, 286–87, 308; and Awami League, *see* Awami

Pakistan, East (cont.):
League; "Bharat," 69; Biharis in, 311; famine, 293; general strike (1970), 240; Hindu minority of, 13, 289; secession attempt, 267; see also Bangla Desh; Bengal, East; Pakistani civil war
Pakistan, West: and attitude toward India, 307, 308, 309; Bengalis in, 311; division of, into provinces, 239, 285; riots in, 94, 213
Pakistan International Airways, 190
Pakistani civil war, 9, 238–41, 282–92, 306, 312; and India, 309–10; international responses to, 241–47; postwar political prospects, 289–92; refugee migration, 237, 241–42; relief efforts, 245, 246, 247, 293; and U.S.S.R., 311; and U.S., 311–12; Yahya on, 309–12
Panch Sheel period, 136–41, 145, 316, 321
Panchen Lama (Tibet), 144
Panikkar, K. M., 66, 132, 136
Paraguay, 263
Paramountcy, device of, 35–36
Partition, 26, 29–35; see also British India
Patel, Sardar V., 31, 72
Pathan tribes (Afghanistan), 78
Pearson Commission, 268, 299, 300; see also Foreign aid
People's Daily, 174
Persian Gulf, 84; Soviet presence in, 258, 324, 327
Peshawar military installation (Pakistan), 162, 216, 223, 233, 252
Philippines, 98
Plebiscite Front (Kashmir), 312
Podgorny, Nikolai, 243
Point Four Program, 91
Poland, 121–22
Population problems, 274, 275, 279; in India, 297–98; in Pakistan, 283
Portugal, 119, 121, 168
Post Dispatch, St. Louis, 96
Prasad, Bisheshwar, 53–54
Pravda, 120, 156–57, 206
Princely states, 35–38
Punjab (India), 29, 30, 34, 39–40, 72; see also Kashmir dispute
Pushtunistan dispute, 45, 77–79, 305

Racial discrimination, 57, 58, 59, 64
Radford, Arthur W., 89, 106
Rann of Kutch, 197–200, 221
Rawalpindi conspiracy, 94
Regional Cooperation for Development (RCD), 191, 344
Roosevelt, Franklin D., 64
Roy, M. N., 109
Rumania, 229
Rusk, Dean, 205
Russian Empire, 52; see also Union of Soviet Socialist Republics

Sadiq, G. M., 193
St. Louis Post Dispatch, 96
San Francisco Conference, 61
Schlesinger, James R., 335
Se La Pass (India), 175
SEATO (Southeast Asia Treaty Organization), 121, 181, 188, 222; British membership in, 127; formation of, 97–98; and Pakistan, 191, 338, 339, 344; and U.S.S.R., 123
Shastri, Lal Bahadur, 193, 197, 199, 207; death of, 212; on Rann of Kutch, 198; on Tashkent meetings, 210
Sikkim, 63, 134, 211; Chinese interest in, 327; foreign relations of, 305; Indian troops in, 153; protectorate status of, 52
Simla Convention (1914), 150
Sind, 197
Singh, Swaran, 243, 246, 310, 335
Sinkiang, 39, 189, 318; Chinese roads to, 234, 240
Sino-Indian border war (1962), 6, 174–82, 320; aftermath of, for India, 192; becomes public, 146–50; and Indian aggressiveness, 170–74; motivations and strategies in, 155–55; Pakistan's reaction to, 183–88; reappraisal of, 316–22; settlements of (proposed), 154–55, 343, 344; and U.S.S.R., 178–79, 321; and U.S., 160–61, 320–22
Sino-Indian relations: (early 1950s), 61–63, 107, (mid-1950s), 139–40, (late 1950s), 142–43; and Chinese intentions, 331; and common frontiers, 149–50, map, 148; and Indian uprisings, 219–20, 328; Indira Gandhi

on, 222, 322; and Kashmir, 159; in Panch Sheel period, *see* Panch Sheel period; and Rann of Kutch, 199; and Sino-Indian conflict (1954), 114; and Tibet, 132–34, 136, 142, 144–50; *see also* Sino-Indian border war

Sino-Pakistani relations, 2, 320; (post-independence), 80, (under Ayub), 187, (early 1960s), 188–90, (mid-1960s), 214–15; and border claims, 173, 189; and India, 317; and Pakistani civil war, 244; and SEATO, 98; and U.S. arms to Pakistan, 96

Sino-Soviet relations, 5, 131, 158, 318, 319; (late 1950s), 140–42, (mid-1960s), 228–29; future of, 262

Sino-Soviet–South Asia axis (potential), 264

Socialism, 46, 79, 117

Soda Plains, *see* Aksai Chin

Srinigar (India), 203

Stalin, Joseph, 64, 84, 109, 113, 114

Stephens, Ian, 22

Stevenson, Adlai, 168

Sudan, 86, 93, 152

Suez base, 86, 87, 99; attack on, 122, 127

Suez canal, 92, 93, 324

Suhrawardy, H. S., 127, 188

Sukarno, 191, 229

Suslov, M., 176

Sutlej River, 149

Taiwan, 121, 130–31, 139, 346; *see also* China, Nationalist

Taiwan Straits, 133, 142

Talbot, Phillips, 167

Tashkent meeting, 8, 210–12

TASS, 156–57

Telengana revolt (Hyderabad), 112, 113

Test-Ban Treaty, 334; *see also* Nuclear capability

Thailand, 98

Thant, U, 206, 247

Thimayya, General, 153, 173

Third World, *see* Afro-Asian nations

Tibet, 39, 51, 62, 130–31, 136, 141, 146, 211; as buffer state, 3, 52, 318; Chinese control of, 67, 132–34, 136, 317, 319–20, 329; economic dependency, 327; Indian mission to, 132;

revolution in, 144–47, 318; Sino-Indian trade agreement on, 173; status of, 62–63, 107; and U.S., 144; *see also* Sino-Indian border war

Tibet-Ladakh Agreement (1684), 150

Tilak, Bal Gangadhar, 16

Times, The (London), 211, 218

Times of India, The, 177, 198

Tito, Josip Broz, 120, 128

Tochi pass (Afghanistan), 79

Trade: of Afghanistan, 305; as aid to development, 269; and Commonwealth, 58; Indian: with Communist countries, 118, 229–32, with Pakistan, 70, table, 230, with West, 232, 298–99; Pakistani: with Britain, 75, with China, 190, 214–15, with India, 70, table, 231, with U.S.S.R., 124, 216; and Sino-Indian agreement on Tibet, 173

Truman, Harry, 66, 91

Truman Doctrine, 85

Turkey, 76, 84, 85, 86, 345; and Cyprus, 223; Khilafat movement, 19, 20; and Middle East security organization, 93; and NATO, 87, 98; and Regional Cooperation for Development, 191; and treaty with Iraq (1955), 99; and treaty with Pakistan (1954), 97, 98, 123

Two-nation theory (Pakistan), 55, 74, 307, 313

U-2 Flights, 162, 252

Uganda, 263

Union of Soviet Socialist Republics (U.S.S.R.): aid, *see* Foreign aid; Azerbaijan, 84; and China, *see* Sino-Soviet relations; Cominform, 120; détente policies of, 113–16, 142, 157–58, 165; and Eastern Europe, 64, 121–23, 229; Five Year plan, 109; German attack on, 47; and India, *see* Indo-Soviet relations; and Middle East, 87; military posture, 326–27; Navy, 324, 326, *see also* Indian Ocean, Persian Gulf; postwar recovery of, 83–85; Security Council boycott, 66; Sputnik, 141; *see also* Asia, and U.S.S.R.

and Pakistan, relations with, 2,

Union of Soviet Socialist Republics (*cont.*):
103; (mid-1950s), 79–80, 123–25, (late 1960s), 232, 235–36, 242–43; *see also* Foreign aid
United Arab Republic (U.A.R.), 178, 191; *see also* Egypt
United Kingdom, *see* Britain
United Nations, 36, 37, 56, 66, 90, 101, 118, 195; and Asian security guarantees, 236; Charter, 137; Chinese representation in, 62, 66, 80, 119, 181, 246; develoment efforts, 299; and Goa, 168; and Hungary, 122; and Indonesia, 60; and Kashmir: 8, 38, 41–42, 56–57, 79, 118, 127, 315, cease-fire resolution, 207, 208, 209, *see also* Kashmir dispute; and Korea, 80; and Middle East, 61, 77; Pakistani admission to, 42, 77; refugee camps, 312; and Tibet, 133
United Nations Economic Commission for Asia and the Far East (ECAFE), 118
United Nations Military Observer Group for India and Pakistan (UNMOGIP), 56, 195
United States: aid, *see* Foreign aid; Air Force, 91; and Bay of Pigs, 167; and Cambodia, 262; and China, 246, 258, 321; Congress: 223, 297, and India, 197, 229, and Indo-Pakistani hostility, 199–200, and Pakistan, 245, and PL480, 228, Senate Appropriations Committee, 205, Senate Foreign Relations Committe, 125; foreign policy: "containment," 84–85, 259, 265–66, under Eisenhower, 89–91, humanitarian concerns of, 268–72, isolationist tradition, 257, under Kennedy, 165–67, "massive retaliation," 89, and national interest, 257–72, overcommitment of, 258–59, 342, *see also* Asia and Vietnam; Guam Doctrine, 234; and India, *see* Indo-U.S. relations; military bases, 324, *see also* Pakistan; National Security Council, 96, 105; Northern Tier scheme, 93–94, 97; and Pakistan, *see* U.S.-Pakistani relations; Point Four Program, 91; racial segregation, 64; Seventh Fleet, 66, 85–86, 133; Sixth Fleet, 324, 325; U-2 incident, 162, 252; and U.S.S.R., *see* Cold war *and* Union of Soviet Socialist Republics, détente policies; *see also* Asia
U.S.-Pakistani relations, 2, 127, 196, 260–62, (early 1950s), 91, (late 1950s), 158–62, (under Kennedy), 168–70, (under Nixon), 233–36; future prospects for, 342–48; Pakistani attacks on U.S., 6, 184–87, 204–5, 208, 214; and Pakistani civil war, 245–47; *see also* Foreign aid
Uri-Punch (Kashmir), 203

V-E Day, 83
Vale of Kashmir, 38, 193, 313; *see also* Kashmir dispute
Van Eekelen, 137
Vietnam, 222, 229, 246, 272, 340; effects of war in, on U.S., 223, 228, 257, 258, 259, 342, 343
Voice of America, 197

Wavell, Lord, 26, 29
Wells of Power, 91
Wilson, Harold, 200, 205
World Bank, *see* International Bank for Reconstruction and Development
World War II, 24–25, 83 ,84

Yahya Khan, 233–34, 239–40; and CENTO, 338; constitution under (1969), 285, 286; and Mujib, 286–88; on Pakistani civil war, 309–12; and visit to Dacca, 288
Yalu River, 133
Yugoslavia, 120

Zafrullah Khan, 42, 98
Zhdanov, Andrei, 111

Recent Publications

FOREIGN AFFAIRS (quarterly), edited by Hamilton Fish Armstrong.

THE UNITED STATES IN WORLD AFFAIRS (annual), by Richard P. Stebbins.

DOCUMENTS ON AMERICAN FOREIGN RELATIONS (annual), by Richard P. Stebbins with the assistance of Elaine P. Adam.

THE REALITY OF FOREIGN AID, by Willard L. Thorp (1971).

POLITICAL HANDBOOK AND ATLAS OF THE WORLD, 1970, edited by Richard P. Stebbins and Alba Amoia (1970).

JAPAN IN POSTWAR ASIA, by Lawrence Olson (1970).

THE CRISIS OF DEVELOPMENT, by Lester B. Pearson (1970).

THE GREAT POWERS AND AFRICA, by Waldemar A. Nielsen (1969).

A NEW FOREIGN POLICY FOR THE UNITED STATES, by Hans J. Morgenthau (1969).

MIDDLE EAST POLITICS: THE MILITARY DIMENSION, by J. C. Hurewitz (1969).

THE ECONOMICS OF INTERDEPENDENCE: Economic Policy in the Atlantic Community, by Richard N. Cooper (1968).

HOW NATIONS BEHAVE: Law and Foreign Policy, by Louis Henkin 1968).

THE INSECURITY OF NATIONS, by Charles W. Yost (1968).

PROSPECTS FOR SOVIET SOCIETY, edited by Allen Kassof (1968).

THE AMERICAN APPROACH TO THE ARAB WORLD, by John S. Badeau (1968)

U.S. POLICY AND THE SECURITY OF ASIA, by Fred Greene (1968).

NEGOTIATING WITH THE CHINESE COMMUNISTS: The U.S. Experience, by Kenneth T. Young (1968).

FROM ATLANTIC TO PACIFIC: A New Interocean Canal, by Immanuel J. Klette (1967).

TITO'S SEPARATE ROAD: America and Yugoslavia in World Politics, by John C. Campbell (1967).

U.S. TRADE POLICY: New Legislation for the Next Round, by John W. Evans (1967).

TRADE LIBERALIZATION AMONG INDUSTRIAL COUNTRIES: Objectives and Alternatives, by Bela Balassa (1967).

THE CHINESE PEOPLE'S LIBERATION ARMY, by Brig. General Samuel B. Griffith II, U.S.M.C. (ret.) (1967).

THE ARTILLERY OF THE PRESS: Its Influence on American Foreign Policy, by James Reston (1967).

TRADE, AID AND DEVELOPMENT: The Rich and Poor Nations, by John Pincus (1967).

BETWEEN TWO WORLDS: Policy, Press and Public Opinion on Asian-American Relations, by John Hohenberg (1967).

THE CONFLICTED RELATIONSHIP: The West and the Transformation of Asia, Africa and Latin America, by Theodore Geiger (1966).

THE ATLANTIC IDEA AND ITS EUROPEAN RIVALS, by H. van B. Cleveland (1966).

EUROPEAN UNIFICATION IN THE SIXTIES: From the Veto to the Crisis, by Miriam Camps (1966).

THE UNITED STATES AND CHINA IN WORLD AFFAIRS, by Robert Blum, edited by A. Doak Barnett (1966).

THE FUTURE OF THE OVERSEAS CHINESE IN SOUTHEAST ASIA, by Lea A. Williams (1966).

ATLANTIC AGRICULTURAL UNITY: Is It Possible?, by John O. Coppock (1966).

TEST BAN AND DISARMAMENT: The Path of Negotiation, by Arthur H. Dean (1966).

COMMUNIST CHINA'S ECONOMIC GROWTH AND FOREIGN TRADE, by Alexander Eckstein (1966).

POLICIES TOWARD CHINA: Views from Six Continents, edited by A. M. Halpern (1966).

THE AMERICAN PEOPLE AND CHINA, by A. T. Steele (1966).

INTERNATIONAL POLITICAL COMMUNICATION, by W. Phillips Davison (1965)

ALTERNATIVE TO PARTITION: For a Broader Conception of America's Role in Europe, by Zbigniew Brzezinski (1965).

THE TROUBLED PARTNERSHIP: A Re-Appraisal of the Atlantic Alliance, by Henry A. Kissinger (1965).